John Hookham Frere, Henry Bartle Edward Frere, William Frere

The Works of the Right Hon. John Hookham Frere

In Verse and Prose. Vol. II

John Hookham Frere, Henry Bartle Edward Frere, William Frere

The Works of the Right Hon. John Hookham Frere
In Verse and Prose. Vol. II

ISBN/EAN: 9783744691772

Printed in Europe, USA, Canada, Australia, Japan

Cover: Foto ©Thomas Meinert / pixelio.de

More available books at **www.hansebooks.com**

THE WORKS OF THE RIGHT HON.

JOHN HOOKHAM FRERE

VOLUME II.

Fre   ick Honourable

THE WORKS

OF THE RIGHT HONOURABLE

JOHN HOOKHAM FRERE

IN VERSE AND PROSE

VOLUME II

ORIGINAL WORKS AND MINOR TRANSLATIONS

EDITED BY W. E. FRERE

Second Edition with Additions

ALDI

DISCIP.

ANGLVS

LONDON
BASIL MONTAGU PICKERING
196 PICCADILLY
1874

CONTENTS.

CONTRIBUTIONS TO THE

MICROCOSM.

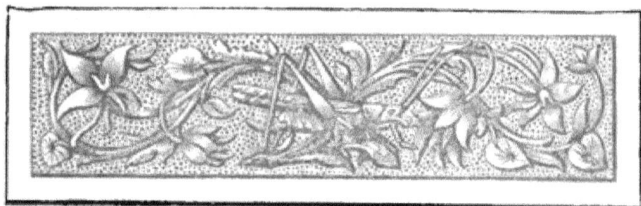

CONTRIBUTIONS TO THE

MICROCOSM.

MONDAY, NOVEMBER 27, 1786.

" —— I, demens, et sævas curre per Alpes,
Ut pueris placeas, et declamatio fias."
JUVENAL, Sat. x. l. 166.

" Climb o'er the Alps, thou rash, ambitious fool,
To please the boys, and be a theme at school."
DRYDEN.

AS the subject of the following discourse is the examination of a passion more peculiarly prevalent in the minds of youth; and as I conceive it would be but an indifferent compliment to the talents of the younger part of my readers to consider it necessary to apologize to them for the more serious nature of it; I shall, without detaining them any further by unnecessary introduction, proceed to my subject, *the Love of Fame*. And this I consider not only as that exalted principle which has in all ages produced patriots and heroes, but when in a depraved state, contributing more perhaps to the promotion of immorality than our most violent passions and most craving appetites. For the observer will discover, that whenever this *primum mobile* of the mind is diverted from the pursuit of more laudable ambition, to the desire of false honour and criminal adulation, its tendency is *only* diverted, while its power remains unimpaired. This principle, capable of carrying us to the highest pitch of human ambition, or, on the other hand, sinking us to the lowest ebb of depravity, is implanted in our natures; it is inherent in, and inseparable from, humanity; the reins are thrown into our hands, and the rest remains with ourselves.

It should seem then, that a reasonable being, conscious that he is possessed of such an internal principle, aware of the consequences immediately attending on a proper or improper use of it, and having the direction of it in his own power, could hardly err in the application; but unfortunately it happens that the distribution of praise lies equally in the hands of all; and from hence it is that the commonalty derive a power for which they are far from being qualified by greater nicety of judgment or accuracy of observation. And these too frequently judging more from outward appearance than an investigation of intrinsic merit, it will happen that by far the greater share of glory attends upon what are called great actions; which, by their superior splendour, attract and dazzle the eyes of the multitude more than a sober train of benevolence which passes over the mind with the smooth uniformity of a polished surface, not marked by any eminent feature, or distinguished by any leading characteristic. Hence a wide barrier is fixed between actions glorious to the individual, and such as are useful to the community; and the effects produced by it are not so much to be wondered at as lamented. The life of a man beneficial to society, is most commonly passed in a continued series of benevolent actions, frequently in a circle extremely contracted; but this is not a life of glory, and though an useful uniformity may demand our praise, it lays no claim to our admiration. So unvaried indeed is the tenour of a life really useful, and not unusually charged with so little incident, that the muse, whose office it is to shed a perfunctory tear over the ashes of the deceased, has frequently been obliged, by the barrenness of the subject, to have recourse to topics of praise entirely fictitious, or relinquish a theme rendered so uninteresting by its uniformity. And if we except that of Pope on Mrs. Corbet, and the original of Crashaw, from which Pope seems to have transfused no inconsiderable part of his own performance, there does not perhaps remain in our language an elegant epitaph on any person undistinguished by military, civil, or literary exertions. I would wish, however, to except the following lines, which, in a parish in Yorkshire, cover the bones of an honest yeoman, whose merits seem to have been understood by the author, though he might have been prevented from recurring to feigned topics by the want of art evident in the construction of the lines. I shall subject them to the perusal of my reader; they are as follows:—

> "John Bell Brokenbow
> Laies under this stane,
> Four of my eene sonnes
> Laied it an my weame,
> I was master of my meat,
> Master of my wife,
> I lived on my own lands
> Without mickle strife."

How much more glorious is this simple testimony to the undistinguished merits of a private man, than if it had announced the bones of a general who, by the singular favour of fortune, had, with the loss of only twenty thousand individuals of the same country with himself, slaughtered two hundred thousand, guilty of being divided from it by a narrow sea or a chain of mountains. The merit of the former character is evidently superior, yet our admiration had undoubtedly sided with the latter.

Not that this meritorious inaction is always undistinguished by observation and applause; the character of Atticus is not perhaps less remarkable for its literary excellence than the inactive acquiescence which he betrayed at a period when any degree of eminence must have been attended with consequences more or less repugnant to the interests of his country. How different is this patriotic conquest over a desire of glory not to be obtained in a manner consistent with his country's welfare, from the obstinacy of another character equally eminent about the same time, who would have

> "Blush'd if Cato's house had stood
> Secure, and flourish'd in a civil war."

It should seem doubtful whether the poet meant this

sentiment for the effect of a natural impulse on the occasion which introduces it, or the result of an affectation eminent in the original character; and which could not have escaped the author, though so much its admirer. Certain I am that it could not proceed from the feelings of nature, even admitting the possibility of any connexion subsisting between an individual and his country, which did not in a stronger manner tie him to his family. I shall not at present arraign the policy, which dictated a law to the Athenians, inflicting disgrace and ignominy on any one, who, in a public dissension, might remain inactive; however, the observer may discover in this edict the source of those disturbances which continually divided the state, and ended but in its ruin.

But to return to my subject—and perhaps it may not be entirely foreign from it to observe that, admitting the desire of glory to have so great an influence as I contend it is possessed of, the higher ranks in life may be cleared of an imputation under which they have long laboured. I allude to an opinion extremely prevalent, that all national depravity and corruption, before it descends to the lower classes, originates among their superiors. The regard paid by the lower ranks to the example and authority of their superiors has been cited, and with some degree of plausibility, to support this opinion; but is not this influence effectually and entirely counterbalanced by the distribution of censure and applause which resides entirely in the hands of the commonalty? or can anyone doubt the influence which the common people have with their superiors, when he sees the forms of government change with the disposition of the people, and the affectation of ignorance and illiberality assumed by the higher orders at home, in their dress, manners, and conversation? We readily grant a propensity in the inferior orders to imitate the actions of their superiors. But is not imitation the height of flattery? and does not a readiness to receive and copy the depraved manners of a superior order suppose a previous depravity in the people?

Perhaps the only true criterion of the utility or dangerous tendency of this passion is the disposition of the times; for the same spirit which, in a more corrupt period, carries the enthusiast for it to the height of excess and extravagance, would, in an era of more simple manners, have produced the exact reverse :—

> " Lucullus, when frugality could charm,
> Had roasted turnips in his Sabine farm ;"

and Cincinnatus, had he lived in a period less disposed to honour a virtuous poverty, might probably have changed the frugality of his simple meal for the luxury of the *Apollo.*

The present path to glory, and consequently that which its votaries pursue, is faction ; and even in this lesser world the observer may discover a demagogue in embryo, distinguished perhaps only for stronger powers of vocife- ration. But here, as upon all other occasions, the MICRO- COSMOPOLITAN would wish to avoid misapprehension ; and while he reprobates a turbulence of behaviour, does not wish his readers entirely to discard their judgment and free will, and to degrade themselves to the rank of nonenti- ties, or according to a more accepted phrase, *cyphers.* The great increase of the above-mentioned species calls for attention, whether it proceeds from a prevailing idea that an individual, like a numerical figure, is made of more consequence by the addition of a cypher, or from a fear in its promoters of a discovery of their own weakness ; as the cruel policy of Semiramis had its origin in an appre- hension, that her sex might be discovered by an unprece- dented want of beard. From whatever cause the present increase of this species arises, it is now grown to so for- midable a height as to require the attention of the public, and more particularly of the MICROCOSMOPOLITAN.

I would wish to present to the perusal of my readers the following lines, not entirely foreign from some part of this essay ; and at the same time admonish them that the ....ne of Melpomene at the birth of a poet is useless, without that of his readers on his publication.

I.

WITHIN the sounding quiver's hollow womb
　　Repose the darts of praise and harmony ;
　Goddess, draw forth the chosen shaft ; at
　　　whom
　　Shall the swift arrows of the Muses fly ?
By the great almighty mind
For man's highly favour'd race
Various blessings were design'd,
Bounties of superior grace ;
Here the fat and fertile ground
Waves the flood of harvest round ;
Or fervid wine's ecstatic juice
Cluster-curved vines produce ;
A sullen land of lazy lakes
Rhine slowly winding to the ocean makes,　·
This rescued from the eager wave
Human art has dared to save,
While o'er each foggy pool and cheerless fen
Hums the busy buzz of men.
A warlike nation bent on deathful deeds
　From daring actions safety seeks, and fame,
Rush through the ranks, where'er the battle bleeds,
　Or whirl their neighing coursers through the flame.
　　The Indian youth beneath the shade
　　　· More loves repose and peace,
　　And underneath his plantain laid
　　　Sings indolence and ease.

II.

　　Thus far with unerring hand
　　All-ruling providence has plann'd,
　　Thus far impartial to divide,
　　Nor all to one, nor one to all denied.
　　　But Order, heaven-descended queen,
　　Where'er you deign to go,
　　　Alone you fix the bounds between
　　Our happiness and woe.
　　Nor wealth, nor peace, nor without thee
　　Heaven's first best bounty, Liberty,
　　　Can bless our native land.

Then come, O nymph! and o'er this isle
Dispense thy soul-subduing smile,
  And stretch thy lenient hand.

III.

Before time was, before the Day
Shot through the skies his golden ray,
A sightless mass, a wasteful wild
Tumultuous gulph, was all this fair creation,
Till you the shapeless chaos reconciled,
Each part commanding to its proper station!
Then hills upheaved their verdant head,   ⎫
Above a purer sky was spread,   ⎬
And Ocean floated in his ample bed;   ⎭
Then first creeping to the main
Rivers drew their tortuous train;
Then from her fertile womb the earth
Brought forth at one ample birth
All that through the waste of sky
Borne on aëry pinions fly,
Or through the deep's dark caverns roam,
And wallowing dash the sea to foam.
Tutor'd by your guiding sway,
The planets trace their pathless way,
The seasons in their order'd dance
In grateful interchange advance!
But when, O Goddess, wilt thou deign
O'er favour'd man to stretch thy reign?
Then shall sedition's tempest cease,
The dashing storm be hush'd to peace,
The angry seas no longer roar,
But gently rolling kiss the shore,
While from the wave-worn rock the troubled waters pour.

IV.

When poised athwart the lurid air,
  The sword of vengeance pours a sanguine ray,
Or comets from their stream of blazing hair
  Shake the blue pestilence, and adverse sway
Of refluous battle, o'er some high-viced land;
  Through the sick air the power of poison flies,
By gentler breezes now no longer fann'd,

Sultry and still ; the native breathes and dies.
    Yet often free from selfish fear
        The son attends his father's bed,
    Nor will disdain the social tear
        In pleasing painful mood to shed.—
When chilling pine and cheerless penury,
    Stretch o'er some needy house their wither'd hand,
Where modest want alone retires to die,
    Yet social love has shed her influence bland,
To cheer the sullen gloom of poverty.
For 'tis decreed, that every social joy
    In its partition should be multiplied,
Still be the same, nor know the least alloy,
    Though sympathy to thousands should divide
Our pleasures ; but when urged by dire distress,
The grief by others felt is made the less.

v.

Not so the ills sedition sows,
Midst sever'd friends, and kindred foes ;
When the horrid joy of all
Embitters every private fall.
Creeping from her secret source
Sedition holds her silent course,
With watery weeds and sordid sedge
Skirting her unnoted edge,
Till scorning all her former bounds
She sweeps along the fertile grounds ;
And as in sullen solemn state she glides,
Receives into her train the tributary tides ;
Then rushing headlong from some craggy steep
She pours impetuous down and hurries to the deep.
Ah ! luckless he, who o'er the tide
Shall hope his fragile bark to guide ;
While secure his sail is spread
The waves shall thunder o'er his head ;
But if, long tempest-tost, once more
His crazy bark regain the shore,
There shall he sit and long lament
His youthful vigour vainly spent ;
And others warn, but warn, alas ! in vain,
In unambitious safety to remain.

Then happy he who to the gale
Nor trusts too much the varying sail,
Nor rashly launching forth amain
Attempts the terrors of the watery plain ;
But watchful, wary, when he sees
The ocean black beneath the breeze,
The cheerless sky with clouds o'erspread,
And darkness gathering round his head,
Trusts not too far, but hastes to seek
The shelter of some winding creek ;
Thence sees the waves by whirlwinds tost,
And rash ambition's vessel lost ;
Hears the mad pilot late deplore
The shifting sail, the faithless oar,
And hears the shriek of death, the shriek that's heard no
    more.

MONDAY, JANUARY 29, 1787.

" —— Sit quod vis, simplex duntaxat et unum."
                                        HOR. *Art. Poet.* l. 23.
" Be what you will, so you be still the same."
                                        ROSCOMMON.

THERE are few precepts dictated like the above
by judgment and experience, which, though
originally confined to a particular application
(as this to the formation of dramatic character)
may not be adopted with success in the seve-
ral branches of the same science, and even transferred into
another. The directions which the poet gives us here, to
preserve a regard for simplicity and uniformity, may be
applied to the general design and main structure of a poem ;
and if we allow them a still greater latitude of interpretation, may be found to convey a very useful rule with respect
to the inferior component parts which constitute a work.

A venerable pile of Gothic architecture, viewed at a distance, or after the sober hand of time has stripped it of
the false glare of meretricious ornament, communicates a

sensation which the same object under a closer inspection, in its highest degree of perfection, was incapable of producing, when the attention, solicited by a thousand minutiæ with which the hand of caprice and superstition had crowded its object, was unavoidably diverted from the contemplation of the main design.

In all points which admit of hesitation, the sister sciences are found to throw a corresponding lustre on each other. The impropriety of admitting ill-judged ornament, though connected as in the above instance with all that is awful and venerable, must be evident to the most superficial observer; and this circumstance should lead us to conjecture, that the same principle existed in a similar though superior science. Originality of sentiment, vivacity of thought, and loftiness of language may conduct the reader to the end of a work, though awkwardly designed and injudiciously constructed; while the nicest adherence to poetic rule would be found insufficient to compensate for meanness of thought, or vulgarity of expression. That these two faults should infallibly destroy all title which any writer might otherwise have to the name of poet, should seem self-evident, and yet a fault which appears to be a composition of them both, has, I think, in some instances passed without reprehension, I mean, allusion to local circumstance: I shall therefore make this paper the vehicle of a few observations on this practice.

Nothing can be more directly adverse to the spirit of poetry, considered under one of its definitions as an universal language, than whatever confines it to the comprehension of a single people, or a particular period of time.

Blackmore, a name now grown to a byword in criticism, in the original structure of his poem, was little, if at all, inferior to the great prototypes of antiquity; but that simplicity and uniformity, so visible in the first design, was in every other respect, conformably to the taste of his time, violated and neglected. It is said, that the most desolate deserts of Africa are distinguished by little insulated spots, clothed with perpetual verdure; and it sometimes happens, that beautiful passages present themselves in the " Prince Arthur," as in the first book :—

> " The heavens serenely smiled, and every sail
> Fill'd its broad bosom with the indulgent gale."

But when lines like these occur, we must consider it, to borrow an expression from a contemporary Poet,—

> " A gift no less
> Than that of manna in the wilderness."

Scriptural allusions like the foregoing were much in fashion among the poets of that period ; and in this particular, so earnest a follower of it was not to be left behind : he has accordingly introduced his enchanter, Merlin, building seven altars, offering upon each a bullock and a ram, and attempting to curse the army of the hero, in imitation of Balaam, and with the same success.

Dryden himself is strongly tinctured with the taste of the times ; and those *Dalilahs of the Town*, to use his own expression, are plentifully scattered throughout his works, esteemed in the present age for those passages only in which he ventured to oppose his own taste to that of his readers, and which have already passed the ordeal of unmerited censure.

Nor is that narrowness of conception, which confines a work to the comprehension of a particular portion of individuals, less reprehensible or less repugnant to the essential principles of poetry ; and of this defect innumerable instances occur in both the authors above cited, with this difference, that in one instance we contemplate with regret the situation of an eminent genius constrained by his exigencies to postpone the powers of his own taste, and submit his judgment to the arbitrary dominion of a prevailing mode ; while in the other, we view with indifference an author, spoilt indeed by the taste of the times in which he lived, but who, had he not adopted theirs, had most probably succeeded as ill by following his own. Nothing is so common as in both these writers to meet with expressions and allusions drawn from the meanest mechanical employments ; at present infinitely disgusting to the general scholar, and (a proof of the necessity of observing the rule we have endeavoured to illustrate) to a foreigner, acquainted only with the learned part of our language, entirely unintelligible.[1]

---

[1] I would not here be understood to hint at any similarity in the original genius of these authors ; were I to draw the line of affinity, I should call Blackmore the caricatura of Dryden.

In the earlier stages of civilization, while the bonds of society hang yet loose upon the individual, before the benefits of mutual assistance and dependence are felt or understood, the savage, elate with the idea of absolute independence, and unacquainted with all the advantages which accompany the arts of society, looks down with supreme contempt on a state whose every individual is entirely dependent upon and connected with the community. The wretched Esquimaux give themselves the exclusive title of *men*, and the Indian of North America, bestows on the Europeans, as compared with himself, the epithet of the *accursed race*.

In a state of absolute barbarism the arts of life are few, and agreeably to that all-sufficiency which the savage so much affects, practised and understood by each individual. The Indian unacquainted with the arts of polished life is to himself what society is to the members which compose it : he raises himself the roof of his humble hut, and ventures upon the ocean in the canoe which his own hands have hollowed; his weapons for war or for the chace are such as his own industry, or sometimes a casual intercourse with politer nations, have furnished for him.[1] The component members of barbarous societies are seldom numerous, owing to the extreme difficulty which attends the education of infancy among the hazards and hardships of savage life, and joined to it produces that extreme tenderness which all uncivilized communities entertain for the life of an individual. Where the members are comparatively few, the principle of patriotism is concentrated—the loss or misconduct of a North American Indian would be more sensibly felt by his tribe, than that of a thousand Englishmen by the parent country.

It remains, after a consideration of the causes, to trace their effects in the artless essays of the more remote periods. Ossian's poems, if allowed to be authentic, are the only specimen of this species generally known ; Homer being, according to the testimony of Aristotle, posterior to a long line of poets, his predecessors and perhaps his patterns : the decided preference given through every poem to the nation, the family, and person of the poet, strongly

---

[1] Robertson's " History of America," book iv.

mark the national character **as well as that of the times.**
Allusions to the inferior arts are so **unusual and so simple**
as must speak them in their first period **of progression ;**
or evince a taste and judgment in the author far beyond
the times in which **he** is supposed **to have** flourished. He
is himself, agreeably to that **idea of** self-importance, the
invariable attendant on savage life, the hero of his own tale.
Filial duty, and a regard to the merits of an illustrious warrior,
might contribute **to** give Fingal a conspicuous character **in**
poems, the productions of his son ; but no other reason **can**
be given **why Ossian, the** *bard of Song,* should be the **hero**
of it. **"The battle,"** says Regnor Lodbrog, a prince, pirate,
and poet of a succeeding age, "is grateful to me as the
smile of a virgin in the bloom of youth, as the kiss of a
young widow in a retired apartment." An egotism which
moderns must suppose agreeable to the character of **those**
times. **The** pride of family, **a** prevailing passion **where**
arts and commerce have not set mankind on a level, **was**
indulged by the **poet, who** comprised in his profession **that**
of the genealogist. Homer frequently traced **the descent**
of his heroes into remote **and fabulous antiquity ; probably**
with a view to gratify such **of his patrons as piqued them-**
selves on their pedigree.

The poetry of ruder ages **is** seldom distinguished **for**
elegance of diction or variety of imagery ; yet there are
advantages so strongly peculiar to it, as must raise it high
in the esteem of all admirers of nature, while yet simple
and unsophisticated. The state of the arts, as yet rude
and imperfect, renders it impossible to deviate from sim-
plicity. The distinctions of property being as yet faintly
delineated, no idea of superiority can obtain but what arises
from personal qualifications ; and poetic praise, unpro-
stituted to power and wealth, must be the genuine tribute
of gratitude and **admiration.** That property **was in a** very
unsettled **state in the days of** Homer, may be gathered
from numberless passages in **his** writings ; among the
calamities which awaited an aged **father** on the death of
his only son, the plunder of his possessions is mentioned ;
and Achilles laments that life, **unlike** every other human
possession, was not to be obtained by **theft.** Accordingly,
in the epithets which accompany the name of each hero,
through **the Iliad and** Odyssey, we see no allusions to the

adventitious circumstances of wealth and power, if we except the title of *lord of rich Mycenæ* sometimes, though
rarely, bestowed on Agamemnon.   While the subtlety of
Ulysses, the swiftness of Achilles, the courage and strength
of Diomed, are mentioned as often as the names of those
heroes occur.

The intermediate step between barbarity and perfection
is perhaps the least favourable to the cultivation of poetry ;
for the *necessity* of writing with simplicity is taken away
long before its *beauty* is discovered or attended to.   The
arts, if we may believe the picture of them, as exhibited in
the shield of Achilles, had attained this intermediate stage
of their progress in the days of Homer ; and accordingly
we find, in the works of that great master, some allusions
to the meaner arts, as well as illustrations drawn from
them ; which, however the antiquary might regard as
throwing light on so remote a period, criticism must reject
as repugnant to that simplicity and universality which form
the essential characteristics of poetry.   When Hector tells
Paris that he deserved *a coat of stone, i.e.* to be stoned to
death, I cannot help suspecting it to have been a cant word
of that time ; and am rather disgusted than satisfied, to find
the security which Neptune gives for Mars was agreeable
to the form of procedure in the Athenian courts.   Though
in this instance a modern, and especially a modern of this
country, may be easily prejudiced ; the laws here, by the
uncouthness of their language, and other numberless particularities, wearing an air of ridicule by no means connected with the idea of laws in general.   Yet, whatever
allowances we admit in consideration of the distant period
which produced this patriarch of poetry and literature, and
however we abstract ourselves from the prevailing prejudices of modern manners, we still find ourselves better
pleased with those images which, from their simplicity in
so long a period, have undergone the smallest variation.
The following lines are perhaps the most pleasing to a
modern reader of any in the whole Iliad :—

> " What time in some sequester'd vale
> The weary woodman spreads his sparing meal ;
> When his tired arms refuse the axe to rear,
> And claim a respite from the sylvan war ;
> But not till half the prostrate forest lay,
> Stretch'd in long ruin, and exposed to day."—POPE.

And it is a curious consideration, that in a period which has exhausted the variety of wealth and vanity, the simple life of the labourer has not undergone the most trifling alteration. Milton, a strict observer, as well as a constant imitator of the ancients, has adopted the same idea in the following lines :—

> " What time the labour'd ox,
> With loosen'd traces from the furrow came,
> And the swink'd hedger at his supper sat."

The father of English poetry, like that of the Grecian, lived in a period little favourable to simplicity in poetry ; and several meannesses occur throughout his works, which in an age more refined or more barbarous he must have avoided. We see among the *worthie* acts of *Duke* Theseus—

> " How he took the nobil cite after,
> And brent the walls and tore down roof and rafter."

And, among the horrid images which crowd the temple of Mars,—

> " The child stranglid in the cradil,
> The coke scaldid for alle his long ladil."

That state or equipose between horror and laughter, which the mind must here experience, may be ranked among its most unpleasing sensations. The period at which the arts attain to their highest degree of perfection, may be esteemed more favourable to the productions of the Muses than either of the foregoing ; the mind is indulged in free retrospect of antiquity, and sometimes in conjectural glimpses of futurity ; with such a field open before him, the objects which we must suppose should more immediately attract the attention of the poet, would be the failure or success of his predecessors, and the causes to which either was to be attributed. Pope has fully availed himself of the dear-bought experience of all who went before him ; there is perhaps no poet more entirely free from this failing. I shall, however, only cite one instance in which he may seem to have carried his regard for simplicity so far as to show himself guilty of inaccuracy and inattention :—

> " The hungry Judges now the sentence sign,
> And wretches hang, that jurymen may dine."

That judges in England never *sign* a sentence is well
known; and hunger, whatever effect it might have had on
the jurymen of ancient days, with those of modern times,
seems to operate rather as an incitement to mercy. *Clifden's
proud alcove* has not at present, and probably never had,
any existence; but the fault, if any there is, seems rather
that of the language than of the poet; or perhaps, after
all, it was mere penury of rhyme, and a distress similar to that which made him in another place hunt his poor
dab-chick into a *copse* where it was never seen but in the
Dunciad.

After so much said on the subject of local allusions and
terms of art, it cannot but occur to me, that I have myself
sometimes fallen into the error which I have here repre-
hended, and adopted phrases and expressions unintelligible,
except to the little circle to which my labours were at first
confined, an error I shall cautiously avoid for the future;
for how little claim soever the lucubrations of GREGORY
GRIFFIN may have to public notice, or a protracted term of
existence, he is unwilling to abridge either by wilful con-
tinuance in an acknowledged error.

MONDAY, MARCH 5, 1787.

" ———— Usus,
Quem penes arbitrium est et jus et norma loquendi."
HOR. *Art. Poet.* l. 71.

" Use is the judge, the law, and rule of speech."

IT is a favourite amusement with me, and one of
which, in the present paper, I shall invite my
readers to participate, to adopt a maxim
established in any single instance, to trace its
influence where it has operated undiscovered,
to examine the secret springs by which it has worked, and
the causes which have contributed to their concealment.
In the course of this pursuit, I may boast that there is

scarce one of these *miniatures* of experience and observation, from the moral maxims of Grecian philosophy, to the
prudential apophthegms of Poor Robin, which has not been
successively the object of my observation and discussion. I
am, however, aware that, in the opinion of their importance,
I may perhaps be singular.

That "life is short," that "the generality of mankind are
vicious," seem ideas that might have suggested themselves
to a mind undistinguished for peculiar sagacity, or an un-
common share of experience. But to carry further the
former of these maxims, and to consider that life is short,
when compared with the multiplicity of its business and the
variety of its pursuits; that it is too much so for the purposes of honour and ambition; that to draw a conclusion
from the attempts of men, we should imagine it longer, is
an observation not so entirely unworthy of a philosopher.
And by pursuing the latter of these thoughts, though on
the first view it may not appear the result of any extraordinary observation, it may be found on a narrower inspection, to convey a strong argument of the impropriety of
popular government.

The scrap of Latin which, in conformity to established
precedent, is prefixed to my paper, exhibits an example of
the influence of Fashion beyond those limits, which are
usually assigned to its prerogative. For were we to accept
the definition of it the most usually accepted, we should
consider it only as the director of diversion and dress, of
unmeaning compliment and unsocial intimacy. And however evidently mistaken such an opinion might appear, we
must look for its source in one of the most prevailing principles of the human mind; a principle (the excess of which
we stigmatize by the name of pedantry) of deducing the
illustrations of every subject of inquiry from the more
immediate objects of our own pursuits, and circumscribing
its bounds within the limits of our own observation. On
the contrary, we shall find that all our attempts to prescribe
bounds to the activity of this so powerful agent, will end
only in surprise at the extent of its authority, in astonishment at the universality of its influence. Its claim to an
undisputed empire over language, is asserted by the author
from whom I have taken the motto of this paper, with what
justice the testimony of a succeeding age may declare,

when a Cæsar, who made and unmade the laws of the world at his pleasure, found the smallest innovation in language beyond the utmost limits of arbitrary power. Nothing indeed but the highest vanity, nourished by the grossest adulation, an idea of the infinitude of sovereign authority and servile obedience, could have given birth to such an attempt.

However paradoxical it may seem that, in a matter of judgment and taste, the vague arbitration of individuals should be preferable to the absolute decision of a learned body; yet the imbecility so evident in the language of a neighbouring nation, and so undoubtedly the effect of establishing such a court of criticism, leaves us little reason to regret that language with us is so entirely the child of chance and custom. The first prize of Rhetoric given to a woman was a bad omen to the future endeavours of the French Academy.

To omit the innumerable inconveniences attending on every attempt to regulate language; to judge of the possible success of such an attempt, from the abstracted probability alone, were to declare it impossible. A multitude of circumstances, equally unforeseen and unavoidable, must concur to the formation of a language. An improvement, or corruption of manners; the reduction of a foreign enemy; or an invasion from abroad, are circumstances that ultimately or immediately tend to produce some change in the language of a people. And even of these the most feeble agents have been found more efficacious than the joint operations of power and policy.

The conquests of this nation on the continent contributed more perhaps to the naturalization of the French language amongst us than the Norman invasion and its attendant consequences—the necessity laid on every individual to acquire the use of that tongue, in which all cases of property were to be determined—and the numberless disadvantages and restrictions imposed on the study of the native language.

At a time when measures so seemingly decisive proved ineffectual, it may be curious to observe the agency of others apparently foreign from any connexion with the improvement or alteration of our language. The residence of our nobility in the conquered provinces of France, the continual wars maintained against that nation, making the study of their language an indispensable qualification in all who aspired to civil or military dignities, unavoidably brought on a change in our own. The accusation, therefore, of a learned etymologist against Chaucer, of introducing into our language "*integra verborum plaustra,* (*whole cartloads of words*)," however elegant in expression, is false in foundation. The language of Chaucer's poetry is that of the court in which he lived ; and that it was not, no probable conclusion can be drawn from any difference of style in authors, his contemporaries. In those who writ under the same advantages no such difference is observable, and those who were excluded from them laboured under extreme disadvantages from the variations of vernacular language and the diversity of provincial dialect, which, as they have now in a great measure ceased to exist, may, together with their primary causes, furnish a subject for curious inquiry.

It appears, from the concurrence of several ingenious antiquaries, as well as from the testimony of Caxton, in one of his prefaces, that the English language was in his time diversified by innumerable provincial peculiarities. He mentions his own choice of the Kentish dialect and the success that attended it. The language of Chaucer's poetry is frequently more intelligible to a modern reader than that of such of his successors as employed themselves on popular subjects. Gawin Douglas, a poetical translator of Virgil, is now, owing to the use of a northern dialect, though a near contemporary of Spenser's, almost unintelligible.

After establishing the existence of a fact, the beaten track of transition will naturally lead us to a consideration of its causes. Among the first effects produced by an extension of empire may be reckoned a barbarous peculiarity of language in the provinces the most remote from the seat of learning and refinement. Livy is said to have had his *Patavinity,* and Claudian is accused of barbarisms, the consequence of his education in a distant province. A difficulty of conveyance, a stagnation of commercial intercourse, will produce the same effects with too wide an extension of empire ; and are as effectual a barrier against a mixture of idioms and dialect as, in a more civilized state, the utmost distance of situation between the most remote provinces.

To causes seemingly so unconnected with the situation of language must we attribute the barbarity of our own during so many centuries. And those which contributed to its refinement may, at first sight, probably seem equally foreign to that effect. No nation, perhaps, contributed less to the revival of literature than our own; a circumstance which in a great measure secured it from that torrent of pedantry which overwhelmed the rest of Europe. The ignorance of our ancestors kept them unacquainted with the ancients, except through the medium of a French translation. The first labours of the English press brought to light the productions of English literature, which, how rude and barbarous soever, were not confined to the intelligence of the scholar or the libraries of the learned, but dispersed throughout the nation, and open to the inspection of all, disseminated a general taste for literature, and gave a slow gradual polish to our language; while, in every other nation of Europe, the conceits of commentators and writers of a similar stamp, whose highest ambition it was to add a Latin termination to a High Dutch name, came into the world covered with ill-sorted shreds of Cicero and Virgil, like the evil spirits which have been said to animate a cast-off carcase, previous to their ascension to the regions of light.

MONDAY, MAY 7, 1787.

"Interdum vulgus rectum videt ; est ubi peccat."
HOR. *Ep.* ii. 1, l. 63.

" ———— The people's voice is odd,
It is, and it is not, the voice of God."—POPE.

PROVERBIAL expressions and received opinions have usually been considered as an abridgment of national wisdom, and are perhaps the best guides to the character or genius of a people. And it is not improbable that the extension of this method of inquiry, to the established opinions and received ideas of mankind in general, may lead us to a more perfect and general knowledge of them.

That the mind of man is not framed for happiness is a principle, of the truth of which perhaps the most certain criterion is its popularity.

At the revival of learning, the idea of gradual and progressive degeneracy obtained very strongly; and whether it contributed in any measure to the study of the ancients, or what is more probable, was derived from the inferiority visible in their imitators, its prevalence was unlimited, and its authority unquestioned. How far a servile reverence and scrupulous imitation of antiquity is compatible with the efforts of learning and genius, may be seen in the attempts of an age whose diligence was unequalled, and whose genius ours has no right to suppose inferior to her own. But it may be objected, that the qualities of the heart, if not those of the head, may be improved by a converse with antiquity; that if the science of barbarous nations is rude, their morality at least is pure. To fall into errors authorized by the example of a superior, has frequently afforded a despicable gratification to men of inferior abilities; and the scrupulous stickler for obsolete antiquity may be pleased to find his error common to the ablest politicians of declining Rome. That great empire in a state of decay, has been aptly characterized by her historian, as the theatre in which the scenes of a more virtuous age were acted over again; but without the principle or spirit of the real personages. This was the error of a physician, who would treat an infirm patient as if he was in youth and health, as the only means of restoring him to both; and the only circumstances which render the former folly the more excusable are its great frequency and that appearance of earnestness which the voluntary assumption of more rigid manners carries with it. Perhaps the result of all serious inquiries on this subject will be, that in the moral, as well as the physical world, there is a correspondent propriety in every member, as far as its relation to the rest is considered; and that the manners of every age and nation have as much propriety in their designation as the passions peculiar to the different periods of life, and the instinctive qualities of the animal world.

The striking analogy which subsists between the two first may afford matter for a digression, which my readers will the more readily pardon as it arises immediately from the subject, contributes in some measure to illustrate it, and throws light on a similitude whose leading features seem to have struck every observer, but whose more minute corresponding peculiarities have never been traced with any degree of accuracy. The first attempts of a rising state, struggling into eminence and observation, the strength of an established constitution, and the weakness of declining empire, have so strong an analogy to the first efforts of infancy, the confirmed vigour of maturity, and the debility of age, that expressions adopted into one from the other are hardly considered as metaphorical; and are to be met with in styles the most unadorned, or even the flow of common conversation.

The progress of national refinement, considered as analogous to the improvement of personal taste, may perhaps furnish a less trite, and more interesting subject of discussion.

The objects with which children are most delighted, are such as strike most forcibly upon the senses; the simplest tunes, the sweetest tastes, a fanciful association of the most gaudy colours, are most agreeable to our infancy; and a fondness for similar objects is a certain indication of a national taste in the first stages of cultivation; an implicit credulity in what they hear, and the utmost deference to the authority of what they read, is another leading characteristic of childhood; insomuch that a system of education which confines its pupils to ignorance, has been grounded on the fear of imbibing early and mistaken opinions. The grand and fundamental error which makes this system entirely impracticable, is the supposition, that the implicit adherence to superior authority was to be destroyed, not by the researches of learning, but the advances of age. Unprejudiced ignorance is always diffident; and to this cause are to be attributed the credulity of childhood and that readiness with which a barbarous age receives the opinions of a superior genius.

A mind too ignorant or too indolent for reflection is pleased to repose itself under the shadow of some great authority, and to adopt a set of dogmas implicitly, without hesitation or inquiry. Hence in our earliest moral writers, almost every sentence is prefaced with an authority for the sentiment it contains; and in Spain, a country some centuries behind the rest of Europe in point of taste and learning, the same species of writing still subsists.

Of all the periods of human life, the passions and opinions of youth are perhaps the most remarkable; the mind perceives a sensible dilation of its faculties, becomes jealous of an unprejudiced freedom of inquiry, and ashamed of that implicit deference it had formerly entertained for the opinions of others. New systems are daily raised, inveterate prejudices examined and rejected, and we flatter ourselves for a while with the sufficiency of private observation and unassisted endeavours, the ardour of innovation at length subsides, and we discover in time that a credulous attention to the opinions of others, and a blind confidence in our own, are equally insufficient for the pursuits of truth and wisdom.

If we should trace back the progress of natural science to the first dawn that dispelled the clouds of prejudice and error, we should discover a number of circumstances parallel to those in the improvement of personal knowledge; the immediate rejection of all received opinions, and the readiness with which a new system is embraced, are circumstances common to both and highly characteristic.

After the existence of a similitude between the progress of personal and of popular taste has been proved, it would be needless to vindicate the propriety of either; I shall therefore confine myself to an examination of the reasons from which an idea of modern inferiority has arisen.

Man, though constantly in pursuit of happiness, so seldom appears to be in possession of his object, that his constant failure of success has been attributed to a supposed defect in his formation; a principle that offers to its followers so compendious a protection from the feelings of conscious humiliation, and the agonies of conviction and remorse, could hardly fail of being popular; the invention of lenitives, similar in their effect, though not equally comprehensive in their operation, had long employed the invention of mankind. The narratives of our first adventurers were filled with descriptions of more favoured realms, where the manners of patriarchal life were supposed to exist among a people unenvied and undisturbed ; in a simplicity as happy as it was innocent ; while the volumes of our earliest moralists were filled with the idea of progressive degeneracy, against which as it was impossible to succeed, so was it useless to contend.

The discoveries of navigation, and the lights of reviving learning, were for a time insufficient to convince our ancestors that there had not been a period in which men were wiser, or a land in which they were happier than themselves. The visionary worlds of Bacon and Sir Thomas More have a situation assigned them, in some part of the globe then unknown ; and Spenser's lines, in which he obviates any objections that might arise to the actual existence of " *his delightfull lond of Faëry,*" are so curious for the subject, and method of reasoning, as to deserve citation.

> " Right well I wote, most mighty Soueraine,
> That all this famous antique history,
> Of some th' aboundance of an idle braine
> Will iudged be, and painted forgery,
> Rather than matter of iust memory ;
> Sith none, that breatheth living aire, does know
> Where is this happy lond of Faëry,
> Which I so much do vaunt, yet no where show,
> But vouch antiquities, which nobody can know.

> " But let that man with better sense advise,
> That to the world least part to vs is red :
> And daily how through hardy enterprize
> Many great regions are discouered,
> Which to late age were never mentioned.
> Who euer heard of the Indian Peru ?
> Or who in venturous vessell measured
> The Amazons huge riuer now found trew ?
> Or fruitfullest Virginia who did euer vew ?

> " Yet all these were, when no man did them know ;
> Yet haue from wisest ages hidden beene :
> And later times things more unknown shall show.
> Why then should witless man so much misweene
> That nothing is, but that which he hath scene ?
> What if within the moons faire shining spheare,
> What if in every other star vnseene,
> Of other worldes he happily should heare ?
> He wonder would much more, yet such to some appeare."

An argument of the actual existence of a country, derived from the impossibility of demonstrating the contrary, was so singular, that I could not resist the temptation of offering it to my readers. These visionary obstacles to perfection did not vanish before the morning of science ; on the contrary, from some circumstances before observed they seem to have gained additional terrors. Milton himself was under apprehensions, that his poem was produced too late for admiration if not for excellence, and our ancestors were long content to believe themselves born in an age too late, or a climate too cold, for the attainment of perfection. In the first it will be sufficient to observe, that countries the least polished by literature or civilized by commercial intercourse, have always been found the most resolute asserters of their ancient dignity, a cause to which we must attribute the prolix catalogue of Scottish monarchs, and the Milesian colony of the Irish antiquaries. The second, as the malice of my inquiry does not war with the dead, I shall not examine ; the very existence of such an opinion may in time become doubtful.

There are perhaps few popular opinions so repugnant as the former to truth and reason, which may not be traced to their origin, in an inventive mind, occupied rather in palliating its omissions by ingenious excuses, than in avoiding them by a determined activity ; and the most specious are seldom recurred to but as the lenitives of reflection on the painful retrospect of wasted time and abilities misapplied.

MONDAY, JULY 9, 1787.

"Sed turpem putat inscite metuitque lituram."
HOR. *Ep.* ii. 1, l. 167.
"———— I but forgot
The last and greatest art, the art to blot."—POPE.

HERE are few instances of imperfection more mortifying to human pride than those incidental ones which occur in the most illustrious and distinguished characters. The traces of occasional oversight are most frequently discovered in those figures whose outlines have been dashed

with the gigantic sublimity of the masterpieces of the most
celebrated painters ; few will remain which we can declare
faultless, after those are excepted in which some trivial oversight has been discovered, and published with all the efforts
of industrious petulance.   The errors of Hannibal and
Charles the Twelfth are such as an inferior genius would
have been preserved from by the mere frigidity of cautious
consideration, however superior the noble daring of a great
mind may be to that cold and faultless mediocrity which is approved without admiration.   Though the puns of " Paradise
Lost," the incidental nodding of the Iliad, and the *parties
carrées* in Somerset Place, vanish before the collected
splendour of the whole design, they must be regarded as
infinitely more mortifying than a series of continued dulness, or a collection of united deformity.

In such a train of reflections I was interrupted by an
unexpected summons from my editor, who informed me
that a stranger of a very extraordinary appearance had of
late made very frequent inquiries for me, and was now at
his house waiting my arrival with considerable impatience.
As I am not by nature either incurious or discourteous I
followed my editor, who after a walk of about a quarter of
an hour introduced me to a little parlour, and a little elderly
man, with a very serious countenance and exceeding foul
linen.   After smoothing his approaches to my acquaintance
by some introductory compliments, he informed me, as indeed I might have guessed, " that he was by profession an
author, that he had been for many years a literary pro-
jector ; that owing to a kind of fatality which had hitherto
attended his attempts, and a firm resolution on his own
side never to indulge the trivial taste of an ill-judging age
in which it was his misfortune to be born—but he would
not trouble me with a detail of the open hostilities committed on his works by avowed criticism, or the more
secret and dangerous attempts of tacit malevolence and
pretended contempt—that he had lately hit upon a project
which by its nature must secure to itself the attention of
the public, and which, if he had not formed a very wrong
estimate of its merit, would draw his former efforts from
the dust of unmerited oblivion into general notice and
universal approbation.

" It could not have escaped an exact observer, and such

a one he might, without hazarding the imputation of flattery, pronounce Mr. Griffin" (whereupon Mr. Griffin bowed) "that the reputation of our great tragic poet was sinking apace, and that not so much from any radical or intrinsic defect in his writings, as from some venial errors and incidental omissions. Our more refined neighbours had never been able to relish the low humour which pervades every scene, or the frequent violation of those unities which they observe with so religious a regard. Mr. Voltaire, with that philosophic candour which so strongly characterized his life and writings, had abandoned his defence ; and though in some instances he had deigned to borrow from him, had condemned him as the poet of a barbarous age, and the favourite of an unenlightened people. Even among a national audience, the most admired of his dramas were received at least without that enthusiastic applause they had formerly excited, and we must expect, that in another century the partiality for our favourite poet will vanish, together with our national antipathies against popery and wooden shoes, and frogs and slavery, and that a taste for French criticism will immediately follow a relish for their cookery.

"Something must be done, Mr. Griffin, and that shortly. The commentators have done little or nothing. Indeed, what could be expected from such a plan ? Could any thing be more ridiculous ? They have absolutely confined themselves to what Shakespeare might possibly have wrote ! I am fully sensible that the task of reducing to poetic rules and critical exactness, what was written in ignorance or contempt of both, requires a genius and ability little inferior to that of the original composer ; yet this is my project, which however arduous in the undertaking, however difficult in execution, I am persuaded to attempt, and to whom can I with greater propriety—— Mr. Griffin, who himself——so early an age——in so extraordinary a manner—&c. &c."

My friend continued, by remarking "that the people of Athens allowed to the judicious critic, who should adapt a tragedy of Æschylus to the stage, an equal proportion of credit and copy-money, with the author of an original drama. Yet he desired me to observe, that the author of Grecian tragedy was far more strictly observant of poetic discipline, than the father of the English stage. In all his tragedies, there is only one in which he has ventured to break the unity of place, an essential point, and as my friend declared, highly necessary, though it is very natural for the spectator to mistake the stage for a palace, actresses for virgin princesses, &c. yet it is impossible for him to imagine that he is in Bohemia, when but the act before he was fully convinced that he was in Sicily."

He at length concluded by drawing out of a tin box some " proposals for publication," which he desired might be communicated to the public through the medium of my paper, at the same time presenting me with a very copious specimen of the work he had undertaken. He reflected on the honour of such a distinction, " but he was naturally partial to rising merit, and Gregory Griffin might see a period when he himself should exist only in his writings."

In the course of conversation my new acquaintance became extremely communicative, desired my opinion of a preface and dedication, and whether he should prefix it to an improved edition of " Sleidan de quatuor imperiis," or " Girton's Complete Pigeon Fancier ; " but, upon recollection, resolved upon an ode which he had lately composed " On the Use of Acorns in Consumptive Cases."

Having occasion, in the course of conversation, to remark the number of classical scholars produced in our public seminaries, and the comparative paucity of those who have directed their attention to the cultivation of their native language, my friend regarded the cause as extremely evident ; " there were several assistances which the classical composer enjoyed, which—but all these difficulties I should see obviated in his " New Dictionary of Rhymes;" it was a work which had cost him considerable labour and study. Those of his predecessors— Bysshe, Gent, and others, were mere farragos, in which the sound only was consulted, without any nicety of taste or accuracy of selection. This chaos, this rude and undigested mass, he had reduced to order, by selecting the rhymes proper for every possible subject, and reducing them to systematical arrangement. However, as this scheme must be unavoidably retarded by the prosecution of his former project, he should be peculiarly happy to

see his system familiarly explained and illustrated in some
of my future lucubrations." This request, from an earnest
desire I entertained of assisting young practitioners in the
pleasing art of poetry, I immediately complied with; however, as I did not fully comprehend his system, I took the
liberty of transcribing the following passages from my
author's manuscript.

" For the eclogue, or pastoral dialogue, let the student
conclude his lines with the rhymes underwritten, always
taking care to finish his sense with the second rhyme, and
at no time to suffer his verse to exceed the just measure
of ten syllables. The rhymes for this purpose be these:

" —— —— shady brake
—— —— Lycidas awake.
—— —— careless rove
—— —— leafy grove.
—— —— fruitful field
—— —— harvest yield.
—— —— tuneful measures
—— —— harmless pleasures.
—— —— nymphs and swains
—— —— flowery plains.
&c.

" Should our student turn his thoughts to panegyric,
we would advise that he adhere to the endings we have
here prescribed, as

" —— The muse
—— A tributary —— refuse
—— good and great
—— ordain'd by fate
—— noble line
—— race divine
—— great —— heir
—— peculiar care.
&c.

" If my practitioner should, perchance, be possessed of
a great fund of humour, and be inclined to employ his
wicked wit in ridiculing the clergy, we would admonish
him to adhere to the following terminations, in order as
they are appointed, being careful only to confine his lines
to eight syllables:

" —— musty
—— rusty
—— college
—— knowledge

———— —— Farce on
———— —— Parson
———— —— vicar
———— —— liquor
———— —— ease
———— —— fees
———— —— fire
———— —— squire
———— —— tale
———— —— ale
———— —— spouse
———— —— carouse
———— —— breed
———— —— feed."

Should the public approve of this specimen of my friend's abilities, I may perhaps, in some future paper, present them with a sample of his projected publication.

MISCELLANIES.

1785—1792.

1*

D

VERSES WRITTEN AT SIXTEEN

" Ingenium ingens
Inculto latet hoc sub corpore."—HOR. lib. i. sat. III. l. 33.

PHILOSOPHERS of old dispute ye
Whether mere virtue without beauty,
Unhewn, unpolish'd, better is
Than *vitium cum illecebris.*
The man who, twenty years undusted,
In books and single life has rusted,
Contemns the world, commends his college,
And talks of solid sense and knowledge.
For through a medium form'd by reading,
Unrectified by sense or breeding,
Who views the world, but must despise?
Who is there will not trust his eyes?
And though ill-form'd, who will suspect
In his own judgment a defect?
A man brought hither from the moon
(For rhyme's sake) in an air balloon,
Would stare to see our people throw
Away their victuals when they sow;
But this good soul who saw corn sowing,
Yet had no notion of its growing,
Were he to laugh at us, I trust,
His censure would be thought unjust.
Who hears a story but half told,
Who knows no learning but the old,
Their judgments equally must fail
In censuring the times or tale:

The world must his contempt despise
Who looks at them with borrow'd eyes.
Now let us hear what says the beau—
" Politeness is a *passe pour tout.*
Latin and Greek, old fogrum stuff,
Don't signify a pinch of snuff."
Suppose a house built, if you please,
With cornice, architrave, and frieze,
Entablature of colonnade,
And knicknacks of the building trade :
Grand and complete, it draws the eye
Of passengers a-riding by;
The very connoisseurs allow
No palace makes a nobler show ;
Yet you would think the man but silly
Who, having built this sumptuous villa,
Had not a tolerable room
To show his friends in when they come.
This is the case of many a beau
Who gives up all for glare and show.
Outside and front all fine and burnish'd,
But the inner rooms are thinly furnish'd.
Suppose another's mind so grovelling
That a most execrable hovel in
He, strangely whimsey-struck, should like
To fix the pictures of Vandyke ;
I say, if such a den he chose,
Each passer-by would turn his nose.
But should he chance to enter in,
'Twere then, indeed, another thing.
He'd talk of attitudes and contours,
Show his own taste and flatter yours ;
And though a little odd your plan,
Call you a reasonable man ;
But thousands that remain without
Think you a madman past all doubt.
This is the only difference on't,
To those who know you or who don't ;
To seem a fool, the difference this
'Twixt pedant and 'twixt coxcomb is ;
The man of real worth and merit,
The praise of either will inherit.

TRANSLATION FROM SIMONIDES.

"Οτε λάρνακι, κ. τ. λ.

WAS night, and silence and a curling breeze
Crept o'er the shuddering surface of the seas;
Closed in her chest, thus Danaë begun,
With tearful eyes, and clasp'd her darling son:
" O child, what grief I suffer! You the while,
As all regardless, sleep, and sleeping smile;
And can you not, my infant, share my woes,
But in this horrid mansion find repose;
Nor heed the passing waves that, as they come,
Dash o'er your silver locks the hoary foam,
Nor hear the passing tempest whistle wild,
Sunk in your purple mantle, lovely child?
But if, my babe, perchance your little ear
Might understand your mother's voice or hear—
Sleep on, sweet infant—sleep the roaring sea—
Sleep the rude tempest.—Come, sweet sleep, tò me.
And grant me, Jove, if not too great the boon,
Speedy revenge, and that, too, from my son."

EPITAPH ON NÆVIUS.

Mortalis immortalis flere, &c.

AULUS GELLIUS, *Noct. Attic., lib.* I. *cap.* xxiv.

F goddesses for mortal men might weep,
A tear on Nævius should the Muse bestow;
Since Rome no longer does her language keep,
Now he is destined to the shades below.

EPITAPH ON PLAUTUS.

Postquam morte datu'st, &c.

AULUS GELLIUS, *id.*

HEN comic Plautus first departed,
The scene was left, the stage deserted;
And wit and merriment, together
With mirth and humour, fled for ever.

CARMINA MARCIANA AS QUOTED BY LIV₁.

L. XXV. C. 12.

Amnem Trojugena Cannam, &c.

TURNED INTO OLD ENGLISH.

AUNCYENT Romaynes, sonnes of Troie old,
Flee fro' the fyld, the whych is Canna called,
For drede your ennemis should you constrayne
Perforce to fyght in Diomedis Playne ;
But you will take no help of what I have sayin
Tyll all the fyld is covered wyth slayn,
And the ryvere shall bere down to the sea
Dead karkasses the fyshes food to be ;
And vultures and birddes shall have fyll
Of mennes bodys—thys is Jove hys wyll.

Hostem, Romani, si expellere vultis, &c.

ROMAYNE, yffe ye wyshe fro' your domayne
To dryve awaie the nacyons forayne,
Herkinith to me, yt ys my rede,
If that ye wyshe goodhap and woldith spede,
Vowith to Phebus, yerely to fynde
Sacryfyce, and yourselffis by othe bynde.
When publickly yᵉ tribute ys payd
For everich one the sacryfyce shall be made,
And the Pretor that ys chyf of the cyty,
Offe the gamyn shall have yᵉ maistery,
And eke the decemviri shall ordere
The sportis alle after the Greke mannere—
If that ye doith this, yt ys no naye,
But ye and yere pepyl shalle rejoyce alwaie,
And the straungers wᵇ now hold dale and down,
That ilka daie shalle perysh everich one.

ODE FROM A FRAGMENT OF ALCÆUS, QUOTED
BY ARISTIDES.

Οὐ λίθοι οὐδὲ ξύλα, κ. τ. λ.

IS not the arch whose ample stride
With easy sweep surmounts the tide,
Nor mole, that shouldering forth obtains
Old ocean, and his storm restrains ;
While, in its arms' encircling sweep
The sullen seas in silence sleep,
And baffled ocean roars around ;
Nor towering cliffs with turrets crown'd,
Nor. fleets that to the stiffening gale
Unfurl the bosom of the sail ;
Nor wealth acquired in busy traue,
   Nor populous cities, wall-begirt,
Can make a state, or save, when made,
   From hostile arms, from hostile hurt.
But men alone, when they inherit
No other wealth than strength and spirit,
No other bulwark than their sword,
Shall never dread a foreign lord.
'Tis men alone that make a state
Or truly rich or truly great.
Why seek we wealth, then ? to what end,
Say, when war's tempest shall descend
Will lances innocently play
Around the crest with plumage gay ?
Will not the wearer rather show
A signal to invite the blow ?
Arms in an adamantine mould,
By fear and dread, were cast of old ;
Now Fear is overcome by Pride—
In wealth, in grandeur they confide.
Vainly secure—do ye not know
These lures do but invite the foe.
   Then hail, great Albion ! for to thee
Her choicest gifts does fate decree.

Nor are the blessings to thee shown
In grandeur or in wealth alone ;
But in a manly, hardy race,
At once thy bulwark and thy grace.
In thee these double blessings end
At once to have, and to defend.

ADMONITU LOCORUM.[1]

UO sensu antiquas hospes perlustrat Athenas,
     Strata videns passim fana, sepulcra, domus !
Aut vix Romanam retinentia mœnia pompam,
     Templaque barbaricas non bene passa
         manus !
Cuncta obit admirans oculis, passimque vaganti
     Nunc trepidant sacro percita corda metu ;
Nunc gemit antiqui miseratus nominis umbram,
     Temperat et lenis gaudia mista dolor.
" Ergone," ait, "veteres artes operumque labores
     Excelsasque ædes una ruina premit ?
Hîc Gracchi, hîc spissâ circùm plaudente coronâ
     Tullius intonuit libera jura foro.
Hîc celebrans claros solenni more triumphos
     Consul quadrijugis nobilis ibat equis."
Inde loca heroùm vel nomina clara sophorum
     Observans tacitâ religione colit.
Mens nempe ipsa memor, quo nescio percita motu
     Hos monitus viso sentit inesse loco.
Quo pariter sensu, longo post tempore, alumnus
     Jam senior campos lustrat, Etona, tuos.
Scilicet hinc turres venerandaque tecta tuenti
     Lætitia (at modico tincta dolore) subit.
" His," ait, " in campis meditatus, sæpe vocabam
     Cultor Pierias in nova jura Deas :
Sæpe etiam ludo spatia hæc celebrata fremebant,
     Sive trochus, baculo seu levis icta pila est.
Durato incisum testatur robore nomen,
     Quasve tenet fidas sculpta columna notas.

---

[1] [These verses were written while the author was at Eton in
1787, and printed in the *Musæ Etonenses*, vol. ii. p. 220.—ED.]

O felix, nova cui proles assurgit, **Etona,**
  Perpetuumque recens læta juventa **viget."**
Sic pius arcano commotus pectora sensu
  Tempora lapsa diu, nec reditura, refert.
At mihi jam dulcesque lares sedesque paranti
  Linquere Pieridum, quid mihi mentis inest?
Scilicet hinc rapior diversæ in munia vitæ,
  Imparilem officiis vimque animumque ferens.
Hei mihi! quæ dicam? faveat modò multa volenti
  Dicere flebilibus mœsta Elegea modis.
Sed desiderio nimiùm mens icta fideli
  Obstupet, ad Musas nec facit ille dolor.
Hos, lector, grati quos scribimus, accipe versus,
  Munera queîs pietas qualiacunque litet.

METRICAL VERSION OF AN ODE ON ATHELSTAN'S VICTORY.

From the Saxon.[1]

HE mightiest of alle manne,
  Was the gude kinge Athelstan,
  All his knytis to hir medis
  Weren riche and ryal wedis.
  Edmond his brother, was a Knyt
Comelich, brave, and fair to syht.
At Brunenbruc in stour they faught;
Fiercer fray was never wraught.
Maille was split, and helmis roven,
The wall of shieldis down they cloven:
The Thanis which cold with Edmond fare
To meet the fomen well were yare.
For it was comen to hem of kynde
Hir londis and tresoúrs to fend.

The kempis, whych was of Irlond,
  On ilka daie, on ilka strond,

[1 Ellis' "Specimens of English Poetry," Lond. 1801, vol. i. pp. 32-34. For the original see Ellis, *ubi suprà*, pp. 13-31.]

Weted with blude, and wounded, fell
Rapely smatin with the stell.
Grislich on the grund they groned;
Aboven, alle the hyls resouned.
What for laboúr, and what for hete,
The kempis swate til they wer wete.
From morrow til the close of day,
Was the tyme of that journée.

Monie mon from Dacie sprong
The deth tholid, I underfong.
The Scottis fell in that bataille,
Whyche wer forwerid of travaille.
The West Saxonis wer ware,
When their foen away wold fare ;
As they fled they did hem sewe
Wyth ghazand swerdis, that wel couth hew.
The cokins they n' olden staie,
For thir douten of that fraye.

The Mercians fought, I understond ;
There was gamen of the hond.
Alle that with Anlaff hir way nom,
Over the seas in the shippes wome,
And the five sonnes of the kynge,
Fel mid dint of swerd-fightinge,
His seven erlis died alswo ;
Many Scottes wer killed tho.
The Normannes, for their migty bost,
Went hame with a lytyl host.
The Kynge and frode syked sore
For hir kempis whyche wer forlore :
The Kynge and frode to schyppe gan flee,
Wyth mickel haste, but hir meguie.
Constantine gude, and Anlaff,
Lytyl bost hadde of the laif.
Maie he nat glosen, ne saie
But he was right wel appaie.
In Dacie of that gaming
Monie wemen hir hondis wring.
The Normannes passed that rivere,
Mid hevy hart, and sory chere.

The brothers to Wessex yode ;
Leving the crowen, and the tode,
Hawkes, doggis, and wolves tho ;
Egles, and monie other mo,
With the ded men for their mede
On hir corses for to fede.

Sen the Saxonis first come
In schippes over the sea-fome,
Of the yeres that ben forgone,
Greater bataile was never none.

IN COMITIIS PRIORIBUS, Feb. 26, 1789.

Et canibus leporem, canibus venabere damas.

E quoque Phœbe canam, nec non sylvestria
    tecum
Officia et studia et notas venantibus artes :
Tu faveas utrisque laboribus ; Eia, age, notos
Sume habitus, habilesque arcus, pharetramque
sonantem,
Si modò te mecum deserta per avia, rerum
Raptet amor ; juvat ignotas in montibus herbas
Carpere Castaliumque bibentia lilia fontem.
    Principio sedes canibus, statioque petenda est
Propter aquam, tardis ingens ubi flexibus errat
Flumen, et arboreâ densum nemus accubat umbrâ ;
Scilicet atque tibi prudens persuadeat auctor
Sordes, et tetro halantes humore paludes
Pellere, et æstivum stabulis avertere solem ;
Carpit enim tenues sensus adjectus odorum,
Nec soliti patitur studii meminisse, nec artis,
Quippe hebetes sensus, et stamina dura resistunt.
    Tu modò quos in spem statuas submittere gentis,
Nequaquam de plebe canum viliuè catervâ
Delige, sed si quos sylvis exercuit altis
Assiduus labor, atque ingentis gloria prædæ.
Ille mihi placeat maculis insignis et albo,
Qui grandes oculos, immensosque oris hiatus

Exhibet, et plantâ vestigia pandit apertâ;
Cui nitidi dentes, cui spinâ cauda retortâ
Erigitur, cui lentæ aures, et grandia colla,
Crus breve, et ingentes scapulæ, lateque patescit
Pectus, et in tenuem rursus succingitur alvum,
Ille mihi ante alios fortunatissimus omnes
Arva sequi, et leporum secreta cubilia nosse;
Primus odorato relegens vestigia prato,
Naribus aërium patulis decerpet odorem;
Implicitasque vias, iterataque signa retexet.
Sin studium est leporem instanti prævertere cursu,
Est canis, in tales tibi qui nec inutilis artes
Serviet, huic arrectæ aures spicantur, et acre
Argutumque caput, tum lumina viva vagantur,
Ille quidem gracilisque artus, tenuisque videri,
Sed validus, firmisque aptus per viscera fibris,
Acer, acerba tuens, prædam per aperta volantem
Insequitur, sed nec per densos ille recessus
Ire, nec elapsam novit sectarier ultrò.
    Hæc duo sunt genera, hic melior, qui præpete cursu
Deficiens, tantumque leves sectatus odores,
Maturata dabit producto gaudia cursu.
    Præterea nec mos, nec gens est una ferarum,   .
Quippe imbelle genus leporum, nec fidere campis
Ignotis audet, fluviosvè innare rapaces;
Sed circum timidè per pascua nota vagatur,
Aut redit exacto sua per vestigia gyro.
Quoque magis clamore virûm, strepituque sequentum
Urgetur, quantoque magis genua ægra fatiscunt,
Tam magis implicitos sese convertit in orbes.
    Quid cervi? quid quæ præbent spectacula vulpes?
Scilicet hi scopulosque et depressas convalles
Lustravere fugâ, et densæ penetralia sylvæ.
Cernis ab invento cervus simul exiit antro,
Vix pede tangit humum, surgentesvè atterit herbas;
Mox autem spatio extremo, sub fine laborum,
Attollit caput exultans, colloque superbit
Arduus, et magno molimine crura reponit.
Tunc animis opus, O socii, tum viribus usus!
Ille fugit, longèque ignotis exulat oris,
Respiciens sylvam in magnam, dulcesque hymenæos
Suspirans nequicquam, agris excessit avitis,

Latrantum strepitu, et vastis clamoribus actus.
Ergo aut ille metu trepidum latus æger anhelans
In fluvium dedit, et magno se condidit alveo;
Aut duro vitam tandem in certamine liquit,
Et gemitu nemus ah! notum, sylvamque replevit,
Vulnera sæva videns, avulsaque viscera vivo.
Hanc olim veteres vitam coluere, priusquam
Moribus, et placidâ se composuere quiete.
Cum neque vomeribus glebas diffringere inertes,
Aut ferrum scibant tractare, aut utier igni.
Ergo inter sese, vestiti pelle ferarum,
Venatu vitam egerunt, passimque ferarum
Consectabantur per agros sylvestria secla,
Stipitibus duris, et acuti pondere saxi.
Ergo illos extensi excepit terminus ævi,
Multaque sæpe virûm vivendo sæcula vicit
Indomitum genus, et magnos induruit artus.
Inde et amicitiam cœperunt jungere, et nates
Proserere, et sacras divûm venerarier aras,   •
Et communia jura pati, castosque hymenæos.
   Sed nos immensos cursu lustravimus agros,
Tempus abire, viri, partamque avertere prædam.[1]

---

[1] [These verses, now published for the first time, have, thanks to
the courtesy of the Rev. H. R. Luard, been carefully collated with the
original in the Registrary's office at Cambridge. No attempt has
been made at correction where they do not conform with the more
advanced Latinity of the present day; and only the most obvious
typographical errors have been corrected. The companion set of
verses on

"Immiscentque manus manibus, pugnamque lacessunt"

was by the famous "F. Wrangham (A. Tr.)" It describes a fight
between Humphrey and Mendoza. Wrangham wrote another copy
for the Comitia Posteriora of the same year, but Wollaston the
Moderator was reprimanded for allowing it to be printed, on account
of its offensive nature. Bobus Smith wrote in 1790 and two following years; William Frere of Trinity in 1795, 1797, 1798; Praed
in 1823; C. Wordsworth in 1828; C. Frere (Corpus), 1841.—Ed.]

ESSAY WHICH GAINED THE MEMBERS' PRIZE,
CAMBRIDGE, 1792.

" An morum emendationem et virtutis cultum in nascenti
Sinûs Botanici republicâ sperare liceat ?"

> " Terra salutares herbas, eademque nocentes,
>   Nutrit : et urticæ proxima sæpe rosa est."
>   OVID. *Rem. Amoris*, l. 45.

UCTO indies et progrediente rei politicæ
studio, haud abs re videretur, pauca quædam
de coloniarum institutis dicere. Argumentum enim habemus, sive utilitatem, sive dignitatem spectes, amplissimum, tum, id quod
in academicâ questione maximé observandum est, ab odio
omni et contentione, quibus hæc studia abundare solent,
semotum maximé et alienum. Hinc enim ab oriente pro-
fecta gens humana totum orbem terrarum sine cæde aut
sanguine occupavit ; et quæcunque nunc, aut opulentiâ,
aut pulchritudine præstant, a feris sylvisque vindicavit.

Primum ergo ut de Græcorum coloniis loquar : nam
illa nimis antiqua et ipsâ vetustate obscura prætermittenda
censeo. Oriebantur hæ plerumque aut e civium copiâ,
aut e seditionibus ; quarum causarum, modo pace externâ
civitas fruatur, necesse est ut altera quidem existat ; (nisi
forté ut Sinenses hodie, quod in civitate liberâ fieri vix
posse arbitrandum est, profluentem incolarum copiam
magno suo malo intrà patriæ terminos coercere velint) ;
quâ re nihil tetrius fædiusve excogitari potest. Ut enim a
peregrinantibus accepimus, iisque recentioribus, et fidei
satis probatæ ; adeo multitudine suâ laborat gens illa, ut
humani operis pretium ad vilissimam mercedem redactum
sit, quæque apud nos machinarum aut jumentorum ope
fiunt, illic hominum vi omnia aguntur, quibusque alimentis
cæteræ omnes gentes abstinent, iis avidissime utuntur
Sinensium tenuiores ; neque majore copiâ et incuriâ apud
nos cadavera bestiarum projecta sunt quam illic infantium
recens natorum corpora ; quâ miserabili frequentiâ quæ
non vastitas et solitudo potior videatur ?

Ut a Sinensibus ad Græcos redeam, horum quidem
coloniæ nihil aliud erant quam effusa in cæteras regiones
nimia aut inquieta multitudo (quod ipsorum vocabulum
ἀποικία verissime exprimit); neque in eas quicquam juris
aut imperii obtinuit, quæ metropolis vocabatur, nisi si
quod in honore et observantiâ positum esset. Multa
tamen sunt a Græcis in coloniarum institutione commodè
et sapienter excogitata; qualia sunt sacrorum consortia,
et quod suprà ostensum est vocabulum maternæ caritatis
inter urbes usurpatum; ut quodam parricidii crimine
teneri viderentur, qui adversus sociam cognatamque
urbem arma moverint; et hæc sanè, etsi levia et futilia
quibusdam videantur, habent tamen mirabilem quandam
vim ad pacis fideique conservationem. Quis enim non
sentit apud gentes intervallo aliquo separatas odii, amici-
tiæque terminos tenuissimo discrimine dirimi, nosque iis
constanter favere, quibus nobiscum aut linguæ aut re-
ligionis aut victûs denique communit⸺ intercesserit?

In coloniis quidem, perinde atque aliis Græcorum
institutis, omnia ad vitæ jucunditatem amœnitatemque et
populare commodum conformata deprehendimus: Romani
autem, quorum omnis politia paucorum dominationem
quodammodo sapit, eâdem necessitate permoti fructum
longè uberiorem ex eâ perceperunt; fructum illum modo
(quod plerique solent) imperii magnitudine quam privatâ
uniuscujusque utilitate metiri malis—neque ullâ re magis
ad imperium totius orbis evecti sunt. A Romulo enim
profecti eodem et instituti hujus et imperii auctore, quod
Dionysius testatur, in urbes bello captas civium Romanorum colonias deducebant, quâ ex re quanta commoda
profluxerint haud facile dictu erit; primum enim egenæ
et inquietæ plebis quasi sentinam ex urbe exhauriebant
ab urbanâ tribu sortitionem exorsi, tum stirpem Latinam
patriamque augebant: Plebes enim agrorum opportunitate
sustentata matrimonia libentius contraxit, prolem facilius
educavit, et id quidem agresti illi et simplici more, militi-
bus senectus in agris assignata, quinetiam subactarum
gentium pervicacia quasi præsidiis impositis repressa,
sæpe porro adversus hostium ferociam veteranorum
coloniæ objectæ, ut Cremona et Placentia duo firmissima
munimenta adversus impetum Gallorum, præcedente
autem seculo per Rhenum et Istrum passim dispositæ

sunt. Hanc autem progeniem suam urbs Romana adeo non manumisit, ut in eos severius imperium exercuisse videatur, pariter enim atque cives Romani, milites, conscribere, stipendia pendere tenebantur; ademtoque omni civitatis et suffragii jure dimidium capitis amiserunt. Italico quidem bello illa omnia conturbata sunt, inque municipia manavit suffragandi potestas; verum ita antiquius usitatum est de Romanis coloniis; nam de Latinis haud satis compertum habemus.

Nescio sane utrum in hac quæstione prætermittendum sit id, quod tum antiquissimis imperiis, tum etiam Romano debili jamdudum et senescenti acceptum fuisse constat; gentes enim barbaras alienigenasque sedibus suis excitas in ipsa imperii penetralia transtulerunt, cujus rei prudentissimum auctorem Darium Ioniæ Thraciæque incolis Cissæum agrum habitandum dedisse tradit. Herodotus, Ægyptique reges coloniis Græcorum Naucratim provinciam assignâsse; eorumque opera adversus civium seditiones haud rarò usos; et erat id quidem sapienter ut in tyrannide excogitatum, ne socius scilicet cognatusque populus morum aut linguæ commercio conspiraret; tum ut advenas viros summis sibi beneficiis obstrictos tanquam militem mercenarium ad omnia jussa exequenda pacatum et in procinctu haberent. Sed Romanos cum id, quod ob unius incolumitatem inventum esset, ad imperii tutamen transferre conarentur, spes fefellit; neque enim pari lege populus populo, atque homini homo, obedit; neque unquam infirmioribus et paucioribus validi et plures inserviunt.

Satis hæc de antiquorum coloniis, pro questione fortasse nimia; quod si rei ipsius magnitudinem et dignitatem spectaveris, jejuna certe, et exilia: ad recentiores tandem deducenda est oratio. Atque hic ferè omnia antiquis absimilia instituerunt, et ad lucrum spectantia, neque imperii obtinendi gratiâ, neque frequentiâ civium, adducti ut in exteras regiones se conferrent; quicquid enim in hâc re profecerunt minores, ad commercii studium referamus oportet; quippe cui ipsas sedes suas et domicilia coloniæ nostræ debeant. Indiam enim per viam breviorem quærentibus primum patuit ille novus orbis, cumque vim maximam auri et argenti navigantibus offerret, coloniis deductis occupabatur, quos non tantum ulla agri ubertas

impulit, ut relictâ patriâ in alias terras secederent, quantum spes divitiarum quam ex metallis conceperant, quod
ex regiis diplomatibus satis constat, quibus Jacobo Primo,
Henrico Quarto regnantibus, Anglis Gallisque in novum
orbem migrandi jus conceditur ; his enim metallorum
decimæ regi reservantur, tum Anglis præcipitur, ut si quem
exitum habeat occidentem versus mare Atlanticum sedulò
explorent. His consiliis fundatæ colonorum res haud ita
magno tempore eò creverunt, ut mercatoribus nostris
quæstuosum fore videretur, si, exclusis aliarum gentium
navigiis, sibi solis liceret ad portus Americanos mercaturæ
causâ commeare ; petierunt ergo illi, et ab hominibus in
re alienâ benignis impetrârunt, atque hujus privilegii
gratiâ (quod reliquis civibus etiam obfuisse constat) imperium in colonias retentum est, maxima bella suscepta,
respublica fœnore obstricta, avulsis autem a dominatione
nostrâ provinciis, summæ opes, quæ prius in privatum
mercatorum commodum redundârant, per patriam popu-
lumque fluxerunt. Quam enim illi sortem capitalem vix
tertio quoque anno tandem receperunt, fœnore quidem
satis amplo adauctam, sed reliquis ferè civibus infructuoso,
ad propinquum magis commercium retulerunt, ex quo aut
bis aut ter in anno reditus fiant ; quâ mutatione factâ,
quantis opibus artificum opificumque omne genus susten-
târint, juvaverint, auxerint, incredibile ferè est et infinitum.
Summas enim quibus jam floremus divitias huc oportet
referamus ; neque sanè mihi temperare possum, quin huic
gratuler plaudamque invento; cum enim propriis bonis
homines jamdudum attoniti sint, originemque eorum alii,
alio derivent, primus, ni fallor, veros fontes aperui, quos
valde demiror viros in re politicâ versatos latere tam diu
potuisse, cum, stante adhuc et vigente in colonias imperio
nostro, quæ ex commercio eorum commoda, quæque ex
privilegio isto incommode fluerent, Smithius luculentè
patefecerit ; ita ut manifestum videretur, illo manente,
sublato altero, summis opibus rempublicam auctam iri ;
quæ res quidem ita evenit, neque aliunde ortùm trahit ; ut
enim summam prudentiam constantiamque regentibus
nostris inesse libens fatear, errare nihilominua videntur,
qui privatas, quibus floremus opes, iis attribuant, utpote
quos constet in vectigalibus augendis, ære alieno sensim
minuendo, per omne imperii spatium occupatos fuisse ;

1 *   E

quorum alterum singulorum civium opes augere certè
nullo modo potest, alterum fœnoris pretio diminuto haud
ita magnum momentum eo conferat; quod si tandem
infrà quadrantem usuræ redigantur, pulcherrimam occa-
sionem habebimus oblatam æris alieni, non carptim ut
nunc, sed compendio quodam abolendi, nullâ fœneratorum
injuriâ: quid vero lætius hoc feliciusve excogitari potest?
Quod tamen non ita longè abesse spondere possumus,
modo pace populus fruatur, et, qua ratione huc usque
opulentiæ crevit, eâ augeri pergat. Quæ vero tum cre-
dendum est hanc civitatem examina missuram? Neque
jam ad metalla indaganda, sterile propositum, et vix tanto
imperio dignum arbitrandum, neque ut ignota marium
perscrutemur, quæ sub auspiciis regis nostri feré omnia
patuerunt; sed, ubi abundantem civium copiam hæc
nostra patria in se continere non poterit, usque in extrema
orbis coloniæ educentur, quæque nunc inculta jacent et
deserta terræ loca, incolis, artibus, opibus florere posteri
nostri videbunt; neque jam ista omnia tam sedulo explo-
rabimus; quæ commercii consuetudo cum quâque coloniâ
institui possit; qui reditus ex eâ fiant; sedem tantum et
habitandi locum auctæ multitudini exquiremus, quæ, si cum
patriæ civitatis commodo constare poterint, ideo præ-
ferenda sunt, sin aliter, ipsâ necessitatis vi jubente præ-
termitti non possunt.

De novæ autem coloniæ situ, recte necne electus fuerit,
omnino nihil affirmare ausim. Agitur enim de omnium,
quot in orbe terrarum sunt, locorum cœlo, solo, incolis,
quæ quidem majora videntur, quam ut privato judicio com-
plecti possint. Hoc tantum contendere licet, neque lucro,
neque commodo eam nobis fore, nisi si quod in exhauriendâ
plebe posthac consistere potuerit. Hoc cur fiat causa in
promtu est; obvium enim cuique et manifestum, sublato,
qui nunc publico sumptu facitur, commeatu, exulibus mercaturæ consortia cum hâc nostrâ patriâ nulla prorsus
interfore. Quî enim merces nostras emere poterunt?
"Frumento (dicet aliquis), coriisque, et cibariis sale con-
ditis, ut olim Americani." At hæc omnia vilia sunt mo-
lisque maximæ, neque unquam pretio vecturam vincent;
præsertim cum hæc omnia minimo pretio præstent Americani, et præstabunt in multa sæcula; quod si iis in coloniæ
gratiam portus nostri occluderentur nosmetipsos manifestâ

injuriâ afficeremus. "Indiam vero navigabunt:" at vetat
lex ; aiunt enim juris-periti civem Anglicanum, ubicunque
terrarum consederit, persecuturas tamen cum patriæ suæ
leges et insectaturas, pariterque ac nos exules nostros ab
Indorum commercio prohiberi.

Sperandum est ergo consulturos de hâc re, qui princi-
patum gerunt, cauturosque ubi primum mercatoriæ societatis privilegia renovantur, ne coloniæ navigia Asiæ littori-
bus arceantur ; sin aliter fiat, dubia nascentis civitatis initia,
tardaque ejus incrementa auspicor. Incolæ enim ad opi-
ficia necessario se convertent, sterile genus laboris et
infructuosum, si cum agri culturâ comparetur, quæque ex
Asiâ fructibus prædiorum redimere possent, perfectæ artis
et elegantiæ opera ipsi sibi omnis artificii rudes plerumque
et indocti conficient ; neque contendat aliquis in duritie ac
pauperie enutritam civitatem validiorem quando evasuram.
Constat enim industriam pro laboris pre⬛ igere, pretium
autem rei cujuscumque est, quod eâ parare possis. Vid-
eant ergo qui coloniæ res gerunt, ut eam omnibus privilegii vinculis quamprimum exuant, quibusque fasciis in-
fantem obvolvi necesse erat, puerum factum ne constrin-
gant. De illo loquor, duro et militari imperio, ut in homines
improbos fortasse necessario : confido tamen moribus in
melius mutatis lenius ac mitius provinciam administrari
posse. Adjuvat fiduciam Americanarum coloniarum exemplum ; nam hæ iisdem feré neque melioribus incolis
primum concelebrabantur : quod si sanctæ illius simpli-
cisque sectæ viros excipias quibus Pensylvania colonis
condita est ; quorumque nonnullos in hanc novam nostram
ituros libentissimè audio ; omnes ferè aut seditiosos aut
criminum convictos patria expulit.

Nihil ergo videtur esse cur de nascentis reipublicæ
moribus quisquam desperet, cum pro iis et amplissimum
exemplum stare videtur, et ipsa ratio quandam vitæ cum
virtute conjunctionem indicat ; abest enim ab illâ fraus
omnis et invidia ; nec enim bonis alienis anguntur, nec
inventa (quod alii artifices faciunt) parcè aut malignè im-
pertire solent, sed in commune humani generis commodum
benignè consulere, rarissimis inimicitiis utuntur, simula-
tione nullâ. Quod si huc accedant cognatæ caritatis vin-
cula, proprietatisque dulcedo, quid sit, quod hominum
mentes in deterius trahere possit, planè non video ; cum

absint præsertim vitiorum irritamenta, popinæ, scorta,
lupanaria, cumque ipsa naturæ species animum ad numinis
contemplationem virtutisque cultum conciliet ; eoque magis
quo rudiores illi homines sunt et indoctiores. Atque hic
vereor, ne quibusdam videar præter hominum opinionem
sententiam protulisse, quod si rem paulo attentius perscrutemur a rectâ eam ratione pendere deprehendemus.
Bestiæ enim nonne iis rebus aguntur quæ sensibus obji-
ciuntur et in quibus versantur? itaque homines, ut stolidi-
tate et inscientiâ ad bestiarum naturam accedunt, exter-
narum rerum facilius impressionem admittunt ; qui vero
semel rerum scientiam hausit, omnia sua (ut aiebat sapiens
ille) secum portat, neque iis afficitur (ut Stoicorum sermone utar) quæ extra ipsum sunt ; atque ille, si virtutis
præceptis rectè imbutus est nullis vitiorum lenociniis ad-
duci potest, ut de rectâ viâ deflectat ; si autem cogitanti
cuidam meditantique vitia sua non displicuerunt, nulla
unquam præcepta, nulla exempla, animo inhærentem in-
veteratamque pravitatem avellere poterunt.

De hominibus ergo utcunque facinorosis non desperan-
dum videtur, modo illud non accedat quod est in malis
ultimum, ut volentes scientes tranquillo animo peccent.
Non prætermittenda videtur in hâc disputatione recenti-
orum philosophorum opinio (accurata quidem, ut mihi
videtur, et experientiæ satis congrua): aiunt enim affec-
tuum humanorum duo esse genera, quorum aliud ex naturâ,
aliud ex societate, oriri, ex natura scilicet prolis curam, et
in affines cognatosque benevolentiam, iram denique, et
misericordiam ; avaritiam vero, et invidiam, odium, ambi-
tionem, hæc omnia â societate proficisci ; quoque ea sit
multiplex magis et in partes distributa, eo crescere magis
et vigere.

Jam vero, si qua est hujus argumenti vis et auctoritas,
(quæ mihi videtur esse maxima, neque tantum decretis
philosophorum, sed et suffragiis nixa multorum hominum
et experientiâ) pro nascentis coloniæ moribus facit, in quâ
et societatis et vivendi rationem simplicem esse oportet ;
quis enim ibi relinquetur ambitioni aut contentioni locus ?
sit autem avaritiæ ; sordidæ illi et odiosæ certè non erit.
Quæ vero inimicitiæ aut nasci aut durare poterunt ? quis
alteri invidebit neque multo plura habenti neque ipse rei
alicujus indigus ?

Hæc de moribus dicta volui; nam religio, cum omnis ejus successus non ab ipsis rebus sed a paucorum ingenio et industriâ pendeat, in disputatione locum habere non potest : valdè tamen demiror, cum res ipsa tanti momenti sit, nullam ejus mentionem, neque in rerum gestarum commentariis, neque in procuratoris epistolis fuisse factam. Quod si mortis formidine exules a scelere deterreri posse putabant, manifesto errore teneri videntur. Quis enim est de illo sceleratorum grege qui mortis timorem non multoties expenderit contempseritque ? Lapso scilicet effætoque animo acriores stimuli subjiciendi sunt, neque iis diutius immorandum quibus animi sensusque hominum obtorpuerunt. Sed ponamus homines in omni scelere et spurcitia volutatos ad bonos mores revocari non posse ; quanquam et de iis melius et de humano ingenio arbitror. Quid est autem quod nascentem sobolem depravet, quibus omnia illa vitiorum lenocinia nisi mentibus ipsorum ingenita esse velis, ignota sint necesse est? Quod si objiciat aliquis perpetuâ colluvie in novam civitatem effluente periculum fore ne contaminentur eorum animi ; ad Americæ exemplum iterum recurramus oportet. Huc enim, donec ab imperio nostro descitum est, quot annis deportabantur criminum convicti, et in statutum servitii tempus venum dati ? quos tamen civitatis mores infecisse nemo arbitrabatur. Quod contrarium ferè evenit ; plerique enim ipsorum ad bonam frugem revocati sunt, ibi consederunt. Quid est ergo quod prohibeat, quo minus nova hæc proles in paupertate rusticoque labore educata simplex et proba evadat ; summis præsertim industriæ præmiis propositis, sceleri nullis. Ager enim apud nos summo pretio habitus prohibet quo minus integro laboris fructu pauperes fruantur ; illic autem in tanta vilitate jacet, ut in vacuum solum venienti etiam gratia habenda sit, unde fit ut, quod apud nos in divitum vectigalia, illic in laboris pretium cedat.

Hactenus de moribus dictum volui ; quin si tenue quibusdam et rarum videatur quod de eis nominatim disputavimus, eos ita reputare velim quicquid de industriâ, de commercio, disseruimus a morum contemplatione non abesse : quamobrem mihi videtur summaque (?) de nascentis imperii fortunis in moribus recte esse posita ; ut quæ alia omnia in se complectatur atque contineat. Si qua sint autem in hâc disputatione quæ obscuriora aliquibus videantur, et quidem ne sint valdè metuo, veniam tamen apud æquos judices consecuturum arbitror, rem conatum arduam apprimè et difficilem, res novas antiquo sermone illustrare ; tum (id quod longè gravius) excerpta quædam theoremata ex Smithii libris huic tractatui inserere, quæque ille continuâ ratiocinationis serie vincit, ab ipsis rei politicæ elementis breviter deducere. Atque hujus viri mentionem ingressus nescio sane quodnam operi meo fastigium potius imponam, quam ut laudes ejus eloquar, qui quam amplexus est, neque minimam, rei politicæ provinciam, neque infœcundam, adeo excoluit, ut quæ prius erroribus perplexa jacerent et verborum farragine obvoluta, non solum aperta jam et purgata videantur, sed spem messis amplissimam ostenderint.

Ille, Ille vir pacis per Europam concordiæque fundamenta jecit, libero commercio viam patefecit atque munivit, plebi erudiendæ, coloniis educendis, præcepta edidit ; omnia denique quæ extrà scholas philosophorum sunt ad bene beateque vivendum necessaria suppeditavit, effecitque ut ad veterum opes (a quibus certè nunc absumus, neque naturæ injuriâ, sed ignorantiâ propriâ exclusi) cito perventuri videamur ; modo, quod ille voluit, non per abrupta et præcipitia eniti tentemus, sed nota sequendo et lenia, quæ ipse præcepit exequamur.[1]

---

[1] This Essay, never before printed, is here given from the original manuscript. It appears to have been somewhat incorrectly written ; but none save the most obvious corrections have been admitted : and one or two difficult passages are still left to exercise the ingenuity of the reader.—_Note to the First Edition._

CONTRIBUTIONS TO THE
ANTI-JACOBIN.

CONTRIBUTIONS TO THE
ANTI-JACOBIN.

N 1852 appeared an edition[1] of the "Poetry of the Anti-jacobin," giving the "Contents, with the names of the Authors," as furnished by

"Canning's own copy of the poetry,"
"Lord Burghersh's copy,"
"Wright the Publisher's copy," and information derived from the amanuensis Upcott.

Lord Burghersh attributes several pieces to "Frere" which he never claimed. In the following pages those only have been ascribed to him, which (in memoranda given by him of the authors) he said were his own, either wholly or in part; and wherever it was possible (as in some places in the "Loves of the Triangles," the "Rovers," and "New Morality"), the particular lines contributed by each author, according to Mr. Frere's memoranda, have been marked.

---

[1] [A second edition, enlarged, was published in 1854.]

IMITATION.[1]

INSCRIPTION

FOR THE DOOR OF THE CELL IN NEWGATE, WHERE MRS.
BROWNRIGG, THE PRENTICE-CIDE, WAS CONFINED
PREVIOUS TO HER EXECUTION.

[NOVEMBER 20, 1797.]

OR one long term, or e'er her trial came,
  Here BROWNRIGG linger'd. Often have these
    cells
  Echo'd her blasphemies, as with shrill voice
  She scream'd for fresh Geneva. Not to her
Did the blithe fields of Tothill, or thy street,
St. Giles, its fair varieties expand ;
Till at the last, in slow-drawn cart, she went
To execution. Dost thou ask her crime?
SHE WHIPP'D TWO FEMALE 'PRENTICES TO DEATH,
AND HID THEM IN THE COAL-HOLE. For her mind
Shaped strictest plans of discipline. Sage schemes!
Such as Lycurgus taught, when at the shrine
Of the Orthyan goddess he bade flog
The little Spartans ; such as erst chastised
Our Milton, when at college. For this act
Did Brownrigg swing. Harsh laws! But time shall come
When France shall reign, and laws be all repeal'd!

                    CANNING AND FRERE.

THE FRIEND OF HUMANITY AND THE
KNIFE-GRINDER.

[NOVEMBER 27, 1797.]

N the specimen of JACOBIN POETRY which we
  gave in our last Number, was developed a
  principle, perhaps one of the most universally
  recognized in the Jacobin creed ; namely,
  " that the animadversion of *human laws* upon
human actions is for the most part nothing but *gross op-*

---

[1] Of Southey's " Inscription for the apartment in Chepstow Castle,
where Henry Marten, the Regicide, was imprisoned thirty years."

pression; and that, in all cases of the administration of **criminal** *justice*, the truly benevolent mind will consider only the *severity of the punishment*, without any reference to the *malignity of the crime."* This principle has of late years been laboured with extraordinary industry, and brought forward in a variety of shapes, for the edification of the public. It has been inculcated in bulky quartos, and illustrated in popular novels. It remained only to fit it with a poetical dress, which had been attempted in the inscription for Chepstow Castle, and which (we flatter ourselves) was accomplished in that for Mrs. Brownrigg's cell.

Another principle, no less devoutly entertained, and no less sedulously disseminated, is the *natural and eternal* **warfare of the** POOR and the RICH. In those orders and gradations of society, which are the natural result of the original difference of talents and of industry among mankind, the Jacobin sees nothing but a graduated scale of violence and cruelty. He considers every rich man as an oppressor, and every person in a lower situation as the victim of avarice, and the slave of aristocratical insolence and contempt. These truths he declares loudly, not to excite compassion, or to soften the consciousness of superiority in the higher, but for the purpose of aggravating discontent in the inferior orders.

A human being, in the lowest state of penury and distress, is a treasure to a reasoner of this cast. He contemplates, he examines, he turns him in every possible light, with a view of extracting from the variety of his wretchedness, new topics of invective against the pride of property. He, indeed, (if he is a true Jacobin,) refrains from *relieving* the object of his compassionate contemplation; as well knowing, that every diminution from the general mass of human misery, must proportionably diminish the force of his argument.

This principle is treated at large by many authors. It is versified in sonnets and elegies without end. We trace it particularly in a poem by the same author from whom we borrowed our former illustration of the Jacobin doctrine of crimes and punishments. In this poem, the pathos of the matter is not a little relieved by the absurdity of the metre. We shall not think it necessary to transcribe the whole of it, as our imitation does not pretend to be so literal as in the last instance, but merely aspires to convey some idea of the manner and sentiment of the original. One stanza, however, we must give, lest we should be suspected of painting from fancy, and not from life.

The learned reader will perceive that the metre is Sapphic, and affords a fine opportunity for his *scanning* and *proving*, if he has not forgotten them.

> Cōld wăs thē nīght wĭnd ; drīftĭng fāst thĕ snōws fĕll ;
> Wīde wĕre thē dōwns, ănd shĕltĕrlēss ănd nākĕd :
> Whēn ă poōr wānd'rĕr strŭgglĕd ŏn hĕr joŭrnĕy,
>   Wēăry ănd wāy-sōre.

This is enough ; unless the reader should wish to be informed how

> Fāst o'ĕr thē blēāk hēāth rāttlĭng drŏve ă chārĭōt ;

or how, not long after,

> Loūd blĕw thē wĭnd, ŭnhĕārd wăs hĕr cŏmplāinĭng—
>   On wĕnt thĕ hŏrsemān.

We proceed to give our imitation, which is of the *Amœ-bæan* or *Collocutory* kind.

IMITATION.   SAPPHICS.

THE FRIEND OF HUMANITY AND THE KNIFE-GRINDER.

FRIEND OF HUMANITY.

NEEDY Knife-grinder! whither are you going? Rough is the road, your wheel is out of order— Bleak blows the blast;—your hat has got a hole in't,
>   So have your breeches!

" Weary Knife-grinder! little think the proud ones, Who in their coaches roll along the turnpike--road, what hard work 'tis crying all day ' Knives and
>   ' Scissors to grind O !'

" Tell me, Knife-grinder, how you came to grind knives?
Did some rich man tyrannically use you?
Was it the squire? or parson of the parish?
                              Or the attorney?

" Was it the squire, for killing of his game? or
Covetous parson, for his tithes distraining?
Or roguish lawyer, made you lose your little
                              All in a lawsuit?

" (Have you not read the Rights of Man, by Tom Paine?)
Drops of compassion tremble on my eyelids,
Ready to fall, as soon as you have told your
                              Pitiful story."

KNIFE-GRINDER.

" Story! God bless you! I have none to tell, sir,
Only last night a-drinking at the Chequers,
This poor old hat and breeches, as you see, were
                              Torn in a scuffle

" Constables came up for to take me into
Custody; they took me before the justice;
Justice Oldmixon put me in the parish-
                              —Stocks for a vagrant.

" I should be glad to drink your Honour's health in
A pot of beer, if you will give me sixpence;
But for my part, I never love to meddle
                              With politics, sir."

FRIEND OF HUMANITY.

" *I* give thee sixpence! I will see thee damn'd first—
Wretch! whom no sense of wrongs can rouse to vengeance—
Sordid, unfeeling, reprobate, degraded,
                              Spiritless outcast!"

[*Kicks the knife-grinder,* **overturns** *his wheel, and exit
in a transport of* **Republican** *enthusiasm and universal philanthropy.*]

                              CANNING AND FRERE.

MEETING OF THE FRIENDS OF FREEDOM.

[NOVEMBER 30, 1797.]

The curiosity, and even anxiety, which several of our readers have expressed respecting the final declaration expected from the party, upon the subject of the events of the 18th Fructidor, have induced us to lay before them an authentic copy of a part of a future Morning Chronicle, which a correspondent of ours has had the good fortune to anticipate.

THE celebration of this great epocha of the French Revolution had excited a general enthusiasm.—The dinner-room was crowded at an early hour, and part of the company, among which was the Duke of NORFOLK, overflowed into the tap-room. At about sixteen minutes after five, Mr. Fox entered the room and walked up to the end of the table amidst the universal plaudits of the company. The general appearance of his health was perfectly satisfactory; it appeared, indeed, to have been improved by his residence in the country. His hair was, as usual, without powder.

After dinner, when a few appropriate toasts had been given, Mr. Fox rose, upon his health being drank, and began by stating that he felt peculiar satisfaction in considering that the character and object of this meeting were perfectly congenial to his feelings and to those principles he had uniformly professed. What was the conclusion which the event which they were now celebrating naturally suggested to every thinking mind? It was this—that the example of one or more revolutions did not always prevent the necessity of another. There was likewise another conclusion which he trusted it would impress very forcibly on the minds of all who heard him. They would learn, he hoped, from the example of all that had passed in France, that vigorous measures were no less requisite for the support of freedom than for its original establishment; and that when these measures were once determined upon, it was mere affectation to be scrupulous or fastidious in the choice of means. Mr. Fox appealed to the whole tenour of his public life—he had acted with very different men, and upon a great variety of political principles; and if, in the course of all his experience, he had acquired any knowledge of his own character, he could declare with confidence that a squeamishness or hesitation in the choice of means, was a weakness, of all others, the most alien to his nature.

How did the case stand between the majority of the Directory (the *Triumvirate*, as some persons in this country had thought proper to style them), and that majority of the nation who were accused (and in his conscience he believed they were justly accused), of a wish to terminate the Revolution? The majority of the nation seemed to have acted pretty much in the style and temper of the minister of this country: proceeding to their ultimate object with infinite art and subtlety, they had entrenched themselves within the forms of the constitution on the one hand, while with the other they were sapping the vitals of liberty, and poisoning its very foundations. As for the Directory, the scene was fairly open before them.—On the one hand, they saw a termination to the Revolution; on the other, there were certain rights to be invaded, and certain principles to be infringed. Placed between these two alternatives, they were not long in forming their resolution, and a manly and vigorous resolution it was:—they determined to break through every obstacle of form, and to save their country in spite of precedent. The seditious journalists, with the refractory members of the two councils, and of the directorial body itself, were seized and imprisoned, or otherwise disposed of.—The vacancies thus made were supplied by other persons, appointed by the directorial majority, upon their own personal knowledge and good opinion.—He was aware, Mr. Fox said, that an objection might be raised to this species of nomination, but, for his part, he conceived that the Directory had acted well and wisely;—they were convinced that the majority of the nation were infected with the new principles of pretended order and moderation—they were aware that in this disorder of the public mind, they had nothing to expect from the re-elections—they saw the necessity and they acquiesced in it.—They inverted that order which prevails in those countries where liberty has been established by a more tedious process—they abrogated the instructions of the constituent to his representative, and they addressed their own instructions to the constituent body.—In all this there was nothing but what was perfectly just and natural; nothing inconsistent with the principles of freedom, nor with those principles which he himself had professed in the outset of his political life (Mr. Fox *here alluded to his well known opinion on the Middlesex Election*).[1]

With regard to the absolute abstract inviolability of the Press—Mr. Fox declared—that he considered himself as particularly fortunate in having had a very early opportunity of asserting his opinions upon that subject also; it was pretty well known, that the first ground of difference between himself and a noble lord (with whom he had originally acted, whom he had afterwards opposed, but with whom he had ultimately united, and of whom he should always speak in the language of friendship), was laid in a subject of this kind. That noble lord had refused, in spite of his remonstrances, to proceed against a printer, and upon that difference they parted, till the necessity of the times, and the voice of the country, calling aloud for a coalition, had brought them together again.

With regard to the morality and justice of this conduct in the Directory, he was aware, Mr. Fox said, that different opinions were avowed; for his own part, he had never entertained the least doubt upon the subject. The question seemed to him to lie in a very narrow compass indeed—he was no friend to the pretended refinements and abstractions of political justice; in his opinion, there were rules sufficient for the direction of every man's conduct, lying upon the surface, and within everybody's reach. Of this kind was that excellent rule, which an eminent writer, the late

---

[1] "Commons' Debates," vol. 25, p. 28, Mr. C. Fox said, "We had not lost the confidence of the people by the Middlesex Election, as was foolishly said, but by suffering with tameness the many insults which had been offered to the Sovereign and that House—that, had he his will, those aldermen and others who presented a remonstrance to the Throne should be taken into custody; that a few years back they sent two aldermen to the Tower, but suffered a paltry printer to hold them in contempt; that it was by these means we lost the good will of our constituents."—Lord North's motion was for sending the printer to the Gate-House—Mr. Fox insisted upon Newgate.

Mr. ADAM SMITH, had established as the only true test upon which we could pretend to decide upon the conduct of other persons. We should put ourselves in their place, and unless we could be thoroughly convinced, that under the same circumstances, we ourselves should have acted differently, we might rest assured that the conscientious disapprobation which we were so ready to affect, was nothing better than a despicable farce of hypocrisy and self-delusion.

He would apply this rule to the conduct of the Directory —Let any man for a moment place himself in the situation of those gentlemen (Messrs. BARRAS and REWBELL), could they, after all they had acted themselves, and all they had inflicted on others in the course of the Revolution—could they, admitting them to be men endowed with the common sentiment of self-preservation—he would put it to the feelings of every gentleman—could they, consistently with that sentiment, permit for a single moment the expression of the public voice, which had almost unanimously declared against them? While human nature was human nature, it was impossible—and it was idle to imagine it. The conduct of the Directory was perfectly just and natural—and he was at a loss for words to express his contempt of the hypocrisy of those who would assert, that under the same circumstances, they themselves would have acted differently.

With regard to the political propriety of the measure, he had ever held, as a fixed and unalterable principle, the maxim which had been advanced upon this subject by MACHIAVEL—it was this, that when a Government, for practical purposes, had become exhausted and effete, there was only one method for renewing its energies; this was by having recourse to those principles upon which it had been originally constituted.— In what did the essence of the French system consist? In the activity of the insurrectionary energy.—Through the whole course of the Revolution, whenever this energy had been suffered to lie dormant for any considerable time, the whole system had invariably been affected with a general torpor and lassitude. That period, the happy issue of which they were now commemorating, was in fact truly critical. If the energy of insurrection had not roused and exerted itself as it did, it must have sunk into the sleep of death;

I*   F

or it would only have been awakened to return again
under monarchical domination.—On the other hand, what
had been the effect of this new stimulus ? Fresh life and
vigour had been infused into the whole system—they had
concluded a peace with the EMPEROR on their own terms
—they had resolutely dismissed our own negotiator from
Lisle, and they were now preparing for the invasion of
this country ! (*Loud applauses.*)

It remained only to speak of the means employed for
effecting such a happy change. The legislative body,
representing the disaffected majority of the nation, had
been dispersed by a party of soldiery, acting under a
temporary discretionary insurrectionary commission.—Mr.
Fox here claimed the attention of his audience.—He was
aware—he said—that an attempt would be made to
impute to him certain principles inconsistent with his
approbation of this measure ; an approbation which he
was by no means disposed to disguise or qualify.—The
principle briefly stated was this—" *The subordination of
the Military to the Civil Power.*" It would be alleged that,
at some time or other, he had maintained, and professed
this principle—He anticipated the calumny, and he would
answer it.

It would be sufficient for him to call back their recollection to a very late event. They all remembered the
Mutiny—(*Loud applause.*)—It was fresh in the recollection
of everybody—How happened it then, if in fact he had
ever entertained this principle, that an event of such a
magnitude should never have called it forth ? Was the
expression of any such principle to be found in the reports
of his speeches at that period ? Had he ever, directly or
indirectly, intimated the least disapprobation of the conduct of the seamen then in a state of insurrection ? Or,
the *mutineers*, as some gentlemen thought proper to call
them.—(*Loud laugh and applause.*) He appealed to the
memory of his auditors—he challenged the malignant
recollection of his enemies, and the spies of Government,
if any such were present. (*Here a considerable tumult.*)
He defied all the quibbling sophistry of the minister himself, to put such an interpretation on any word he had
said. He had been upon his guard at the time—he was
aware of the use that might have been made of his name,

and this consideration had suggested the necessity of
caution.—Political caution he considered as no less necessary in public life than political courage—He had always
thought and felt so, and never had this sentiment been
impressed upon his mind with a more tremendous conviction, than at the period he was alluding to.

After concluding his defence of the conduct of the
Directory, and of his own consistency in approving it, Mr.
Fox entered into the discussion of a very delicate point.
"Since I am upon the subject of the Mutiny," said Mr.
Fox, ("and I give it that name without meaning to connect with it any idea of criminality or reproach, but
merely for the sake of a distinction, which we may here-
after have occasion for, between civil and military insurrection ;) I am naturally led to take notice of a difference
of opinion between myself and an hon. friend with whom I
have long acted ; that gentleman thought it his duty to
declare in Parliament that he disliked mutinies ;—now, for
my part, I like them—and for this plain reason, because
in every mutiny, as it arises, I see the possibility, at least,
of the accomplishment of our great ultimate object—a
change of system. But if I should be—as I trust I ever
shall be—the last man to discourage a mutiny on practical
grounds, still less should I object to it on principles of
pure theory. What does a mutiny prove ? If it proves
anything it proves this : *that the principles of liberty in the
human mind are inextinguishable.* You must either
govern in conformity with the will of the mass of the
people, and of the individuals composing that mass, or you
must employ force—there is no alternative—while the
individual is left at liberty to make his own laws, and
when he is permitted to repeal them as he finds occasion—
in such a case I am unable to conceive how it is possible
that, under any circumstances, he should be tempted to
disobey them.

"'But no,' says the Government ; 'this will not answer our purpose—we will strip you of this privilege—
we will go a step farther—we will not even permit you to
make your own laws. Even this will not satisfy us—you
are a single insulated being, and we have you in our
power—we will fetter you with laws and precedents—we
will bind you down with usages and statutes which were

enacted before you were born!'—What must be the state
of things where such a system is established? where it is
acted upon without disguise? where it is openly defended
and avowed? what is to be expected, but that which we
daily witness in this country? a state of sullen, ill-dis-
sembled discontent! This discontent displays itself in
actions which are the natural expression of such a sentiment.—Now mark how all this follows—Government,
instead of removing the discontent, can see no remedy but
in coercion; but how is coercion to be obtained? Why,
by the very means which have occasioned the discontent—
by a still grosser violation of individual liberty: they take a
number of individuals, and when they have subjected
them to a military discipline, they flatter themselves that
they can employ them as a means for suppressing discontent in others. —But what is the necessary consequence
of all this?—The spirit of freedom, which they are
endeavouring to keep down, explodes first in that body in
which it had been compressed, with the greatest violence.
—The military system is blown to pieces, and the whole
ill-constructed scaffolding is brought down in ruin upon
the heads of its architects.

"I sincerely hope," said Mr. Fox, "that no such explosion may take place to the destruction of a constitution
which I venerate;—but ministers have already made the
first step in this vicious circle of politics.—The original
defect was undoubtedly to be found in the constitution
itself, even as it existed in better times. These defects
were the natural subject of a peaceable and salutary
reform.—But what have ministers done? Instead of
reforming the constitution—by removing the abuse, they
have exaggerated the abuse till they have destroyed the
constitution; by their last infamous Bills they have put
the finishing stroke to our liberties—they have taken
away from every Englishman his NATURAL INDIVIDUAL
COMPETENCE IN MATTERS OF LEGISLATION."

Mr. Fox here concluded a very animated and impressive speech, by recommending to his auditors, *that they
should immediately strike a blow for the destruction of the
present system:* as a pledge of his earnest wishes for the
accomplishment of this object he would give them for a
toast—" RFWBFLL *and a free Representation!*"

We have no hesitation in declaring our opinion, that
this Speech was one of the best that Mr. Fox ever
delivered; it abounds in all those characteristic traits
which distinguish and elevate the tone of that gentleman's
eloquence, above that of all his rivals and opponents. The
references to MACHIAVEL and ADAM SMITH evinced the
extraordinary facility which he possesses, of drawing an
unforeseen inference from some acknowledged truth; that
ardent deprecation of the all-violent and repressive
measures, with the irrefragable demonstration of the
absurdity and inutility of coercion in every possible case—
all these, and above all, the spirited and undaunted appeal
to his own past life and conduct, were *in Mr. Fox's very
best manner.* We have only to regret, that while we do
justice to his sentiments, and general style of argument,
it is impossible for us, in a report of this kind, to give our
readers any idea of the language in which those sentiments were conveyed.—(*We must here conclude our extract. The Examiner of Monday next will contain the
Speeches of Mr. ERSKINE, &c. &c., which we shall likewise
take the liberty of borrowing from the Morning Chronicle
of the same date, but which we are obliged, at present, to
postpone for want of room.*)

FRERE.

MEETING OF THE FRIENDS OF FREEDOM.

[DECEMBER 4, 1797.]

(Continued from No. III.)

THE "*House of Russell*" being given, LORD
JOHN and LORD WILLIAM rose both at once.

LORD JOHN made a very neat, and LORD
WILLIAM a very appropriate, speech.

ALDERMAN COMBE made a very impressive
speech.

Mr. TIERNEY made a very pointed speech.

Mr. GREY made a very fine speech. He described the
ministers as "bold, bad men"—their measures he repeatedly
declared to be, not only "weak, but wicked."

Mr. Byng said a few words.

" General Tarleton and *the Electors of Liverpool*" being given, the General, after an eulogium on Mr. Fox, begged to anticipate their favourite concluding toast, and to give " *The cause of Freedom all over the World.*" This toast unfortunately gave rise to an altercation which threatened to disturb the harmony of the evening. Olaudah Equiano, the African, and Henry Yorke, the mulatto, insisted upon being heard; but as it appeared that they were entering upon a subject which would have entirely altered the complexion of the meeting, they were, though not without some difficulty, withheld from proceeding further.

Mr. Erskine now rose, in consequence of some allusions which had been made to the trial by jury. He professed himself to be highly flattered by the encomiums which had been lavished upon him; at the same time he was conscious that he could not, without some degree of reserve, consent to arrogate to himself those qualities which the partiality of his friends had attributed to him. He had on former occasions declared himself to be clothed with the infirmities of man's nature; and he now begged leave, in all humility, to reiterate that confession: He should never cease to consider himself as a feeble, and with respect to the extent of his faculties, in many respects, a finite, being.—He had ever borne in mind, and he hoped he should ever continue to bear in mind, those words of the inspired penman—"Thou hast made him less than the angels, to crown him with glory and honour." These lines were indeed applicable to the state of man in general, but of no man more than himself; they appeared to him pointed and personal, and little less than prophetic; they were always present to his mind; he could wish to wear them in his breast as a sort of amulet against the enchantment of public applause, and the witcheries of vanity and self-delusion. Yet, if he were indeed possessed of those superhuman powers—all pretensions to which he again begged leave most earnestly to disclaim—if he were endowed with the eloquence of an angel, and with all those other faculties which we attribute to angelic natures, it would be impossible for him to do justice to the eloquence with which the hon. gentleman who opened the meeting had defended the Cause of Freedom, identified, as he conceived it to be, with the persons and government of the Directory. In his present terrestrial state he could only address it as a prayer to God, and as counsel to Man, that the words which they had heard from that hon. gentleman might work inwardly in their hearts, and, in due time, produce the fruit of Liberty and Revolution.

He had not the advantage of being personally acquainted with any of the gentlemen of the Directory;—He understood, however, that one of them (Mr. MERLIN), previous to the last change, had stood in a situation similar to his own—he was, in fact, nothing less than a leading advocate and barrister in the midst of a free, powerful, and enlightened people.

The conduct of the Directory with regard to the exiled deputies, had been objected to by some persons on the score of a pretended rigour. For his part, he should only say that, having been, as he had been, both a soldier and a sailor, if it had been his fortune to have stood in either of those two relations to the Directory—as a man, and as a major-general, he should not have scrupled to direct his artillery against the national representation:—as a naval officer, he would undoubtedly have undertaken for the removal of the exiled deputies; admitting the exigency, under all its relations, as it appeared to him to exist, and the then circumstances of the times, with all their bearings and dependencies, branching out into an infinity of collateral considerations, and involving in each a variety of objects, political, physical, and moral; and these again under their distinct and separate heads, ramifying into endless subdivisions, which it was foreign to his purpose to consider.

Having thus disposed of this part of his subject, Mr. ERSKINE passed, in a strain of rapid and brilliant allusion, over a variety of points characteristic of the conduct and disposition of the present Ministry: Mr. BURKE's metaphor of "the Swinish Multitude;" Mr. REEVES's metaphor of the "Tree of Monarchy;" "the Battle of Tranent," and "the March to Paris;" the phrase of "Acquitted Felons," and the exclamation of "Perish Commerce"—which last expression he declared he should never cease to attribute to Mr. WINDHAM, so long at least as it should please the Sovereign Dispenser to continue to him the power of utterance and the enjoyment of his present

faculties. He condemned the "Expedition to Quiberon;"
he regretted the "Fate of Messrs. MUIR and PALMER;"
he exulted in the "Acquittal of Citizens TOOKE, HARDY,
THELWALL, HOLCROFT, and others;" and he blessed that
Providence to which (as it had originally allotted to him
(Mr. ERSKINE) the talents which had been exerted in their
defence) the preservation of those citizens might perhaps
be indirectly attributed. He then descanted upon the
captivity of LA FAYETTE and the dividend of the Imperial
Loan.

After fully exhausting these subjects, Mr. ERSKINE re-
sumed a topic on which he had only slightly glanced
before. In a most delicate and sportive vein of humour,
he contended that, if the people were a "swinish multitude," those who represented them must necessarily be a
swinish representation. It would be in vain to attempt to do
justice to the polite and easy pleasantry which pervaded
this part of Mr. ERSKINE's speech. Suffice it to say that
the taste of the audience showed itself in complete unison
with the genius of the orator; and the whole of this passage was covered with loud and reiterated plaudits.

After a speech of unexampled exertion, Mr. ERSKINE
now began to enter much at length into a recital of
select passages from our most approved English authors;
concluding with a copious extract from the several publica-
tions of the late Mr. BURKE; but such was the variety and
richness of his quotations, which he continued to an extent
far exceeding the limits of this paper, that we found ourselves under the necessity, either of considerably abridging
our original matter, or of omitting them altogether, which
latter alternative we adopted the more readily, as the
greater part of these brilliant citations have already past
through the ordeal of a public and patriotic auditory; and
as there is every probability that the circumstances of
the times will again call them forth on some future emer-
gency.

Mr. ERSKINE concluded by recapitulating, in a strain of
agonizing and impressive eloquence, the several more prominent heads of his speech :—He had been a soldier and
a sailor, and had a son at Winchester School—he had been
called by special retainers during the summer into many
different and distant parts of the country — travelling

chiefly in post-chaises.—He felt himself called upon to declare that his poor faculties were at the service of his country—of the free and enlightened part of it at least. —He stood here as a man.—He stood in the eye, indeed, in the hand of God—to whom (in the presence of the company and waiters) he solemnly appealed.—He was of noble, perhaps royal blood—he had a house at Hampstead —was convinced of the necessity of a thorough and radical Reform—his pamphlets had gone through thirty editions—skipping alternately the odd and even numbers— he loved the Constitution, to which he would cling and grapple—and he was clothed with the infirmities of man's nature—he would apply to the present French rulers (particularly BARRAS and REWBELL) the words of the poet :—

> " Be to their faults a little blind,
> Be to their virtues very kind,
> Let all their ways be unconfined
> And clap the padlock on their mind !"—

And for these reasons, thanking the gentlemen who had done him the honour to drink his health, he should propose " MERLIN *the late Minister of Justice, and Trial by Jury !*"

Mr. ERSKINE here concluded a speech which had occupied the attention and excited the applause of his audience during the space of little less than three hours, allowing for about three quarters of an hour, which were occupied by successive fits of fainting between the principal subdivisions of his discourse.—Mr. ERSKINE descended from the table and was conveyed down stairs by the assistance of his friends.—On arriving at the corner of the piazzas they were surprised by a very unexpected embarrassment. Mr. ERSKINE's horses had been taken from the carriage, and a number of able chairmen engaged to supply their place ; but, these fellows having contrived to intoxicate themselves with the money which the coachman had advanced to them upon account, were become so restive and unruly, and withal so exorbitant in their demands (positively refusing to abide by their former engagement), that Mr. ERSKINE deemed it unsafe to trust himself in their hands, and determined to wait the return of his own more tractable and less chargeable animals. This unpleasant scene continued for above an hour.

Mr. SHERIDAN's health was now drunk in his absence, and received with an appearance of general approbation: —when, in the midst of the applause, Mr. Fox arose, in apparent agitation, and directed the attention of the Company to the rising, manly virtues of Mr. MACFUNGUS.

Mr. MACFUNGUS declared that, to pretend that he was not elated by the encomiums with which Mr. Fox had honoured him, was an affectation which he disdained: such encomiums would ever form the proudest recompense of his patriotic labours;—he confessed they were cheering to him—he felt them warm at his heart—and, while a single fibre of his frame preserved its vibration, it would throb in unison to the approbation of that hon. gentleman.— The applause of the company was no less flattering to him —he felt his faculties invigorated by it, and stimulated to the exertion of new energies in the race of mind. Every other sensation was obliterated and absorbed by it;—for the present, however, he would endeavour to suppress his feelings, and concentre his energies, for the purpose of explaining to the company why he assisted now, for the first time, at the celebration of the Fifth Revolution which had been effected in regenerated France. The various and extraordinary talents of the right hon. gentleman— his vehement and overpowering perception, his vigorous and splendid intuition, would for ever attract the admiration of all those who were in any degree endowed with those faculties themselves, or capable of estimating them in others; as such, he had ever been among the most ardent admirers, and on many occasions, among the most ardent supporters, of the right hon. gentleman;—he agreed with him in many points—in his general love of liberty and revolution; in his execration of the war; in his detestation of ministers; but he entertained his doubts, and till those doubts were cleared up, he could not, consistently with his principles, attend at the celebration of any revolution whatever.

These doubts, however, were now satisfactorily done away. A pledge had been entered into for accomplishing an effectual radical revolution; not for the mere overthrow of the present system, nor for the establishment of any other in its place, but for the effecting such a series of revolutions, as might be sufficient for the establishment of a free system.

Mr. MACFUNGUS continued—He was incapable of compromising with first principles—of acquiescing in shortsighted, temporary, palliative expedients ; if such had been his temper, he should assuredly have rested satisfied with the pledge which that right hon. gentleman had entered into about six months ago, on the subject of Parliamentary Reform, in which pledge he considered the promise of that previous and preliminary Revolution to which he had before alluded as essentially implicated.—" Whenever this Reform takes place," exclaimed Mr. MACFUNGUS, " the present degraded and degrading system must fall into dissolution ; it must sink and perish with the corruptions which have supported it. The national energies will awake, and, shaking off their lethargy, as their fetters drop from them, they will follow the Angel of their Revolution, while the Genius of Freedom, soaring aloft beneath the orb of Gallic Illumination, will brush away, as with the wing of an Eagle, all the cobwebs of Aristocracy.—But, before the Temple of Freedom can be erected in their place, the surface which they have occupied must be smoothed and levelled —it must be cleared by repeated Revolutionary Explosions, from all the lumber and rubbish with which Aristocracy and Fanaticism will endeavour to encumber it, and to impede the progress of the holy work.—The sacred level, the symbol of Fraternal Equality, must be past over the whole.—The completion of the Edifice will indeed be the more tardy, but it will not be the less durable, for having been longer delayed.—Cemented with the blood of Tyrants and the tears of the Aristocracy, it will rise a Monument for the astonishment and veneration of future Ages.—The remotest Posterity, with our Children yet unborn, and the most distant portions of the Globe, will crowd around its Gates, and demand admission into its Sanctuary.—The Tree of Liberty will be planted in the midst of it, and its branches will extend to the ends of the Earth, while the Friends of Freedom meet and fraternize and amalgamate under its consolatory shade.

" There our Infants shall be taught to lisp in tender accents the Revolutionary Hymn—there, with wreaths of

myrtle, and oak, and poplar, and vine, and olive and
cypress, and ivy; with violets and roses, and daffodils and
dandelions in our hands, we will swear respect to childhood, and manhood, and old age, and virginity, and
womanhood, and widowhood, but, above all, to the Supreme Being.—There we will decree and sanction the
Immortality of the soul.—There pillars, and obelisks, and
arches, and pyramids, will awaken the love of Glory and
of our Country.—There Painters and Statuaries, with
their chisels and colours, and Engravers with their engraving tools, will perpetuate the interesting features of
our Revolutionary Heroes; while our Poets and Musicians,
with an honourable emulation, strive to immortalize their
Memories.   Their bones will be entombed in the Vault
below, while their sacred Shades continue hovering over
our heads—Those venerated Manes which, from time to
time, will require to be appeased by the blood of the
remaining Aristocrats.—Then Peace, and Freedom, and
Fraternity, and Equality will pervade the whole Earth;
while the Vows of Republicanism, the Altar of Patriotism,
and the Revolutionary Pontiff, with the thrilling volcanic
Sympathies, whether of Holy Fury or of ardent Fraternal
Civism, uniting and identifying, as it were, an electric
energy."

Mr. MACFUNGUS here paused for a few moments, seemingly overpowered by the excess of sensibility, and the
force of the ideas which he was labouring to convey.—
The whole company appeared to sympathize with his unaffected emotions.   After a short interval he recovered
himself from a very impressive silence, and continued as
follows:—

"These prospects, Fellow-Citizens, may possibly be
deferred.   The Machiavelism of Governments may for the
time prevail, and this unnatural and execrable contest may
yet be prolonged; but the hour is not far distant; Persecution will only serve to accelerate it, and the blood of
Patriotism, streaming from the severing axe, will call down
vengeance on our oppressors in a voice of Thunder.   I
expect the contest, and I am prepared for it.—I hope I
shall never shrink, nor swerve, nor start aside wherever
duty and inclination may place me.   My services, my life

itself, are at your disposal.—Whether to act or to suffer, I am yours—with HAMPDEN in the Field, or with SIDNEY on the Scaffold.—My example may be more useful to you than my talents, and this Head may perhaps serve your cause more effectually, if placed on a pole upon Temple Bar, than if it was occupied in organizing your Committees, in preparing your Revolutionary Explosions, and conducting your Correspondence."

Mr. MACFUNGUS said he should give, as an unequivocal test of his sentiments, " BUONAPARTE AND A RADICAL RE-FORM."

The conclusion of Mr. MACFUNGUS's speech was followed by a simultaneous burst of rapturous approbation from every part of the room. The applause continued for several minutes, during which Mr. MACFUNGUS repeatedly rose to express his feelings.

The conversation now became more mixed and animated: several excellent songs were sung, and toasts drank, while the progressive and patriotic festivity of the evening was heightened by the vocal powers of several of the most popular singers. A new song, written for the occasion by Captain MORRIS, received its sanction in the warmest expression of applause. The whole company joined with enthusiasm in their old favourite chorus of " Bow! Wow!! Wow!!!"

FRERE.

LA SAINTE GUILLOTINE.

[DECEMBER 4, 1797.]

WE have been favoured with the following specimen of Jacobin poetry, which we give to the world without any comment or imitation. We are informed (we know not how truly) that it will be sung at the meeting of the Friends of Freedom; an account of which is anticipated in our present paper.

LA SAINTE GUILLOTINE.

A NEW SONG.

Attempted from the French.

Tune—" O'er the vine-cover'd hills and gay regions of France."

I.

FROM the blood-bedew'd valleys and mountains
of France
See the genius of Gallic invasion advance !
Old Ocean shall waft her, unruffled by storm,
While our shores are all lined with the *Friends
of Reform*.[1]

Confiscation and Murder attend in her train,
With meek-eyed Sedition, the daughter of Paine ;[2]
While her sportive *Poissardes* with light footsteps are seen
To dance in a ring round the gay *Guillotine*.[3]

II.

To *London*, " the rich, the defenceless,"[4] she comes—
Hark ! my boys, to the sound of the Jacobin drums !
See Corruption, Prescription, and Privilege fly,
Pierced through by the glance of her blood-darting eye.

While patriots, from prison and prejudice freed,
In soft accents shall lisp the Republican creed,
And with tricolor'd fillets and cravats of green,
Shall crowd round the altar of *Saint Guillotine*.

III.

See the level of Freedom sweeps over the land—
The vile Aristocracy's doom is at hand !
Not a seat shall be left in a House *that we know*,
But for *Earl* BUONAPARTE and *Baron* MOREAU.

---

[1] See proclamation of the Directory.
[2] The " *too long calumniated* author of the ' Rights of Man.' "—
See a Sir Something Burdett's speech at the " Shakespeare," as referred to in the " Courier " of November 30.
[3] The Guillotine at Arras was, as is well known to every Jacobin,
painted " *Couleur de Rose.*"
[4] See " Weekly Examiner," No. II.   Extract from the " Courier."

But the rights of the Commons shall still be respected,
Buonaparte himself shall approve the elected ;
And the Speaker shall march with majestical mien,
And make his three bows to the grave *Guillotine.*

IV.

Two heads, says our proverb, are better than one,
But the Jacobin choice is for Five Heads or none.
By Directories only can Liberty thrive ;
Then down with the ONE, boys! and up with the FIVE!

How our bishops and judges will stare with amazement,
When their heads are thrust out at the *National Casement!*[1]
When the *National Razor*[1] has shaved them quite clean,
What a handsome oblation to *Saint Guillotine!*

CANNING AND FRERE.

THE SOLDIER'S FRIEND.

[DECEMBER 11, 1797.]

E have already hinted at the principle by which the followers of the Jacobinical sect are restrained from the exercise of their own favourite virtue of charity. The force of this prohibition, and the strictness with which it is observed, are strongly exemplified in the following poem. It is the production of the same author, whose happy effort in English Sapphics we presumed to imitate ; the present effusion is in Dactylics, and equally subject to the laws of Latin prosody.

THE SOLDIER'S WIFE.

Wēarȳ wăy-wāndĕrĕr, lānguĭd ănd sick ăt hĕart,
Trāvĕllĭng pāinfŭllȳ ŏvĕr thĕ rūggĕd rŏăd ;
Wild visāg'd wāndĕrĕr—āh fŏr thȳ hĕavȳ chănce.

We think that we see him fumbling in the pocket of his

---

[1] *La petite Fenêtre,* and *le Rasoire National,* fondling expressions applied to the Guillotine by the Jacobins in France, and their pupils here.

blue pantaloons; that the splendid shilling is about to make
its appearance, and to glitter in the eyes, and glad the heart
of the poor sufferer. But no such thing—the bard very
calmly contemplates her situation, which he describes in a
pair of very pathetical stanzas; and, after the following
well-imagined topic of consolation, concludes by leaving
her to Providence.

> Thy husband will never return from the war again;
> Cold is thy hopeless heart, *even as charity;*
> Cold are thy famish'd babes—*God help thee,* widow'd one!

We conceived that it would be necessary to follow up
this general rule with the particular exception, and to point
out one of those cases in which the embargo upon Jacobin
bounty is sometimes suspended; with this view we have
subjoined the poem of—

THE SOLDIER'S FRIEND.

DACTYLICS.

OME, little Drummer Boy, lay down your
⸱   knapsack here:
I am the soldier's friend—here are some books
for you;
Nice clever books by Tom Paine, the philan-
thropist.

Here's half-a-crown for you—here are some handbills
too—
Go to the barracks, and give all the soldiers some.
Tell them the sailors are all in a mutiny.

> [*Exit Drummer Boy, with handbills, and half-a-*
> *crown. Manet Soldier's Friend.*

Liberty's friends thus all learn to amalgamate,
Freedom's volcanic explosion prepares itself,
Despots shall bow to the fasces of liberty.

> Reason, philosophy, "fiddledum, diddledum,"
> Peace and fraternity, higgledy, piggledy,
> Higgledy, piggledy, "fiddledum, diddledum."

> > *Et cætera, et cætera, et cætera.*

> > > CANNING AND FRERE.

SONG.

[JANUARY 8, 1798.]

HE following song is recommended to be sung at all *convivial* Meetings, convened for the purpose of opposing the Assessed Tax Bill. The correspondent who has transmitted it to us, informs us that he has tried it with great success among many of his well-disposed neighbours, who had been at first led to apprehend that the 120th part of their income was too great a sacrifice for the preservation of the remainder of their property from French confiscation.

You have heard of REWBELL,
That demon of hell,
   And of BARRAS, his brother Director ;
Of the canting LEPAUX,
And that scoundrel MOREAU,
   Who betray'd his old friend and protector.

Would you know how these friends,
For their own private ends,
   Would subvert our religion and throne ?—
Do you doubt of their skill
To change laws at their will ?—
   You shall hear how they treated their own.

'Twas their pleasure to look,
In a little blue book,
   At the code of their famed legislation,
That with truth they might say,
In the space of one day
   They had broke every law of the nation.

The first law that they see,
Is " *the press shall be free !*"
   The next is " *the trial by jury :*"
Then, " *the people's free choice ;* "
Then, " *the members' free voice*"—
   When REWBELL exclaim'd in a fury—

1*   G

" On a method we'll fall
For infringing them all—
 We'll seize on each printer and member :
No period so fit
For a desperate hit,
 As our old bloody month of *September*.

" We'll annul each election
Which wants our correction,
 And name our own creatures instead.
When once we've our will,
No blood we will spill
 (Let CARNOT be knock'd on the head).

" To *Rochefort* we'll drive
Our victims alive,
 And as soon as on board we have got 'em,
Since we destine the ship
For no more than one trip,
 We can just make a hole in the bottom.

" By this excellent plan,
On the *true Rights of Man*,
 When we've founded our *fifth Revolution*,
Though *England's* our foe,
An army shall go
 To *improve* HER corrupt Constitution.

" We'll address to the nation
A fine proclamation,
 With offers of friendship so warm :
Who can give BUONAPARTÉ
A welcome so hearty
 As the friends of a THOROUGH REFORM ?"

CANNING, ELLIS, AND FRERE.

THE PROGRESS OF MAN.

[February 19, 1798.]

A DIDACTIC POEM, IN FORTY CANTOS, WITH NOTES CRITICAL
AND EXPLANATORY: CHIEFLY OF A PHILOSOPHICAL
TENDENCY.

DEDICATED TO R. P. KNIGHT, ESQ.

CANTO FIRST.

CONTENTS.—The Subject proposed.—Doubts and Waverings.—
Queries not to be answered.—Formation of the stupendous Whole.
—Cosmogony; or the Creation of the World:—the Devil—Man
—Various classes of Being :—ANIMATED BEINGS—Birds—Fish—
Beasts—the Influence of the Sexual Appetite—on Tigers—on
Whales—on Crimpt Cod—on Perch—on Shrimps—on Oysters.—
Various Stations assigned to different Animals :—Birds—Bears—
Mackerel.—Bears remarkable for their fur—Mackerel cried on a
Sunday—Birds do not graze—nor Fishes fly—nor Beasts live in
the Water.—PLANTS equally contented with their lot :—Potatoes
—Cabbage—Lettuce—Leeks—Cucumbers.—MAN only discon-
tented—born a Savage ; not choosing to continue so, becomes
polished—resigns his Liberty—Priest-craft—King-craft—Tyranny
of Laws and Institutions.—Savage life—description thereof :—The
Savage free—roaming Woods—feeds on Hips and Haws—Animal
Food—first notion of it from seeing a Tiger tearing his prey—
wonders if it is good—resolves to try—makes a Bow and Arrow—
kills a Pig or two—resolves to roast a part of them—lights a fire
—APOSTROPHE to fires—Spits and Jacks not yet invented.—Digression.—CORINTH—SHEFFIELD.—Love, the most natural desire after Food.—Savage Courtship.—Concubinage recommended.
—Satirical Reflections on Parents and Children—Husbands and
Wives—against collateral Consanguinity.—FREEDOM the only
Morality, &c. &c. &c.

THE PROGRESS OF MAN.

CANTO I.

HETHER some great, supreme, o'er-ruling
Power
Stretch'd forth its arm at Nature's natal hour,
Composed this mighty Whole[1] with plastic
skill,
Wielding the jarring elements at will?

---

[1] Line 3. A modern author of great penetration and judgment,

Or whether sprung from CHAOS' mingling storm,   5
The mass of matter started into form ?
Or CHANCE o'er earth's green lap spontaneous fling
The fruits of autumn and the flowers of spring ?
Whether MATERIAL SUBSTANCE, unrefined,
Owns the strong impulse of instinctive MIND,   10
Which to one centre points diverging lines,
Confounds, refracts, invigorates, and combines ? [1]
Whether the joys of *earth*, the hopes of *heaven*,
By MAN to GOD, or GOD to MAN, were given ? [2]
If virtue leads to bliss, or vice to woe ?   15
Who rules above ? or who reside below ?" [3]
Vain questions all—shall man presume to know ?
On all these points, and points obscure as these,
Think they who will,—and think whate'er they please !

Let us a plainer, steadier theme pursue—   20
Mark the grim savage scoop his light canoe ;
Mark the dark rook, on pendent branches hung,
With anxious fondness feed her cawing young.—
Mark the fell leopard through the desert prowl,
Fish prey on fish, and fowl regale on fowl ;—   25
How Lybian tigers' chawdrons Love assails, [4]
And warms, midst seas of ice, the melting whales ;— [5]

---

observes very shrewdly, that "the cosmogony of the world has
puzzled the philosophers of all ages. What a medley of opinions
have they not broached upon the creation of the world ! Sanchonia-
thon, Manetho, Berosus, and Ocellus Lucanus, have all attempted
it in vain. The latter has these words—*Anarchon ara kai ateleutaion
to pan*—which imply, that all things have neither beginning nor end."
See Goldsmith's " Vicar of Wakefield ;" see also Mr. Knight's Poem
on the " Progress of Civil Society."

[1] Line 12. The influence of Mind upon Matter, comprehending
the whole question of the Existence of Mind as independent of
Matter, or as co-existent with it, and of Matter considered as an intelligent and self-dependent Essence, will make the subject of a
larger Poem in 127 Books, now preparing under the *same* auspices.

[2] Line 14. See Godwin's " Enquirer ;" Darwin's "Zoonomia ;"
Paine; Priestley, &c., &c.; also all the French Encyclopædists.

[3] Line 16. *Quæstio spinosa et contortula.*

[4] Line 26. " Add thereto a tiger's chawdron."—*Macbeth.*

[5] Lines 26, 27. " In softer notes bids Libyan lions roar,
       And warms the whale on Zembla's frozen shore."
              Progress of Civil Society, Book I. ver. 98.

Cools the crimpt cod, fierce pangs to perch imparts,
Shrinks shrivell'd shrimps, but opens oysters' hearts ; [1]
Then say, how all these things together tend   30
To one great truth, prime object, and good end?

First—to each living thing, whate'er its kind,
Some lot, some part, some station is assign'd.
The feather'd race with pinions skim the *air*—[2]
Not so the mackerel, and still less the bear : [3]   35
This roams the *wood*, carnivorous, for his prey ! [4]
That with soft roe pursues his *watery* way : [5]
This slain by hunters, yields his shaggy hide ; [6]
That, caught by fishers, is on Sundays cried.— [7]

But each, contented with his humble sphere,   40
Moves unambitious through the circling year ;
Nor e'er forgets the fortunes of his race,
Nor pines to quit, or strives to change, his place.
Ah ! who has seen the mailed lobster rise,
Clap his broad wings, and soaring claim the skies?   45
When did the owl, descending from her bower,
Crop, midst the fleecy flocks, the tender flower?
Or the young heifer plunge, with pliant limb,
In the salt wave,[8] and fish-like strive to swim? [9]

The same with plants[10]—potatoes 'tatoes breed—[11] ⎫
Uncostly cabbage springs from cabbage seed ;   ⎬   50
Lettuce to lettuce, leeks to leeks succeed ;   ⎭

---

[1] Line 29. "An oyster may be crossed in love."—
[2] Line 34. Birds fly.   MR. SHERIDAN's *Critic*.
[3] Line 35. But neither fish, nor beasts—particularly as here exemplified.   [4] Line 36. The bear.
[5] Line 37. The mackerel—There are also *hard-roed* mackerel. *Sed de his alio loco.*
[6] Line 38. Bear's *grease*, or *fat*, is also in great request ; being supposed to have a *criniparous*, or hair-producing quality.
[7] Line 39. There is a special Act of Parliament which permits mackerel to be cried on Sundays.
[8] Line 49. *Salt wave*—wave of the sea—"*briny wave.*"—*Poetæ passim.*
[9] Line 45 to 49. Every animal contented with the lot which it has drawn in life. A fine contrast to man, who is always discontented.
[10] Line 50. A still stronger contrast, and a greater shame to man, is found in plants ; they too are contented—he restless and changing.
     Mens agitat mihi ; nec placidâ contenta quiete est.
[11] Line 50. *Potatoes 'tatoes breed.* Elision for the sake of the verse,

Nor e'er did cooling cucumbers presume
To flower like myrtle, or like violets bloom,
—MAN only,—rash, refined, presumptuous MAN,   55
Starts from his rank, and mars creation's plan.
Born the free heir of nature's wide domain,
To art's strict limits bounds his narrow'd reign ;
Resigns his native rights for meaner things,
For *faith* and *fetters*—LAWS, and PRIESTS, and KINGS.   60

(*To be continued.*)

We are sorry to be obliged to break off here. The remainder of this admirable and instructive Poem is in the
press, and will be continued the first opportunity.—THE
EDITOR.

CANNING.

THE PROGRESS OF MAN.

[FEBRUARY 26, 1798.]

IN consequence of the poem on the "Progress
of Man," of which we favoured our Readers
with a specimen in our last Number, we have
received a variety of letters, which we confess
have not a little surprised us, from the un-
founded, and even contradictory charges they contain. In
one, we are accused of malevolence, in bringing back to
notice a work that had been quietly consigned to oblivion ;
—in another, of plagiarism by copying its most beautiful
passages ;—in a third, of vanity, for striving to imitate what
was in itself inimitable, &c. &c. But why this alarm ?
has the author of the *Progress of Civil Society* an exclusive patent for fabricating *Didactic* poems ? or can we not
write against order and government without incurring the
guilt of imitation ? We trust we were not so ignorant of the
nature of a didactic poem (so called from *didaskein*, to
teach, and *poema*, a poem ; because it teaches nothing, and
is not poetical) even before the *Progress of Civil Society*

---

not meant to imply that the root degenerates.—Not so with man—
           Mox daturos
      Progeniem vitiosiorem.

appeared, but that we were capable of such an undertaking.

We shall only say further, that we do not intend to proceed regularly with our poem ; but having the remaining thirty-nine cantos by us, shall content ourselves with giving, from time to time, such extracts as may happen to suit our purpose.

The following passage, which, as the reader will see by turning to the CONTENTS prefixed to the head of the Poem, is part of the first canto, contains so happy a deduction of MAN's present state of Depravity, from the first slips and failings of his Original state, and inculcates so forcibly the mischievous consequences of *social* or *civilized*, as opposed to *natural* society, that no dread of imputed imitation can prevent us from giving it to our readers.

THE PROGRESS OF MAN.

EE the rude savage, free from civil strife,
Keeps the smooth tenour of his guiltless life ;
Restrain'd by none, save Nature's lenient laws,
Quaffs the clear stream, and feeds on hips and haws.

Light to his daily sports behold him rise !   65
The bloodless banquet health and strength supplies.[1]
Bloodless not long—one morn he haps to stray[2]
Through the lone wood—and close beside the way,
See the gaunt tiger tear his trembling prey ;
Beneath whose gory fangs a leveret bleeds,   70
Or pig—such pig as fertile China breeds.[3]

Struck with the sight, the wondering savage stands,
Rolls his broad eyes, and clasps his lifted hands!
Then restless roams—and loathes his wonted food ;
Shuns the salubrious stream, and thirsts for blood.   75

---

[1] Line 61 to 66. Simple state of savage life—previous to the pastoral, or even the hunter state. First savages disciples of Pythagoras.

[2] Line 67, &c. Desire of animal food natural only to beasts, or to man in a state of civilized society. First suggested by the circumstance here related.

[3] Line 71. Pigs of the *Chinese* breed most in request.

By thought matured, and quicken'd by desire,[1]
New arts, new arms, his wayward wants require.
From the tough yew a slender branch he tears,
With self-taught skill the twisted grass prepares ;[2]
Th' unfashion'd bow, with labouring efforts bends   80
In circling form, and joins th' unwilling ends.
Next some tall reed he seeks—with sharp-edged stone
Shapes the fell dart, and points with whiten'd bone.[3]
Then forth he fares—around, in careless play,
Kids, pigs, and lambkins unsuspecting stray.   85
With grim delight he views the sportive band,
Intent on blood, and lifts his murderous hand,
Twangs the bent bow—resounds the fateful dart
Swift-wing'd, and trembles in a porker's heart.

Ah, hapless porker! what can now avail[4]   90
Thy back's stiff bristles, or thy curly tail?
Ah! what avail those eyes so small and round,
Long pendent ears, and snout that loves the ground?[5]

Not unrevenged thou diest!—in after times[6]
From thy spilt blood shall spring unnumber'd crimes.   95
Soon shall the slaughterous arms that wrought thy woe,
Improved by malice, deal a deadlier blow ;[7]
When *social* man shall pant for nobler game,
And 'gainst his fellow man the vengeful weapon aim.

As love, as gold, as jealousy inspires,   100
As wrathful hate, or wild ambition fires,[8]
Urged by the statesman's craft, the tyrant's rage,
Embattled nations endless wars shall wage,

---

[1] Line 76. First formation of a bow.   Introduction to the science
of archery.
[2] Line 79. Grass twisted, used for a string, owing to the want of
other materials not yet invented.
[3] Line 83. Bone—fish's bone found on the sea-shore, shark's teeth,
&c. &c.
[4] Line 90. Ah ! what avails, &c.   See Pope's " Description of
the Death of a Pheasant."
[5] Line 93. " With leaden eye that loves the ground."
[6] Line 94. The first effusion of blood attended with the most
dreadful consequences to mankind.
[7] Line 97. *Social* man's wickedness opposed to the simplicity of
savage life.
[8] Lines 100 and 101. Different causes of war among men.

Vast seas of blood the ravaged field shall stain,
And millions perish—that a KING may reign! 105

For blood once shed, new wants and wishes rise!
Each rising want invention quick supplies.
To roast his victuals is man's next desire,
So two dry sticks he rubs, and lights a fire; [1]
Hail, fire, &c. &c.

CANNING.

THE PROGRESS OF MAN.

[APRIL 2, 1798.]

E promised in our Sixteenth Number, that though we should not proceed regularly with the publication of the Didactic Poem, THE PROGRESS OF MAN, a work which, indeed, both from its bulk, and from the erudite nature of the subject, would hardly suit with the purposes of a Weekly Paper;—we should, nevertheless, give from time to time such extracts from it, as we thought were likely to be useful to our readers, and as were in any degree connected with the topics or events of the times.

The following extract is from the 23rd Canto of this admirable and instructive Poem;—in which the author (whom, by a series of accidents, which we have neither the space, nor indeed the liberty, to enumerate at present, we have discovered to be Mr. HIGGINS, of *St. Mary Axe*) describes the vicious refinement of what is called civilized society, in respect to marriage, contends with infinite spirit and philosophy against the factitious sacredness and indissolubility of that institution, and paints in glowing colours the happiness and utility (in a moral as well as political view) of an arrangement of an opposite sort, such as prevails in countries which are yet under the influence of pure and unsophisticated nature.

In illustration of his principles upon this subject, the author alludes to a popular production of the German

---

[1] Line 109. Invention of fire—first employed in cookery, and produced by rubbing dry sticks together.

Drama, the title of which is the " REFORMED HOUSEKEEPER,"
which he expresses a hope to see transfused into the language of this country. As we are not much conversant
with German literature, and still less, (such is the course
of our occupations) with the British stage, we are not
informed how far Mr. HIGGINS's hopes may have any chance
of being realized. The recommendation of so judicious an
author cannot fail to have its weight; and for our part,
were we to have any voice in the matter, we have too
great a respect for the order of females from among whom
the heroine of the piece in question is selected (having
ourselves great obligations to the lady who lives with Mr.
Wright our publisher in that capacity, for her decision in
respect to the PRIZE OF DULNESS)[1] not to feel very much
interested in the events of a drama, any way affecting the
reputation of that sisterhood.

THE PROGRESS OF MAN.

CANTO TWENTY-THIRD.

CONTENTS.—ON MARRIAGE.—Marriage being indissoluble the cause
of its being so often unhappy.—Nature's laws not consulted in this
point.—Civilized nations mistaken.—OTAHEITE: Happiness of
the natives thereof—visited by Captain Cook, in his Majesty's ship
Endeavour—Character of Captain Cook.—Address to CIRCUM-
NAVIGATION.— Description of his Majesty's ship *Endeavour*—
Mast, rigging, sea sickness, prow, poop, mess-room, surgeon's
mate—History of one.—Episode concerning naval chirurgery.—
Catching a Thunny Fish.— Arrival at Otaheite—cast anchor—land
—Natives astonished.—Love—Liberty—Moral—Natural—Reli-
gious—Contrasted with EUROPEAN manners.—Strictness—Licence
—DOCTORS COMMONS.— Dissolubility of MARRIAGE recom-
mended—Illustrated by a game at Cards—WHIST—CRIBBAGE—
Partners changed—Why not the same in Marriage?—Illustrated
by a River.—Love free.—Priests, Kings—German Drama.—
KOTZEBUE's "Housekeeper Reformed"—to be translated.—Moral
employments of Housekeeping described.—HOTTENTOTS sit and
stare at each other—Query, WHY?—Address to the HOTTENTOTS.
—History of the Cape of Good Hope.—Résumé of the Arguments
against Marriage.—Conclusion.

---

[1] See the "Anti-Jacobin," No. 16, 26th February, 1798, p. 125,
original copy.

THE PROGRESS OF MAN.

EXTRACT.

HAIL! beauteous lands[1] that crown the Southern
    Seas;
Dear happy seats of Liberty and Ease!
Hail! whose green coasts the peaceful ocean
    laves,
Incessant washing with its watery waves!
Delicious islands! to whose envied shore
Thee, gallant COOK! the ship *Endeavour*[2] bore.

There laughs the sky, there zephyr's frolic train,
And light-wing'd loves, and blameless pleasures reign:
There, when two souls congenial ties unite,
No hireling *Bonzes* chant the mystic rite;
Free every thought, each action unconfined,
And light those fetters which no rivets bind.

There in each grove, each sloping bank along,
And flowers and shrubs and odorous herbs among,
Each shepherd[3] clasp'd, with undisguised delight,
His yielding fair one,—in the Captain's sight;
Each yielding fair, as chance or fancy led,
Preferr'd new lovers to her sylvan bed.

---

[1] The ceremony of invocation (in didactic poems especially) is in some measure analogous to the custom of drinking toasts; the corporeal representatives of which are always supposed to be absent, and unconscious of the irrigation bestowed upon their names. Hence it is, that our Author addresses himself to the natives of an island who are not likely to hear, and who, if they did, would not understand him.

[2] His Majesty's ship *Endeavour.*

[3] In justice to our Author we must observe, that there is a delicacy in this picture, which the words, in their common acceptation, do not convey. The amours of an English shepherd would probably be preparatory to marriage (which is contrary to our Author's principles), or they might disgust us by the vulgarity of their object. But in Otaheite, where the place of a shepherd is a perfect sinecure (there being no sheep on the island), the mind of the reader is not offended by any disagreeable allusion.

Learn hence, each nymph, whose free aspiring mind
Europe's cold laws,[1] and colder customs[2] bind—
O! learn, what Nature's genial laws decree—
What Otaheite[3] is, let Britain be!
  *   *   *   *   *

Of WHIST or CRIBBAGE mark th' amusing game—
The PARTNERS *changing*, but the sport the *same*.
Else would the gamester's anxious ardour cool,
Dull every deal, and stagnant every pool.[1]
Yet must *one*[5] Man, with one *unceasing* Wife,
Play the LONG RUBBER of connubial life.
Yes! human laws, and laws esteem'd divine,
The generous passion straiten and confine ;
And, as a stream, when art constrains its course,
Pours its fierce torrent with augmented force,
So, Passion,[6] narrow'd to one channel small,
Unlike the former, does not flow at all.
For Love *then* only flaps his purple wings,
When uncontroll'd by priestcraft or by kings.

Such the strict rules, that, in these barbarous climes,
Choke youth's fair flowers, and feelings turn to crimes :
And people every walk of polish'd life[7]
With that two-headed monster, MAN and WIFE.

Yet bright examples sometimes we observe,
Which from the general practice seem to swerve ;

---

[1] Laws made by parliaments or kings.

[2] Customs voted or imposed by ditto, not the customs here alluded to (*by the Author*).

[3] M. Bailly and other astronomers have observed, that in consequence of the varying obliquity of the Ecliptic, the climates of the circumpolar and tropical climates may, in process of time, be materially changed. Perhaps it is not very likely that even by these means Britain may ever become a small island in the South Seas. But this is not the meaning of the verse—the similarity here proposed relates to manners, not to local situation. (*Note by the Author.*)

[4] "*Multam accepit rimosa paludem.*"—VIRGIL.

[5] The word *one* here, means all the inhabitants of Europe (excepting the French, who have remedied this inconvenience), not any particular individual. The Author begs leave to disclaim every allusion that can be construed as personal.

[6] As a stream—simile of dissimilitude, a mode of illustration familiar to the ancients.

[7] Walks of polished life, see " Kensington Gardens," a poem.

Such as presented to Germania's [1] view,
A Kotzebue's bold emphatic pencil drew :
Such as, translated in some future age,
Shall add new glories to the British stage ;
—While the moved audience sit in dumb despair,
" Like Hottentots,[2] *and at each other stare.*"

With look sedate, and staid beyond her years,
In matron weeds a *Housekeeper* appears.
The jingling keys her comely girdle deck—
Her 'kerchief colour'd, and her apron *check.*
Can that be Adelaide, that " soul of whim,"
Reform'd in practice, and in manner prim?
—On household cares intent,[3] with many a sigh
She turns the pancake, and she moulds the pie ;
Melts into sauces rich the savoury ham ;
From the crush'd berry strains the lucid jam ;
Bids brandied cherries,[4] by infusion slow,
Imbibe new flavour, and their own forego,
Sole cordial of her heart, sole solace of her woe !
While still, responsive to each mournful moan,
The saucepan simmers in a softer tone.

CANNING AND FRERE.

---

[1] Germania—Germany ; a country in Europe, peopled by the Germani : alluded to in Cæsar's Commentaries, page 1, vol. ii. edit. prin. See also several DIDACTIC POEMS.

[2] A beautiful figure of German literature. The Hottentots remarkable for staring at each other—God knows why.

[3] This delightful and instructive picture of domestic life, is recommended to all keepers of boarding schools, and other seminaries of the same nature.

[4] It is a singular quality of brandied cherries, that they exchange their flavour for that of the liquor in which they are immersed.

THE LOVES OF THE TRIANGLES.

[APRIL 16, 1798.]

E cannot better explain to our readers the design of the poem from which the following extracts are taken, than by borrowing the expressions of the author, MR. HIGGINS, of St. Mary Axe, in the letter which accompanied the manuscript.

We must premise, that we had found ourselves called upon to remonstrate with Mr. H. on the freedom of some of the positions laid down in his other DIDACTIC POEM, the "PROGRESS OF MAN;" and had in the course of our remonstrance hinted something to the disadvantage of the *new principles* which are now afloat in the world, and which are, in our opinion, working so much prejudice to the happiness of mankind. To this Mr. H. takes occasion to reply—

"What you call the *new principles* are, in fact, nothing less than *new*. They are the principles of primeval nature, the system of original and unadulterated man.

"If you mean by my addiction to *new principles* that the object which I have in view in my larger work [meaning the "PROGRESS OF MAN"] and in the several other *concomitant* and *subsidiary* DIDACTIC POEMS which are necessary to complete my plan, is to restore this first, and pure simplicity; to rescue and to recover the interesting nakedness of human nature, by ridding her of the cumbrous establishments which the folly, and pride, and self-interest of the worst part of our species have heaped upon her;—you are right. Such is my object. I do not disavow it. Nor is it mine alone. There are abundance of abler hands at work upon it. *Encyclopedias, Treatises, Novels, Magazines, Reviews,* and *New Annual Registers,* have, as you are well aware, done their part with activity and with effect. It remained to bring the *heavy* artillery of a DIDACTIC POEM to bear upon the same object.

"If I have selected your paper as the channel for conveying my labours to the public, it was not because I was unaware of the hostility of your principles to mine, of the

bigotry of your attachment to '*things as they are*,'—but
because, I will fairly own, I found some sort of cover and
disguise necessary for securing the favourable reception of
my sentiments; the usual pretexts of humanity, and philanthropy, and fine feeling by which we have for some time
obtained a passport to the hearts and understandings of
men, being now worn out or exploded.   I could not choose
but smile at my success in the first instance, in inducing
you to adopt my poem as your own.

   " But you have called for an explanation of these principles of ours, and you have a right to demand it.   Our
first principle is, then—the reverse of the trite and dull
maxim of Pope—' *Whatever is, is right.*'   We contend, that
' *Whatever is, is* WRONG ;' that institutions, civil and religious, that social order (as it is called in *your* cant) and
regular government, and law, and I know not what other
fantastic inventions, are but so many cramps and fetters on
the free agency of man's *natural intellect* and *moral sensibility ;* so many badges of his degradation from the primal
purity and excellence of his nature.

   " Our second principle is, the '*eternal and absolute* PER-
FECTIBILITY OF MAN.'   We contend, that if, as is demon-
strable, we have risen from a level with the *cabbages of the
field* to our present comparatively intelligent and dignified
state of existence, by the mere exertion of our own *energies ;*
we should, if these *energies* were not repressed and subdued by the operation of prejudice, and folly, by KING-
CRAFT and PRIEST-CRAFT, and the other evils incident to
what is called civilized society, continue to exert and
expand ourselves in a proportion infinitely greater than
anything of which we yet have any notion :—in a *ratio*
hardly capable of being calculated by any science of which
we are now masters, but which would in time raise man
from his present biped state, to a rank more worthy of his
endowments and aspirations ; to a rank in which he would
be, as it were, all MIND ; would enjoy unclouded perspica-
city and perpetual vitality ; feed on PHLOGISTON, and never
DIE, but *by his own consent.*

   " But though the poem of the PROGRESS OF MAN alone
would be sufficient to teach this system, and enforce these
doctrines, the whole practical effect of them cannot be
expected to be produced, but by the gradual perfecting of

each of the sublimer sciences ; at the husk and shell of
which we are now nibbling, and at the kernel whereof, in
our present state, we cannot hope to arrive.   These
several sciences will be the subjects of the several
auxiliary DIDACTIC POEMS which I have now in hand (one
of which, entitled THE LOVES OF THE TRIANGLES, I herewith transmit to you), and for the better arrangement and
execution of which, I beseech you to direct your bookseller to furnish me with a handsome Chambers's Dictionary ; in order that I may be enabled to go through
the several articles alphabetically, beginning with *Abraca-*
dabra, under the first letter, and going down to *Zodiac*,
which is to be found under the last.

"I am persuaded that there is no SCIENCE, however
abstruse, nay, no TRADE OR MANUFACTURE, which may not
be taught by a DIDACTIC POEM.   In that before you, an
attempt is made (not unsuccessfully) to *enlist the* IMAGI-
NATION *under the banners of* GEOMETRY.   BOTANY I found
done to my hands.   And though the more rigid and un-
bending stiffness of a mathematical subject does not admit
of the same appeals to the warmer passions, which naturally arise out of the *sexual* (or, as I have heard several
worthy gentlewomen of my acquaintance, who delight
much in the poem to which I allude, term it, by a slight
misnomer no way difficult to be accounted for—the *sen-*
sual) system of Linnæus ;—yet I trust that the range and
variety of illustration with which I have endeavoured to
ornament and enlighten the arid truths of EUCLID and
ALGEBRA, will be found to have smoothed the road of
Demonstration, to have softened the rugged features of
Elementary Propositions, and, as it were, to have strewed
the *Asses' Bridge* with flowers."

Such is the account which Mr. HIGGINS gives of his own
undertaking and of the motives which have led him to it.
For our parts, though we have not the same sanguine
persuasion of the *absolute perfectibility* of our species, and
are at the same time liable to the imputation of being
more satisfied with *things as they are*, than Mr. HIGGINS
and his associates ; yet, as we are, in at least the same
proportion, less convinced of the practical influence of
DIDACTIC POEMS, we apprehend little danger to our readers'
morals from laying before them Mr. HIGGINS's Doctrine in

its most fascinating shape. The poem **abounds, indeed,** with beauties of the most striking kind,—various **and** vivid imagery, bold and unsparing impersonifications; **and** similitudes and illustrations brought **from the most ordinary and** the most **extraordinary occurrences of nature,—from history** and **fable,—appealing equally to the heart and to the** understanding, **and calculated to make the subject of which the poem professes to treat, rather amusing than intelligible. We shall be agreeably surprised** to hear that **it has assisted any young student at** either **University in his Mathematical Studies.**

We need hardly **add, that the** plates **illustrative** of this **poem (the** engravings **of** which would have been too expensive for our **publication) are** to be found in EUCLID's **Elements, and other** books **of a** similar **nature** and **tendency.**

THE LOVES OF THE TRIANGLES.

ARGUMENT OF THE FIRST CANTO.

Warning **to the** profane not to approach—NYMPHS and DEITIES of MATHEMATICAL MYTHOLOGY—CYCLOIS of a pensive disposition—PENDULUMS, **the contrary,** playful—and WHY?—Sentimental Union of the NAIADS and HYDROSTATICS—Marriage of EUCLID and ALGEBRA—PULLEY the emblem of MECHANICS—OPTICS of a licentious disposition—distinguished by her telescope **and green** spectacles.—HYDE PARK GATE on a Sunday morning —Cockneys—Coaches—DIDACTIC POETRY—NONSENSIA—Love delights in ANGLES or Corners—Theory of Fluxions **explained**—TROCHAIS, the Nymph of the Wheel—SMOKE-JACK described—Personification of elementary or culinary FIRE—LITTLE JACK HORNER—Story of CINDERELLA—RECTANGLE, a MAGICIAN, **educated** by PLATO and MENECMUS — in love with THREE CURVES at the same time—served by GINS, or GENII—transforms himself into a CONE—the THREE CURVES requite his **passion—Description of** them—PARABOLA, HYPERBOLA, and ELLIPSIS — ASYMPTOTES — Conjugated Axes — Illustrations — REWBELL, BARRAS, and LEPAUX, the THREE virtuous Directors —MACBETH and the THREE Witches—the THREE Fates—the THREE Graces—King LEAR and his THREE Daughters—Catherine Wheel.—Catastrophe of Mr. GINGHAM, with his Wife and THREE Daughters **overturned** in a One-horse Chaise—DISLOCATION and CONTUSION two kindred Fiends—Mail Coaches—**Exhortation** to Drivers to be careful—Genius of the Post-Office—Invention of Letters—DIGAMMA—DOUBLE Letters—Remarkable

I*   H

Direction of One—HIPPONA the Goddess of Hackhorses—Anec-
dote of the Derby Diligence—PARAMETER and ABSCISSA unite to
overpower the ORDINATE, who retreats down the AXIS MAJOR,
and forms himself in a SQUARE—ISOSCELES, a Giant — Dr.
RHOMBOIDES—Fifth Proposition, or ASSES' BRIDGE—Bridge of
LODI—BUONAPARTE—Raft and Windmills—Exhortation to the
recovery of our Freedom—Conclusion.

THE LOVES OF THE TRIANGLES.

A MATHEMATICAL AND PHILOSOPHICAL POEM.

INSCRIBED TO DR. DARWIN.

CANTO I.

TAY your rude steps, or e'er your feet invade
The Muses' haunts, ye sons of WAR and TRADE!
Nor you, ye legion fiends of CHURCH and LAW,
Pollute these pages with unhallow'd paw![1]
Debased, corrupted, grovelling, and confined,
No DEFINITIONS[2] touch *your* senseless mind ;
To *you* no POSTULATES[3] prefer their claim,
No ardent AXIOMS[1] *your* dull souls inflame ;
For *you*, no TANGENTS[5] touch, no ANGLES meet,
No CIRCLES[6] join in osculation[7] sweet !

---

[1] Imitated from the introductory couplet to the "Economy of
Vegetation : "
" Stay your rude steps, whose throbbing breasts infold
   The legion fiends of glory and of gold."
This sentiment is here expanded into four lines.

[2] *Definition.*—A distinct notion explaining the genesis of a thing.
—*Wolfius.*

[3] *Postulate.*—A self-evident proposition.

[4] *Axiom.*—An indemonstrable truth.

[5] *Tangents.*—So called from touching, because they touch circles,
and never cut them.

[6] *Circles.*—See Chambers's Dictionary, article "Circle."

[7] *Osculation.* — For the *os-culation*, or kissing of circles and other
curves, see *Huygens*, who has veiled this delicate and inflammatory
subject in the decent obscurity of a learned language.

For *me*, ye CISSOIDS,[1] round my temples bend
Your wandering curves ; ye CONCHOIDS[2] extend ;
Let playful PENDULES quick vibration feel,
While silent CYCLOIS rests upon her wheel ;
Let HYDROSTATICS,[3] simpering as they go,
Lead the light Naiads on fantastic toe ;
Let shrill ACOUSTICS[4] tune the tiny lyre ;
With EUCLID sage fair ALGEBRA[5] conspire ;
The obedient pulley[6] strong MECHANICS ply,
And wanton OPTICS roll the melting eye !

I see the fair fantastic forms appear,
The flaunting drapery, and the languid leer ;
Fair sylphish forms[7]—who, tall, erect, and slim,
Dart the keen glance, and stretch the length of limb ;
To viewless harpings weave the meanless dance,
Wave the gay wreath, and titter as they prance.

Such rich confusion[8] charms the ravish'd sight,

---

[1] *Cissois.*—A curve supposed to resemble the sprig of ivy, from which it has its name, and therefore peculiarly adapted to poetry.

[2] *Conchois,* or *Conchylis.*—A most beautiful and picturesque curve ; it bears a fanciful resemblance to a *conch* shell. The conchois is capable of infinite extension, and presents a striking analogy between the animal and mathematical creation—every individual of this species containing within itself a series of *young* conchoids for several generations, in the same manner as the Aphides and other insect tribes are observed to do.

[3] *Hydrostatics.*—Water has been supposed, by several of our philosophers, to be capable of the passion of love. Some later experiments appear to favour this idea. Water, when pressed by a moderate degree of heat, has been observed to *simper*, or *simmer* (as it is more usually called). The same does not hold true of any other element.

[4] *Acoustics.*—The doctrine or theory of sound.

[5] *Euclid and Algebra.*—The loves and nuptials of these two interesting personages forming a considerable episode in the third canto, are purposely omitted here.

[6] *Pulley.*—So called from our Saxon word PULL, signifying to pull or draw.

[7] *Fair sylphish forms.*—*Vide* modern prints of nymphs and shepherds dancing to nothing at all.

[8] *Such rich confusion.*—Imitated from the following genteel and sprightly lines in the first canto of the " Loves of the Plants : "—

" So bright its folding canopy withdrawn,
Glides the gilt landau o'er the velvet lawn,
Of beaux and belles displays the glittering throng,
And soft airs fan them as they glide along."

When vernal Sabbaths to the Park invite.
Mounts the thick dust, the coaches crowd along,
Presses round Grosvenor Gate th' impatient throng ;
White-muslin'd misses and mammas are seen,
Link'd with gay cockneys, glittering o'er the green :
The rising breeze unnumber'd charms displays,
And the tight ancle strikes th' astonish'd gaze.

But chief, thou Nurse of the DIDACTIC MUSE,
Divine NONSENSIA, all thy soul infuse ;
The charms of *Secants* and of *Tangents* tell,
How Loves and Graces in an *Angle*[1] dwell ;
How slow progressive *Points*[2] protract the *Line*,
As pendent spiders spin the filmy twine ;
How lengthen'd *Lines*, impetuous sweeping round,
Spread the wide *Plane*, and mark its circling bound ;
How *Planes*, their substance with their motion grown,
Form the huge *Cube*, the *Cylinder*, the *Cone*.

---

[1] *Angle*—Gratus puellæ risus ab ANGULO.—*Hor.*

[2] *How slow progressive Points.*—The Author has reserved the picturesque imagery which the *theory of fluxions* naturally suggested, for his "Algebraic Garden," where the *fluents* are described as rolling with an even current between a margin of *curves* of the higher order over a pebbly channel, inlaid with *differential calculi.*

In the following six lines he has confined himself to a strict explanation of the theory, according to which LINES are supposed to be generated by the motion of POINTS, PLANES by the lateral motion of LINES, and SOLIDS from PLANES, by a similar process.

Quære—Whether a practical application of this theory would not enable us to account for the genesis or original formation of SPACE itself, in the same manner in which DR. DARWIN has traced the whole of the organized creation to his SIX FILAMENTS—Vide "ZOO-NOMIA." We may conceive the whole of our present universe to have been originally concentred in a single POINT ; we may conceive this primeval POINT, or PUNCTUM SALIENS of the universe, evolving itself by its own energies, to have moved forwards in a right line, *ad infinitum*, till it grew tired ; after which the right LINE which it had generated would begin to put itself in motion in a lateral direction, describing an AREA of infinite extent. This AREA, as soon as it became conscious of its own existence, would begin to ascend or descend, according as its specific gravity might determine it, forming an immense solid space filled with VACUUM, and capable of containing the present existing universe.

SPACE being thus obtained, and presenting a suitable NIDUS, or receptacle for the generation of CHAOTIC MATTER, an immense deposit of it would gradually be accumulated ; after which, the FILA-

Lo! where the chimney's sooty tube ascends,
The fair TROCHAIS[1] from the corner bends!
Her coal-black eyes upturn'd, incessant mark
The eddying smoke, quick flame, and volant spark;
Dart her quick ken, where flashing in between,
Her much-loved *Smoke-Jack* glimmers thro' the scene;
Mark how his various parts together tend,
Point to one purpose,—in one object end;
The spiral *grooves* in smooth meanders flow,
Drags the long *chain*, the polish'd axles glow,
While slowly circumvolves the piece of beef below:
The conscious fire[2] with bickering radiance burns,
Eyes the rich joint, and roasts it as it turns.

MENT of *fire* being produced in the chaotic mass, by an *idiosyncrasy*, or self-formed habit analogous to fermentation, *explosion* would take place; suns would be shot from the central chaos; planets from *suns*; and *satellites* from *planets*. In this state of things the FILAMENT of *organization* would begin to exert itself, in those independent masses which, in proportion to their bulk, exposed the greatest surface to the action of *light* and *heat*. This FILAMENT, after an infinite series of ages, would begin to *ramify*, and its viviparous offspring would diversify their forms and habits, so as to accommodate themselves to the various *incunabula* which Nature had prepared for them. Upon this view of things it seems highly probable that the first effort of Nature terminated in the production of VEGETABLES, and that these being abandoned to their own *energies*, by degrees detached themselves from the surface of the earth, and supplied themselves with wings or feet, according as their different propensities determined them in favour of aërial or terrestrial existence. Others, by an inherent disposition to society and civilization, and by a stronger effort of *volition*, would become MEN. These, in time, would restrict themselves to the use of their *hind feet:* their *tails* would gradually rub off, by sitting in their caves or huts as soon as they arrived at a domesticated state; they would invent *language* and the use of *fire*, with our present and hitherto imperfect system of *society*. In the meanwhile, the *Fuci* and *Algæ*, with the *Corallines* and *Madrepores*, would transform themselves into *fish*, and would gradually populate all the submarine portion of the globe.

[1] *Trochais.*—The Nymph of the Wheel, supposed to be in love with SMOKE-JACK.

[2] *The conscious fire.*—The sylphs and genii of the different elements have a variety of innocent occupations assigned them; those of FIRE are supposed to divert themselves with writing the name of *Kunkel* in phosphorus.—See "ECONOMY OF VEGETATION:"

"Or mark, with shining letters, KUNKEL'S name
In the slow *phosphor's* self-consuming flame."

So youthful Horner roll'd the roguish eye,
Cull'd the dark plum from out his Christmas pie,
And cried, in self-applause—" How good a boy am I."

So, the sad victim of domestic spite,
Fair Cinderella, pass'd the wintry night,
In the lone chimney's darksome nook immured,
Her form disfigured, and her charms obscured.
Sudden her godmother appears in sight,
Lifts the charm'd rod, and chants the mystic rite ;
The chanted rite the maid attentive hears,
And feels new ear-rings deck her listening ears ;[1]
While 'midst her towering tresses, aptly set,
Shines bright, with quivering glance, the smart aigrette ;
Brocaded silks the splendid dress complete,
And the Glass Slipper grasps her fairy feet.
Six cock-tail'd mice[2] transport her to the ball,
And liveried lizards wait upon her call.

FRERE.

---

[1] *Listening ears.*—Listening, and therefore peculiarly suited to a pair of diamond ear-rings. See the description of Nebuchadnezzar in his transformed state—

" Nor flattery's self can pierce his *pendent ears.*"

In poetical diction, a person is said to "*breathe the* BLUE *air*," and to "*drink the* HOARSE *wave!*"—not that the colour of the sky or the noise of the water has any reference to drinking or breathing, but because the poet obtains the advantage of thus describing his subject under a *double relation*, in the same manner in which material objects present themselves to our different senses at the same time.

[2] *Cock-tailed mice*—COCTILIBUS MURIS. *Ovid.*—There is reason to believe, that the *murine*, or *mouse* species, were anciently much more numerous than at the present day. It appears from the sequel of the line, that SEMIRAMIS surrounded the *city of Babylon* with a number of these animals.

Dicitur altam
COCTILIBUS MURIS *cinxisse Semiramis urbem.*

It is not easy at present to form any conjecture with respect to the end, whether of ornament or defence, which they could be supposed to answer. I should be inclined to believe, that in this instance the mice were dead, and that so vast a collection of them must have been furnished by way of tribute, to free the country from these destructive animals. This superabundance of the *murine* race must have been owing to their immense fecundity, and to the comparatively tardy reproduction of the *feline* species. The traces of this disproportion are to be found in the early history of every country. The ancient laws of Wales estimate a CAT at the price of as much

THE LOVES OF THE TRIANGLES.

A MATHEMATICAL AND PHILOSOPHICAL POEM.

(*Continued.*)

[APRIL 23, 1798.]

CANTO I.

ALAS! that partial Science should approve
The sly RECTANGLE'S[1] too licentious love!
For *three* bright nymphs the wily wizard
burns;—
Three bright-eyed nymphs requite his flame
by turns.
Strange force of magic skill! combined of yore
With PLATO's science and MENECMUS' lore.[2]
In *Afric's* schools, amid those sultry sands
High on its base where POMPEY's pillar stands,
This learnt THE SEER; and learnt, alas! too well,
Each scribbled talisman and smoky spell:
What mutter'd charms, what soul-subduing arts,
Fell ZATANAI[3] to his sons imparts.

---

corn as would be sufficient to cover her, if she were suspended by the tail with her fore-feet touching the ground.—See HOWEL DHA.—In Germany, it is recorded that an army of rats, a larger animal of the *mus* tribe, were employed as the ministers of Divine Vengeance against a feudal tyrant; and the commercial legend of our own WHITTINGTON might probably be traced to an equally authentic origin.

[1] *Rectangle.*—"A figure which has one angle, *or more*, of ninety degrees."—*Johnson's Dictionary*. It here means a RIGHT-ANGLED TRIANGLE, which is therefore incapable of having more than one angle of ninety degrees, but which may, according to our author's *Prosopopœia*, be supposed to be in love with THREE, or any greater number of NYMPHS.

[2] *Plato's science and Menecmus' lore.*—Proclus attributes the discovery of the CONIC SECTIONS to PLATO, but obscurely. Eratosthenes seems to adjudge it to MENECMUS. "*Neque Menecmos necesse erit in CONO secare ternarios.*" (Vide *Montucla*.) From *Greece* they were carried to *Alexandria*, where (according to our author's beautiful fiction) RECTANGLE either did or might learn magic.

[3] *Zatanai.*—Supposed to be the same with Satan.—Vide the "New Arabian Nights," translated by Cazotte, author of "*Le Diable amoureux.*"

GINS[1]—black and huge! who in DOM-DANIEL'S[2] cave
Writhe your scorch'd limbs on sulphur's[3] azure wave;
Or, shivering, yell amidst eternal snows,
Where cloud-capp'd CAF[4] protrudes his granite toes;
(Bound by *his* will, *Judæa's* fabled king,[5]
Lord of *Aladdin's* lamp and mystic ring.)
GINS! YE remember!—for YOUR toil convey'd
Whate'er of drugs the powerful charm could aid;
Air, earth, and sea ye search'd, and where below
Flame embryo lavas, young volcanoes[6] glow,—
GINS! ye beheld appall'd th' enchanter's hand
Wave in dark air th' *Hypothenusal* wand:
Saw him the mystic *Circle* trace, and wheel
With head erect, and far-extended heel;[7]

---

[1] *Gins*—the Eastern name for GENII.—Vide *Tales of ditto*.

[2] *Dom-Daniel*—a sub-marine palace near Tunis, where Zatanai usually held his court.—Vide " New Arabian Nights."

[3] *Sulphur.*—A substance which, when cold, reflects the yellow rays, and is therefore said to be yellow. When raised to a temperature at which it *attracts oxygen* (a process usually called *burning*), it emits a blue flame. This may be beautifully exemplified, and at a moderate expense, by igniting those *fasciculi* of brimstone *matches*, frequently sold (so frequently, indeed, as to form one of the London cries) by women of an advanced age, in this metropolis. They will be found to yield an *azure*, or blue light.

[4] *Caf.*—The Indian *Caucasus.*—Vide " *Bailly's Lettres sur l'Atlantide*," in which he proves that this was the native country of GOG and MAGOG (now resident in GUILDHALL), as well as of the PERIS, or *fairies* of the Asiatic romances.

[5] *Judæa's fabled king.*—MR. HIGGINS does not mean to deny that SOLOMON was really King of JUDÆA. The epithet *fabled* applies to that empire over the Genii, which the retrospective generosity of the Arabian fabulists has bestowed upon this monarch.

[6] *Young volcanoes.*—The genesis of burning mountains was never, till lately, well explained. Those with which we are best acquainted, are certainly not viviparous; it is therefore probable, that there exists, in the centre of the earth, a considerable reservoir of their eggs, which, during the obstetrical convulsions of general earthquakes, produce new volcanoes.

[7] *Far-extended heel.*—The personification of the TRIANGLE, besides answering a poetical purpose, was necessary to illustrate MR. HIGGINS'S philosophical opinions. The ancient mathematicians conceived that a CONE was generated by the revolution of a TRIANGLE; but this, as our author justly observes, would be impossible, without supposing in the TRIANGLE that *expansive nisus*, discovered by BLUMENBACH, and improved by DARWIN, which is peculiar to animated matter, and which alone explains the whole mystery of or-

Saw him, with speed that mock'd the dazzled eye,
Self-whirl'd, in quick gyrations eddying fly:
Till done the potent spell—behold him grown
Fair *Venus'* emblem—the *Phœnician* CONE.[1]

Triumphs THE SEER, and now secure observes
The kindling passions of the *rival* CURVES.

And first, the fair PARABOLA[2] behold,
Her timid arms, with virgin blush, unfold!
Though, on one *focus* fix'd, her eyes betray
A heart that glows with love's resistless sway,
Though, climbing oft, she strive with bolder grace
Round his tall neck to clasp her fond embrace,
Still ere she reach it, from his polish'd side
Her trembling hands in devious TANGENTS glide.

Not thus HYPERBOLA:[3]—with subtlest art
The blue-eyed wanton plays her changeful part;
Quick as her *conjugated* axes move
Through every posture of luxurious love,
Her sportive limbs with easiest grace expand;
Her charms unveil'd provoke the lover's hand:

---

ganization. Our enchanter sits on the ground, with his heels stretched out, his head erect, his wand (or *hypothenuse*) resting on the extremities of his feet and the tip of his nose (as is finely expressed in the engraving in the original work), and revolves upon his bottom with great velocity. His skin, by magical means, has acquired an indefinite power of expansion, as well as that of assimilating to itself all the *azote* of the air, which he decomposes by expiration from the lungs—an immense quantity, and which, in our present unimproved and uneconomical mode of breathing, is quite thrown away—by this simple process the transformation is very naturally accounted for.

[1] *Phænician Cone.*—It was under this shape that *Venus* was worshipped in *Phænicia.* MR. HIGGINS thinks it was the *Venus Urania*, or Celestial Venus; in allusion to which, he supposes that the *Phænician* grocers first introduced the practice of preserving sugar-loaves in blue or sky-coloured paper—he also believes that the *conical* form of the original grenadiers' caps was typical of the loves of MARS and VENUS.

[2] *Parabola.*—The curve described by projectiles of all sorts, as bombs, shuttlecocks, &c.

[3] *Hyperbola.*—Not figuratively speaking, as in rhetoric, but mathematically; and therefore blue-eyed.

Unveil'd, except in many a filmy ray,
Where light *Asymptotes*[1] o'er her bosom play,
Nor touch her glowing skin, nor intercept the day.

Yet why, Ellipsis,[2] at thy fate repine?
More lasting bliss, securer joys are thine.
Though to each fair his treacherous wish may stray,
Though each, in turn, may seize a transient sway,
'Tis thine with mild coercion to restrain,
Twine round his struggling heart, and bind with endless
    chain.

ELLIS.

Thus, happy FRANCE! in thy regenerate land,
Where TASTE with RAPINE saunters hand in hand;
Where, nursed in seats of innocence and bliss,
REFORM greets TERROR with fraternal kiss;
Where mild PHILOSOPHY first taught to scan
The *wrongs* of PROVIDENCE, and *rights* of MAN;
Where MEMORY broods o'er FREEDOM's earlier scene,
The *Lantern* bright, and brighter *Guillotine ;*
Three gentle swains evolve their longing arms,
And woo the *young* REPUBLIC's virgin charms;
And though proud BARRAS with the fair succeed,
Though not in vain th' Attorney REWBELL plead,
Oft doth th' impartial nymph their love forego,
To clasp thy crooked shoulders, blest LEPAUX!

So, with dark dirge athwart the blasted heath,
Three SISTER WITCHES hail'd the appall'd MACBETH.

So, the *Three* FATES beneath grim *Pluto's* roof,
Strain the dun warp, and weave the murky woof;
Till deadly Atropos with fatal shears
Slits the thin promise of th' expected years,
While midst the dungeon's gloom or battle's din,
Ambition's victims perish, as they spin.

---

[1] *Asymptotes.*—"Lines which, though they may approach still
nearer together till they are nearer than the least assignable distance,
yet being still produced infinitely, will never meet."—*Johnson's
Dictionary.*

[2] *Ellipsis.*—A curve, the revolution of which on its axis produces
an ellipsoid, or solid resembling the eggs of birds, particularly those
of the gallinaceous tribe. *Ellipsis* is the only curve that embraces
the cone.

Thus, **the** *Three* Graces on the *Idalian* green
Bow with deft homage to *Cythera's* Queen;
Her polish'd arms with pearly bracelets deck,
Part her light locks, and bare her **ivory neck;**
Round her fair form ethereal odours throw,
And teach th' unconscious zephyrs where to blow;
Floats the thin gauze, and glittering as they play,
The bright folds flutter in phlogistic day.

So, with his daughters *Three,* th' unsceptred LEAR
Heaved the loud sigh, and pour'd the glistering **tear:** [1]
His DAUGHTERS *Three,* **save one alone, conspire**
(**Rich in** *his* **gifts) to spurn their** generous **sire;**
Bid the rude storm his hoary tresses drench,
Stint the spare meal, **the** hundred knights retrench;
Mock his mad sorrow, and with alter'd mien
Renounce the daughter, and assert the queen.
A father's griefs his feeble frame convulse,
Rack his white head, and fire **his feverous pulse;**
Till kind CORDELIA soothes **his soul to rest,**
And **folds** the **parent-monarch to her breast.**

                              CANNING, ELLIS, AND FRERE.

Thus some fair spinster grieves in wild affright,
Vex'd **with dull megrim, or vertigo light;**
Pleased **round the fair** *Three* **dawdling** doctors stand,
Wave the **white wig, and stretch the** asking hand,
State the grave **doubt, the nauseous** draught decree,
And all receive, though none deserve, a fee.

So down thy hill, romantic **Ashbourn, glides**
The Derby dilly, carrying *Three* INSIDES.
One in each corner sits, **and lolls at ease,**
With **folded arms,** propt back, **and outstretch'd knees;**
While **the press'd** *Bodkin,* punch'd and squeezed to death,
Sweats in the mid-most place, and scolds, and pants for
        breath. [2]

---

[1] *Glistering tear.*—This is not a medical metaphor. The word *glistering* is here used as the participle of the verb to *glister,* and is not in any way connected with the substantive of the same name. "**All** that glisters is not gold," **are** the words of our old but immortal bard.

[2] These **last twelve lines [by Mr.** Canning] were **not in the "Anti-** Jacobin" as printed on the 23rd April, 1798.

THE LOVES OF THE TRIANGLES.

[MAY 7, 1798.]

HE frequent solicitations which we have received for a continuation of the LOVES OF THE TRIANGLES, have induced us to lay before the public (with Mr. Higgins's permission) the concluding lines of the Canto. The catastrophe of Mr. and Mrs. GINGHAM, and the episode of HIPPONA, contained, in our apprehension, several reflections of too free a nature. The conspiracy of PARAMETER and ABSCISSA against the ORDINATE, is written in a strain of poetry so very splendid and dazzling, as not to suit the more tranquil majesty of diction which our readers admire in Mr. HIGGINS. We have therefore begun our extract with the Loves of the Giant ISOSCELES, and the Picture of the *Asses'-Bridge*, and its several illustrations.

CANTO I.

EXTRACT.

WAS thine alone, O youth of giant frame,
ISOSCELES![1] that rebel heart to tame !
In vain coy MATHESIS[2] thy presence flies :
Still turn her fond hallucinating[3] eyes ;
Thrills with *Galvanic* fires[4] each tortuous
    nerve,
Throb her blue veins, and dies her cold reserve.

---

[1] *Isosceles.*—An equi-crural triangle. It is represented as a *Giant*, because Mr. HIGGINS says he has observed that procerity is much promoted by the equal length of the legs, more especially when they are long legs.

[2] *Mathesis.*—The doctrine of mathematics—Pope calls her *mad Mathesis.*—Vide "Johnson's Dictionary."

[3] *Hallucinating.*—The disorder with which MATHESIS is affected is a disease of *increased volition*, called *erotomania*, or *sentimental love*. It is the fourth species of the second genus of the first order and third class ; in consequence of which Mr. Hackman shot Miss Ray in the lobby of the playhouse.—Vide "Zoonomia," vol. ii. pp. 363, 365.

[4] *Galvanic fires.*—Dr. GALVANI is a celebrated philosopher at

—Yet strives the **fair**, till in **the** giant's breast
She sees the mutual passion flame confess'd :
Where'er he moves, she sees his **tall** limbs **trace**
Internal Angles[1] *equal at the base ;*
Again she doubts him : but *produced at* **will,**
She sees *th' external Angles equal still.*

Say, blest ISOSCELES ! what favouring power,
Or love, or chance, at night's auspicious hour,
While to **the** *Asses'-Bridge*[2] entranced you stray'd,
Led to the *Asses'-Bridge* the enamour'd maid ?—
The *Asses'-Bridge,* for ages doom'd to hear
The deafening surge assault his wooden ear,
With joy repeats sweet sounds of mutual bliss,
The soft susurrant sigh, and gently-murmuring kiss.

So thy dark arches, LONDON *Bridge,* bestride
Indignant THAMES, and part his angry tide,
There oft returning from those green retreats,
Where fair *Vauxhallia* decks her sylvan seats ;—
Where each spruce nymph, from city compters free,
Sips the froth'd syllabub, or fragrant tea ;
While with sliced ham, scraped beef, and burnt champagne,
Her 'prentice lover soothes his amorous pain ;
There oft, in well-trimm'd wherry, glide along
Smart beaux and giggling belles, a glittering throng :

Turin. He has proved that the electric fluid is the proximate cause
of nervous sensibility ; and Mr. HIGGINS is of opinion that, by
means of this discovery, the sphere of our disagreeable sensations
may be, in future, considerably enlarged. " Since dead frogs " (says
he) " are awakened by this fluid to such a degree of posthumous sensibility as to jump out of the glass in which they are placed, why not
men, who are sometimes so much more sensible when alive ? And
if so, why not employ this new stimulus to deter mankind from
dying (which they so pertinaciously continue to do) of various old-
fashioned diseases, notwithstanding all the brilliant discoveries of
modern philosophy, and the example of Count CAGLIOSTRO ?"

[1] *Internal Angles,* &c.—This is an exact versification of Euclid's
fifth theorem.—Vide Euclid, *in loco.*

[2] *Asses' Bridge*—Pons Asinorum.—The name usually given to
the before-mentioned theorem—though, as Mr. Higgins thinks,
absurdly. He says, that having frequently watched companies of
asses during their passage of a bridge, he never discovered in them
any symptoms of geometrical instinct upon the occasion. But he
thinks that with Spanish asses, which are much larger (vide Towns-
end's " Travels through Spain "), the case may possibly be different.

Smells the tarr'd rope—with undulation fine
Flaps the loose sail—the silken awnings shine ;
" Shoot we the bridge !" the venturous boatmen cry ;
" Shoot we the bridge !" the exulting fare [1] reply.
—Down the steep fall the headlong waters go,
Curls the white foam, the breakers roar below.
The veering helm the dextrous steersman stops,
Shifts the thin oars, the fluttering canvas drops ;
Then with closed eyes, clench'd hands, and quick-drawn
    breath,
Darts at the central arch, nor heeds the gulf beneath.
—Full 'gainst the pier the unsteady timbers knock,
The thin planks, starting, own the impetuous shock ;
The shifted oar, dropp'd sail, and steadied helm,
With angry surge the closing waters whelm—
—Laughs the glad THAMES, and clasps each fair one's
    charms,
That screams and scrambles in his oozy arms.
—Drench'd each thin garb, and clogg'd each struggling
    limb,
Far o'er the stream the Cockneys sink or swim ;
While each badged boatman,[2] clinging to his oar,
Bounds o'er the buoyant wave, and climbs the applauding
    shore.

So, towering ALP![3] from thy majestic ridge
Young FREEDOM gazed on LODI's blood-stain'd Bridge ;
Saw, in thick throngs, conflicting armies rush,
Ranks close on ranks, and squadrons squadrons crush ;
Burst in bright radiance through the battle's storm,
Waved her broad hands, display'd her awful form ;
Bade at her feet regenerate nations bow,
And twined the wreath round BUONAPARTE's brow.

---

[1] *Fare.*—A person, or a number of persons conveyed in a hired vehicle by land or water.

[2] *Badged boatman.*—Boatmen sometimes wear a *badge*, to distinguish them ; especially those who belong to the WATERMEN'S COMPANY.

[3] *Alp, or Alps.*—A ridge of mountains which separate the North of Italy from the South of Germany. They are evidently primeval and volcanic, consisting of granite, toadstone, and basalt, and several other substances, containing animal and vegetable recrements, and affording numberless undoubted proofs of the infinite antiquity of the earth, and of the consequent falsehood of the Mosaic chronology.

—Quick with new lights, fresh hopes, and alter'd zeal,
The slaves of despots dropp'd the soften'd steel:
Exulting Victory crown'd her favourite child,
And freed Liguria clapp'd her hands, and smiled.

Nor long the time ere Britain's shores shall greet
The warrior-sage, with gratulation sweet:
Eager to grasp the wreath of naval fame,
The Great Republic plans the *Floating Frame!*
—O'er the huge frame gigantic Terror stalks,
And counts with joy the close-compacted balks:
Of young-eyed Massacres the Cherub crew
Round their grim chief the mimic task pursue;
Turn the stiff screw, [1] apply the strengthening clamp,
Drive the long bolt, or fix the stubborn cramp,
Lash the reluctant beam, the cable splice,
Join the firm dove-tail with adjustment nice,
Through yawning fissures urge the willing wedge,
Or give the smoothing adze a sharper edge.
—Or group'd in fairy bands, with playful care,
The unconscious bullet to the furnace bear,
Or gaily tittering, tip the match with fire,
Prime the big mortar, bid the shell aspire;
Applaud, with tiny hands, and laughing eyes,
And watch the bright destruction as it flies.

Now the fierce forges gleam with angry glare—
The windmill [2] waves his woven wings in air;
Swells the proud sail, the exulting streamers fly,
Their nimble fins unnumber'd paddles ply:
—Ye soft airs breathe, ye gentle billows waft,
And, fraught with Freedom, bear the expected Raft!

---

[1] *Turn the stiff screw,* &c.—The harmony and imagery of these lines are imperfectly imitated from the following exquisite passage in the "Economy of Vegetation:"

> "Gnomes, as you now dissect, with hammers fine,
> The granite rock, the noduled flint calcine;
> Grind with strong arm the circling Chertz betwixt,
> Your pure ka—o—lins and Pe—tunt—ses mixt.
>   Canto ii. line 297.

[2] *The windmill,* &c.—This line affords a striking instance of the sound conveying an echo to the sense. I would defy the most unfeeling reader to repeat it over without accompanying it by some corresponding gesture imitative of the action described.—*Editor.*

Perch'd on her back, behold the Patriot train,
MUIR, ASHLEY, BARLOW, BUONAPARTE, PAINE!
While ROWAN's hand directs the blood-empurpled rein. }

Ye Imps of MURDER! guard her angel form,
Check the rude surge, and chase the hovering storm ;
Shield from contusive rocks her timber limbs,
And guide the SWEET ENTHUSIAST[1] as she swims ;
—And now, with web-foot oars, she gains the land,
And foreign footsteps press the yielding sand:
—The *Communes* spread, the gay *Departments* smile,
Fair *Freedom's Plant* o'ershades the laughing isle :
Fired with new hopes, the exulting peasant sees
The Gallic streamer woo the British breeze ;
While, pleased to watch its undulating charms,
The smiling infant[2] spreads his little arms.

Ye Sylphs of DEATH! on demon pinions flit
Where the tall *Guillotine* is raised for PITT :
To the poised plank tie fast the monster's back,[3]
Close the nice slider, ope the expectant sack ;
Then twitch, with fairy hands, the frolic pin—
Down falls the impatient axe with deafening din ;
The liberated head rolls off below,
And simpering FREEDOM hails the happy blow!

CANNING, ELLIS, AND FRERE.

---

[1] *Sweet Enthusiast*, &c.—A term usually applied in allegoric or technical poetry to any person or object to which no other qualification can be assigned.—*Chambers's Dictionary.*

[2] *The smiling infant.*—Infancy is particularly interested in the diffusion of the new principles. See the "Bloody Buoy." See also the following description and prediction :—

> " Here Time's huge fingers grasp his giant mace,
> And dash proud Superstition from her base ;
> Rend her strong towers and gorgeous fanes, &c.
>   &c.   &c.   &c.   &c.
> While each light moment, as it passes by,
> With feathery foot and pleasure-twinkling eye,
> Feeds from its baby-hand with many a kiss
> The callow nestlings of domestic bliss."
>   *Botanic Garden.*

[3] *The monster's back.*—LE MONSTRE PITT, l'ennemi du genre humain. See Debates of the legislators of the Great Nation *passim.*

ELEGY ON THE DEATH OF JEAN
BON ST. ANDRE.

[MAY 14, 1798.]

HE following exquisite tribute to the Memory of an unfortunate Republican, is written with such a touching sensibility, that those who can command salt tears, must prepare to shed them. The Narrative is simple and unaffected; the Event in itself interesting; the Moral obvious and awful.—We have only to observe, that as this account of the transaction is taken from the French papers, it may possibly be somewhat partial.—The DEY's own statement of the affair has not yet been received. Every friend of ˙Humanity will join with us, in expressing a candid and benevolent hope, that this business may not tend to kindle the flames of War between these two Unchristian Powers; but that, by mutual concession and accommodation, they may come to some point (short of the restoration of JEAN BON's head to his shoulders, which in this stage of the discussion is hardly practicable) by which the peace of the Pagan World may be preserved. For our part, we pretend not to decide from which quarter the concessions ought principally to be made. There are probably faults on *both sides*, in this, as in most other cases. For the character of the DEY we profess a sincere respect on the one hand; and on the other, we should naturally have wished that the head of JEAN BON ST. ANDRE should have been reserved for his own *guillotine*.

ELEGY, OR DIRGE.

I.

LL in the town of *Tunis*,
   In *Africa* the torrid,
     On a *Frenchman* of rank
     Was play'd such a prank,
As LEPAUX must think quite horrid.

1*   I

II.

No story half so shocking,
By kitchen-fire or laundry,
 Was ever heard tell,—
 As that which befel
The great JEAN BON ST. ANDRE.

III.

Poor JOHN was a gallant Captain,
In battles much delighting;
 He fled full soon
 On the *first of June*—
But he bade the rest keep fighting.

IV.

To *Paris* then returning,
And recover'd from his panic,
 He translated the plan
 Of "*Paine's Rights of Man*"
Into language *Mauritanic*.

V.

He went to teach at *Tunis*—
Where as Consul he was settled—
 Amongst other things,
 "That the PEOPLE are KINGS!"
Whereat the DEY was nettled.

VI.

The *Moors* being rather stupid,
And in temper somewhat mulish,
 Understood not a word
 Of the doctrine they heard,
And thought the *Consul* foolish.

VII.

He form'd a *Club* of *Brothers*,
And moved some resolutions—
 "Ho! ho! (says the DEY,)
 So this is the way
That the *French* make *Revolutions*."

VIII.

The DEY then gave his orders
In *Arabic* and *Persian*—
 "Let no more be said—
 But bring me his head!—
These *Clubs* are my aversion."

IX.

The CONSUL quoted WICQUEFORT,
And PUFFENDORF and GROTIUS;
 And proved from VATTEL
 Exceedingly well,
Such a deed would be quite atrocious.

X.

'Twould have moved a *Christian's* bowels
To hear the doubts he stated;—
 But the *Moors* they did
 As they were bid,
And strangled him while he prated.

XI.

His head with a sharp-edged sabre
They sever'd from his shoulders,
 And stuck it on high,
 Where it caught the eye,
To the wonder of all beholders.

XII.

This sure is a doleful story
As e'er you heard or read of;—
 If at *Tunis* you prate
 Of matters of state,
Anon they cut your head off!

XIII.

But we hear the FRENCH DIRECTORS
Have thought the point so knotty,
 That the DEY having shown
 He *dislikes* JEAN BON,
They have sent him BERNADOTTÉ.

On recurring to the French papers to verify our Correspondent's statement of this singular adventure of JEAN
BON ST. ANDRE, we discovered, to our great mortification,
that it happened at *Algiers*, and not at *Tunis*. We should
have corrected this mistake, but for two reasons—*first*,
that *Algiers* would not stand in the verse ; and, *secondly*,
that we are informed by the young man who conducts the
Geographical Department of the " *Morning Chronicle*,"
that both the towns are in Africa, or Asia (he is not quite
certain which), and, what is more to the purpose, that both
are peopled by Moors. *Tunis*, therefore, may stand.

CANNING, ELLIS, AND FRERE.

THE ROVERS; OR, THE DOUBLE ARRANGEMENT.

[JUNE 4, 1798.]

UR ingenious correspondent, Mr. HIGGINS, has
not been idle. The deserved popularity of
the Extracts which we have been enabled to
give from his two DIDACTIC POEMS, the " PRO-
GRESS OF MAN," and the "LOVES OF THE
TRIANGLES," has obtained for us the communication
of several other Works which he has in hand, all framed
upon the same principle, and directed to the same end.
The propagation of the NEW SYSTEM of PHILOSOPHY forms,
as he has himself candidly avowed to Us, the main object
of all his writings. A SYSTEM, comprehending not Politics
only and Religion, but Morals and Manners, and generally
whatever goes to the composition or holding together of
Human Society ; in all of which a total change and Revolution is absolutely necessary (as he contends) for the
advancement of our common nature to its true dignity, and
to the summit of that perfection which the combination of
matter, called MAN, is by its innate energies capable of
attaining.

Of this SYSTEM, while the sublimer and more scientific
branches are to be taught by the splendid and striking
medium of Didactic Poetry, or *ratiocination in rhyme*,
illustrated with such paintings and portraitures of Essences

and their Attributes, as may lay hold of the Imagination while they perplex the Judgment—the more ordinary parts, such as relate to the conduct of common life, and the regulation of social feelings, are naturally the subject of a less elevated style of writing—of a style which speaks to the eye as well as to the ear—in short, of Dramatic Poetry and Scenic Representation.

" With this view," says Mr. HIGGINS (for we love to quote the very words of this extraordinary and indefatigable writer)—in a Letter dated from his Study in St. Mary Axe, the window of which looks upon the Parish-pump—" with this view I have turned my thoughts more particularly to the GERMAN STAGE, and have composed, in imitation of the most popular pieces of that country, which have already met with so general reception and admiration in this, a Play; which, if it has a proper run, will, I think, do much to unhinge the present notions of men with regard to the obligations of Civil Society, and to substitute in lieu of a sober contentment, and regular discharge of the duties incident to each man's particular situation, a wild desire of undefinable latitude and extravagance; an aspiration after shapeless somethings, that can neither be described nor understood, a contemptuous disgust at all that is, and a persuasion that nothing is as it ought to be —to operate, in short, a general discharge of every man (in his own estimation) from every thing that laws, divine or human, that local customs, immemorial habits, and multiplied examples impose upon him; and to set them about doing what they like, where they like, when they like, and how they like—without reference to any Law but their own Will, or to any consideration of how others may be affected by their conduct.

" When this is done, my dear Sir," continues Mr. H. (for he writes very confidentially)—" you see that a great step is gained towards the dissolution of the frame of every existing Community. I say nothing of *Governments*, as *their* fall is of course implicated in that of the social system—and you have long known that I hold every Government (that acts by coercion and restriction—by Laws made by the few to bind the many) as a *malum in se* —an evil to be eradicated—a nuisance to be abated, by force, if force be practicable, if not, by the artillery of

Reason, by Pamphlets, Speeches, Toasts at Club-dinners, and though last, not least, by *didactic* POEMS.

" But where would be the advantage of the destruction of this or that Government, if the form of Society itself were to be suffered to continue such, as that another must necessarily arise out of it, and over it ?—Society, my dear Sir, in its present state, is a *hydra*. Cut off one head— another presently sprouts out, and your labour is to begin again. At best you can only hope to find it a *polypus*— where, by cutting off the *head*, you are sometimes fortunate enough to find a *tail* (which answers all the same purposes) spring up in its place. This, We know, has been the case in *France*—the only Country in which the great experiment of regeneration has been tried with anything like a fair chance of success.

" DESTROY the frame of society—decompose its parts —and set the elements fighting one against another, insulated and individual, every man for himself (stripped of prejudice, of bigotry, and of feeling for others) against the remainder of his species ;—and there is then some hope of a totally new *order of things*—of a *Radical Reform* in the present corrupt system of the World.

" The GERMAN THEATRE appears to proceed on this judicious plan. And I have endeavoured to contribute my mite towards extending its effect and its popularity. There is one obvious advantage attending this mode of teaching—that it can proportion the infractions of Law, Religion, or Morality, which it recommends, to the capacity of a Reader or Spectator. If you tell a Student, or an Apprentice, or a Merchant's Clerk, of the virtue of a BRUTUS, or of the splendour of a LA FAYETTE, you may excite his *desire* to be equally conspicuous ; but how is he to set about it ? Where is he to find the Tyrant to murder ? How is he to provide the Monarch to be imprisoned, and the National Guards to be reviewed on a White Horse ?— But paint the beauties of *Forgery* to him in glowing colours ; show him that the presumption of Virtue is in favour of Rapine and occasional Murder on the highway, and he presently understands you. The highway is at hand—the till or the counter is within reach. These *Haberdashers' heroics* ' come home to the business and the bosoms of men.' And you may readily make ten *Footpads*, where you would not have materials nor opportunity for a single *tyrannicide*.

" The subject of the Piece which I herewith transmit to you, is taken from common or middling life ; and its merit is that of teaching the most lofty truths in the most humble style, and deducing them from the most ordinary occurrences. Its moral is obvious and easy, and is one frequently inculcated by the German dramas which I have had the good fortune to see ; being no other than ' *the reciprocal duties of one or more Husbands to one or more Wives, and to the children who may happen to arise out of this complicated and endearing connexion.*' The Plot, indeed, is formed by the combination of the Plots of *two* of the most popular of these Plays (in the same way as TERENCE was wont to combine two stories of MENANDER'S). The Characters are such as the admirers of these Plays will recognize for their familiar acquaintances. There are the usual ingredients of Imprisonments, Post-houses and horns, and appeals to Angels and Devils. I have omitted only the *Swearing*, to which English ears are not yet sufficiently accustomed.

"I transmit at the same time a *Prologue,* which in some degree breaks the matter to the Audience. About the Song of ROGERO, at the end of the first act, I am less anxious than about any other part of the performance, as it is, in fact, literally translated from the composition of a young German Friend of mine, an *Illuminé*, of whom I bought the original for three-and-sixpence. It will be a satisfaction to those of your Readers who may not at first sight hit upon the tune, to learn, that it is setting by a hand of the first eminence.—I send also a rough sketch of the plot, and a few occasional Notes.—The *Geography* is by the young Gentleman of the ' *Morning Chronicle.*' "

THE ROVERS; OR, THE DOUBLE ARRANGEMENT.

DRAMATIS PERSONÆ.

PRIOR of the ABBEY of QUEDLINBURG, very corpulent and cruel.

ROGERO, a prisoner in the Abbey, in love with MATILDA POT-TINGEN.

CASIMERE, a Polish emigrant, in Dembrowsky's legion, married to CECILIA, but having several children by MATILDA.

PUDDINGFIELD and BEEFINGTON, English noblemen, exiled by the tyranny of KING JOHN, previous to the signature of Magna Charta.

RODERIC, Count of SAXE WEIMAR, a bloody tyrant, with red hair and amorous complexion.

GASPAR, the minister of the Count; author of ROGERO's confinement.

Young POTTINGEN, brother to MATILDA.

MATILDA POTTINGEN, in love with ROGERO, and mother to CASIMERE's children.

CECILIA MÜCKENFELDT, wife to CASIMERE.

Landlady, Waiter, Grenadiers, Troubadours, &c. &c.

PANTALOWSKY and BRITCHINDA, children of MATILDA, by CASIMERE.

JOACHIM, JABEL, and AMARANTHA, children of MATILDA, by ROGERO.

CHILDREN of CASIMERE and CECILIA, with their respective Nurses.

SEVERAL CHILDREN, fathers and mothers unknown.

The Scene lies in the town of Weimar, and the neighbourhood of the Abbey of Quedlinburg.

Time from the 12th to the present century.

PROLOGUE.

IN CHARACTER.

OO long the triumphs of our early times,
With Civil Discord and with Regal crimes,
Have stain'd these boards; while SHAKE-
SPEARE's pen has shown
Thoughts, manners, men, to modern days un-
known.
Too long have ROME and ATHENS been *the rage;* [*Applause.*
And classic Buskins soil'd a BRITISH stage.

To-night our bard, who scorns pedantic rules,
His plot has borrow'd from the GERMAN schools;

The GERMAN schools—where no dull maxims bind
The bold expansion of th' electric mind.
Fix'd to no period, circled by no space,
He leaps the flaming bounds of time and place:
Round the dark confines of the Forest raves,
With *gentle* ROBBERS[1] stocks his gloomy caves;
Tells how bad MINISTERS[2] are shocking things,
And *reigning Dukes* are just like tyrant Kings;
How to *two* swains[3] *one* nymph her vows may give,
And how *two* damsels[3] with *one* lover live!
Delicious scenes!—such scenes *our* BARD displays,
Which, crown'd with *German*, sue for *British*, praise.

Slow are the steeds, that through GERMANIA's roads
With hempen rein the slumbering post-boy goads;
Slow is the slumbering post-boy, who proceeds
Through deep sands floundering, on these tardy steeds;
More slow, more tedious, from his husky throat
Twangs through the twisted horn the struggling note.

These truths confess'd—Oh! yet, ye TRAVELL'D FEW,
GERMANIA's *plays* with eyes unjaundiced view!
View and approve!—though in each passage fine
The faint Translation[4] mock the genuine line,
Though the nice ear the erring sight belie,
For *U twice dotted* is pronounced like *I*;[4]   [*Applause.*

---

[1] See the "ROBBERS," a German tragedy, in which ROBBERY is
put in so fascinating a light, that the whole of a German University
went upon the highway in consequence of it.
[2] See "CABAL AND LOVE," a German tragedy, very severe
against ministers and reigning Dukes of Brunswick. This admirable
performance very judiciously reprobates the hire of German Troops
for the *American* war in the reign of QUEEN ELIZABETH—a practice which would undoubtedly have been highly discreditable to that
wise and patriotic Princess, not to say wholly unnecessary, there
being no American war at that particular time.
[3] See the "STRANGER; OR, REFORMED HOUSEKEEPER," in
which the former of these morals is beautifully illustrated; and
"STELLA," a genteel German comedy, which ends with placing a
man *bodkin* between *two wives*, like *Thames* between his *two banks*,
in the "Critic." Nothing can be more edifying than these two
dramas. I am shocked to hear that there are some people who
think them ridiculous.
[4] These are the warnings very properly given to readers, to
beware how they judge of what they cannot understand. Thus if

Yet oft the scene shall nature's fire impart, ·
Warm *from* the breast, and glowing *to* the heart!

Ye TRAVELL'D FEW, attend!—On *you* our BARD
Builds his fond hope! Do you his genius guard!
                                    [*Applause.*

Nor let succeeding generations say
A BRITISH AUDIENCE *damn'd* a GERMAN PLAY!
                        [*Loud and continued applauses.*

[*Flash of lightning.—The Ghost of* PROLOGUE'S GRAND-
   MOTHER *by the Father's side, appears to soft music,
   in a white tiffany riding-hood.* PROLOGUE *kneels to
   receive her blessing, which she gives in a solemn and
   affecting manner, the audience clapping and crying
   all the while.—Flash of lightning.—*PROLOGUE *and
   his* GRANDMOTHER *sink through the trap-doors.*[1]

THE ROVERS; OR, THE DOUBLE ARRANGEMENT.

ACT I.   SCENE I.

SCENE *represents a room at an inn, at* WEIMAR—*On one
   side of the stage the bar-room, with jellies, lemons in nets,
   syllabubs, and part of a cold roast fowl, &c.—On the opposite side, a window looking into the street, through which
   persons (inhabitants of* WEIMAR) *are seen passing to and
   fro in apparent agitation—*MATILDA *appears in a great
   coat and riding-habit, seated at the corner of the dinner-
   table, which is covered with a clean huckaback cloth—
   plates and napkins, with buck's-horn-handled knives and
   forks, are laid as if for four persons.*

---

the translation runs, "*lightning of my soul, fulguration of angels,
sulphur of hell,*" we should recollect that this is not coarse or strange
in the German language, when applied by a lover to his mistress;
but the English has nothing precisely parallel to the original MUYLV-
CHAUSE ARCHANGELICHEN, which means rather *emanation of the
archangelical nature,—*or to SMELLMYNKERN VANKELFER, which,
if literally rendered, would signify *made of stuff of the same odour
whereof the devil makes flambeaux.* See *Schüttenbrüchtess* on the
GERMAN IDIOM.

[1] "Flash of lightning—Prologue sinks thro' the trap-door" was
all the stage direction printed in "The Anti-Jacobin" of June 4,
1798.

Matilda.

S it impossible that I can have dinner sooner?

Land. Madam, the *Brunswick* post-waggon is not yet come in, and the Ordinary is never before two o'clock.

Mat. (with a look expressive of disappointment, but immediately recomposing herself). Well, then, I must have patience—(*Exit Landlady.*) Oh CASIMERE! how often have the thoughts of thee served to amuse these moments of expectation!—What a difference, alas!—Dinner—it is taken away as soon as over, and we regret it not!—It returns again with the return of appetite.—The beef of to-morrow will succeed to the mutton of to-day, as the mutton of to-day succeeded to the veal of yesterday.— But when once the heart has been occupied by a beloved object, in vain would we attempt to supply the chasm by another. How easily are our desires transferred from dish to dish!—Love only, dear, delusive, delightful love, restrains our wandering appetites, and confines them to a particular gratification! . . . .

Post-horn blows; re-enter LANDLADY.

Land. Madam, the post-waggon is just come in with only a single gentlewoman.

Mat. Then show her up—and let us have dinner instantly; (LANDLADY *going*) and remember—(*after a moment's recollection, and with great earnestness*)—remember the toasted cheese. [*Exit* LANDLADY.

CECILIA *enters, in a brown cloth riding-dress, as if just alighted from the post-waggon.*

Mat. Madam, you seem to have had an unpleasant journey, if I may judge from the dust on your riding-habit.

Cec. The way was dusty, madam, but the weather was delightful. It recalled to me those blissful moments when the rays of desire first vibrated through my soul.

Mat. (aside). Thank Heaven! I have at last found a heart which is in unison with my own—(*To Cecilia*)— Yes, I understand you—the first pulsation of sentiment— the silver tones upon the yet unsounded harp. . . . .

Cec. The dawn of life—when this blossom—(*putting her hand upon her heart*) first expanded its petals to the penetrating dart of love !

Mat. Yes—the time—the golden time, when the first beams of the morning meet and embrace one another !— The blooming blue upon the yet unplucked plum ! . . . .

Cec. Your countenance grows animated, my dear madam.

Mat. And yours too is glowing with illumination.

Cec. I had long been looking out for a congenial spirit !— my heart was withered—but the beams of yours have re-kindled it.

Mat. A sudden thought strikes me—Let us swear an eternal friendship.

Cec. Let us agree to live together !

Mat. (*with rapidity and earnestness*). Willingly.

Cec. Let us embrace.   [*They embrace.*

Mat. Yes ; I too have loved ! you, too, like me, have been forsaken !—

　　　[*Doubtingly, and as if with a desire to be informed.*

Cec. Too true !

Both. Ah, these men ! these men !

LANDLADY *enters, and places a leg of mutton on the table, with sour krout and prune sauce*—CECILIA *and* MATILDA *appear to take no notice of her.*

Mat. Oh, Casimere !

Cec. (*aside*). Casimere ! that name !—Oh my heart, how it is distracted with anxiety.

Mat. Heavens ! Madam, you turn pale.

Cec. Nothing—a slight meagrim—with your leave, I will retire—

Mat. I will attend you.

　　　[*Exeunt* MATILDA *and* CECILIA ; *Manent* LANDLADY *and* WAITER, *with the dinner on the table.*

Land. Have you carried the dinner to the prisoner in the vaults of the abbey ?

Waiter. Yes. Pease-soup, as usual—with the scrag end of a neck of mutton—The Emissary of the Count was here again this morning, and offered me a large sum of money if I would consent to poison him.

Land. (*with hesitation and anxiety*). Which you refused ?

Waiter (*with indignation*). Can you doubt it?

Land. (*recovering herself, and drawing up with an expression of dignity*). The conscience of a poor man is as valuable to him as that of a prince. . . . .

Waiter. It ought to be still more so, in proportion as it is generally more pure.

Land. Thou say'st truly, Job.

Waiter (*with enthusiasm*). He who can spurn at wealth when proffered as the price of crime, is greater than a prince.

> [*Post-horn blows.*—*Enter* CASIMERE (*in a travelling dress*—*a light blue great coat with large metal buttons*—*his hair in a long queue, but twisted at the end; a large Kevenhuller hat : a cane in his hand*).

Cas. Here, Waiter, pull off my boots, and bring me a pair of slippers. (*Exit* WAITER.) And hark'ye, my lad, a bason of water (*rubbing his hands*) and a bit of soap. I have not washed since I began my journey.

Waiter (*answering from behind the door*). Yes, Sir.

Cas. Well, Landlady, what company are we to have?

Land. Only two gentlewomen, Sir. They are just stept into the next room—they will be back again in a minute.

Cas. Where do they come from?

> [*All this while the* WAITER *re-enters with the bason and water ;* CASIMERE *pulls off his boots, takes a napkin from the table, and washes his face and hands.*

Land. There is one of them, I think, comes from *Nuremburg.*

Cas. (*aside*). From *Nuremburg !*—(*with eagerness*)—her name?

Land. MATILDA.

Cas. (*aside*). How does this idiot woman torment me! —What else?

Land. I can't recollect.

Cas. (*in a paroxysm of agitation*). Oh agony!

Waiter. See here, her name upon the travelling trunk —MATILDA POTTINGEN.

Cas. (*embracing the Waiter*). Ecstasy! ecstasy!

Land. You seem to be acquainted with the lady—shall I call her?

Cas. Instantly—instantly—tell her her loved, her long-lost—tell her—

Land. Shall I tell her dinner is ready?

Cas. Do so—and in the meanwhile I will look after my portmanteau.   [*Exeunt severally.*

[SCENE *changes to a subterranean vault in the Abbey of Quedlinburg, with coffins, 'scutcheons, death's-heads and cross-bones—toads and other loathsome reptiles are seen traversing the obscurer parts of the stage.* ROGERO *appears, in chains, in a suit of rusty armour, with his beard grown, and a cap of a grotesque form upon his head.—Beside him a crock, or pitcher, supposed to contain his daily allowance of sustenance. —A long silence, during which the wind is heard to whistle through the caverns.—*ROGERO *rises, and comes slowly forward, with his arms folded.*

Rog. Eleven years! it is now eleven years since I was first immured in this living sepulchre—the cruelty of a Minister—the perfidy of a Monk— yes, Matilda! for thy sake—alive amidst the dead—chained—coffined—confined —cut off from the converse of my fellow-men.   Soft!— what have we here! (*stumbles over a bundle of sticks*). This cavern is so dark, that I can scarcely distinguish the objects under my feet.   Oh!—the register of my captivity. Let me see ; how stands the account? (*Takes up the sticks and turns them over with a melancholy air ; then stands silent for a few moments, as if absorbed in calculation.*) Eleven years and fifteen days!—Hah! the twenty-eighth of August!   How does the recollection of it vibrate on my heart!   It was on this day that I took my last leave of my MATILDA.—It was a summer evening—her melting hand seemed to dissolve in mine, as I pressed it to my bosom— Some demon whispered me that I should never see her more.—I stood gazing on the hated vehicle which was conveying her away for ever.—The tears were petrified under my eyelids.—My heart was crystallized with agony. —Anon—I looked along the road.—The diligence seemed to diminish every instant—I felt my heart beat against its prison, as if anxious to leap out and overtake it.—My soul whirled round as I watched the rotation of the hinder wheels.—A long train of glory followed after her, and

mingled with the **dust**—it was the Emanation of Divinity,
luminous with love and beauty—like the splendour of the
setting sun—but it told **me that the sun** of my joys **was
sunk** for ever—Yes, here in the depths of an eternal **Dungeon**—in the Nursing Cradle of Hell, **the Suburbs of Per-
dition**—in a nest of Demons, where **Despair** in vain sits
brooding over the putrid eggs of Hope; where Agony **wooes
the** embrace of Death ; where **Patience,** beside the bottom-
less pool of Despondency, sits angling for Impossibilities.
Yet, even *here* to behold her, to embrace her—Yes, MATILDA,
whether in this dark abode, amidst toads and spiders, or
in a Royal Palace, amidst the more loathsome Reptiles of
a Court, would be indifferent to **me**—Angels would **shower**
down their hymns of gratulation upon our heads—while
fiends would envy the eternity of suffering Love. . . . .
Soft, what air was that? it seemed a sound of more than
human warblings?—Again—(*listens attentively for some
minutes*)—Only the wind—it is well, however—it reminds
me of that melancholy air, which has so often solaced the
hours of my captivity—Let me see whether the damps of
this dungeon have not yet injured my guitar—(*Takes his
guitar, tunes it, and begins the following air, with a full
accompaniment of violins from the orchestra.*)

AIR—" Lanterna Magica."

FRERE.

SONG.

BY ROGERO.

I.

Whene'er with haggard eyes I view
   This dungeon that I'm rotting in,
I think of those companions true
   Who studied with **me** at the **U**—
         —niversity of *Gottingen,*—
         —niversity of *Gottingen.*

[*Weeps,* **and pulls out a blue** *kerchief, with which
   he wipes* **his eyes;** *gazing tenderly at it, he
   proceeds—*

II.

Sweet kerchief, check'd with heavenly blue,
    Which once my love sat knotting in!—
Alas! MATILDA *then* was true!
    At least I thought so at the U—
            —niversity of *Gottingen*—
            —niversity of *Gottingen.*

[*At the repetition of this line* ROGERO *clanks his
chains in cadence.*

III.

Barbs! barbs! alas! how swift you flew,
    Her neat post-waggon trotting in!
Ye bore MATILDA from my view;
    Forlorn I languish'd at the U—
            —niversity of *Gottingen*—
            —niversity of *Gottingen.*

IV.

This faded form! this pallid hue!
    This blood my veins is clotting in,
My years are many—they were few
    When first I enter'd at the U—
            —niversity of *Gottingen*—
            —niversity of *Gottingen.*

V.

There first for thee my passion grew,
    Sweet! sweet MATILDA POTTINGEN!
Thou wast the daughter of my tu—
    —tor, *law professor* at the U—
            —niversity of *Gottingen*—
            —niversity of *Gottingen.*

VI.

Sun, moon, and thou vain world, adieu,
    That kings and priests are plotting in:
Here doom'd to starve on water gru—
    —el,¹ never shall I see the U—
            —niversity of *Gottingen*—
            —niversity of *Gottingen.*

_____

A manifest error, since it appears from the Waiter's conversation
(page 124) that Rogero was not doomed to starve on water-gruel,

[*During the* **last** *stanza* ROGERO **dashes his head re-**
peatedly against the walls of **his prison ; and, finally,**
so *hard as* **to** *produce* **a visible contusion ; he then**
throws himself **on the floor in an agony.** *The curtain*
drops ; the music still continuing to play till it is
wholly fallen.

END OF ACT I.

CANNING AND ELLIS.

THE ROVERS.

[JUNE 11, 1798.]

E have received, in the course of the last
week, several long, and to say the truth,
dull letters, from unknown hands, reflecting,
in very severe terms, on Mr. HIGGINS, for
having, as it is affirmed, attempted to pass
upon the world, as a faithful sample of the productions of
the *German* **theatre**, a performance no way resembling any
of those pieces which have of late excited, and which bid
fair to engross, the admiration of the British public.

As we cannot but consider ourselves as the guardians of
Mr. HIGGINS's literary reputation, in respect to every work
of his which is conveyed to the world through the medium
of our paper (though, what we think of the danger of his
principles we have already sufficiently explained for ourselves, and have, we trust, succeeded in putting our
readers upon their guard against them)—we hold ourselves bound, not only to justify the fidelity of the imitation, but (contrary to our original intention) to give a
further specimen of it in our present number, in order to
bring the question more fairly to issue between our author
and his calumniators.

---

but on pease-soup, which is a much better thing. Possibly the length
of Rogero's imprisonment had impaired his memory; or he might
wish to make things appear worse than they really were ; which is
very natural, I think, in such a case as this poor unfortunate gentleman's.—*Printer's Devil.*

This last stanza and the note accompanying it were not in the Anti-
Jacobin as printed on June 4th, 1798.

I* K

In the first place, we are to observe that Mr. HIGGINS professes to have taken his notion of German plays wholly from the *translations* which have appeared in our language. If *they* are totally dissimilar from the originals, Mr. H. may undoubtedly have been led into error; but the fault is in the translators, not in him. That he does not differ widely from the models which he proposed to himself, we have it in our power to prove satisfactorily; and might have done so in our last number, by subjoining to each particular passage of his play the scene in some one or other of the German plays, which he had in view when he wrote it. These parallel passages were faithfully pointed out to us by Mr. H. with that candour which marks his character; and if they were suppressed by us (as in truth they were), on our heads be the blame, whatever it may be. Little, indeed, did we think of the imputation which the omission would bring upon Mr. H., as in fact our principal reason for it, was the apprehension, that from the extreme closeness of the imitation in most instances, he would lose in praise for invention more than he would gain in credit for fidelity.

The meeting between MATILDA and CECILIA, for example, in the first act of the " ROVERS," and their sudden intimacy, has been censured as unnatural. Be it so. It is taken, *almost word for word*, from " STELLA," a German (or professedly a German) piece now much in vogue; from which also the catastrophe of Mr. HIGGINS's play is in part borrowed, so far as relates to the agreement to which the ladies come, as the reader will see by-and-by, to share CASIMERE between them.

The dinner-scene is copied partly from the published translation of the " STRANGER," and partly from the first scene of " STELLA." The *song* of ROGERO, with which the first act concludes, is admitted on all hands to be in the very first taste; and if no German original is to be found for it, so much the worse for the credit of German literature.

An objection has been made by one anonymous letter-writer to the names of PUDDINGFIELD and BEEFINGTON, as little likely to have been assigned to English characters by any author of taste or discernment.—In answer to this objection we have, in the first place, to admit, that a small, and we hope not an unwarrantable, alteration has been made by us since the MS. has been in our hands. These names stood originally PUDDINCRANTZ and BEEFINSTERN, which sounded to our ears as being liable, especially the latter, to a ridiculous inflection—a difficulty that could only be removed by furnishing them with English terminations. With regard to the more substantial syllables of the names, our author proceeded, in all probability, on the authority of GOLDONI, who, though not a German, is an Italian writer of considerable reputation ; and who, having heard that the English were distinguished for their love of liberty and beef, has judiciously compounded the two words *Runnymede* and *beef,* and thereby produced an English nobleman, whom he styles *Lord Runnybeef.*

To dwell no longer on particular passages—the best way perhaps of explaining the whole scope and view of Mr. H.'s imitation, will be to transcribe the short sketch of the plot which that gentleman transmitted to us together with his drama, and which it is perhaps the more necessary to do, as, the limits of our paper not allowing of the publication of the whole piece, some general knowledge of its main design may be acceptable to our readers, in order to enable them to judge of the several extracts which we lay before them.

PLOT.

ROGERO, son of the late minister of the COUNT of SAXE-WEIMAR, having, while he was at college, fallen desperately in love with MATILDA POTTINGEN, daughter of his tutor, Doctor ENGELBERTUS POTTINGEN, Professor of Civil Law ; and MATILDA evidently returning his passion, the DOCTOR, to prevent ill consequences, sends his daughter on a visit to her aunt in *Wetteravia,* where she becomes acquainted with CASIMERE, a Polish officer, who happens to be quartered near her aunt's ; and has several children by him.

RODERIC, Count of SAXE-WEIMAR, a prince of a tyrannical and licentious disposition, has for his Prime Minister and favourite, GASPAR, a crafty villain, who had risen to his post by first ruining, and then putting to death, ROGERO's father.—GASPAR, apprehensive of the power and popularity which the young ROGERO may enjoy at his

return to Court, seizes the occasion of his intrigue with
MATILDA (of which he is apprised officially by Doctor
POTTINGEN) to procure from his master an order for the
recall of ROGERO from college, and for committing him to
the care of the PRIOR of the *Abbey* of *Quedlinburg*, a
priest, rapacious, savage, and sensual, and devoted to
GASPAR's interests—sending at the same time private
orders to the PRIOR to confine him in a dungeon.

Here ROGERO languishes many years.   His daily sustenance is administered to him through a grated opening
at the top of a Cavern, by the *Landlady* of the "*Golden
Eagle*" at WEIMAR, with whom GASPAR contracts, in the
prince's name, for his support, intending, and more than
once endeavouring, to corrupt the WAITER to mingle
poison with the food, in order that he may get rid of
ROGERO for ever.

In the meantime, CASIMERE, having been called away
from the neighbourhood of MATILDA's residence to other
quarters, becomes enamoured of and marries CECILIA, by
whom he has a family; and whom he likewise deserts,
after a few years' co-habitation, on pretence of business
which calls him to *Kamschatka*.

Doctor POTTINGEN, now grown old and infirm, and
feeling the want of his daughter's society, sends young
POTTINGEN in search of her, with strict injunctions not to
return without her; and to bring with her either her
present lover CASIMERE, or, should not that be possible,
ROGERO himself, if he can find him; the DOCTOR having
set his heart upon seeing his children comfortably settled
before his death.   MATILDA, about the same period, quits
her aunt's in search of CASIMERE; and CECILIA, having
been advertised (by an anonymous letter) of the falsehood
of his KAMSCHATKAN journey, sets out in the post-waggon
on a similar pursuit.

It is at this point of time the play opens—with the accidental meeting of CECILIA and MATILDA at the Inn at
WEIMAR.   CASIMERE arrives there soon after, and falls in
first with MATILDA, and then with CECILIA.   Successive
éclaircissements take place, and an arrangement is finally
made, by which the two ladies are to live jointly with
CASIMERE.

Young POTTINGEN, wearied with a few weeks' search,

during which he **has not** been able **to find** either **of** the objects of it, resolves to stop at WEIMAR, and wait events there. **It** so happens that he takes **up** his lodging in the **same** house with PUDDINGCRANTZ **and** BEEFINSTERN, **two** English noblemen, whom the **tyranny** of KING JOHN has obliged to fly from their country ; **and who,** after wandering about the Continent for **some time,** have fixed their residence **at** WEIMAR.

The **news of** the **signature of** MAGNA CHARTA arriving, determines PUDDING. and- BEEF. **to return to** *England.* Young POTTINGEN opens his case to them, and entreats them **to stay to assist him in the object of his** search.— This **they refuse** ; **but coming to** the inn where they are to **set off for** *Hamburg,* **they** meet CASIMERE, from whom they **had** both received **many** civilities in *Poland.*

CASIMERE, by this time tired of his **" DOUBLE ARRANGE-MENT,"** and having learnt from the **waiter that** ROGERO **is** confined in the vaults of the neighbouring **abbey** *for love,* resolves to attempt his rescue, and **to** make **over** MATILDA to him as the price of his deliverance. **He communicates** his scheme **to** PUDDINGFIELD and BEEFINGTON, **who** agree to assist him ; **as also does** young POTTINGEN. The WAITER of the Inn **proving to be a** *Knight Templar* **in** disguise, is appointed **leader of** the expedition. **A** band of TROUBA-DOURS, **who happen** to be returning **from** the CRUSADES, **and a company of** Austrian **and** Prussian GRENADIERS **returning from the** SEVEN YEARS' WAR, **are** engaged **as troops.**

The **attack on the** Abbey **is made with** great success. **The Count of** WEIMAR and GASPAR, who are feasting with **the** PRIOR, **are seized and** beheaded **in the** refectory. The PRIOR **is** thrown **into the** dungeon, **from which** ROGERO **is** rescued. MATILDA **and** CECILIA **rush in. The** former recognizes ROGERO, and agrees **to live with** him. The children are produced on all sides—and **young** POTTINGEN is commissioned to write to his **father, the** DOCTOR, **to** detail the joyful events which have taken place, and to invite **him** to WEIMAR **to** partake of the general felicity.

THE ROVERS; OR, THE DOUBLE ARRANGEMENT.

ACT II.

SCENE—*a Room in an ordinary Lodging-house at* WEIMAR— PUDDINGFIELD *and* BEEFINGTON *discovered sitting at a small deal table, and playing at* ALL-FOURS—*Young* POTTINGEN *at another table in the corner of the room, with a pipe in his mouth, and a Saxon mug of a singular shape beside him, which he repeatedly applies to his lips, turning back his head, and casting his eyes towards the firmament —at the last trial he holds the mug for some moments in a directly inverted position; then he replaces it on the table with an air of dejection, and gradually sinks into a profound slumber—the pipe falls from his hand, and is broken.*

Beefington.

BEG.

   Pudd. (*deals three cards to Beefington*). Are you satisfied?

   Beef. Enough. What have you?

   Pudd. High—low—and the game.

   Beef. Damnation! 'Tis my deal. (*Deals; turns up a knave.*) One for his heels!   [*Triumphantly.*

   Pudd. Is King highest?

   Beef. No (*sternly*)—The game is mine—The Knave gives it me.

   Pudd. Are Knaves so prosperous?

   Beef. Ay, marry are they, in this world. They have the game in their hands. Your kings are but *noddies*[1] to them.

   Pudd. Ha! ha! ha!—Still the same proud spirit, Beefington, which procured thee thine exile from England.

---

[1] This is an excellent joke in German; the point and spirit of which is but ill-*Rendered* in a translation. A NODDY, the reader will observe, has two significations, the one a *knave at All-fours*, the other a *fool* or *booby*. See the translation by Mr. Render of "COUNT BENYOWSKY, OR THE CONSPIRACY OF KAMSCHATKA," a German Tragi-Comi-Comi-Tragedy; where the play opens with a scene of a game at chess (from which the whole of this scene is copied), and a joke of the same point and merriment about PAWNS, *i.e.*, BOORS, being *a match for* KINGS.

Beef. England! my native land!—when shall I revisit thee?

> [*During this time* PUDDINGFIELD *deals, and begins to arrange his hand.*

Beef. (*continues*). Phoo—hang ALL-FOURS; what are they to a mind ill at ease? Can they cure the heartache? Can they soothe banishment? Can they lighten ignominy? —Can ALL-FOURS do this? O, my Puddingfield! thy limber and lightsome spirit bounds up against affliction— with the elasticity of a well-bent bow; but mine—O! mine—

> [*Falls into an agony, and sinks back in his chair. Young* POTTINGEN, *awakened by the noise, rises, and advances with a grave demeanour towards* BEEF. *and* PUDD.—*The former begins to recover.*

Y. Pot. What is the matter, comrades,[1] you seem agitated. Have you lost or won?

Beef. Lost!—I have lost my country.

Y. Pot. And I my sister.—I came hither in search of her.

Beef. O, England!

Y. Pot. O, MATILDA!

Beef. Exiled by the tyranny of an usurper, I seek the means of revenge, and of restoration to my country.

Y. Pot. Oppressed by the tyranny of an abbot, persecuted by the jealousy of a count, the betrothed husband of my sister languishes in a loathsome captivity—her lover is fled no one knows whither—and I, her brother, am torn from my paternal roof, and from my studies in chirurgery, to seek him and her, I know not where—to rescue Rogero, I know not how.—Comrades, your counsel.—My search fruitless—my money gone—my baggage stolen! What am I to do?—In yonder abbey—in the dank, dark vaults, there, my friends—there lies Rogero—there MATILDA's heart.

CANNING.

---

[1] This word in the original is strictly *fellow-lodgers*—" *Co-occupants of the same room, in a house let out at a small rent by the week.*" There is no single word in English which expresses so complicated a relation, except perhaps the cant term of *chum,* formerly in use at our universities.

Enter WAITER.

Waiter. Sir, here is a person who desires to speak with you.

Beef. (*goes to the door and returns with a letter, which he opens. On perusing it his countenance becomes illuminated, and expands prodigiously*). Hah, my friend, what joy!

[*Turning to* PUDDINGFIELD.

Pudd. What? tell me—let your PUDDINGFIELD partake it.

Beef. (*produces a printed paper*). See here.

Pudd. (*with impatience*). What?

Beef. (*in a significant tone*). A newspaper!

Pudd. Hah, what say'st thou?—A newspaper!

Beef. Yes, Puddingfield, and see here—(*shows it partially*), from *England.*

Pudd. (*with extreme earnestness*). Its name?

Beef. The "*Daily Advertiser*—"

Pudd. Oh, ecstasy!

Beef. (*with a dignified severity*). Puddingfield, calm yourself—repress those transports—remember that you are a man.

Pudd. (*after a pause, with suppressed emotion*). Well, I will be—I am calm—yet, tell me, BEEFINGTON, does it contain any news?

Beef. Glorious news, my dear PUDDINGFIELD—the Barons are victorious—KING JOHN has been defeated—MAGNA CHARTA, that venerable immemorial inheritance of Britons, was signed last Friday was three weeks, the third of July Old Style.

Pudd. I can scarce believe my ears—but let me satisfy my eyes—show me the paragraph.

Beef. Here it is, just above the advertisements.

Pudd. (*reads*). "The great demand for *Packwood's* Razor Straps"—

Beef. Pshaw! what, ever blundering!—you drive me from my patience.—See here, at the head of the column.

Pudd. (*reads*).

"A hireling print, devoted to the court, has dared to question our veracity respecting the events of yesterday;

but by to-day's accounts, our information appears to have been perfectly correct. The Charter of our Liberties received the royal signature at five o'clock, when messengers **were** instantly dispatched to Cardinal PANDULFO; and their majesties, after partaking of a cold collation, returned to Windsor."—I am satisfied.

Beef. Yet here again—there are some further particulars (*turns to another* **part of the** *paper*). "Extract of a letter from Egham—My dear friend, we **are** all **here in** high **spirits—the interesting event** which took place **this** morning at **Runnymede,** in the neighbourhood **of this** town"—

Pudd. Hah, **Runnymede!** enough—no more—my doubts are vanished—then are we free indeed!

Beef. I **have,** besides, a letter in my pocket from our friend, the immortal BACON, who has been appointed Chancellor.—Our outlawry is reversed!—What says **my friend** —shall we return by the next packet?

Pudd. Instantly, instantly!

Both. Liberty! ADELAIDE! revenge!

> [*Exeunt, young* POTTINGEN *following,*[1] *and waving* **his** *hat, but obviously without much consciousness of the* **meaning of** *what* **has passed.**

FRERE.

SCENE *changes* **to** *the* **outside of the Abbey.** *A Summer's Evening—Moonlight.*

Companies of AUSTRIAN *and* PRUSSIAN *Grenadiers march* **across** *the stage, confusedly,* **as** *if* **returning** *from the* **Seven Years'** *War.—Shouts and* **martial music.**

The Abbey Gates are opened ; *the* MONKS **are seen** *passing* **in procession, with the** PRIOR *at their head ;* **the** *choir is* **heard chaunting** *vespers. After which a pause—then* **a** **bell is** *heard, as if ringing for supper. Soon after,* **a** *noise of singing and jollity.*

Enter from the Abbey, pushed out *of the gates by the* PORTER, *a* TROUBADOUR, *with a bundle under his cloak, and a Lady under his arm—*TROUBADOUR *seems* **much** *in liquor, but caresses the* FEMALE MINSTREL.

---

[1] This was all the stage direction printed in "The Anti-Jacobin," on June 11, 1798.

Fem. Min. Trust me, Gieronymo, thou seemest melancholy. What has thou got under thy cloak?

Trou. Pshaw, women will be inquiring. Melancholy! not I—I will sing thee a song, and the subject of it shall be thy question—"What have I got under my cloak?" It is a riddle, MARGARET—I learnt it of an almanack-maker at GOTHA—if thou guessest it after the first stanza, thou shalt have never a drop for thy pains. Hear me—and, d'ye mark! twirl thy thingumbob while I sing.

Fem. Min. 'Tis a pretty tune, and hums dolefully.

> [*Plays on her balalaika.*[1] TROUBADOUR *sings.*

> I bear a secret comfort *here,*

>> [*Putting his hand on the bundle, but*
>> *without showing it.*

> A joy I'll ne'er impart;
> It is not wine, it is not beer,
> But it consoles my heart.

Fem. Min. (interrupting him).—I'll be hanged if you don't mean the bottle of cherry-brandy that you stole out of the vaults in the abbey cellar.

Trou. I mean!—Peace, wench, thou disturbest the current of my feelings—

> [FEM. MIN. *attempts to lay hold on the bottle;* TROU-
> BADOUR *pushes her aside, and continues singing*
> *without interruption.*

> This cherry-bounce, this loved noyeau,
> My drink for ever be;
> But, sweet my love, thy wish forego;
> I'll give no drop to thee!

> (*Both together.*)

Trou.	This			this	
F. M.	That	cherry-bounce		that	loved noyeau,
Trou.	My				
F. M.	Thy	drink for ever be;			
Trou.		But, sweet my love,		thy wish forego!	
F. M.				one drop bestow,	
Trou.	I			ME!	
F. M.	Nor	keep it all for		THEE!	

---

[1] The balalaika is a Russian instrument, resembling the guitar. See the play of "Count Benyowsky," *Rendered* into English.

*[Exeunt struggling for the bottle, but without anger
or animosity, the* FEM. MIN. *appearing by degrees
to obtain a superiority in the contest.*

END OF ACT II.

ACT THE THIRD—contains the *éclaircissements* and final
arrangement between CASIMERE, MATILDA, and CECILIA,
which so nearly resemble the concluding act of "STELLA,"
that we forbear to lay it before our readers.

CANNING.

ACT IV.

SCENE.—*the Inn door—Diligence drawn up.*—CASIMERE *appears as if superintending the package of his portman-
teaux, and giving directions to the* PORTERS.

Enter BEEFINGTON *and* PUDDINGFIELD.

Puddingfield.

ELL, Coachey, have you got two inside places ?
Coach. Yes, your honour.
Pudd. (seems to be struck with CASIMERE's
*appearance. He surveys him earnestly, with-
out paying any attention to the* COACHMAN,
then doubtingly pronounces) Casimere !
Cas. (turning round rapidly, recognizes PUDDINGFIELD,
and embraces him). My Puddingfield !
Pudd. My Casimere !
Cas. What, Beefington too ! *(discovering him)*—then is
my joy complete.
Beef. Our fellow-traveller, as it seems ?
Cas. Yes, Beefington—but wherefore to Hamburg ?
Beef. Oh, Casimere ¹—to fly—to fly—to return—Eng-

¹ See "Count Benyowsky; or, the Conspiracy of Kamschatka,"
where Crustiew, an old gentleman of much sagacity, talks the following nonsense:
CRUSTIEW *(with youthful energy, and an air of secrecy and confidence).* "To fly, to fly, to the isles of Marian—the island of Tinian
—a terrestrial paradise. Free—free—a mild climate—a new-created
sun —wholesome fruits—harmless inhabitants—and liberty—tranquillity."

land—our country—Magna Charta—it is liberated—a new
æra—House of Commons—Crown and Anchor—Opposition—

Cas. What a contrast! You are flying to liberty and
your home—I, driven from my home by tyranny, am exposed to domestic slavery in a foreign country.

Beef. How domestic slavery?

Cas. Too true—two wives—(*slowly, and with a dejected
air—then after a pause*)—you knew my Cecilia?

Pudd. Yes, five years ago.

Cas. Soon after that period I went upon a visit to a lady
in Wetteravia—my Matilda was under her protection.
Alighting at a peasant's cabin, I saw her on a charitable
visit, spreading bread-and-butter for the children, in a
light blue riding-habit. The simplicity of her appearance,
the fineness of the weather, all conspired to interest me—
my heart moved to hers, as if by a magnetic sympathy—
we wept, embraced, and went home together—she became
the mother of my Pantalowsky.—But five years of enjoyment have not stifled the reproaches of my conscience—
her Rogero is languishing in captivity—if I could but
restore her to *him!*

Beef. Let us rescue him.

Cas. Will without power [1] is like children playing at
soldiers.

Beef. Courage without power [2] is like a consumptive
running footman.

Cas. Courage without power is a contradiction.[3] Ten
brave men might set all Quedlinburg at defiance.

Beef. Ten brave men—but where are they to be found?

Cas. I will tell you—marked you the waiter?

Beef. (*doubtingly*). The waiter?

Cas. (*in a confidential tone*). No waiter, but a *Knight
Templar.* Returning from the Crusade, he found his
Order dissolved and his person proscribed.—He dissembled
his rank, and embraced the profession of a waiter.—I have

---

[1] See "Count Benyowsky," as before.
[2] See "Count Benyowsky."
[3] See "Count Benyowsky" again, from which play this and the
preceding references are taken word for word. We acquit the Germans of such reprobate silly stuff. It must be the translator's.

made sure of him already.—There are, besides, an Austrian and a Prussian grenadier. I have made them abjure their national enmity, and they have sworn to fight henceforth in the cause of freedom. These, with young Pottingen, the waiter, and ourselves, make seven—the Troubadour, with his two attendant minstrels, will complete the **ten**.

Beef. (*with enthusiasm*). Now **then for** the execution.

Pudd. Yes, **my** boys—for **the** execution.

[*Clapping them on the back.*

Waiter. But hist! we are observed.

Trou. Let us by a song conceal our purposes.

RECITATIVE ACCOMPANIED.[1]

Casimere.	Hist! hist! nor let the airs that blow
	From night's cold lungs our purpose know!
Puddingfield.	Let Silence, mother of the dumb,
Beefington.	Press on each lip her palsied thumb!
Waiter.	Let Privacy, allied to Sin,
	That loves to haunt the **tranquil inn**—
Grenadier. }	And Conscience start, **when she shall view,**
Troubadour. }	The mighty deed **we mean** to do!

GENERAL **CHORUS**—*Con spirito.*

	Then **friendship** swear, ye **faithful** bands,
	Swear to save a shackled **hero!**
	See **where yon abbey** frowning stands!
	Rescue, **rescue brave** Rogero!
Casimere.	Thrall'd **in** a monkish tyrant's **fetters**
	Shall great Rogero hopeless **lie?**
Young **Pot.**	**In my pocket** I have letters,
	Saying, " Help me, or I die!"

Allegro Allegretto.

CAS. BEEF. PUDD. **GRENS.** }	Let us fly, let us fly,
TROUB. WAIT. and **POT.** *with* }	Let us help, ere he die!
enthusiasm.	

[*Exeunt omnes, waving their bats.*

---

[1] We believe this song to be copied, with a small variation in metre and **meaning, from a** song in "Count Benyowsky; or, the Conspiracy **of Kamschatka," where** the conspirators join in a chorus, *for fear of being overheard.*

SCENE—*the Abbey Gate, with Ditches, Drawbridges, and Spikes; TIME—about an hour before Sunrise.—The conspirators appear as if in ambuscade, whispering and consulting together, in expectation of the signal for attack.— The WAITER is habited as a Knight Templar, in the dress of his Order, with the Cross on his breast, and the scallop on his shoulder.—PUDDINGFIELD and BEEFINGTON armed with blunderbusses and pocket-pistols; the GRENADIERS in their proper uniforms.—The TROUBADOUR with his attendant MINSTRELS bring up the rear—martial music— the conspirators come forward, and present themselves before the Gate of the Abbey.—Alarum—firing of pistols —the Convent appear in Arms upon the Walls—the Drawbridge is let down—a body of choristers and lay brothers attempt a sally, but are beaten back, and the Verger killed.—The besieged attempt to raise the Drawbridge—PUDDINGFIELD and BEEFINGTON press forward with alacrity, throw themselves upon the Drawbridge, and by the exertion of their weight preserve it in a state of depression—the other besiegers join them, and attempt to force the entrance, but without effect.—PUDDINGFIELD makes the signal for the battering-ram.—Enter QUINTUS CURTIUS and MARCUS CURIUS DENTATUS, in their proper military habits, preceded by the Roman Eagle—the rest of their Legion are employed in bringing forward a battering-ram, which plays for a few minutes to slow time, till the entrance is forced.—After a short resistance, the besiegers rush in with shouts of Victory.*

Scene changes to the interior of the Abbey.—*The inhabitants of the Convent are seen flying in all directions.*

PRIOR *is brought forward between two Grenadiers.*

The COUNT *of* WEIMAR, *who had been found feasting in the Refectory, is brought in manacled. He appears transported with rage, and gnaws his chains.—The* PRIOR *remains insensible, as if stupefied with grief.—*BEEFINGTON *takes the keys of the Dungeon, which are hanging at the* PRIOR'S *girdle, and makes a sign for them both to be led away into confinement.—Exeunt* PRIOR *and* COUNT, *properly guarded.—The rest of the conspirators disperse in search of the Dungeon where* ROGERO *is confined.*

END OF ACT IV.

FRERE.

JUNE 25TH, 1798.

AFTER the splendid account of BUONAPARTE'S successes in the East, which our readers will find in another part of this paper, and which they will peruse with equal wonder and apprehension, it is some consolation to us to have to state, not only from authority, but in verse, that our government has not been behindhand with that of France ; but that, aware of the wise and enterprising spirit of the enemy, and of the danger which might arise to our distant possessions from the export of learning and learned men being entirely in their hands, have long ago determined on an expedition of a similar nature, and have actually embarked at Portsmouth on board one of the East India Company's ships taken up for that purpose (the ship *Capricorn*, Mr. Thomas Truman, Commander), several tons of *savans*, the growth of this country. The whole was conducted with the utmost secrecy and dispatch, and it was not till we were favoured with the following copy of a letter (obligingly communicated to us by the *Tunisian* gentleman to whom it is addressed) that we had any suspicion of the extent and nature of the design, or indeed of any such design being in contemplation.

The several great names which are combined to render this Expedition the most surprising and splendid ever undertaken, could not indeed have been spared from the country to which they are an ornament, for any other purpose, than one the most obviously connected with the interests of the empire, and the most widely beneficial to mankind.

The secrecy with which they have been withdrawn from the British public without being so much as missed or inquired after, reflects the highest honour on the planners of the enterprise. Even the celebrity of DOCTOR PARR has not led to any discovery or investigation : and the silent admirers of that great man have never once thought of asking what was become of him; till it is now all at once come to light, that he has been for weeks past on shipboard, the brightest star in the bright constellation of talents which stud the quarter-deck of the *Capricorn*, Mr. T. Truman (as before mentioned), Commander.

The resignation of the late worthy President of a certain Board, might indeed have taught mankind to look for some extraordinary event in the world of science and adventure ; and those who had the good fortune to see the deportation from his house, of the several wonderful anomalies which had for years formed its most distinguished inmates,—the stuffed ram, the dried boar, the cow with three horns, and other fanciful productions of a like nature, could not but speculate with some degree of seriousness on the purpose of their removal, and on the place of their destination.

It now appears that there was in truth no light object in view. They were destined, with the rest of the *savans*, on whom this country prides itself (and long may it have reason to indulge the honest exultation) ! to undertake a voyage of no less grandeur than peril ; to counteract the designs of the DIRECTORY, and to frustrate or forestall the conquests of BUONAPARTE.

The young gentleman who writes the following letter to his friend in London, is, as may be seen, interpreter to the Expedition. We have understood further, that he is nearly connected with the young man who writes for the *Morning Chronicle*, and conducts the *Critical, Argumentative*, and *Geographical* departments. Some say it is the young man himself, who has assumed a feigned name, and, under the disguise of a Turkish dress and circumcision, is gone, at the express instigation of his employers, to improve himself in geographical knowledge. We have our doubts upon this subject, as we think we recognize the style of this deplorable young man in that article of last week's *Morning Chronicle*, which we have had occasion to answer in a preceding column of our present paper. Be that as it may, the information contained in the following letter may be depended upon.

We cannot take leave of the subject without remarking what a fine contrast and companion the vessel and cargo described in the following poem affords to the "NAVIS STULTIFERA," the "SHIPPE OF FOOLES" of the celebrated BARCLAY; and we cannot forbear hoping that the *Argenis* of an author of the same name may furnish a hint for an account of this stupendous Expedition in a learned language, from the only pen which in modern days is capable of writing *Latin* with a purity and elegance worthy of so exalted a theme, and that the author of a classical *preface* may become the writer of a no less celebrated voyage.

TRANSLATION OF A LETTER

(IN ORIENTAL CHARACTERS)

FROM BOBBA-DARA-ADUL-PHOOLA,

DRAGOMAN TO THE EXPEDITION,

TO NEEK-AWL-ARETCHID-KOOEEZ,

SECRETARY TO THE TUNISIAN EMBASSY.

DEAR NEEK-AWL,

OU'LL rejoice that at length I am able
 To date these few lines from the captain's
  own table.
Mr. Truman himself, of his proper sugges-
  tion,
Has in favour of science decided the question ;
So we walk the main-deck, and are mess'd with the captain,
I leave you to judge of the joy we are wrapt in.

At Spithead they embark'd us, how precious a cargo !
And we sail'd before day to escape the embargo.
There was SHUCKBOROUGH, the wonderful mathematician ;
And DARWIN, the poet, the sage, and physician ;
There was BEDDOES, and BRUIN, and GODWIN, whose trust is,
He may part with his work on *Political Justice*
To some Iman or Bonze, or Judaical Rabbin ;
So with huge quarto volumes he piles up the cabin.
There was great Dr. PARR, whom we style *Bellendenus,*
The Doctor and I have a hammock between us—
Tho' 'tis rather unpleasant thus crowding together,
On account of the motion and heat of the weather ;
Two souls in one berth we might easily cram,
But Sir John *will* insist on a place for his *ram.*

I*   L

Though the Doctor, I find, is determined to think
'Tis the animal's hide that occasions the stink ;
In spite of th' experienced opinion of Truman,
Who contends that the scent is exclusively human.
But BEDDOES and DARWIN engage to repair
This slight inconvenience with *oxygene air.*

    Whither bound ? (you will ask). 'Tis a question, my
       friend,
On which I long doubted; my doubt's at an end.
To Arabia the stony, Sabæa the gummy,
To the land where each man that you meet is a mummy ;
To the mouths of the Nile, to the banks of Araxes,
To the *Red* and the *Yellow,* the *White* and the *Black* seas,
With telescopes, globes, and a quadrant and sextant,
And the works of all authors whose writings are extant ;
With surveys and plans, topographical maps,
Theodolites, watches, spring-guns and steel-traps,
Phials, crucibles, air-pumps, electric machinery,
And pencils for painting the natives and scenery.
In short, we are sent to oppose all we know,
To the knowledge and mischievous arts of the foe,
Who, though placing in arms a well-grounded reliance,
Go to war with a flying artillery of science.

    The French *savans,* it seems, recommended this measure,
With a view to replenish the national treasure.
First, the true *Rights of Man* they will preach in all places,
But chief (when 'tis found) in the Egyptian Oasis :
And this doctrine, 'tis hoped, in a very few weeks
Will persuade the wild Arabs to murder their Sheiks,
And, to aid the *Great Nation's* beneficent plans,
Plunder pyramids, catacombs, towns, caravans,
Then enlist under Arcole's gallant commander,
Who will conquer the world like his model ISKANDER.
His army each day growing bolder and finer,
With the Turcoman tribes he subdues Asia Minor,
Beats Paul and his Scythians, his journey pursues
'Cross the Indus, with tribes of Armenians and Jews,
And Bucharians, and Affghans, and Persians, and Tartars,—
Chokes the wretched Mogul in his grandmother's garters,
And will hang him to dry in the Luxembourg hall,
'Midst the plunder of Carthage and spoils of Bengal.

Such, we hear, was the plan ; but I trust, if we meet 'em,
That, *savant* to *savant*, our cargo will beat 'em.
Our plan of proceeding I'll presently tell ;—
But soft—I am call'd—I must bid you farewell ;
To attend on our *savans* my pen I resign,
For it seems that they *duck* them on *crossing* the Line.

We deeply regret this interruption of our Oriental poet,
and the more so, as the prose letters which we have received from a less learned correspondent do not enable us
to explain the tactics of our belligerent philosophers so
distinctly as we could have wished. It appears, in general,
that the learned Doctor who has the honour of sharing the
hammock of the amiable Oriental, trusted principally to
his superior knowledge in the Greek language, by means
of which he hoped to entangle his antagonists in inextricable confusion. Dr. DARWIN proposed (as might be
expected) his celebrated experiment of the ice-island,
which, being towed on the coast of Africa, could not fail of
spoiling the climate, and immediately terrifying and em-
barrassing the sailors of Buonaparte's fleet, accustomed
to the mild temperature and gentle gales of the Mediterranean, and therefore ill qualified to struggle with this
new importation of tempests. Dr. BEDDOES was satisfied
with the project of communicating to Buonaparte a con-
sumption, of the same nature with that which he formerly
tried on himself, but superior in virulence, and therefore
calculated to make the most rapid and fatal ravages in the
hectic constitution of the Gallic hero. The rest of the
plan is quite unintelligible, excepting a hint about Sir J. S.'s
intention of proceeding with his ram to the celebrated
Oasis, and of bringing away, for the convenience of the
Bank, the treasures contained in the temple of Jupiter
Ammon.

CANNING, ELLIS, AND FRERE.

NEW MORALITY.

[JULY 9, 1798.]

FROM mental mists to purge a nation's eyes ;
To animate the weak, unite the wise ;
To trace the deep infection that pervades
The crowded town, and taints the rural shades ;
To mark how wide extends the mighty waste
O'er the fair realms of Science, Learning, Taste ;
To drive and scatter all the brood of lies,
And chase the varying falsehood as it flies ;
The long arrears of ridicule to pay,
To drag reluctant dulness back to-day ;
Much yet remains.—To you these themes belong,
Ye favour'd sons of virtue and of song !

Say, is the field too narrow ? are the times
Barren of folly, and devoid of crimes ?

Yet, venial vices, in a milder age,
Could rouse the warmth of POPE's satiric rage :
The doting miser, and the lavish heir,
The follies and the foibles of the fair,
Sir Job, Sir Balaam, and old Euclio's thrift,
And Sappho's diamonds with her dirty shift,
Blunt, Charteris, Hopkins—meaner subjects fired
The keen-eyed Poet, while the Muse inspired
Her ardent child—entwining, as he sate,
His laurell'd chaplet with the thorns of hate.

But say,—indignant does the Muse retire,
Her shrine deserted, and extinct its fire ?
No pious hand to feed the sacred flame,
No raptured soul a poet's charge to claim ?

Bethink thee, GIFFORD ; when some future age
Shall trace the promise of thy playful page ;—
" The hand which brush'd a swarm of fools away,
Should rouse to grasp a more reluctant prey !"—
Think then, will pleaded indolence excuse
The tame secession of thy languid Muse ?

Ah! where is now that promise ? why so long
Sleep the keen shafts of satire and of song ?
Oh ! come, with taste and virtue at thy side,
With ardent zeal inflamed, and patriot pride ;
With keen poetic glance direct the blow,
And empty all thy quiver on the foe :—
No pause—no rest—till weltering on the ground
The poisonous hydra lies, and pierced with many a wound.

Thou too !—the nameless Bard,[1]—whose honest zeal
For law, for morals, for the public weal,
Pours down impetuous on thy country's foes
The stream of verse, and many-languaged prose ;
Thou too !—though oft thy ill-advised dislike,
The guiltless head with random censure strike,—
Though quaint allusions, vague and undefined,
Play faintly round the ear, but mock the mind ;—
Through the mix'd mass yet truth and learning shine,
And manly vigour stamps the nervous line ;
And patriot rage the generous verse inspires,
And wakes and points the desultory fires !

Yet more remain unknown :—for who can tell
What bashful genius, in some rural cell,
As year to year, and day succeeds to day,
In joyless leisure wastes his life away?
In him the flame of early fancy shone ;
His genuine worth his old companions own ;
In childhood and in youth their chief confess'd,
His master's pride, his pattern to the rest.
Now, far aloof retiring from the strife
Of busy talents, and of active life,
As from the loop-holes of retreat he views
Our stage, verse, pamphlets, politics, and news,
He loathes the world,—or, with reflection sad,
Concludes it irrecoverably mad ;
Of taste, of learning, morals, all bereft,
No hope, no prospect to redeem it left.

FRERE.

---

[1] The author of "The Pursuits of Literature."
[The above note was not in the "Anti-Jacobin" of July 9, 1798.]

Awake! for shame! or ere thy nobler sense
Sink in th' oblivious pool of indolence!
Must wit be found alone on falsehood's side,
Unknown to truth, to virtue unallied?
Arise! nor scorn thy country's just alarms;
Wield in her cause thy long-neglected arms:
Of lofty satire pour th' indignant strain,
Leagued with her friends, and ardent to maintain
'Gainst Learning's, Virtue's, Truth's, Religion's foes,
A kingdom's safety, and the world's repose.

If Vice appal thee,—if thou view with awe
Insults that brave, and crimes that 'scape the law;
Yet may the specious bastard brood, which claim
A spurious homage under Virtue's name,
Sprung from a parent nurse of thousand crimes,
The *New Philosophy* of modern times,—
Yet, these may rouse thee!—With unsparing hand,
Oh, lash the vile impostures from the land!

First, stern PHILANTHROPY:—not she, who dries
The orphan's tears, and wipes the widow's eyes;
Not she, who, sainted Charity her guide,
Of British bounty pours the annual tide:—
But *French* Philanthropy;—whose boundless mind
Glows with the general love of all mankind;—
Philanthropy,—beneath whose baneful sway
Each patriot passion sinks, and dies away.

Taught in her school to imbibe thy mawkish strain,
CONDORCET, filter'd through the dregs of PAINE,
Each pedant prig disowns a Briton's part,
And plucks the name of England from his heart.

What! shall a name, a word, a sound, control
Th' aspiring thought, and cramp th' expansive soul?
Shall one half-peopled Island's rocky round
A love, that glows for all creation, bound?
And social charities contract the plan
Framed for thy freedom, universal man!
No—through th' extended globe his feelings run
As broad and general as th' unbounded sun!
No narrow bigot *he*;—*his* reason'd view
Thy interests, England, ranks with thine, Peru!

France **at our** doors, *he* sees no danger nigh,
But heaves for Turkey's woes th' impartial sigh ;
A steady patriot of the world alone,
The friend of every country—but his own.

Next comes a gentler Virtue.—Ah ! **beware**
Lest the harsh verse **her** shrinking **softness scare.**
Visit her not too roughly ;—the warm **sigh**
Dwells on her lips ; the tear-drop gems **her eye.**
Sweet SENSIBILITY, **that dwells** enshrined
In the fine foldings **of the** feeling mind ;
With delicate Mimosa's **sense** endued,
That shrinks instinctive from a hand **too** rude ;
Or, like the pimpernel, whose prescient flower
Shuts her soft leaves at evening's chilly hour.
Sweet child of sickly Fancy !—her of yore
From her loved France ROUSSEAU to exile bore ;
And, while 'midst lakes and mountains wild he **ran,**
Full of himself, and shunn'd the **haunts of** man,
Taught her o'er each lone vale **and Alpine steep**
To lisp the stories of his **wrongs, and weep;**
Taught her to cherish **still in either eye,**
Of tender **tears a plentiful supply,**
And pour **them in the brooks that babbled by ;**
Taught her **to mete by rule her feelings strong,**
False **by degrees, and** delicately **wrong ;**
For the crush'd beetle *first,*—the **widow'd dove,**
And all the warbled sorrows **of the grove** ;
Next for poor suffering *guilt ;* and *last* of all,
For parents, friends, a king **and** country's fall.

Mark her fair votaries, prodigal of grief,
With cureless pangs, and woes that mock **relief,**
Droop in soft sorrow o'er a faded **flower ;**
O'er a dead jack-ass[1] pour the pearly shower ;
But hear, unmoved, of *Loire's* ensanguined flood,
Choked up with slain ; of *Lyons* drench'd in blood ;
Of crimes that blot the age, the world, with shame,
Foul crimes, but sicklied o'er with Freedom's name ;
Altars and thrones subverted ; social life
Trampled to earth,—the husband from **the wife,**

---

[1] **Vide** " Sentimental Journey."

Parent from child, with ruthless fury torn ;
Of talents, honour, virtue, wit, forlorn
In friendless exile,—of the wise and good
Staining the daily scaffold with their blood ;
Of savage cruelties, that scare the mind,
The rage of madness with hell's lusts combined,—
Of hearts torn reeking from the mangled breast,
They hear—and hope that ALL IS FOR THE BEST.

Fond hope ! but JUSTICE sanctifies the prayer—
JUSTICE ! here, Satire, strike ! 'twere sin to spare !
Not she in British Courts that takes her stand,
The dawdling balance dangling in her hand,
Adjusting punishments to fraud and vice,
With scrupulous quirks, and disquisition nice :
But firm, erect, with keen reverted glance,
Th' avenging angel of regenerate France,
Who visits ancient sins on modern times,
And punishes the POPE for CÆSAR's crimes.[1]
Such is the liberal JUSTICE which presides
In these our days, and modern patriots guides ;
JUSTICE, whose blood-stain'd book one sole decree,
One statute fills—" the People shall be Free !"
Free by what means ?—by folly, madness, guilt,
By boundless rapines, blood in oceans spilt ;
By confiscation, in whose sweeping toils
The poor man's pittance with the rich man's spoils,
Mix'd in one common mass, are swept away,
To glut the short-lived tyrant of the day :
By laws, religion, morals, all o'erthrown,
—Rouse then, ye sovereign people, claim your own—

---

[1] The Manes of Vercingetorix are supposed to have been very much gratified by the invasion of Italy and the plunder of the Roman territory. The defeat of the Burgundians is to be revenged on the modern inhabitants of Switzerland. But the Swiss were a free people, defending their liberties against a tyrant. Moreover, they happened to be in alliance with France at the time. No matter ; Burgundy is since become a province of France, and the French have acquired a property in all the injuries and defeats which the people of that country may have sustained, together with a title to revenge and retaliation to be exercised in the present or any future centuries, as may be found most glorious and convenient.

The licence that enthrals, the truth that blinds,
The wealth that starves you, and the power that grinds !
—So JUSTICE bids.—'Twas her enlighten'd doom,
LOUIS, thy head devoted to the tomb—
'Twas JUSTICE, claim'd, in that accursed hour,
The fatal forfeit of too lenient power.
Mourn for the Man we may ;—but for the King,—
Freedom, oh ! Freedom's such a charming thing !

" Much may be said on both sides."—Hark ! I hear
A well-known voice that murmurs in my ear,—
The voice of CANDOUR.—Hail ! most solemn sage, ⎫
Thou drivelling virtue of this moral age,   ⎬
CANDOUR, which softens party's headlong rage.   ⎭
CANDOUR,—which spares its foes ; nor e'er descends
With bigot zeal to combat for its friends.
CANDOUR,—which loves in see-saw strain to tell
Of *acting foolishly*, but *meaning well ;*
Too nice to praise by wholesale, or to blame,
Convinced that *all* men's *motives* are the same ;
And finds, with keen discriminating sight,
BLACK's not *so* black ;—nor WHITE *so very* white.

" Fox, to be sure, was vehement and wrong :
But then, PITT's words, you'll own, were *rather* strong.
Great men will have their foibles ; 'twas just so
With Fox and PITT full forty years ago !
So WALPOLE, PULTENEY—factions in all times
Have had their follies, ministers their crimes."

Give me th' avow'd, th' erect, the manly foe,
Bold I can meet—perhaps may turn his blow ;
But of all plagues, good Heav'n, thy wrath can send,
Save, save, oh ! save me from the *Candid Friend !*

" BARRAS loves plunder—MERLIN takes a bribe,—
What then ?—shall CANDOUR these good men proscribe ?
No ! ere we join the loud-accusing throng,
Prove,—not the facts,—but, that *they thought them wrong.*

" Why hang O'QUIGLEY ?—he, misguided man,
In sober thought his country's weal *might* plan :
And, though his deep-laid Treason sapp'd the throne,
Might act from *taste in morals*, all his own."

Peace to such Reasoners—let them have their way ;
Shut their dull eyes against the blaze of day—
PRIESTLEY's a Saint, and STONE a Patriot still ;
And LA FAYETTE a Hero, if they will.

I love the bold uncompromising mind,
Whose principles are fix'd, whose views defined :
Who, sick of modern cant, discredits quite
All *taste in morals*, innate sense of right,
And Nature's impulse, all uncheck'd by art,
And feelings fine, that float about the heart.
Content, for good men's guidance, bad men's awe,
On moral truth to rest, and Gospel law ;
Who owns, when Traitors feel th' avenging rod,
Just retribution, and the hand of God—
Who hears the groans through Olmutz' roofs that ring,
Of him who chain'd and who betray'd his king—
Hears unappall'd—though Freedom's zealots preach—
Unmoved, unsoften'd by FITZPATRICK's speech.
That speech on which the melting Commons hung,
" While truths divine came mended from *his* tongue ;"
How loving husband clings to duteous wife,—
How pure Religion soothes the ills of life,—
How Popish ladies trust their pious fears
And naughty actions in their chaplain's ears.
Half novel and half sermon, on it flow'd ;
With pious zeal THE OPPOSITION glow'd ;
And as o'er each the soft infection crept,
Sigh'd as he whined, and as he whimper'd, wept ;
E'en CURWEN[1] dropt a sentimental tear,
And stout ST. ANDREW yelp'd a softer " Hear ! "

Parent of crimes and fashions ! which in vain
Our colder servile spirits would attain,
How do we ape thee, France ! but, bungling still,
Disgrace the pattern by our want of skill.
The borrow'd step our awkward gait reveals :
As clumsy COURTNEY mars the verse he steals.

---

[1] Now all the while did not this stony-hearted *cur* shed one tear.
Merchant of Venice.

How do we ape thee, France!—nor claim alone
Thy arts, thy tastes, thy morals, for our own,
But to thy worthies render homage due,
Their " hair-breadth 'scapes "[1] with anxious interest view ;
Statesmen and heroines whom this age adores,
Though plainer times would call them rogues and whores.

    See LOUVET, patriot, pamphleteer, and sage,
Tempering with amorous fire his virtuous rage.
Form'd for all tasks, his various talents see—
The luscious novel, the severe decree—
Then mark him weltering in his nasty sty,
Bare his lewd transports to the public eye—
Not *his* the love in silent groves that strays,
Quits the rude world, and shuns the vulgar gaze.
In LODOISKA's full possession blest,
One craving void still aches within his breast—
Plunged in the filth and fondness of her arms,
Not to himself alone he stints her charms—
Clasp'd in each other's foul embrace they lie,
But know no joy, unless the world stands by.
The fool of vanity, for her alone
He lives, loves, writes, and dies but to be known.
His widow'd mourner flies to poison's aid,
Eager to join her LOUVET's parted shade
In those bright realms where sainted lovers stray—
But harsh emetics tear that hope away.
Yet, hapless LOUVET! where thy bones are laid,
The easy nymphs shall consecrate the shade.[2]
There, in the laughing morn of genial spring,
Unwedded pairs shall tender couplets sing ;
Eringoes o'er the hallow'd spot shall bloom,
And flies of Spain buzz softly round the tomb.[3]

---

[1] See *Récit de mes Périls*, by Louvet ; *Mémoires d'un Détenu*, by
Riouffe. The avidity with which these productions were read,
might, we should hope, be accounted for upon principles of mere
curiosity (as we read the Newgate Calendar, and the History of the
Buccaneers), not from any interest in favour of a set of wretches,
infinitely more detestable than all the robbers and pirates that ever
existed.

[2] *Faciles Napææ.*—VIRG. G. iv. 535.

[3] See Anthologia, *passim.*

Or does severer virtue charm ?   We choose—
ROLAND the just, with ribands in his shoes [1]—
And ROLAND's spouse, who paints with chaste delight
The doubtful conflict of her nuptial night ;—
Her virgin charms what fierce attacks assail'd,
And how the rigid Minister [2] prevail'd.

But ah ! what verse can paint thy stately mien,
Guide of the world, preferment's golden queen,
NECKER's fair daughter,—STAEL the Epicene !
Bright o'er whose flaming cheek and purple nose
The bloom of young desire unceasing glows !
Fain would the Muse—but ah ! she dares no more,
A mournful voice from lone Guyana's shore, [3]
Sad QUATREMER—the bold presumption checks,
Forbid to question thy ambiguous sex.

CANNING.

To thee, proud BARRAS bows—thy charms control
REWBELL's brute rage, and MERLIN's subtle soul—
Raised by thy hands, and fashion'd to thy will,
Thy power, thy guiding influence, governs still,
Where at the blood-stain'd board assiduous plies,
The lame artificer of fraud and lies ;
He with the mitred head and cloven heel—
Doom'd the coarse edge of REWBELL's jests to feel ; [4]

---

[1] Such was the strictness of this minister's principles, that he positively refused to go to court in shoe-buckles.   See Dumourier's Memoirs.

[2] See MADAME ROLAND's Memoirs.—"*Rigide Ministre,*" Brissot à ses Commettans.

[3] These lines contain the Secret History of QUATREMER'S deportation.

Fal. Thou art neither fish nor flesh—a man cannot tell where to have thee.

Quick. Thou art an unjust man for saying so—thou or any man knows where to have me.

[4] For instance, in the course of a political discussion REWBELL observed to the EX-BISHOP, "*that his understanding was as crooked as his legs*"—"Vil émigré, tu n'as pas le sens plus droit que les pieds"—and therewithal threw an inkstand at him.   It whizzed along, as we have been informed, like the fragment of a rock from the hand of one of Ossian's heroes—but the wily apostate shrunk beneath the table, and the weapon passed over him, innocuous and guiltless of his blood or brains.

To stand the playful buffet, and to hear
The frequent ink-stand whizzing past his ear;
While all the five Directors laugh to see
"The limping priest so deft at his new ministry."[1]

Last of th' ANOINTED FIVE behold, and least,
The Directorial Lama, Sovereign Priest,—
LEPAUX:—whom atheists worship:—at whose nod
Bow their meek heads—*the men without a God.*[2]

Ere long, perhaps, to this astonish'd isle,
Fresh from the shores of subjugated Nile,
Shall BUONAPARTE's victor fleet protect
The genuine Theo-philanthropic sect,—
The sect of MARAT, MIRABEAU, VOLTAIRE,—
Led by their Pontiff, good LA RÉVEILLÈRE.
Rejoiced our CLUBS shall greet him, and install
The holy Hunchback in thy dome, St. Paul!
While countless votaries, thronging in his train,
Wave their red caps, and hymn this jocund strain:
" *Couriers* and *Stars*, Sedition's evening host,
Thou *Morning Chronicle* and *Morning Post,*
Whether ye make the Rights of Man your theme,
Your country libel, and your God blaspheme,
Or dirt on private worth and virtue throw,
Still blasphemous or blackguard, praise LEPAUX.

" And ye five other wandering bards, that move
In sweet accord of harmony and love,
COLERIDGE and SOUTHEY, LLOYD, and LAMB and Co.
Tune all your mystic harps to praise LEPAUX!

---

[1] See Homer's description of Vulcan. First Iliad.
  Inextinguibilis vero exoriebatur risus beatis numinibus
  Ut viderunt Vulcanum per domos *ministrantem.*
[2] *The men without a God*—one of the new sects. Their religion is intended to consist in the adoration of a Great Book, in which all the virtuous actions of the society are to be entered and registered. "In times of civil commotion they are to come forward to exhort the citizens to unanimity, and to read them a chapter out of the Great Book. When oppressed or proscribed, they are to retire to a burying-ground, to wrap themselves up in their great coats, and wait the approach of death," &c.

" PRIESTLEY and WAKEFIELD, humble, holy men,
Give praises to his name with tongue and pen!

" THELWALL, and ye that lecture as ye go,
And for your pains get pelted, praise LEPAUX!

" Praise him each Jacobin, or fool, or knave,
And your cropp'd heads in sign of worship wave!

" All creeping creatures, venomous and low,
PAINE, WILLIAMS, GODWIN, HOLCROFT, praise LEPAUX!

FRERE.

" And thou, *Leviathan!* on ocean's brim
Hugest of living things that sleep and swim;
Thou, in whose nose, by BURKE's gigantic hand,
The hook was fix'd to drag thee to the land,
With ——, ——, and —— in thy train,
And —— wallowing in the yeasty main,[1]—
Still as ye snort, and puff, and spout, and blow,
In puffing, and in spouting, praise LEPAUX!'"

Britain, beware; nor let th' insidious foe,
Of force despairing, aim a deadlier blow;
Thy peace, thy strength, with devilish wiles assail,
And when her arms are vain, by arts prevail.
True, thou art rich, art powerful!—thro' thine Isle
Industrious skill, contented labour, smile—
Far seas are studded with thy countless sails—
What wind but wafts them, and what shore but hails?
True, thou art brave—o'er all the busy land
In patriot ranks embattled myriads stand!
Thy foes behold with impotent amaze,
And drop the lifted weapon as they gaze.

But what avails to guard each outward part,
If subtlest poison, circling at thy heart,
Spite of thy courage, of thy power, and wealth,
Mine the sound fabric of thy vital health?

---

[1] Though the *yeasty* sea
Consume and swallow navigation up.
Macbeth.

The ship boring the moon with her main mast; and anon swallowed with yeast and foam, as you would thrust a cork into a hogshead.—*Winter's Tale.*

So thine own oak, by some fair streamlet's side,
Waves its broad arms, and spreads its leafy pride,
Shades the green earth, and towering to the skies
Its conscious strength, the tempest's wrath defies :
The fowls of Heaven its ample branches share,
To its cool shade the panting herds repair—
The limpid current works its noiseless way—
The fibres loosen, and the roots decay ;
Prostrate the mighty ruin lies ; and all
That shared its shelter, perish in its fall.

O thou—lamented SAGE—whose prescient scan
Laid bare foul Anarchy's gigantic plan,
Prompt to incredulous hearers to disclose
The guilt of France, and Europe's world of woes—
Thou, on whose name far distant times shall gaze,
The mighty sea-mark of those troubled days,
O large of soul, of genius unconfined,
Born to delight, instruct, and mend mankind—
BURKE ! in whose breast a Roman ardour glow'd :
Whose copious tongue with Grecian richness flow'd ;
Well hast thou found (if such thy country's doom)
A timely refuge in the sheltering tomb !

As, in far realms, beneath the cypress shade,
Where Eastern kings in pomp of death are laid,
The perfumed lamp with unextinguish'd light
Flames through the vault, and cheers the gloom of night:
So, mighty BURKE ! in thy sepulchral urn,
To Fancy's view, the lamp of Truth shall burn.
Thither late times shall turn their reverent eyes,
Led by thy light, and by thy wisdom wise.

There *are*, to whom (*their* taste such pleasures cloy)
No light thy wisdom yields, thy wit no joy.
Peace to their heavy heads, and callous hearts,
Peace—such as sloth, as ignorance imparts ;
Pleased may they live to plan their country's good,
And crop with calm content their flowery food !

What though thy venturous spirit loved to urge
The labouring theme to Reason's utmost verge,
Kindling and mounting from th' enraptured sight ;
Still anxious wonder watch'd thy daring flight !

While vulgar souls, with mean malignant stare,
Gazed up, the triumph of thy fall to share !
Poor triumph ! which for oft extorted praise,
To Envy still too daring Genius pays.

Oh ! for thy playful smile, thy potent frown,
T' abash bold Vice, and laugh pert Folly down !
So should the Muse in Humour's happiest vein
Frame with light verse the metaphoric strain,
With apt allusions from the rural trade,
Tell of *what wood young* JACOBINS *are made ;*
How the skill'd gardener grafts with nicest rule
The *slip* of coxcomb on the *stock* of fool—
Forth in bright blossom bursts the tender sprig,
A thing to wonder at, perhaps a *Whig :*
Should tell, how wise each new-fledged pedant prates
Of weightiest matters, grave distractions states—
How rules of policy, and public good,
In Saxon times were rightly understood ;
That kings are proper, *may be* useful things,
But then some gentlemen object to kings ;
How in all times the minister 's to blame ;
How British liberty's an empty name ;
Till each fair burgh, numerically free,
Shall choose its members by *the Rule of Three.*

So should the Muse, with verse in thunder clothed,
Proclaim the crimes by God and Nature loathed.
Which—when fell poison revels in the veins—
The poison fell, that frantic Gallia drains
From the cursed fruit of Freedom's blasted tree—
Blot the fair records of Humanity.

To feebler nations let proud France afford
Her damning choice,—the chalice or the sword,
To drink or die ;—Oh fraud ! Oh specious lie !
Delusive choice ! for *if* they drink, they die.

The sword we dread not :—of ourselves secure,
Firm were our strength, our peace and freedom sure.
Let all the world confederate all its powers,
" Be they not back'd by those that should be ours,"
High on his rock shall BRITAIN's GENIUS stand,
Scatter the crowded hosts, and vindicate the land.

Guard we but our own hearts : with constant view
To ancient morals, ancient manners true,
Guard we the manlier virtues, such as nerved
Our fathers' breasts, and this proud Isle preserved
For many a rugged age—and scorn the while,
(Her arms we fear not,) Gallia's specious wiles,
The soft seductions, the refinements nice
Of gay morality, and easy vice—
So shall we brave the storm—our 'stablish'd power
Thy refuge, Europe, in some happier hour.
But French *in heart*—though victory crown our brow,
Low at our feet though prostrate nations bow,
Wealth gild our cities, commerce crowd our shore,
London may shine, but England is no more.

CANNING.

REMARKS ON THE NINTH BOOK
OF THE ILIAD
AND REVIEW OF MITCHELL'S
ARISTOPHANES.

REMARKS ON THE NINTH BOOK
OF THE ILIAD.

To the EDITOR *of the* MUSEUM CRITICUM.

MY DEAR SIR,

PROPOSE to fulfil the promise which you obligingly exacted from me, by sending a few pages relative to a supposed discovery in *Homer*, which had been before communicated to you, and which I would wish you to make use of in any way which may appear most proper in your own judgment, and in that of your critical friends.

The subject relates to what I shall venture to call by anticipation, the *Lay of Meleager ;* namely, the narrative respecting that Hero, which occurs in the speech of Phœnix, in the ninth Book of the Iliad.

Agamemnon has deputed Phœnix, Ulysses, and Ajax, to prevail upon Achilles to return to the War. They find him sitting before his tent, amusing himself with his lyre ; and here a singular passage occurs : (Il. I. 189.)

Τῇ ὅγε θυμὸν ἔτερπεν, ἄειδε δ' ἄρα κλέα ἀνδρῶν.

Literally, *He* (Achilles) *was singing the* FAMES *of the Heroes.* Phœnix, in his endeavours to mollify the resentment of his pupil, with great propriety, as I apprehend, both as an *argumentum ad hominem*, and in reference to the ideas

which (from the amusement in which they found him
engaged) he might suppose to be uppermost in his mind,
urges upon him the example of *the heroes of whom we have
heard the* FAMES; Οὕτω καὶ τῶν πρόσθεν ἐπευθόμεθα κλέα
ἀνδρῶν Ἡρώων (Il. I. 520). Κλέος, like its corresponding
word *Fame* in English, is one of those to which, from the
nature of their signification, the plural number is not
applicable, and I am not aware that it occurs elsewhere,
except in the Odyssey, where it is applied to the song of
Demodocus (Odyss. Θ. 73)—

Μοῦσ' ἄρ' ἀοιδὸν ἀνῆκεν ἀειδέμεναι κλέα ἀνδρῶν,
Οἴμης, τῆς τότ' ἄρα κλέος οὐρανὸν εὐρὺν ἵκανε.

Οἴμη being in this instance understood to signify such a
portion of a long poem, as might be recited without a pause
by one sustained effort, and corresponding in its signification and origin to the old minstrel term FIT, which though
apparently vague and undetermined, (inasmuch as the
οἴμη, i. e. Enthusiastic impulse or *Fit* of recitation would
necessarily vary according to the natural powers and anima-
tion of different reciters), came nevertheless to be adopted
as a precise and technical term, to denote the regular
divisions or *cantos* (as we should call them, in reference to
an etymology not very different), into which the ancient
minstrel poems were divided. The words οἴμης, τῆς τότ',
&c. therefore (signifying that *Fit* or section of the poem)
imply a distinct and specific reference, which must of
course presuppose the existence of the thing referred to;
and our conclusion must be, that the song of Demodocus
was not a poem *in nubibus*, like the song of Iopas in the
Æneid, or that of Mopas in Prince Arthur, but a poem
actually known, and popular at the time when the description of it in the Odyssey was composed.

The origin of the term κλέα ἀνδρῶν, as applied to any
particular species of poetic composition, I apprehend to be
this; there were then in existence a set of lays or short
poems, each of which might be called very properly and
appositely, from the name of the Hero who was the subject of it, Κλέος Τυδέος, Κλέος Βελλεροφόντου, Κλέος Ἰολάου,
or as in the present instance Κλέος Μελεάγρου : as we had
formerly the *Lay of Lanval*, the *Lay of Tristram*, the *Lay
of Lancelot*, and others. These poems, when mentioned

collectively, would of course be called in the plural number
Κλέα or Κλέα ἀνδρῶν. From this origin the term κλέα
ἀνδρῶν appears to have migrated into the more extended
sense, in which we find it employed in the Odyssey, where
it is evidently applied to a long poem divided into distinct
portions, and comprehending a complicated series of action,
in the course of which many heroes must have had their
share of celebration.

In the passage of the Iliad which is before us, the term
appears more distinctly connected with the origin which
we have assigned to it. Achilles is represented as singing
the κλέα ἀνδρῶν, and Phœnix *in reference* to them, as was
before remarked, relates a short narrative of which Meleager
is the principal personage, and which might properly
enough have been called Κλέος Μελεάγρου, according to
the supposed etymology before stated ; and it would then
be understood, that the poems with which Achilles was
amusing himself, were similar to that which Phœnix re-
cites, *i. e.* short narratives, or detached pieces (like the
Spanish romances, each of which was a brief independent
narrative of some heroic adventure), a species of composition which should seem best calculated to occupy the
temporary attention of an hero, whose habits do not appear to have been of a sedentary nature. And here let
me remark, that the comparison which I have made of
these supposed poems to the old metrical Romances of
Spain, affords a parallel likewise in the application of a
plural to a word naturally singular ; for Romance, in its
primary sense, meant the Roman language or ordinary
dialect commonly spoken in the provinces of the Empire,
in contradistinction to the correct and classical Latin. In
Spain the term was made use of afterwards, to designate
the common speech of the country, as distinguished from
that species of Latinity which was still the language of the
Church and of the Law. Hence, a poem composed in the
common language of the country, was called a Romance,
to distinguish it from the Hymns of the Church, and the
metrical Latin songs of the Monks ; and the word in this
sense became capable of a plural, as we have supposed the
case to have been in the transition from κλέος to κλέα.

But without insisting farther upon the probability of
this etymology, or the impossibility of accounting for so

paradoxical a plural in any other way, I should conceive
that this mode of interpretation gives a greater degree of
pertinency and propriety to the narrative of Phœnix, than
would belong to it, if we suppose Achilles to have been
singing the praises of Heroes in general—*Heroum laudes
imitandaque facta.* Secondly, since the term κλέα ἀνδρῶν,
as used in the Odyssey, evidently points to a known existing
poem, we cannot well avoid inferring that the same phrase
must, in like manner, be understood elsewhere as denoting
some specific object ; and in both instances it seems contrary to the rules of good criticism, to resolve the expression into a vague indefinite sense.

It is, I believe, an established axiom among critical
antiquarians, that the poets of a barbarous age (such as
that of Homer) are in no respect more uniformly dis-
tinguishable, than in the absence of those general forms,
both of expression and description, which result from a
more enlarged view of society and manners ; while the
fastidiousness of a more refined age, dissatisfied with the
objects which surround it, imposes upon its contemporary
poets the necessity of resorting to a mode of expression
more vague and indefinite, the terms of which presuppose
the existence of such general knowledge.   The translator
of Homer, for instance, was censured for having used the
words *House of Lords* in some lines addressed to his friend
Murray.   The expression, in the opinion of the critics of
that age, was not sufficiently dignified.   The same idea
ought to have been conveyed in some more general form :
the Senate probably would have been deemed unexception-
able.   But in Homer we may be assured, that every thing
is called by the name which properly and specifically belonged to it ; and we may conclude, *e converso*, that no
term is employed without a reference to something which
in art, nature, or popular imagination and belief, might be
endowed with a separate and specific existence.

Extending the same observation from words to images,
we find Voltaire censured for having introduced too specific
a description in his lines on the battle of Fontenoy :

" *Et le vieux nouvelliste, la canne à la main,
Trace au Palais Royal Ypres, Courtrai, Menin.*"

He defends himself with great ingenuity by saying, truly

enough, that a similar image, if found in an ancient author, would have been considered as eminently classical. He might have added that the contemporaries of Homer proceeded upon a different principle, and were rather pleased than disgusted at recognizing, in the verses recited to them by their bards, the same objects and images which were familiar to them in daily life. It is not, I apprehend, too much to assume, that in examining the works of poets who existed in an uncultivated age, we should in general lean to a specific and definite mode of interpretation. An English antiquary, if he were to find in an old metrical Chronicle or Romance, that the King or Hero was reading the *Gestis of the Romans*, would understand what was said, not generally as referring to the study of Roman History, but specifically, as signifying the perusal of the particular work called *Gesta Romanorum*, which was popular in the middle ages. In the same manner, though we know that the praises of heroes have in all ages and nations been the subject of poetry and song, it seems more natural to suppose, that Homer, in mentioning the κλέα ἀνδρῶν, referred to something which was familiar to his audience, instead of trusting to their knowledge of the general habits of human nature.

If you should allow any degree of weight to the observations above stated, and feel disposed to admit the probability of the existence of such a description of Poems as has been above supposed, this probability will be strengthened by the discovery of any peculiarities of metre in the narrative, which Phœnix is supposed to recite from his recollection of one of them ; and reciprocally, it will appear probable that such peculiarities are not the effects of accident, when they are discovered in the very spot which our previous speculations had induced us to explore.

The nature of this peculiarity will be best explained by the following arrangement of the lines themselves. (Il. I. 525.)

Κουρῆτές τ'	ἐμάχοντο	καὶ Αἰτωλοὶ	μενέχαρμαι
Ἀμφὶ πόλιν	Καλυδῶνα	καὶ ἀλλήλους	ἐνάριζον·
Αἰτωλοὶ μὲν	ἀμυνόμενοι	Καλυδῶνος	ἐρανννῆς,
Κουρῆτες δὲ	διαπραθέειν	μεμαῶτες	Ἄρηϊ.

```
  *  *  *  *   |  *  *   |   *  *  *   |  *  *  *
```
Καὶ γὰρ τοῖσι | κακὸν | χρυσόθρονος |ʼΑρτεμις | ὧρσεν.

A line is here marked as wanting; for τοῖσι according to
the construction should refer to Κουρῆτες, whereas the
sense evidently applies it to the Ætolians, whose chief,
Meleager, had incurred the vengeance of the goddess. It
should seem, that the line, which is now wanting, mentioned
the injury suffered by the Curetes from the Ætolians, without which we are somewhat at a loss to account for the
origin of the war ; and that the sense of the remaining line,
as connected with that which is lost, should run thus :
" they too " (the Ætolians, who had inflicted this injury on
the Curetes) " had themselves suffered from a calamity
which Diana inflicted upon them."

The next line is Dactylic :

Χωσαμένη, ὅ οἱ οὔτι θαλύσια γουνῷ ἀλωῆς

Οἰνεὺς ῥέξ', | ἄλλοι δὲ | θεοὶ | δαίνυνθ' | ἑκατόμβας,
Οἴῃ δ' οὐκ | ἔρρεξε | Διὸς | κούρῃ | μεγάλοιο.

The following line,

ʼΗ λάθετ', ἤ οὐκ ἐνόησεν· ἀάσατο δὲ μέγα θυμῷ

is Dactylic.

ʼΗ δὲ | χολωσἄμἕνῆ | Δῖον γένος | ʼΙοχέαιρα,
ʼΩρσεν | ἔπι χλοὕνῆν | σῦν ἄγριον | ἀργιόδοντα.

Throughout the rest of the narrative, I have detected only
one perfect instance of the species of parallelism above
noted, and the couplet is preceded and followed by lines
which are dactylic with the exception of the first foot.
(v. 572.)

ʼΕξελθεῖν καὶ ἀμῦναι, ὑποσχόμενοι μέγα δῶρον·

ʼΟππόθι | πῖσταρον | πεδίον | Καλυδῶνος | ἐραννῆς,
ʼΕνθα μιν | ἤνωγον | τέμενος | περικαλλὲς | ἑλέσθαι

Πεντηκοντόγυον, τὸ μὲν ἥμισυ οἰνοπέδοιο.

And here it may be observed in general, that in those passages in which a dactylic metre appears to be affected, the
spondees, where they occur, will be found more frequently
in the first foot than in any other. There are however
many passages which approach so nearly to it, as to make

it probable that they were composed with a view to the same species of metrical effect. Thus (v. 542.)

Τόσσος ἔην, πολλοὺς δὲ	πυρῆς	ἐπέβησ'	ἀλεγεινῆς.
Ἡ δ' ἀμφ' αὐτῷ θῆκε	πολὺν	κέλαδον	καὶ ἀϋτήν.
Κουρήτων τε μεσηγὺ	καὶ Αἰτωλῶν		μεγαθύμων.
Ὄφρα μὲν οὖν Μελέαγρος	ἀρηΐφιλος		πολέμιζε,
Τόφρα δὲ Κουρήτεσσι	κακῶς ἦν, οὐδ'		ἐθέλεσκον.

And throughout the whole of the narrative, especially in those parts which are essential to the story, there is a peculiarity of cadence, very pleasing in itself, and strikingly distinct from the dramatic rhythm of the speeches.

But before we close the subject, or enter into a new one which is much too wide for me, we must return once more to good old Phœnix. He introduces the narrative by saying, (v. 523.)

Μέμνημαι τόδε ἔργον ἐγὼ πάλαι, οὔτι νέον γε,
Ὡς ἦν, ἐν δ' ὑμῖν ἐρέω πάντεσσι φίλοισι.

" I remember *the thing* as it was at the time, not lately, but a long while ago."—

τόδε ἔργον must relate to some antecedent ; but if we translate it ' fact' or ' event,' we find that no fact or event has been mentioned : if we understand it prospectively, besides the drawling tone which it gives to the construction, it leaves two lines wholly destitute of that characteristic colloquial spirit, which belongs to the whole of this scene of the conference with Achilles. The sense (if sense it could be called) would then stand thus : " I remember the following fact as it happened a long while ago, not of late years ; and here among my friends I will mention it." The recollection of an event can have only one date, that of the event itself : if therefore Phœnix's recollection of the fact was of old date, it seems somewhat superfluous to say, that it was not recent ; and I am not aware of any great propriety in his prefacing his narrative by saying, that he would relate it among friends : such a confidential intimation appears hardly necessary, if we suppose it simply intended to introduce a narrative of events, which had passed in the time of their fathers and grandfathers. If, on the other hand, we suppose Phœnix to be speaking

of an old piece of poetry, we see what is perfectly consonant to the mixture of gravity and garrulity which is characteristic of old age; the old gentleman refers his recollection of poetry to his early years, and disclaims any later
acquaintance with it.

Let us venture this safe assumption, that the character
of the human race is invariable; and let us, by referring
them to modern and familiar illustration, subject the two
modes of interpretation to our natural and familiar sense
of what is rational and consistent with character. Let us
suppose an old gentleman, (a very old one, if you please,
one old enough to remember the times of Sir Robert Walpole)—Let us suppose him talking in company to this
effect: "There was a circumstance which I remember as it
happened a long while ago, and not lately; and since we
are among friends, I will mention it. About the time that
Sir Robert Walpole went out of administration, &c. &c."
If the story thus introduced was one of public notoriety,
and one of which the communication neither required
secrecy nor implied confidence, the auditors would, I apprehend, conclude that the worthy gentleman's faculties were
considerably impaired. But let us suppose, that in the
course of conversation he quotes a couple of lines from
Akenside's Epistle to Sir W. Pulteney, and then goes on:
"I remember *the thing* at the time: it is a long while
ago, and I have never thought of it since; but as we are
all among friends, I'll try if I cannot recollect some more
of it." Here we have, in my opinion, a much finer and
heartier personage than the former; and we are obliged
to him, moreover, for having given us a solution of our
difficulty respecting τόδε ἔργον, which, as we now see, refers
to lines that he has been quoting. If we recollect that
most of our old Romances begin with a mention of other
Romances (a peculiarity which is noticed in Chamers's
burlesque imitation of them,

"Men talken of Romans of price,")

and that the oldest Romance in existence, that of the Nie-
belungen, begins with a reference to some older Romances, we must surely admit that there is no reason *à
priori*, why the ancient popular heroic poetry of the Greeks
should not have done so too. Phœnix, I apprehend, has

already quoted some lines of the poem, which were introductory of the narrative : (v. 520.)

Οὕτω καὶ	τῶν πρόσθεν	ἐπευθόμεθα	κλέα ἀνδρῶν
Ἡρώων·	ὅτε κέν τιν'	ἐπιζάφελος	χόλος ἵκοι,
Δωρητοί	τε πέλοντο	παραρρήτοις τ'	ἐπέεσσι.

The phrase τόδε ἔργον is used then by Phœnix in reference
to the introductory lines which he had been quoting. He
then goes on, " I remember the old ditty a long while ago ;
and since we are among friends, I will repeat it." If this
paraphrase appears below the dignity of the speaker or
the gravity of the subject, we must bear in mind, that in
Homer's time verse was the only record of past events, and
that there is no more absurdity in Phœnix's reference to
an old tale in verse, than in the appeals made by Shakespeare's heroes to the authority of Chronicles and public
Acts.

If you are disposed to obelize the last of these lines as
an interpolation introduced by Phœnix and not originally
belonging to a real genuine old Κλέος, I shall willingly give
it up ; and will only beg of you in that case to include the
last part of the preceding line (v. 519.)

| νεμεσσητὸν | κεχολῶσθαι.

and to attribute the preservation of such a degree of
parallelism through four lines, to a design on the part of
the composer to mark the reference to another species of
poetry, by an impressive uniformity of metre.

With respect to this last supposed instance of a quotation not formally announced, but introduced casually and
rapidly in the current of discourse, it does not appear to
me to stand alone ; there are, if I mistake not, two others
in this dramatic scene of the tent of Achilles ; one in the
speech of Ulysses, and another in that of Achilles himself ;
both of them, if considered in that light, admirably consonant to the character of the speakers. But I have fatigued
myself, and shall, I am afraid, have wearied your readers :
I will therefore only remark, that the character and spirit
of Ulysses' speech is poisoned by the interpolation of the
line 231.

Νῆας ἐϋσσέλμους, εἰ μὴ σύ γε δύσεαι ἀλκήν.

If you feel as much as I do, how totally it destroys the

character of manly reserve which marks the first part of
that speech, you will, I hope, transfix it with your Obelus.
It seems to have been introduced for no reason but to accommodate ἀπολέσθαι with an accusative case to govern.
I will now absolutely conclude.

Believe me, with great respect,
Very sincerely yours,
J. H. FRERE.

Roydon, September 26, 1815.

DEAR SIR,

N perusing the proof sheet of my Reverees,
which you have been so obliging as to forward
to me, I find them so much shrunk in bulk
under the hands of your Printer, that the
apprehension of inordinate length, which induced me to conclude rather abruptly, is done away, and
I am inclined (instead of leaving your Readers to look for
the *solution of the Conundrum in our next*) to give the lines
in the speeches of Ulysses and Achilles, which appear to
me to have the character of quotation.

In the first place I beg leave to premise, that the whole
of the scene which takes place in the tent of Achilles, is
remarkably free from interpolation, and exempt from those
absurdities and incongruities, which are in general so conveniently accounted for as *Nutations* of the great Bard.
The application therefore of tests drawn from nature, and
the truth of character, is admissible for the detection of
the few interpolations which are evidently inconsistent with
the intention of the Author ; an intention which, from the
general integrity of the context, is sufficiently manifest.
The speech of Ulysses may be considered as a kind of
model, exhibiting the utmost degree of artifice and address,
which is consistent with perfect manliness of character.
It was not the intention of the Poet to represent Ulysses as
descending from the heroic elevation of mind, which belonged to him in common with Ajax and Diomede ; but as
combining with it a degree of prudence and management
which was peculiar to himself. Accordingly, if we ex-
punge that single line of silly and premature importunity,

the general tone of Ulysses' speech will run thus ; " You must excuse us, if we do not partake of the banquet which you have set before us ; but the dangers and difficulties which we are exposed to at this moment, leave us neither leisure nor inclination to enjoy ourselves." He then describes these dangers, taking care at the same time to make Hector the prominent figure; but disguising this artifice by a general air of desperate unconcern. He then adds, " But if it was originally your intention to reserve yourself for the last extremity, and to interfere ultimately to prevent your countrymen from being overwhelmed and trampled down by the uproar of these Trojans, remember the old lines—

> *Repentance and Regret will wring your mind ;*
> *Succour delay'd arrives but to deplore*
> *The ills accomplish'd, while it lagg'd behind :*
> *Give aid in time of need, or long before.*

If you · ever entertained any such designs, it is become necessary for you to interfere for the preservation of the Greeks."

The lines of the original will then stand thus : (Il. I. 247.)

'Αλλ' ἄνα, εἰ μέμονάς γε, καὶ ὀψέ περ, υἷας 'Αχαιῶν
Τειρομένους ἐρύεσθαι ὑπὸ Τρώων ὀρυμαγδοῦ·

| " Αὐτῷ τοι | μετόπισθ'. | ἄχος | ἔσσεται | οὐδέ | τι μῆχος |
| " Ῥεχθέντος | κακοῦ ἔστ' | ἄκος | εὑρεῖν | ἀλλὰ | πολὺ πρίν. |

Φράζευ, ὅπως Δαναοῖσιν ἀλεξήσεις κακὸν ἦμαρ.

The lines which are marked as a quotation, are inserted parenthetically, as is commonly the case with quotations introduced in rapid and earnest discourse ; and the word φράζευ follows in the same construction which would belong to it, if the parenthetical passage were omitted. If we connect φράζευ with the preceding words πολὺ πρίν, the result gives a sense inconsistent with the character of the speaker, and offensive to the temper of the person whom he is addressing: the tone becomes that of an impertinent assumption of a general right to admonish and advise. It is moreover in direct contradiction to the whole of Ulysses' argument ; for if Achilles still had it in his power to interpose *long before* the apprehended catastrophe, it is obvious, that the danger could not be so imminent or immediate as it had been represented.

The construction which is here conceived to be the correct one, is that by which Ulysses, after appealing simply
to the supposed intentions of Achilles, instead of impor-
tuning him on his own behalf, or on the part of those who
had sent him, alleges as a general maxim two proverbial
lines upon the mortification and disappointment attendant
upon the delay of an intended benefit, and applies them to
the case in point.   He does not venture in his own person
to threaten Achilles with the future visitations of remorse.
After this reference to Achilles' supposed intentions, he
proceeds to cite the opinion which of all others (next to
those proceeding from his own mind) Achilles was the most
likely to listen to with complacency, that of his father
Peleus, and the advice which he had given him at parting:
upon the authority of this advice, he ventures to add,

'Ὡς ἐπέτελλ' ὁ γέρων· σὺ δὲ λήθεαι· ἀλλ' ἔτι καὶ νῦν
Παῦε, ἔα δὲ χόλον θυμαλγία· σοὶ δ' Ἀγαμέμνων .
Ἄξια δῶρα δίδωσι, &c.   (Il. I. 259.)

It is not till the conclusion that Ulysses descends, and
for a single line only, to direct supplication: (v. 301.)

———— σὺ δ' ἄλλους περ Παναχαιοὺς
Τειρομένους ἐλέαιρε κατὰ στρατὸν, οἵ σε, θεὸν ὡς,
Τίσουσ'· ————

while at the same time he ventures more openly to stimu-
late him by a prospect of the glory which he might derive
from the destruction of Hector; an artifice which Achilles
is represented as detecting and resenting in his reply.

Upon the whole it may be safely assumed, I believe, as
a general principle, that men are disposed to qualify whatever may appear importunate to their hearers, or be felt
as in any degree degrading to themselves, by the allega-
tion of some general maxim.   The proverb, *Bis dat qui
cito dat* is one of perpetual recurrence in petitions, as the
most decent form of urgent application; and Ulysses' supposed quotation is only a more prolix proverb to the same
effect.

The quotation (for such I conceive it to be) in the speech
of Achilles, is to be found in the lines in which he rejects
the offer of Agamemnon's daughter.

The insolent humour of Lauzun was never more strongly

characterized, than when, upon the death of Mademoiselle, his mistress and supposed or intended wife, he took occasion to express his concern or unconcern in two lines of an **old tune** :

> Elle est morte, la vache au panier,
> Elle est morte, il n'en faut plus parler.

I conceive that Achilles was represented as expressing his refusal **with a** similar sublimity of impertinence : **v. 388.**

> Κούρην δ' οὐ γαμέω Ἀγαμέμνονος Ἀτρείδαο·
> Οὐδ' εἰ χρυσείη | Ἀφροδίτη | κάλλος ἐρίζοι,
> Ἔργα δ' Ἀθηναίη | γλαυκώπιδι | ἰσοφαρίζοι,
> Οὐδέ μιν ὡς γαμέω· | ὁ δ' Ἀχαιῶν | ἄλλον ἑλέσθω.

If we conceive these **lines** to be **a** quotation from some **more ancient and** Hexametrical Archilochus, we shall **see that he was** either restricted to, or occasionally **indulged in,** Rhyme at the Cæsura and the termination.

If I may be allowed to appeal to **a very poor** authority, **but to** a very impartial one (for it was **my own,** some **time** before the idea of a quotation had occurred to me) these lines as they are generally understood, and as I then understood them, are destitute of that spirit of mocking and insolence, which marks the rest of Achilles' speech in those passages which have **a** personal reference to Agamemnon.

Accordingly, **in an** attempt[1] to translate **some** lines of it **into what I** conceived **to** be **a** style **of** language corresponding **to the character of** the original, the supposed **defect in this passage was** disguised, by making Achilles **mention Agamemnon's daughters in** the plural :

> "His girls may equal Venus in their bloom,
> And Pallas in the labours of the loom,
> Adorn'd with graces and with charms **divine ;**
> But never shall he **see** them wives of mine :
> Some suitable alliance let him seek,
> **Some** other nobler, more distinguish'd Greek."

Before I conclude, I will not **omit** an odd coincidence upon the subject of rhyme : **in** a passage in the story of

---

[1] This "attempt," which was to translate from line 308 to line **487** of this Book of the Iliad, will be found at length later on in this volume.

I *

Meleager above-mentioned, where a common place is
mentioned as common place, and of course as a poetical
common place, a strong rhyme occurs at the Cæsura ; v.
587.

$$
\text{——— καί οἱ κατέλεξεν ἅπαντα}
$$
Κήὃε', ὅσ' ἀνθρώποισι πέλει, τῶν ἄστυ ἀλψ́η·
῎Ανὃρας μὲν κτείνουσι ———
Τέκνα ὃέ τ' ἄλλοι ἄγουσι ———

· Believe me,
My dear Sir,
Very sincerely yours,
J. H. FRERE.

REVIEW OF MITCHELL'S ARISTOPHANES.[1]

From the " Quarterly Review," vol. 23, *p.* 474.

SOME of our readers may be disposed to think
that the subject of the Aristophanic comedy
has of late occupied a sufficient space in our
pages : we must, however, persevere, and insist like Falstaff—" Play on the play.   We
have much to say in behalf of that same Aristophanes."
With respect to the present translation, it may truly be
said to be much the best that has hitherto appeared in our
own, or, as far as our acquaintance extends, in any other
modern language.   It may even be said, with truth, that
to an English reader, the first perusal of this translation
may afford as much pleasure as the perusal of the original
is calculated to give to a proficient in the Greek language,
who undertakes, for the first time, to read a play of
Aristophanes in the original.   Those, however, who have
indulged in a continued study of the original, and
(prompted by the perpetual development of new and

---

[1] *The Comedies of Aristophanes.* By T. Mitchell, A. M., late
Fellow of Sidney-Sussex College, Cambridge.   Vol. I.   London,
1820.

unobserved beauties in the change and play of style, and
in the brief and pointed expression of comic character),
have become entirely familiar with the author, will continue to derive a pleasure from repeated reperusals of the
original, such as we cannot venture to promise **to the**
English scholar, if he should be induced to recur, for **a**
second or third time, to the work now before us. We shall,
however, before **we conclude,** have **the** satisfaction of
pointing out some passages which, **like those of the original, fix themselves (the** great test of excellence) involun-
tarily in the memory, and which may be recalled to it
and repeated with undiminished gratification. The **main
cause of the** defect alluded to, and of the disappointment
which will be experienced by those who are best acquainted
with the original, if they expect to find the various forms
of language, and the phrases expressive of character, represented in a satisfactory manner by English equivalents,
is **to be** attributed to the adoption of a particular style;
the style of our ancient comedy in the beginning of the
17th century. We shall proceed to give the reasons which
lead us to consider this style as peculiarly proper for the
purposes to which our own early dramatic poets applied it;
and which, at the same **time, and** for the same reasons, if
they are just ones, must **render it** wholly unsuitable for
representing **or** reproducing that peculiar species of drama
to which the comedies of Aristophanes belong.

   The **early** comedy of modern Europe, that **of the** first
half **of the 17th** century, is **a** fancy **portrait of** the society
of the **time. The** pleasure which it afforded was similar to
that which **we** experience when we contemplate a picture,
in which the resemblance of a countenance familiar to us
is expressed with **that** addition of harmony and grace
which embellish the resemblance, without much detracting
from its truth. Such was the character and principle of
the dramas of Calderon and his contemporaries ; and, before him, of Lope ; and of Fletcher, Shirley, and others,
amongst ourselves. In all these, dignity of character is
uniformly maintained—the cavaliers **are represented as**
daring and generous, delicate and faithful to excess : the
highest tone of sentiment is kept up : the tone of the language also, (which is more to our purpose,) is proportionably **elevated** above the common parlance of those times.

Hence, as in tragedy (and for the same reasons), the
appearance of truth and nature in the whole composition
is preserved by the easy and probable arrangement of
events, quarrels, jealousies, discoveries, and sudden turns
of fortune, which constitute what is called the plot. The
excellence of these comedies, and the merit of the author,
were estimated, in great measure, from the construction of
the plot ; for as by the rules which belong to that species
of drama, the language and characters were idealized, and,
therefore, to a certain degree, removed from reality and
experience, the admission of this improbability would require to be compensated by a greater apparent probability
in the only part which remained, viz. the action and events.[1]

But the ancient Aristophanic comedy proceeded upon a
principle of compensation totally different. In this species
of composition, the utter extravagance and impossibility of
the supposed action is an indispensable requisite ; the
portion of truth and reality, which is admitted as a counterpoise, consists wholly in the character and language.
It is a grave, humorous, impossible, GREAT LIE, related
with an accurate mimicry of the language and manner of
the persons introduced, and great exactness of circumstance in the inferior details. In its simpler state, it
appears to be one of the commonest and most spontaneous

---

[1] In what we have said on this subject, we have followed the
course by which we are persuaded that the authors we have mentioned arrived at the conclusions which guided their practice ; but
for mere illustration it would be equally obvious to invert the statement, and to say that where the incidents are probable, the language
and sentiments must be elevated above ordinary nature, and in this
order it would seem that the inferior tribe of dramatists have, in
general, proceeded, taking probability of character and incident as
their basis, and endeavouring to ennoble it by displays of style and
sentiment. The result of the direct and of the inverted process may
be exemplified in the Electras of Sophocles and Euripides ; in the
first, the display of character is evidently the principal object ; the
probability of the story is artfully elaborated ; but we see that it was
a secondary consideration. In Euripides, on the contrary, probability is evidently the primary object, while the characters are left
to display themselves as circumstances may permit. We have taken
our illustration of the two opposite processes from tragedy, because,
in fact, this system of counterpoise, in which the probability of the
story is placed as a weight in one of the scales, belongs equally to
tragedy and to the higher species of comedy.

products of the human mind ; and usually arises in some
strong expression, which, a moment after, is taken literally,
converted into a reality, and invested with all the circumstances of action and dialogue. We shall show that the
plays now before us, the Acharnæ and the Knights (or
Demagogues), are capable of being traced to the kind of
conversation, out of which, in all probability, they did
originate.

There are other plays, which appear to have grown up
from mere sport, when, in a playful conversation, fancied
events are developed into an imaginary detail.

If we were possessed of the Boswells of antiquity, who
are cited by Athenæus, we might, perhaps, find some
notices which would illustrate the history of the comic stage ;
but for want of them, let us suppose an ancient prototype
of our entertaining countryman, giving an account of the
origin and first suggestion of the Thesmophoriazousæ.

After supper Philonides, meaning to rouse Aristophanes, who
had been cracking his nuts without much attending to the conversation, began to talk about Euripides, and, turning to Aristophanes,
asked him—what he thought of his last tragedy?

Arist. " Why, it has his usual faults and his usual merits, only I
think he's more than usually severe upon the women."

Phil. " He's worse than ever—why, he'll drive them to despera-
tion—yes, they will be driven to some desperate measure against
him—we have had so many plots and conspiracies of late, the
women will take the hint—we shall have a conspiracy of the women
against Euripides."

Arist. " Well, now is their time—they have three days to themselves at the Thesmophoria—considering how the art of plotting
is improved, there is time enough to form a very promising conspiracy."

Phil. " Upon my word, I begin to suspect that there must be
something of the kind in agitation—I almost think it would be right
to speak to some friend of Euripides to desire him to be upon his
guard.—But what would he do, do you think, upon the first
alarm?"

M. or *N. (across the table)*. " Why, I suppose he would consult
with that fine rough-handed fellow his father-in-law Mnesilochus."

Arist. " No, he would not consult him ; he would only tell him
to keep himself in readiness to receive his orders."

Phil. " But what would be the first thing he would do?"

Arist. " The first thing, of course, would be to compose one of
his long apological harangues, according to all the established
rules of rhetoric, and in direct opposition to decorum and common
sense."

Phil. " But after all, this harangue must be delivered among the

assembled females—how is he to contrive that?—The women are
so exasperated against him, none of them would be persuaded to
appear as his advocate."

M. or *N.* (*as before*). "Might not Agathon, the poet, go amongst
them in disguise, with that smooth face of his?"

Arist. "Oh no, Agathon would take care of himself, depend
upon it; he will never get himself into a scrape for anybody."

Phil. "Well then, it must be old Mnesilochus himself,—Euripides
must shave him and dress him up for the purpose. But what will
become of him when he is detected?"

Arist. "Then, of course, Euripides must exert himself, and employ
his whole system of tragical devices for his escape."

Phil. (*after a pause*). "Well, now, Aristophanes, I can't help
thinking, if all that we have been saying was put together, and
worked up in your way, it would turn out a very tolerable comedy."

Arist. "Why perhaps it might, as good as some of mine are;
and better than some others; and better than other people's."

Phil. "Then perhaps you will think of it, if nothing better should
occur, as a subject in time for the next festival?"

Arist. "Why perhaps I may."

For the sake of those who may not have read it, or who
do not immediately recollect it, it may be necessary to
state that this supposed dialogue comprehends all the
material incidents of the comedy.

The origin of the Acharnæ is simpler. Let us suppose
an honest warm-tempered man obliged, (as many were at the
time,) like Dicæopolis in this play, to abandon his landed
property to destruction, and to take refuge in the town—
we may suppose that he would be likely to express his
feelings nearly in this way:—

"If our great politicians, and your leading people here in Athens,
choose to waste the public treasure in embassies and expeditions,
that is their own affair; but I do not see what right they have to
bring down a Peloponnesian army to drive me out of my farm—
there's no quarrel that we country-people ever had with them to my
knowledge—we should all be glad enough to let-alone for let-alone
—for my part, if these enemies of ours (as they call them) would
allow me to live on my farm, and buy and sell as I used to do, I'd
give 'em up all the money I'm worth, and thank 'em into the bargain—and I'd go there to-morrow:—but as for our Statesmen, I'm
persuaded if a Deity were to come down from Heaven, on purpose
to propose a Peace to them, they would never listen to him."

We have here a natural and passionate form of expression,
which, uttered in the hearing of a poet such as Aristophanes,
was sufficient to suggest the plot of the Acharnæ and the
scene of the Demigod Amphitheus; the rest of the play,

with all its wild and fanciful circumstances, being, in fact, nothing more than a whimsical exemplification of the first supposition; namely, that a private citizen **had succeeded in** concluding and maintaining a separate peace.

With respect to the play of the Knights (or Demagogues), the very conversation out of which it originated is to be traced in the passage from line **125 to** 144 of the original. The **conversation turned upon** "**the** degradation of **the** democracy **since the death of Pericles,** whose successors in administration **had been a lintseller,** Eucrates, **a** sheepseller, **Lysicles, and a leatherseller, Cleon,** ($\sigma\tau\upsilon\pi\pi\epsilon\iota o\pi\dot{\omega}\lambda\eta\varsigma$ —$\pi\rho o\beta a\tau o\pi\dot{\omega}\lambda\eta\varsigma$—$\beta\upsilon\rho\sigma o\pi\dot{\omega}\lambda\eta\varsigma$,) who had **superseded each** each **other in a** rapid succession." Then some speculation **arose as to what** branch of trade was likely to furnish the leading statesmen to whom the destinies of the state were **to be next** entrusted, when (in reference to the **occupation** of one Hyperbolus, whose rising **impudence and rascality** appeared to mark him out for popular eminence) **it was** said, "Depend upon it, it will be a lampseller—$\lambda\upsilon\chi\nu o\pi\dot{\omega}\lambda\eta\varsigma$ $\tau\iota\varsigma$ $\ddot{\eta}$ $\lambda a\mu\pi a\delta o\pi\dot{\omega}\lambda\eta\varsigma$;—to which the **answer was** M$\dot{a}$ $\Delta\dot{\iota}a\cdot$ $\dot{a}\lambda\lambda'$ $\dot{a}\lambda\lambda a\nu\tau o\pi\dot{\omega}\lambda\eta\varsigma$—"Depend upon **it, we** cannot expect to stop short in the downfall of all decency and dignity— the lowest occupation will have the best chance—we shall have a sausage-seller." The **particular** occupation " a sausage-seller" would be suggested **by** something of a **similarity in** the sound of **the words in Greek.**

We have here the whole action of the play, which supposes **a sausage-seller** to succeed in supplanting Cleon, and to **assume the** administration in his place : the perso**nification of the** Athenian democracy is an invention of the **highest poetical and moral** merit ; but **it would seem to have been secondary in** point of time, and to have been **adopted as one of the** means of arriving at the predetermined **result.** We think that the **primary** idea, from which the **whole** organization of the **play was** evolved, must have **existed** in a conversation **somewhat similar** to that which **we have** supposed.

We have been somewhat **diffuse in our illustration of the mode** of Invention which belongs **to** this species of Comedy, **because it** has in general been regarded as utterly extravagant and **unaccountable** ; at least by all those who have considered **it in reference to the** established rules of dra-

matic composition and invention ; we shall now resume,
briefly, but with a more comprehensive view, the subject
with which we set out, and from which we have so long
digressed.

The object of the poetic and dramatic art is to instruct
without offence ; to give men hints of their faults and errors,
sufficiently strong to enable them, each for himself, to
make the personal application to his own case, but so, that
neither the author nor the actor shall appear in the character of an accuser, or even of a monitor, which, among
equals, is always odious.[1] In order to effect this, truth
must be mixed up with some ingredients of unreality ;
either the persons must be obviously fictitious, as in fable,
or the events must be impossible, as in the Aristophanic
comedy ; or supposing the events to be combined with
probability, the language and sentiments must be removed
from the reality of ordinary life, as is the case in tragedy,
and (to a certain degree) in our own old regular comedy of
the seventeenth century, the comedy of Jonson and Fletcher.
Thus, absolute Reality is to be avoided as too directly
offensive ; but absolute Unreality is equally objectionable,
it is vague, feeble, and applies to nothing. The two opposites must be combined. Where the events are coherent
and possible, the language must be ideal—where the fiction
is wild and extravagant, its extravagance must be compensated by a reality in the language. In Shakespeare's play
of the Tempest, we perceive a tendency to a fault arising
out of a neglect of this rule, and the correction which his
great judgment applied to it ; the impossibility of the
events, combined with the ideality of the language and
characters, begin to give a character of vagueness and
vacuity to the scene, till the strong infusion of vulgar reality

---

[1] This is the true medium, and whenever the Drama professes to
do more (like most extravagant professors) it commonly betrays its
trust.—Comedy at once moral and probable, is found, generally
speaking, to be nothing more than a formal sententious sycophant,
inveighing against vices and errors which are no longer in vogue ;
and celebrating exclusively those virtues which are most nearly
allied to the prevailing follies and disorders of the time. It is the
morality of the *Hermite de la Chaussée d'Antin*, which (as a friend
observed) is precisely that of a grave, sober, discreet, obliging, grey-
headed keeper of a bagnio.

in the character of Trinculo, and his speculations on the profit which might be made in London by exhibiting his friend Caliban, restore the equilibrium at once, and place the spectator in that due medium between truth and false-hood which the laws of composition require.

In Aristophanes it may be observed that in those parts of his plays in which the circumstances are the most out-rageously impossible, the truth and reality of the dialogue are the most studiously laboured. It is then that he de-lights to exhibit the little unavowed struggle for ascendancy, with its alternate triumphs, efforts and defeats, and, above all, the pride of local information by which the new-comer, whether at the mansion of Jupiter or of Pluto, is kept at arms-length and obliged to bow to the superior knowledge and importance of the established resident. But as all the plays of Aristophanes involve more or less the assumption of some impossibility, so throughout, the perfect reality of the dialogue, both in the little artifices of conversation, and in the forms and turns of expression, is maintained ; we might say, uniformly ; but that occasionally, passages are interspersed, consisting either of burlesque of particular passages in the tragic writers, or of the tragic style in general. Now as these passages are perfectly distinguish-able in the original, they ought undoubtedly to be at least recognizable in the translation ; and here we think, that the choice which Mr. Mitchell has made, of a style borrowed from our early comedies, has subjected him to particular disadvantages : the tone of his general style having been pitched too high, and partaking of an artificial character, it becomes impossible almost, to mark, by any corre-sponding change, those transitions, by which the original passes from natural into artificial language. Hence, in the dialogue between Dicæopolis and Euripides, and in the harangue of the former, the variation and play of style, passing perpetually from the natural to the burlesque, and, in the scene between Demosthenes and the Sausage-seller, the strong declamatory language of the one, and the vulgar interruptions of the other, are represented in the transla-tion by the same uniform and artificial language. It is not too much to say that if Ben Jonson himself, who was certainly a mighty master both of learning and humour, had attempted a translation of Aristophanes, in the same style which he has employed in his own comedies, the very nature of the attempt would have made it impossible for him to produce an adequate representation of the original. But Jonson would have possessed many advantages, which cannot belong to a modern who undertakes to perform the same task in language imitated from him. The language of Jonson, though not purely natural, was at least founded upon, and immediately deduced from nature; it was not an imitation of daily speech, but was conformable to it, and never lost sight of it as a test by which the proper employment of words, and the natural combination of them, was to be determined. Hence, though we are sensible that the language is neither simple nor natural, we are never shocked by anomalous or discordant arrangements of words; the aberration is confined within a certain limit—a limit which was traced out to the author by that usage—

"Quem penes arbitrium est et jus et norma loquendi."

But the author, who attempts to write in the language of times that are past, has no such guide; he has no resource beyond his books, and if they fail him or mislead him, he is in perpetual danger of committing offences against the propriety of language. In a work of so much merit and labour, we should be unwilling to quote particular passages for reprobation; but there are many in which the English idiom is so strained, that a reader to whose recollection the original is not immediately present, would be led to conclude, that the harshness of the translation must have arisen from a verbal adherence to the idiom of the original; and he is surprised, on turning to it, to find that the phrase which he has condemned is given as the English equivalent for an idiom of a different construction. But even if the style and language of our own old comedies were suited to represent the character of the ancient Aristophanic comedy; which from the essential differences subsisting between the two genera, we think, that it is *not ;*—and even supposing that ancient style to be perfectly imitated, we should still feel an objection, arising from the very perfection of the imitation; as it would have a constant tendency to destroy that illusion which it is the object of the translator to create: the translation might be admirable, but the reader would be constantly reminded, that he was reading an admirable translation—he would never be allowed to lose himself in the thoughts and images, and forget for a moment the language in which they were conveyed to him.

The language of translation ought, we think, as far as possible, to be a pure, impalpable and invisible element, the medium of thought and feeling, and nothing more ; it ought never to attract attention to itself; hence all phrases that are remarkable in themselves, either as old or new ; all importations from foreign languages, and quotations, are as far as possible to be avoided. This may appear somewhat too strict to some of our readers ; but we are persuaded that Mr. Mitchell himself is too well acquainted with the principles of translation, not to be aware, upon reflection, that such phrases as he has sometimes admitted, " *solus cum solo,*" for instance, "*petits pâtés,*" &c., have the immediate effect of reminding the reader that he is reading a translation, and that the illusion of originality, which the spirited or natural turn of a sentence immediately preceding might have excited, is instantly dissipated by it.

We think that licences of this kind have in themselves a character of petulance and flippancy—that they are wholly unworthy of the judgment and good taste which Mr. Mitchell has in general shown :—they belong more properly to that class of translators who are denominated *Spirited Translators*, whose spirit and ability consist in substituting a modern variety or peculiarity for an ancient one, to the utter confusion of all unity of time, place, and character ; leaving the mind of the reader bewildered as in a masquerade, crowded and confused with ancient and modern costumes. Of this class of translators, and of their ancient and inveterate antagonists, the *Faithful Translators*, we should wish to say something, because we think that it may tend to illustrate the principle of translation generally.—The proper domain of the Translator is, we conceive, to be found in that vast mass of feeling, passion, interest, action and habit which is common to mankind in all countries and in all ages ; and which, in all languages, is invested with its appropriate forms of expression, capable of representing it in all its infinite varieties, in all the permanent distinctions of age, profession, and temperament, which have remained immutable, and of which the identity is to be traced almost in every page of the author before us.

Nothing can be more convincing or more deeply astonishing than the result which must remain upon the mind of every man who has read the remains of Aristophanes with the attention which they deserve. It is evident that every shade of the human character, and the very mode in which each is manifested, remain the same ; not a genus or a species is become extinct ; many even which might naturally have been considered as mere accidental varieties, are still preserved, or have been reproduced.

The original author who is addressing his contemporaries must of course make use of phrases according to their conventional import ; he will likewise, for the sake of immediate effect, convey his general observations in the form of local or even personal allusion. It is the office, we presume, of the Translator to represent the forms of language according to the intention with which they are employed ; he will therefore in his translation make use of the phrases in his own language, to which habit and custom have assigned a similar conventional import, taking care, however, to avoid those, which, from their form or any other circumstances, are connected with associations exclusively belonging to modern manners ; he will likewise, if he is capable of executing his task upon a philosophic principle, endeavour to resolve the personal and local allusions into the genera, of which the local or personal variety employed by the original author is merely the accidental type ; and to reproduce them in one of those permanent forms which are connected with the universal and immutable habits of mankind. The Faithful Translator will not venture to take liberties of this kind ; he *renders* into English all the conversational phrases according to their grammatical and logical form, without any reference to the current usage which had affixed to them an arbitrary sense, and appropriated them to a particular and definite purpose. He retains scrupulously all the local and personal peculiarities, and in the most rapid and transient allusions thinks it his duty to arrest the attention of the reader with a tedious explanatory note. The Spirited Translator, on the contrary, employs the corresponding modern phrases ; but he is apt to imagine that a peculiar liveliness and vivacity

may be imparted to his performance, by the employment
of such phrases as are particularly connected with modern
manners; and if at any time he feels more than usually
anxious to avoid the appearance of pedantry, he thinks he
cannot escape from it in any way more effectually, than
by adopting the slang and jargon of the day. The peculiarities of ancient times he endeavours to represent, by
substituting in their place the peculiarities of his own time
and nation.

But after all that we have said, an instance in the two
opposite styles will perhaps make our meaning more intelligible: Bacchus is interposing to calm the controversy
between Æschylus and Euripides, which is rising into violence on both sides, and he represents to them—

$$\lambda o \iota \delta o \rho \varepsilon \tilde{\iota} \sigma \vartheta a \iota \; \delta' \; o \dot{\upsilon} \; \pi \rho \dot{\varepsilon} \pi \varepsilon \iota$$
$$"\mathrm{A} \nu \delta \rho a \varsigma \; \pi o \iota \eta \tau \dot{a} \varsigma \; \ddot{\omega} \sigma \pi \varepsilon \rho \; \dot{a} \rho \tau o \pi \dot{\omega} \lambda \iota \delta a \varsigma.$$

literally—

" It ill beseems
Illustrious bards to scold like bakers' wives. "

And, so, accordingly, the literal and Faithful Translator will
render it, with the addition of a note, in which he makes it
clear, by the testimony of various learned authorities, that
the bakers' wives in Athens were addicted to scolding above
their fellows. Not so the Spirited Translator; he looks
for a modern peculiarity to countervail the ancient, and
puts boldly, " to scold like oyster wenches."

But he, the lawful and true Translator, such as we con-
ceive him—$\tau \dot{o} \nu \; \phi \rho \dot{o} \nu \iota \mu o \nu \; \ddot{a} \nu \delta \rho a \; \tau \dot{o} \nu \; \dot{\upsilon} \pi \dot{\varepsilon} \rho \sigma o \phi o \nu$—proceeding
upon the philosophic principle before mentioned, and re-
volving in his mind those characteristics, which (from the
necessary order of sublunary things) must inseparably adhere to the practice of inferior traffic in a place of open
competition; and more especially where the articles exposed for sale are in themselves of a perishable and transitory nature; he will infer *a priori*, that among the ven-
dors of such commodities, so circumstanced, a spirit of
objurgatory altercation must of necessity prevail; the
authority of antiquity, the concurring reports of enlightened
and veracious travellers, the testimony of his own ears, in
passing through the various Agorai of our own metropolis,
will satisfy him, that the conclusion to which he before

arrived by induction, is a just one ; and that the race of Market Scolds are a permanent and imperishable species. Emboldened by this discovery, he proceeds to resolve the variety into the species, and ventures to translate ἀρτοπώλι-δας "hucksters" or "market-women," as may happen to suit the verse ; and though the passage so rendered be neither brilliant nor spirited, nor literally faithful, he is satisfied, that by avoiding both the ancient and the modern peculiarity, he does not, (during the perusal of one line at least,) oblige his reader to recollect, that the work which he has before him is a mere translation.

But in order to convey more perfectly our own idea of what we should consider as an adequate translation, we will suppose an imaginary case :—An ancient manuscript containing one of the plays of Aristophanes, hitherto supposed to have been lost, falls by some accident into the hands of a person capable of translating it upon the principle which we should consider as the true one. He translates accordingly, and publishes his translation ; but determines for a time to keep the original to himself. The learned readers of such a translation, when they had finished their perusal, might be able to infer, from the total absence of any of those peculiarities, unintelligible to an English reader, which belong to antiquity, but which are no wise characteristic of it, which distract the attention without affording employment for the imagination—they would infer, we say, from the total absence of all these types of authenticity, that the translation could not have been executed in strict and literal conformity to the text of the supposed manuscript. But if on the other hand, the tone and character of antiquity, and the general spirit of the original author, should have been so perfectly maintained throughout, as to make it impossible to fix upon any one passage, of which it could confidently be said, "that it was a deviation from the original," or if in so fixing upon a particular passage, the learned before-mentioned should happen to be wrong ; we should conceive in such a case, that the translator had in no degree transgressed the limits of that licence, which is fairly allowable to him ; that he had fulfilled at least one important condition, in preserving the unity and propriety of costume ; and that he ought in justice to be exempt from that condemnation, to which the race of spirited translators, before-mentioned, are, we think, deservedly consigned.

We shall now return to a part of our **subject of which** we had almost lost sight. The principle of generalization will be found, we imagine, to be more or less applicable to translation, in proportion as the mind of the original author may be found to have proceeded habitually upon the same principles. Shakespeare appears at the first glance to be an author, beyond **all others,** encumbered and beset with accidental peculiarities, **(the** peculiarities of his **own** age and nation,) **and** might accordingly **be** considered as incapable of being properly translated ; but a deeper insight into his **works** discovers a spirit of generalization, in which **the** local **and peculiar** allusions served but as types and **abstracts of universal** and permanent forms : hence we **should see** no reason why a mind capable of truly com**prehending** him, and possessing **a practical** command **of** any modern language, might not succeed (as the Germans **are** said to have done) in producing an adequate **translation of** his works. The same remark will apply to **Aristo**phanes ; the impossibility of producing a good **translation** of him has been so long repeated, that it has come **at last to** be admitted as an established **critical** dogma : he is, in**deed,** like Shakespeare, (and even **in a** much greater de**gree,)** encumbered with local **and** individual allusions, and might from that difficulty alone, **if it were an** insuperable **one, be abandoned at once as** untranslateable ; but the greater **portion of his works has** evidently been conceived in a deep **and** comprehensive spirit of generalization : if therefore **we suppose a** competent portion of dexterity in **the management of** any modern language, to be super**added to a** thorough comprehension of the original ; we, **for our** parts, **are** unable to see why an adequate transla**tion,** of such parts at least of **the** original as have been composed upon these principles, may not by possibility be produced ; the talent and attainments requisite are not of the highest order, and if we add to these a natural feeling of taste, and **a** disposition to execute the task, with the degree of perfection of which it is capable, it should seem that little else would be requisite.

We have ventured to say, that Aristophanes composed **for** the most **part** upon principles of generalization ; and,

we repeat it. His representation is, indeed, a caricature
of the Genus; but still it is Generic. Lamachus, for instance, in the play before us (the Acharnians), is not the
individual *Lamachus;* he is as pure an abstract as his
opponent Dicæopolis; the one proud, haughty, courteous,
romantic, adventurous, and imaginative ; the other shrewd,
calculating, peaceful and sensual, humble or saucy, as circumstances may require or permit : they are the permanent contrasts of human nature, and like their parallels,
Don Quixote and Sancho, belong equally to all nations and
times.

The pretensions and airs of the Envoys returned from
two Courts of a different description, are not accidental
but permanent traits. If we substitute the Court of the
Czar Peter and that of Louis XIV. for Thrace and Persia,
we shall see that the Envoy returned from the one, would
be disposed to boast of his familiarity with the barbarous
Autocrat, the rude conviviality in which they had lived
together, and the sincerity and heartiness of his royal
friend's politics ; while the other, in an affected tone of
complaint, would detail the intolerable excess of luxury
and magnificence and accommodation, which had been ob-
truded upon him, at Versailles and the voyage de Marly.

The two Country People who are introduced as attending
Dicæopolis's market, are not merely a Megarian and a
Theban, distinguished by a difference of dialect and behaviour ; they are the two extremes of rustic character—the
one (the Megarian) depressed by indigence into meanness, is shifting and selfish, with habits of coarse fraud and
vulgar jocularity. The caricature, to be sure, is extravagant ; but it is a caricature of the Genus.—The Theban is
the direct opposite—a primitive, hearty, frank, unsuspicious,
easy-minded fellow ; he comes to market with his followers,
in a kind of old-fashioned rustic triumph, with his bag-
pipers attending him: Dicæopolis (the Athenian, the medium
between the two extremes before described) immediately
exhibits his superior refinement, by suppressing their min-
strelsy ; and the honest Theban, instead of being offended,
joins in condemning them. He then displays his wares,
and the Athenian, with a burlesque tragical rant, takes one
of his best articles (a Copaic eel) and delivers it to his own
attendants to be conveyed within doors. The Theban, with

great simplicity, asks how he is to be paid for it, and the Athenian, in a tone of grave superiority, but with some awkwardness, informs him that he claims it, as a toll due to the market. The Theban does not remonstrate, but after some conversation agrees to dispose of all his wares, and to take other goods in return ; but here a difficulty arises, for the same articles which the Athenian proposes in exchange, happen to be equally abundant in Bœotia ; the scene here passes into burlesque, but it is a burlesque expressive of the character which is assigned to the Theban ; a character of primitive simplicity, utterly unacquainted with all the pests by which existence was poisoned in the corrupt community of Athens. A common Sycophant or Informer is proposed as an article which the Athenian soil produced in great abundance, but which would be considered as a rarity in Bœotia. The Theban agrees to the exchange, saying, that if he could get such an animal to take home, he thinks he could make a handsome profit by exhibiting him. A noted informer (Nicarchus by name) immediately appears ; the Theban replies to his first inquiry with the utmost simplicity, and the informer in return denounces his merchandize as enemies' property. Upon this the Athenian proceeds to execute his bargain by seizing him, and (with the assistance of his attendants) tying him round with cords like an oil jar ; this operation is performed in cadence to a lively song of no great meaning (not much unlike that of Nancy Dawson), after which he is properly adjusted as a burden on the back of the Theban's attendants, who departs with his purchase.

As this scene has been omitted by Mr. Mitchell, we shall insert an attempt which has been made to translate it, on the principles which have been recommended above.

" SCENE.—DICÆOPOLIS, *the Athenian, in his new Market-place, which (by virtue of a private Treaty) he has opened to the Citizens of those States which were at war with Athens.—Enter a* THEBAN *with his Attendants all bearing Burdens, and followed by a Train of Bag-pipers.*

Theban. Good troth, I'm right-down shoulder-gall'd ; my Lad, Set down your bundles—You—take care o' the herbs, Gently—be sure don't bruise 'em, and now You Minstrels That needs must follow us all the way from Thebes, Blow wind i' the tail of your Bag-pipes—Puff away.
Dicæ. Get out !—what wind has brought 'em here, I wonder ?— .

I*   O

A parcel of Hornets buzzing about the door !
You humble-bumble drones—Get out—Get out—
  Theb. As Iolaus shall help me ; that's well done,
Friend, and I thank you ;—coming out of Thebes
They blew me away the blossoms from all these herbs—
You've served 'em right—So now, would you please to buy
What likes you best of all my Chaffer here,
All kinds, four-footed things and feather'd fowl.
  Dica.[1] My little tight Bœotian ! Welcome kindly
My little pudding-eater ! What have you brought ?
  Theb. In a manner, every thing, as a body may say,
All the good cheer of Thebes and the primest wares,
Mats, trefoil, wicks for lamps, sweet marjoram,
Coots, didappers, and water-hens—What not ?
Widgeon and teal.
  Dica. Why you're come here amongst us
Like a northwind in Winter, with your wild fowl.
  Theb. Moreover I've brought geese, and hares moreover,
And Eels from the lake Copais which is more.
  Dica. O thou bestower of the best of spitchcocks
That ever yet was given to mortal man,
Permit me to salute those charming Eels.
  Theb. (*addressing the Eel, and delivering it to Dicæopolis*).—
Daughter, come forth and greet the courteous stranger
First-born of Fifty Damsels of the Lake.
  Dica. O long regretted and recover'd late,
Welcome ; thrice welcome to the comic quire,
Welcome to me, to Morychus and all ;
—(Ye slaves, prepare the chafing-dish and stove.)
Children, behold her here, the best of Eels,
The loveliest and the best, at length return'd
After six years of absence ! I myself
Will furnish you with charcoal for her sake.
Salute her with respect, and wait upon
Her entrance there within, with due conveyance :
            [*The Eel is here carried off by Dicæopolis's servants.*
—Grant me, ye Gods ! so to possess thee still,
While my life lasts, and at my latest hour,
Fresh even and sweet as now—with...Savory Sauce.[2]

---

  [1] Dicæopolis is made to practise the common trick of ascendancy ;
taking no notice of the new comer for some time, and then recognizing him suddenly with a kind of hearty jolly condescension.
  [2] The conclusion in broader burlesque is expressed in the original
by the word ἰντιτιυτλανωμίνης. Aristophanes gives it to shew the
rhythm suited to the conclusion of such a passage, and to mark more
strongly the defect of the line in Euripides, from which it is paro-
died, ending with three words, each of them a separate Iambic
foot, τῆς μόνης πιστῆς ἰμοί. The burlesque word has the true
tender faltering cadence—μηδὶ γὰρ θανών ποτε Σοῦ χωρίς εἴην
ἰντιτιυτλανωμίνης.

Theb. But how am I to be paid for it? Won't you tell me?
Dicæ. Why with respect to this Eel, in the present instance,
I mean to take it as a perquisite,
As a kind of toll to the market, you understand me—
—These other things—I suppose you mean to sell them?
Theb. Yes sure—I sell 'em all.
Dicæ. Well, what do you ask?
Or would you take commodities in exchange?
Theb. Ay; think of something of your country produce
That's plentiful Down Here, and scarce Up There.
Dicæ. Well you shall take our Pilchards or our Pottery.
Theb. Pilchards and Pottery!—Naw! we've plenty of they—
But think of something, as I said before,
That's plentiful Down Here, and scarce Up There—
Dicæ. (*after a moment's reflection*).
I have it!—A true-bred Sycophant, an Informer—
I'll give you one, tied neatly and corded up,
Like an oil-jar.
Theb. Ay; that's fair; by the Holy Twins!
He'd bring in money, I warrant; money enough,
Amongst our folks at home, with shewing him,
Like a mischief-full kind of a foreign Ape.
Dicæ. Well, there's Nicarchus bustling on this way,
Laying his Informations—There he comes.
Theb. (*contemplating him with the eye of a purchaser*).
'A seems but a small one to look at.
Dicæ. Ay, but I promise ye,
He's full of tricks and roguery, every inch of him.

Enter NICARCHUS.

Nic. (*in the pert peremptory tone of his profession as an Informer*).
Whose goods are these? these articles?
Theb. Mine sure;
We be come here from Thebes.
Nic. Then I denounce them
As enemies' property—
Theb. (*with an immediate outcry*). Why, what harm have they done,
The birds and creatures?—Why do you quarrel with 'em?
Nic. And I'll denounce you too.
Theb. What, me? What for?
Nic. To satisfy the bystanders I'll explain—
You've brought in Wicks for Lamps, from an enemy's country.
Dicæ. (*ironically*). And so, you bring 'em to *light*?
Nic. I bring to light
A plot!—a plot to burn the arsenal!
Dicæ. (*ironically*). With the Wick of Lamp?
Nic. Undoubtedly—
Dicæ. In what way?
Nic. (*with great gravity*). A Bœotian might be capable of fixing it
On the back of a Cockroach, who might float with it
Into the Arsenal, with a north-east wind,

And if once the fire caught hold of a single vessel,
The whole would be in a blaze !
   Dicæ. (*seizing hold of him*).   You Dog—You Villain,
Would a Cockroach burn the Ships and the Arsenal ?
  Nic. Bear witness, all of ye.
   Dicæ.   There stop his mouth ;
And bring me a band of straw to bind him up,
And send him safely away for fear of breaking,
Gently and steadily, like a potter's jar.

    Chor.   To preserve him safe and sound,
         You must have him fairly bound,
         With a cordage nicely wound
         Up and down and round and round ;
                      Se-curely pack'd.
    Dicæ.   I shall have a special care,
         For he's a piece of paltry ware,
         And as you strike him Here—or There—(*Striking him.*)
         The noises he returns declare—(*The Informer screaming.*)
                   He's partly crack'd.
    Chor.   How then is he fit for use ?
    Dicæ.   As a store-jar of abuse,
         Fit to slander and traduce,
         Plots and lies he cooks and brews,
                  Or any thing.
    Chor.   Have you stow'd him safe enough ?
    Dicæ.   Never fear, he's hearty stuff,
         Fit for usage hard and rough,
         Fit to beat and fit to cuff,
                To toss and fling.

   (*The Informer, being by this time reduced to a Chrysalis state, by
    successive involutions of cordage, is flung about and hung up
    and down in illustration and confirmation of Dicæopolis's
    warranty of him.*)

         You can hang him up or down,
         By the heels or by the crown.
    Theb.   I'm for harvest business bown.
    Chor.   Fare ye well, my jolly clown,
                We wish ye joy.
         You've a purchase tight and neat,
         A rogue, a sycophant complete —
         Fit to bang about and beat,
         Fit to bear the cold and heat—
             And all employ.

  Dicæ. I'd a hard job with the rascal tying him up !
—Come, my Bœotian, take away your bargain.
   Theb. (*speaking to one of his servants*). Ismenias, stoop your back,
    and hoist him up,
Gently and steadily—So—now carry him off—
   Dicæ. He's an unlucky commodity ; notwithstanding,
If he earns you a profit, you can have to say

What few can say—' you've been a gainer by him
And better'd your affairs by an informer.' "—[1]

Having endeavoured to explain as well as we could,
what we conceive to be the principles applicable to a translation of Aristophanes, and having moreover exemplified
them to the best of our ability, we find it still necessary
to take notice of one point which, for the sake of those
readers who may be disposed to compare our version with
the original, may be, perhaps, more conveniently discussed
after a perusal of the translation. The principles which
we before stated will account for the omission of all local
peculiarities, which, however interesting as matters of
curiosity to the antiquary, would, if inserted in a translation, have no other effect than that of distracting the
attention, or diverting it from the broad general expression of character and humour which is evidently the primary object of the poet; but it may, perhaps, be thought,
that in one or two instances we have taken an unwarrantable liberty in expanding the text of the original. Our
defence must be that the text of the original is not *the
original*—it is the *text* of the original and nothing more :
it contains the original always *potentialiter*, but not
always *actualiter*. The true actual Original, which the ancient dramatic poets had in view, and upon the success of
which their hopes of applause and popularity were founded,
consisted of the entire Performance, as exhibited, and in
the dialogue as represented by Actors trained and disci-
plined under the immediate direction of the Author himself ; a sentence, therefore, of three words, or even a single
word, if pronounced with the tone and gesture appropriated
to it by the author, would in many, we may say in most
cases, convey an expression, which would not belong to
the same words barely printed or written, and presenting
themselves, without any accompaniment, to the mere eye
of the reader : wherever, therefore, in such cases, the tone
and intended expression of the original can be ascertained
or fairly inferred, we conceive that the translator (if he
considers it as a part of his office to convey to the modern
reader the sense and intention of his author) must of
necessity expand his sentences into a dimension capable

---

[1] The above is from Mr. Frere's own translation, then in manuscript (see vol. ii. p. 45-49).

of bearing a distinct and intelligible impress of character.
The original Author made use of a sort of comic short-
hand; which was explained to the Actor, and through his
medium was rendered intelligible, and even obvious to the
audience: but the translator has no such intermediate
agent at his command; words are his only instrument—
words, in the form of dull, naked, uniform letter-press;
he must, therefore, make use of them as well as he can,
and he must make use of more of them, if he wishes to
give his readers a tolerably easy chance of comprehending
the conception which he has formed of the original design
of the author whom he professes to reproduce.

In considering the mode in which Aristophanes should
be translated, there is one point of more than literary importance, which we must not overlook. As we would not
consent to expel Swift from the shelves of an English
library, so, with respect to mere grossness, vulgarity and
nastiness, in a translation of Aristophanes, an occasional
spice of each, sparingly applied, (more sparingly a great
deal than in the literary banquet of the Dean,) may be
necessary to give a notion of the genuine flavour of the
original.—Mere physical impurity has not changed its
nature, and the ancients and the moderns do not in this
respect materially differ from each other—not more, perhaps, than the higher and lower classes in the same society.
Aristophanes, it must be recollected, was often under the
necessity of addressing himself exclusively to the lower
class. But the σοφοὶ and the δεξιοὶ, the persons of taste
and judgment, to whom the author occasionally appeals,
form, in modern times, the tribunal to which his translator
must address himself; the utmost which they can be expected to endure may, perhaps, be estimated by the degree of grossness which they tolerate as characteristic,
in the vulgar (which are not altogether the worst) comedies of Molière; and within this limit we should think that
a translator of Aristophanes would do well to confine himself. But with respect to moral impurity the case is
widely different; the distance between the modern Christian
world and Heathen antiquity is immense, and the retrench-
ment must be absolute; for this reason, at least, if for no
other—that the impression is not the same, and consequently can no longer correspond with the intention of the
Author.

We would not willingly particularize instances of this kind; but it would not be difficult to point out lines of extreme grossness, which have evidently been inserted, for the purpose of pacifying the vulgar part of the audience, during passages in which their anger or impatience, or disappointment, was likely to break out : they are evidently forced compromises on the part of the author; breaking in upon the unity of that true comic humour which he was directing to the more refined and intelligent part of his audience. When considered in connexion with the context, and in relation to what is called the business of the stage, it is probable that they were delivered (parenthetically as it were) with some peculiar broadness of gesture and tone, sufficient to separate them from that genuine vein of comic humour, which the more intelligent auditors might still be able to follow, in spite of a burlesque interruption, as a Spanish·audience follow up the interest of a serious dialogue, without finding their attention disturbed by the buffooneries and by-play of the Gracioso. In discarding such passages, therefore, the translator is merely doing that for his author, which he would willingly have done for himself. It is only in the opening scenes of his plays that material chasms would occur, for, as the poet found it necessary (like the orator) to begin "by captivating the benevolence of his auditory," these popular and conciliatory efforts are occasionally accompanied by a most profuse largesse of filth and trash.

It is now time for us to proceed to the examination of the manner in which Mr. Mitchell has executed his work. We do not mean to follow him through the Preliminary Discourse, which occupies his first hundred pages ; indeed, we could only do so, for the purpose of amplification and illustration. He seems to have formed, and he has communicated in a very perspicuous style, a just estimate of the genius, the character, and the patriotic intention of his author, and he has swept away with great vigour, the heaps of calumnious rubbish, which have been accumulating against him for so many centuries.

We will now begin at the beginning. We do not see why the phrase in the fifth line of the original should not have been translated agreeably to Brunck's interpretation. Mr. Mitchell has himself translated τῇ πόλει γὰρ ἄξιον (v. 205) agreeably to the sense which is always implied by

the word ἄξιος when followed by a dative case ; " what is
necessary for," " advantageous to," though he has at the
same time with great good taste preserved the tinge of
associated meaning, derived from its more general use,
and which is always found to adhere to a word when
employed in a sense remote from its habitual meaning.

τῇ πόλει γὰρ ἄξιον.
" It concerns her pride and honour that our town his motions know."

In this instance the strict grammatical import of the
word ἄξιος,[1] and the associated impression connected with
it, are very happily reconciled. We think that in v. 3 the
same combination might have been effected with the same
felicity, and that at any rate the real and strict sense
of the passage ought at least to be discoverable in the
translation. In the next line, it appears as if the translator had not perceived the humour of the original, and
the double sense in which the word τραγῳδικὸν " (tragical) " is employed. We will endeavour to make it more
palpable by re-arranging and concentrating the passage.
Dicæopolis says, " I met with a *tragical* misfortune lately,
for I went to the theatre expecting to hear a *tragedy* of
Æschylus's ; and when I got there, they were going to act
a new *tragedy* of Theognis's. Now that is what I call
altogether quite a *tragical* disappointment."

In verses 17 and 18 of the original, the translator (if we
understand rightly the sense of his note) seems to be of
opinion, that the humour of the passage consists in the
want of connexion between the proposition and its antecedent ; but Dicæopolis is not, we conceive, *complaining of
the dust*, either in jest or earnest. The whole passage
appears to be a metaphor, drawn from one of *the Miseries
of Human Life* in Athens, when persons bathing, and
sprinkled with an alkaline powder in the bath, had the
misfortune to get it into their eyes : children (whose skins
did not require the same process) were exempt from this
inconvenience, hence he says ἐξ ὅτου. On turning to

---

[1] The real meaning of the word is *what is called for*. We are
inclined to believe with Mr. Whiter, that there is no Greek verb
which may not be followed through its various significations by a
radical form in our own language ; ἀξιόω, the verb, though apparently derived from the adjective, retains the primary sense, and
signifies to *ask*, or, as we find it in old language, to *axe*.

Brunck's interpretation we find this sense recognized in the word *lixivium*—we again turn to the translator's note; but neither in the note nor the translation can we discover anything which explains the metaphor; or which even implies that the passage is altogether a metaphorical one. It is possible, that this may be a fault of misexplanation, rather than of misconception; but in either case, the result of embarrassment and disappointment to the reader remains the same. It is, after all, one of those many expressions which are best represented by an equivalent.

We do not mean to pursue this minute species of remark any further; we might have objected to the translation of the word παρέκυψε, as if expressing a continued attitude instead of a momentary action; but taking the line—

"That fellow, Chæris, stooping, Sirs, and slouching,"

as an amplification, sufficiently in harmony with the intention of the author, and characteristic of the appearance of a person performing on such an instrument, we are unwilling to object to it, though we wish that the strict sense (which we conceive to be that of unexpected and inopportune "appearance"), had been preserved at the same time. We should, however, leave our readers under a false impression of the merits of this translation, if they should infer that defects similar to those which we have noticed, occur in the same proportion in other parts of the work; it is unfortunate that they should present themselves in the first pages, and we therefore suggest them for reconsideration in a future edition—ἀρχομένου δ' ἔργου πρόσωπον χρὴ θέμεν τηλαυγές.

We shall take our leave of the long soliloquy upon which we have hitherto animadverted, by inserting the concluding lines, which (" excepting as before excepted") appear to us to be very happily translated.

" For my part, Sirs, sure as the morning comes,
So sure am I the first at the assembly.
Solus cum solo there I take my seat;
And first I groan a little,—then I yawn
A little,—stretch a little,—hawk a little :—
Then comes a fit of vapours,—then I fall
To tracing figures in the sand, or pluck
An idle hair or so, or puzzle me
In sums and items of Arithmetic;
While ever and anon I cast an eye

> Upon the blooming fields, and breathe a prayer
> Of earnestness for peace.   As for the town,—
> Fogs and east winds light on't !—I lack of nothing
> But my snug country-box and pleasant acres.
> No talk from them of buying coals and oil
> And vinegar ; *buy! buy!* thank heaven the word's
> Unknown to them, they yield their produce all
> For nothing, they : nor ever stoop to twit me
> With that cursed *by-word, buy.*   Here then come I—
> Hands, feet and lungs prepared ; and if a word
> Our orators let fall, save what pertains
> To peace, I'll raise a storm of words, and rain
> A very tempest of abuse upon them !"—pp. 17—19.

We may appear, perhaps, too minute in our criticism, but the words "snug country-box" do not quite satisfy us.   A "snug country-box" conveys the idea of a place of occasional retirement for a person whose occupation and resources are fixed in a neighbouring city ; it implies no connexion with agriculture as a means of subsistence to the occupant. But Dicæopolis is lamenting the loss of his entire livelihood, his farm, not the mere convenience of a villa ; a single word ill chosen is often sufficient, as in the present instance, to impair materially the breadth and harmony of a beautiful passage.[1]

We select with pleasure, and without any drawback of criticism, a Semi-Chorus characteristic of the patriotic inveteracy and vehemence of the Old Acharnians, in pursuit of poor Dicæopolis, who has been detected in concluding a separate peace.

> " Toil and search are in vain,
> He is gone—fled amain.
> Now shame to my age,
> And to life's parting stage.
> Other tale it had been,
> When my years were yet green,
> And my youth in her pride
> Followed fast at the side
> Of Phayllus the racer!
> A fleet-going pacer,
> Though coals a full sack
> Press'd hard at my back.

---

[1] The first origin of a phrase will always continue to mark its character.   A citizen becomes the proprietor of a villa ; he does not choose that his opulence should be estimated by the scale of his new purchase ; he therefore applies a disqualifying term to it—"a mere box,"—" my box in the country."

> Then had not this maker
> Of peace, and a breaker
> With his best friends, I ween,
> Long space put between
> His country's undoer
> And me his pursuer,
> Nor should we thus part
> For a leap and a start."—pp. 38, 39.

Dicæopolis, after an altercation in long trochaics, some of which are most admirably translated, " makes a voluntary proposal : a block is to be brought forward, and if he cannot justify himself for having entered into this separate treaty of peace with the enemies of his country, his head is to pay the forfeit of his indiscretion. Such is the homeliness of humour with which the countrymen of Pericles and Plato were to be cheated into their proper interests."

We think that in the concluding observation the translator gives up the cause of his client rather too easily. We have little doubt that this incident is a mere burlesque of a rhetorical scene, in one of the many tragedies of Euripides of which we know nothing, in which the preparations for execution were made on the stage, and in the presence of the hero who was to harangue for his life.

In Dicæopolis's harangue which follows, the sense of the word ἐνασπιδώσομαι seems to have escaped Brunck and the present translator ; the former interprets it " *clypeo me non muniam hercle ;*" the true version would have been " *intra clypeum non me continebo:*" the metaphor is taken from a military phrase, expressing the behaviour of a cowardly soldier, who is contented with lying snug behind his own shield, without venturing to expose himself by attacking the enemy in return. This interpretation agrees perfectly with the context, the tenor of which implies that the future harangue is intended to be accusatory rather than exculpatory.

The prefatory discourse terminates to Dicæopolis's advantage ; he obtains permission to prepare for his defence, by equipping himself in a pathetical costume, which is to be borrowed from Euripides. His interview with Euripides follows ; but the translation represents it to great disadvantage. It appears as if Dicæopolis, in applying to Euripides for assistance, began by wantonly affronting him ; whereas the original expresses only the impertinence

which involuntarily escapes from a man in an excess of
eagerness and hurry. We shall attempt to make our
meaning more intelligible by a loose imitation. " Oh dear!
Euripides, what, you're there, are you? You're writing
your tragedies up stairs? You write them there always?
Always upstairs in the garret, hah! You prefer it to the
ground floor? Well, now, is it not You? an't you the Man
that makes those tragedies with the cripples and the lame
characters? Ah, if you had but a suit of tatters, belonging
to one of your old tragedies, that you would lend me, to
make me look pathetic! You're the poet, an't you, that
makes the tragedies with the beggars in them?"

The interview which Dicæopolis enters upon thus blun-
deringly and abruptly, terminates to his satisfaction; he
procures a complete tragical equipment, and returns to
make his defence. At the close the Chorus are divided in
opinion; they form themselves into a double Semi-Chorus,
and commence a scuffle. When *Lamachus* arrives, he (of
course, as a soldier) takes part against Dicæopolis, and a
personal struggle (which is marked in the original, v. 590)
takes place between them. Lamachus's military assault
is baffled by some knack in wrestling, characteristic of his
rustic opponent; and they proceed to dispute, in a tone
which implies an ascendancy on the part of Dicæopolis;
his arguments are directed to captivate the favour of the
Chorus, composed (as their names indicate) of the charcoal-
burners of Acharnæ—Prinides, Marilades, &c. He addresses them in the lowest style of popular rhetoric.

" Why should not they be employed in Commands and Embassies?—They are old enough; they are steady, honest, industrious
men—why should Lamachus, and the other showy expensive young
fellows monopolize all the salaried offices and employments?"

Lamachus is worked up to a fury by this discourse, and
departs. But why (it may be asked) should Aristophanes
have put topics of such extravagant low democracy into
the mouth of his principal character?—We cannot help
thinking that in this passage there is a spirit of deep and
bitter irony;—we will suppose *Lamachus* himself, the individual *Lamachus*, to have asked the question of the author.

" *L.* Well, Aristophanes, I have not seen you, I think, since your
last comedy.—You have made very good fun of me; but there is

nothing I ought to take amiss—nothing degrading in it, as far as I
am concerned.

A. I am glad you think so—it is not very easy to hit that precise
point—it cost me some trouble, I assure you.

L. But why should you make your friend Dicæopolis talk such
low vulgar trash to the Chorus; as if men without birth or education
were as well fitted for public employment as persons of my sort?
We have had a good education, at least, and are used to live in a
liberal society :—it seems so contrary to your principles, that I am
at a loss to comprehend your drift.

. *A.* Then I will tell you ; it is precisely the men of your sort (the
young rising promising set) that have brought us into our present
difficulties.—Pericles was employing the public resources splendidly
and usefully—embellishing the city ; giving occupation to a multitude of the poorer class ; creating future resources for us; and (as he
thought) strengthening his own interest, by the patronage attached
to this peaceful harmless sort of expenditure. But he and his administration were grown old ;—a new generation had sprung up, who
thought themselves active enough and clever enough, to begin
fingering the public money. They could not endure that the whole
· public expenditure should pass directly from Pericles's hands, to be
distributed among mere architects and artists and mechanics. The
young rising political and military geniuses (precisely the men of
your sort) felt it as a kind of contempt that he should presume to
govern without their participation or assistance. His scheme of
policy was deficient in point of office and salary for persons of their
description. They began, therefore, by attacking the system ;
Phidias was accused and ruined, and he himself was threatened with
opposition at the approaching audit of his accounts ; finally, he was
driven to a compromise, and was obliged to make war, in order to
have the means of stopping your mouths with appointments and
commissions.—I have seen all this ; and now, I see you (the very
same young gentlemen) extremely indignant at finding yourselves
occasionally hustled and jostled and ousted in your contests for
office, by the very individual ragamuffins who were your agents
among the populace at the time when you succeeded in raising an
uproar against Pericles. Now, for my own part, I feel quite incapable of sympathising with those exalted and indignant sentiments;
I prefer you, (no doubt), to your new rivals ; but whenever they
happen to get the better of you, I console myself with the reflection,
that your present mortifications are the results of your own measures
—that you have, in fact, nothing to complain of, except that you are
deprived (perhaps with some mortifying circumstances) of the fruits
of your own unjustifiable policy.—And lastly ; that after all, the
remedy is in your own hands ; if you will unite yourselves to make a
peace, your own salaries, and this offensive rivalry on the part of
your inferiors, will cease together at once, and so I think Dicæopolis
has told you " (v. 619).

We shall now close our account of the Acharnæ ; but
we shall first extract a burlesque lyrical passage which
appears to us perfectly well translated.

" O, for a muse of fire,
Of true Acharnian breed !
A muse that might some strain inspire,
Brightness, tone and voice supplying,
Like sparks which, when our fish are frying,
The windy breath of bellows raise
From forth the sturdy holm-oak's blaze :
What time our cravings to supply,
Some sift the meal and some the Thasian mixture try."—

p. 90.

We do not mean to enter so much at length into the examination of the Knights (or Demagogues, as they are more properly called). We shall content ourselves with noticing a few oversights not peculiar to the present translator. In the first scene, there is a manifest tone of drunkenness in Demosthenes's part, it is the caricaturist's mark by which he indicates that the figure on the stage is meant to represent Demosthenes—timidity and superstition, in like manner, serve to mark out Nicias—just as, in the caricatures of fifty years ago, a fox's tail projecting between the flaps of a full dressed coat, supplied the defective resemblance of a young orator. The poet follows the rule of association, which is more suited to burlesque than the law of cause and effect. Demosthenes is represented drinking on the stage, but the tone of drunkenness begins as soon as he begins to talk about drinking—

" The verse too stammers and the line is drunk."

Ὁρᾷς . . . ὅταν πίνουσιν ἄνθρωποι . . . τότε . . .

observe, too, the similar endings in the following lines perfectly suited to express the pronunciation of a drunken man.

According to the same rule, the poet, before he leaves the stage has no scruple in representing him as sober and even eloquent.—It is usual with Aristophanes, in the first instance, to mark the person ; and afterwards to modify him. Thus Don Quixote, in the first chapters, is a mere madman ; towards the conclusion he is modified, and becomes a vehicle for communicating many of the author's own sentiments and opinions. We shall now extract some lines of the attack upon Cleon, which appear to be admirably well translated.

" Where's the officer at audit but has felt your cursed gripe ?
Squeezed and tried with nice discernment, whether yet the wretch
be ripe.

Like the men our figs who gather, you are skilful to discern,
Which is green and which is ripe, and which is just upon the turn.
Is there one well-pursed among us, lamb-like both in heart and life,
Link'd and wedded to retirement, hating business, hating strife?
Soon your greedy eye's upon him—when his mind is least at home,—
Room and place—from farthest Thrace, at your bidding he must come.
Foot and hand are straight upon him—neck and shoulder in your grip,
To the ground anon he's thrown, and you smite him on the hip."

pp. 185, 186.

In the passage which follows, "*old* deeds of valour" is a most unlucky epithet. The party opposed to Cleon had been lately much strengthened in popularity and influence by the result of the expedition to Corinth. Cleon was aware of it—and (as it appears by this passage) had been truckling to them and began talking about "his intention of proposing a proposal for a plan for erecting a monument in memory of the event." In the last two lines of the original there is a studied vagueness of expression.

In verse 327, ὁ δ' Ἱπποδάμου λείβεται θεώμενος, Brunck translates *liquitur lacrimis*, and the present translator has adopted the same sense. We would rather follow the scholiast, who thinks that a slap is given to Hippodamus, by the bye—the phrase should seem equivalent to τάκεται ὀφθαλμούς, not as expressing *sorrow*, but *envious longing*.[1] —At line 450, the translator observes—

" If the reader should think that the abuse of this pair has reached its climax, he has yet to learn the perseverance and extent of Grecian invective—the two rivals compass half the circle of Grecian science for terms of reproach, before they conclude ;—the builder's art, the powers of the nail and the hammer, the glue-pot, the carpenter's yard, the art of running and casting metal, the crafts of the founder, the brazier, the cheesemonger, and the currier, all furnish terms which render their sarcasms more poignant, and alternately turn the tide of victory."—p. 199.

This, we think, is an imperfect view of the subject ; in the passage, the omission of which is supplied by this observation, it is evidently the object of the poet to mark a departure from the ancient decorum of public oratory, by an affectation of employing metaphors derived from the mechanical arts.—A similar style of affected homeliness has

---

[1] " Hence you squeeze and drain alone the rich milch kine of our allies,
While the son of Hippodamus licks his lips with longing eyes."
[See vol. ii. p. 87.]

occasionally been in fashion in parliamentary speaking, and would furnish sufficient equivalents for a translation.

But an example is more satisfactory, and commonly more concise, than an explanation. We shall endeavour to give the passage according to our notion of the poet's intention.

CLEON says,—

> " By the Holy Goddess, it's not new to me,
> This scheme of yours—I've known the job long since,
> The measurement and the scantling of it all,
> And where it was shaped out and tack'd together.
>
> [*The* CHORUS *are alarmed at this new vein of popular metaphor,
> and encourage their advocate to do his best in the same style.*
>
> *Ch.* Ah, there it is !—you must exert yourself,
> Come, try to match him again with a carpenter's phrase.
> *Sausage-seller.* Does he think I have not track'd him in his
>   intrigues
> At Argos? his pretence to make a treaty
> With the people there, and his clandestine meetings
> With the Spartans? Then he works and blows the coals,
> And has plenty of other irons in the fire.
> *Chorus.* Well done ! the blacksmith beats the carpenter." [1]

The contest in this instance is no longer a mere reciprocation of abuse and menace ; it is an imitation of public oratory as infected and debased by vulgar jargon. What follows is in the same style, and is still more evidently an imitation of the accusatory and menacing style of the orators at that time, when actually speaking before the people. We should suspect that the Sausage-seller's style was copied from " *Hyperbolus's vein.*"

But our readers, if they have followed us thus far, will be glad to turn to a very beautiful specimen of Mr. Mitchell's translation, in which the higher and more austere lyrical poetry is imitated with a slight infusion of burlesque.

> " Lord of the Waters ! king of might,
> Whose eyes and ears take stern delight
> From neighing steeds and stormy fight
>   And galley swift pursuing ;
>
> From starting car and chariot gay,
> And contests on that festive day,
> When Athens' sprightly youth display
>   Their pride and their—undoing ;
> Lord of the dolphins and the spear—
> Geræstian—Sunian—or more dear,

---

[1] This again is from Mr. Frere's own version (see vol. ii. p. 95).

> If Cronus' name salute thy ear,
>   And Phormion's gallant daring;
>
> O come amongst us in thy power,
> Great Neptune; in her trying hour
> Athens knows none so swift to shower
>   Aids of immortal bearing."—pp. 209, 210.

In p. 213 (v. 595 of the original) the translator justly controverts the opinion of Casaubon as to the intention of the poet in this burlesque description of the expedition to Corinth. The truth seems to be that neither compliment nor censure was intended. Aristophanes was the poetical advocate of his party; it was his business to serve them by bringing their merits to the recollection of his audience, and he thought that this might be done more effectually and less invidiously in the fanciful style of humour which he has here adopted. His statement of the political character and merits of his clients was given distinctly in the Epirrema; here in the Antepirrema, it is enforced by example, but extravagantly and whimsically; in the first place, to avoid tediousness and uniformity; and secondly, from the consideration (manifest in the concluding lines of the Epirrema), that the party for which he was pleading was particularly obnoxious to popular disgust and envy. It would have been politic in Cleon, as their adversary, to tempt them to acquiesce in an offensive display of their services by a public monument. Their advocate, on the contrary (but from the same considerations), makes his poetic record as humorous and as inoffensive as possible. The Chorus, composed of knights, could hardly have been allowed seriously to celebrate their own exploits.

We shall here insert, as a curious scene in itself, and as a fair specimen of the translation, the Sausage-seller's narrative of his contest with Cleon before the senate, with the chorus of congratulation on his success:—

> " Straight as he went from hence, I clapt all sail
> And follow'd close behind. Within I found him
> Launching his bolts and thunder-driving words,
> Denouncing all the Knights, as traitors, vile
> Conspirators—jags, crags, and masses huge
> Of stone were nothing to the monstrous words
> His foaming mouth heaved up. All these to hear
> Did the grave Council seriously incline;
> They love a tale of scandal to their hearts,

1*   P

And his had been as quick in birth as golden-herb.
Mustard was in their faces, and their brows
With frowns were furrow'd up. I saw the storm,
Mark'd how his words had sunk upon them, taking
Their very senses prisoners:—and, oh !
In knavery's name, thought I,—by all the fools
And scrubs and rogues and scoundrels in the town,—
By that same forum, where my early youth
Received its first instruction, let me gather
True courage now : be oil upon my tongue,
And shameless Impudence direct my speech.
Just as these thoughts pass'd over me, I heard
A sound of thunder pealing on my right—
I mark'd the omen,—grateful, kiss'd the ground—
And pushing briskly thro' the lattice-work—
Raised my voice to its highest pitch, and thus
Began upon them—'Messieurs of the Senate,
I bring good news, and hope your favour for it.
Anchovies, such as since the war began
Ne'er cross'd my eyes for cheapness, do this day
Adorn our markets'—at the words a calm
Came over every face, and all was hush'd—
A crown was voted me upon the spot.
Then I (the thought was of the moment's birth),
Making a mighty secret of it, bade them
Put pots and pans in instant requisition,
And then—one obol loads you with anchovies,
Said I: anon most violent applause,
And clapping hands ensued ; and every face
Grew unto mine, gaping in idiot vacancy.
My Paphlagonian discern'd the humour
O' the time ; and seeing how the members all
Were tickled most with words, thus utter'd him :
' Sirs—Gentlemen—'tis my good will and pleasure,
That for this kindly news we sacrifice
One hundred oxen to our patron-goddess.'
Straight the tide turn'd ; each head within the Senate
Nodded assent and warm good-will to Cleon :
' What ! shall a little bull-flesh gain the day ?'
Thought I within me : then aloud, and shooting
Beyond his mark :—' I double, sirs, this vote,—
Nay more, sirs, should to-morrow's sun see sprats
One hundred to the penny sold, I move
That we make offering of a thousand goats
Unto Diana.'—Every head was raised ;
And all turn'd eyes incontinent on me.
This was a blow he ne'er recover'd : straight
He fell to muttering fooleries and words
Of no account—the chairmen and the officers
Were now upon him.—All meantime was uproar
In th' Assembly—Nought talk'd of but anchovies.—
How fared our statesman ? he with suppliant tones

Begg'd a few moments' pause.—' Rest ye, sirs, rest ye
Awhile—I have a tale will pay the hearing—
A herald is arrived from Sparta, claiming
An audience—he brings terms of peace, and craves
Your leave to utter them before ye.'   ' Peace !'
Cried all, (their voices one,) ' is this a time
To talk of peace ?—out, dotard !   What, the rogues
Have heard the price anchovies bear !—marry—
Our needs, sir, ask not peace.—War, war, for us,
And, chairmen, break the assembly up.'   'Twas done,
Upon their bidding, straight—who might oppose
Such clamour ?—then, what haste and expedition
On every side ! one moment clears the rails !
I the meantime steal privately away
And buy me all the leeks and coriander
In the market—these I straight make largess of,
And gratis give as sauce to dress their fish.
Who may recount the praises infinite
And groom-like courtesies this bounty gain'd me !
In short you see a man, that for one pennyworth
Of coriander vile has purchased him
An entire senate—not a man among them
But is at my behest and does me reverence.

It will readily be imagined that this speech elicits a song of applause
from the delighted CHORUS.

Chorus. Well, my son, hast thou begun, and well hast thou com-
     peted ;
    Rich bliss and gain wilt thou attain, thy mighty task com-
     pleted.
         He, thy rival, shall admire,   ⎫
         Choked with passion, pale with ire, ⎬
         Thy audacity and fire :   ⎭
         He shall own, abash'd, in thee   ⎫
         Power and peerless mastery   ⎬
         In all crafts and tricks that be.   ⎭
         At all points art thou equipt,   ⎫
         Eye and tongue with treachery tipt, ⎬
         Soul and body both are dipt   ⎭
           In deceit and knavery.
    Forward, son of mine, undaunted—complete thy bold be-
     ginning :
    No aid from me shall be delay'd—which may the prize be
     winning."—pp. 217—223.

The passage, from the sixth to the twelfth line of the
Chorus, is, we think, in the true tone which should belong
to the choruses of this extraordinary play.   In the three
first especially,

> " He shall own, abash'd, in thee ⎫
> Power and peerless mastery   ⎬
> In all crafts and tricks that be "-- ⎭

Mr. Mitchell has hit the very key-note of Aristophanes, whose choruses throughout this play are contrived to afford a relief and contrast to the vulgar acrimony of his dialogue; not in their logical and grammatical sense, but in their form and rhythm, and in the selection of the words; which, if heard imperfectly, would appear to belong (as in the present instance) to a grave, or tender, or beautiful subject.

We may except from this general observation the first chorus, ᾿Ω μιαρὲ καὶ βδελυρὲ, as it forms a transition from the eager and vehement part which the chorus has taken just before. This also is translated by Mr. Mitchell with great power and effect.

> " *Cho.* Wretch ! without a parallel—
> Son of thunder—child of hell,—
> Creature of one mighty sense,
> Concentrated impudence !—
> From earth's centre to the sea,
> Nature stinks of that and thee.
>   It stalks at the bar,
>   It lurks at the tolls ;
> In th' Assembly, black war
> And defiance it rolls.
> It speaks to our ears
> In an accent of thunder ;
> It climbs to the spheres
> And rives heaven asunder.
> Athens deafens at the sound in her ears still drumming ;
>   While seated high,
>   You keep an eye
> Upon the tolls, like those who spy
> If tunny-fish be coming."—pp. 188, 189.

Having extracted already the contest between Cleon and his adversary in the senate, we shall subjoin a part of their subsequent altercation before the assembly of the people, personified in the character of Demus.

> " *Cl.* (*to Demus*). For service and zeal I to facts, sir, appeal :
>   say of all that e'er sway'd this proud city,
> Who had ever more skill your snug coffer to fill,
>   undisturb'd by respectance or pity?
> For one and for two I've the rope and the screw,
>   to a third I make soft supplication ;
> And I spurn at all ties, and all laws I despise,
>   so that Demus find gratification.

Saus. Mere smoke this and dust ! Demus, take it on trust,
      that my service and zeal can run faster :
I am he that can steal at the mouth a man's meal,
      and set it before my own master.
Other proofs than of love in this knave's grate and stove,
      noble lord, may your eyes be discerning :
There the coal and the fuel that should warm your own gruel,
      to your slave's ease and comfort are burning.
Nay, since Marathon's day, when thy sword (*to Demus*) paved the way
      to Persia's disgrace and declension,
(That bountiful mint in which bards without stint
      fashion words of six-footed dimension,)
Like a stone or a stock, hast not sat on a rock,
      cold, comfortless, bare and derided :—
While this chief of the land never yet to your hand
      a cushion or seat hath provided ?
But take this (*giving a cushion*) to the ease of your hams and your knees:
      for since Salamis' proud day of story,
With a fleet ruin-hurl'd, they took rank in the world,
      and should seat them in comfort and glory.
  Dem. What vision art thou ! let me read on thy brow,
      what lineage and kindred have won thee !
Thou wert born for my weal, and the impress and seal
      Of Harmodius are surely upon thee.
    Cleon (*mortified*). O feat easy done ! and is Demus thus won
      by diminutive gifts and oblations ?
    Saus. Small my baits I allow, but in size they outgo
      your own little douceurs and donations.
    Cl. (*fiercely*). Small or great be my bait, ne'er my boast I abate,
      but for proof head and shoulders I offer,
That in act and in will to Demus here still
      a love unexampled I proffer.
    Saus. (*dactylics*). You proffer love indeed ! you that have seen him
      bleed ;
      buffing and roughing it years twice four ;
A tub-and-cask tenant,—vulture-lodged—sixth-floor man ;
      batter'd and tatter'd, and bruised and sore !
There was he pent and shent with a most vile intent,
      his milk and honey sweet from him to squeeze ;
Pity none e'er he won, tho' the smoke pinch'd his eyes,
      and his sweet wine it was drawn to the lees.
When Archeptolemus lately brought PEACE to us ;
      who but you (*to* CLEON) scatter'd and scared the virgin,
While your foot rudely placed, where Honour's soul is cased,
      spurn'd at all such as acceptance were urging ?
    Cl. (*fawning*). And, my good sir, the cause ?—Marry that Demus'
      laws
      Greece universal might obey :
Oracles here have I, and they in verity
      bear that this lord of ours must hold sway,
Judging in Arcady, and for his salary,
      earning him easily a five-obol coin.

Let him but wait his fate ; and in meantime his state,
    food and support shall be care of mine."—pp. 230—233.

Upon the whole, the specimens of lyrical execution which
we have given above, will justify us in venturing the opinion
(which Goldsmith's friend suggested to the travelling connoisseur as a safe one in all cases), that " the picture would
have been better, if the painter had taken more pains."
There is evidently a very just comprehension of the intended effect of the original, and a full power of expressing
it, but this power is not uniformly exerted. With respect
to the dialogue, we have already noticed the defects which
are inseparable from an obsolete and unfamiliar language,
and which, in our opinion, would make it impossible for any
talent to produce an adequate representation of Aristophanes
in a style so unsuited to this species of Comedy. This,
however, is an estimate of the work merely as compared
with the original ;—as compared with former translations,
it stands on the highest ground—and even the original does
not, at the first perusal, reveal to the young student so much,
perhaps, as the mere English reader may collect from Mr.
Mitchell's translation. His estimate of the character of his
author, as detailed in the Preliminary Dissertation, is (in
our opinion) perfectly correct and curious, and interesting
in the highest degree. The notes, though we have pointed
out one or two defects, are in general spirited, judicious, and
learned :—and even if we were inclined to attribute to the
translator a degree of poetical merit much inferior to that
which he may justly claim ; we should still consider British
literature as under the highest obligations to him, for an
addition of such a mass of curious, interesting, and instructive matter ; which has hitherto been inaccessible and which
is now laid open to every English reader, to a point beyond
which many professed scholars have not thought it worth
their while to proceed. Since the publication of Mr. Mit-
ford, nothing has appeared, so calculated to convey a true
impression of the character of antiquity, or to efface those
theatrical and pedantic notions, which are become the
source not only of infinite absurdity and distortion of mind
among scholars, but of much practical mischief and error,
in proportion as the blunders of the learned are diffused
among the vulgar.   W.

PROSPECTUS AND SPECIMEN

OF AN INTENDED

National Work,

BY

WILLIAM AND ROBERT WHISTLECRAFT,

OF STOW-MARKET, IN SUFFOLK, HARNESS AND COLLAR-MAKERS,

INTENDED TO COMPRISE

THE MOST INTERESTING PARTICULARS

RELATING TO

King Arthur and his Round Table.

THE following stanzas being for the most part the production of my late brother William Whistlecraft, as composed by him in the year 1813, I have judged (by the advice of my friends) that it would be more suitable to publish them without alteration in any respect, and to which I have adhered strictly, as may be seen by a reference to the thirteenth stanza. This I thought it due to have stated, in consideration of our having proposed the Two Boards for Verse and Prose, which in the present crisis might be stigmatized; but it is well known that the public opinion was more consonant to magnificence and useful encouragement at that time than it has been for the last twelve months, or is likely to be the case again, unless the funds should experience a further advance, together with an improvement in the branches of Customs and Excise. The occasion of their remaining unpublished was in compliance with the advice of friends, though at present, in conformity with the pressure of the times, they have thought it advisable that the following publication should take place, which, if an indulgent public should espouse it, it is intended that it should be followed in due course with a suitable continuation.

.

'VE often wish'd that I could write a book,
  Such as all English people might peruse ;
I never should regret the pains it took,
  That's just the sort of fame that I should
    choose :
To sail about the world like Captain Cook,
  I'd sling a cot up for my favourite Muse,
And we'd take verses out to Demerara,
To New South Wales, and up to Niagara.

II.

Poets consume exciseable commodities,
  They raise the nation's spirit when victorious,
They drive an export trade in whims and oddities,
  Making our commerce and revenue glorious ;
As an industrious and pains-taking body 'tis
  That Poets should be reckon'd meritorious :
And therefore I submissively propose
To erect one Board for Verse and one for Prose.

III.

Princes protecting Sciences and Art
  I've often seen, in copper-plate and print ;
I never saw them elsewhere, for my part,
  And therefore I conclude there's nothing in't ;
But everybody knows the Regent's heart ;
  I trust he won't reject a well-meant hint ;
Each Board to have twelve members, with a seat
To bring them in per ann. five-hundred neat :—

IV.

From Princes I descend to the Nobility :
  In former times all persons of high stations,
Lords, Baronets, and Persons of gentility
  Paid twenty guineas for the dedications :
This practice was attended with utility;
  The patrons lived to future generations,
The poets lived by their industrious earning,—
So men alive and dead could live by Learning.

V.

Then, twenty guineas was a little fortune ;
  Now, we must starve unless the times should mend :
Our poets now-a-days are deem'd importune
  If their addresses are diffusely penn'd ;
Most fashionable authors make a short one
  To their own wife, or child, or private friend,
To show their independence, I suppose ;
And that may do for Gentlemen like those.

VI.

Lastly, the common people I beseech—
  Dear People ! if you think my verses clever,
Preserve with care your noble Parts of speech,
  And take it as a maxim to endeavour
To talk as your good mothers used to teach,
  And then these lines of mine may last for ever ;
And don't confound the language of the nation
With long-tail'd words in *osity* and *ation*.

VII.

I think that Poets (whether Whig or Tory)
  (Whether they go to meeting or to church)
Should study to promote their country's glory
  With patriotic, diligent research ;
That children yet unborn may learn the story,
  With grammars, dictionaries, canes, and birch :
It stands to reason—This was Homer's plan,
And we must do—like him—the best we can.

VIII.

Madoc and Marmion, and many more,
  Are out in print, and most of them have sold;
Perhaps together they may make a score;
  Richard the First has had his story told,
But there were Lords and Princes long before,
  That had behaved themselves like warriors bold;
Among the rest there was the great KING ARTHUR,
What hero's fame was ever carried farther?

IX.

King Arthur, and the Knights of his Round Table,
  Were reckon'd the best King, and bravest Lords,
Of all that flourish'd since the Tower of Babel,
  At least of all that history records;
Therefore I shall endeavour, if I'm able,
  To paint their famous actions by my words:
Heroes exert themselves in hopes of Fame,
And having such a strong decisive claim,

X.

It grieves me much, that Names that were respected
  In former ages, Persons of such mark,
And Countrymen of ours, should lie neglected,
  Just like old portraits lumbering in the dark:
An error such as this should be corrected,
  And if my Muse can strike a single spark,
Why then (as poets say) I'll string my lyre;
And then I'll light a great poetic Fire;

XI.

I'll air them all, and rub down the Round Table,
  And wash the Canvas clean, and scour the Frames,
And put a coat of varnish on the Fable,
  And try to puzzle out the Dates and Names;
Then (as I said before) I'll heave my cable,
  And take a pilot, and drop down the Thames—
—These first eleven stanzas make a Proem,
And now I must sit down and write my Poem.

CANTO I.

I.

BEGINNING (as my Bookseller desires)
    Like an old Minstrel with his gown and
        beard,
" Fair Ladies, gallant Knights, and gentle
        Squires,
" Now the last service from the Board is clear'd,
" And if this noble Company requires,
    " And if amidst your mirth I may be heard,
" Of sundry strange adventures I could tell,
" That oft were told before, but never told so well."

II.

THE GREAT KING ARTHUR made a sumptuous Feast,
    And held his Royal Christmas at Carlisle,
And thither came the Vassals, most and least,
    From every corner of this British Isle ;
And all were entertain'd, both man and beast,
    According to their rank, in proper style ;
The steeds were fed and litter'd in the stable,
The ladies and the knights sat down to table.

III.

The bill of fare (as you may well suppose)
    Was suited to those plentiful old times,
Before our modern luxuries arose,
    With truffles and ragoûts, and various crimes ;
And therefore, from the original in prose
    I shall arrange the catalogue in rhymes :
They served up salmon, venison, and wild boars
By hundreds, and by dozens, and by scores.

IV.

Hogsheads of honey, kilderkins of mustard,
    Muttons, and fatted beeves, and bacon swine ;
Herons and bitterns, peacock, swan and bustard,
    Teal, mailard, pigeons, widgeons, and in fine

Plum-puddings, pancakes, apple-pies and custard :
  And therewithal they drank good Gascon wine,
With mead, and ale, and cider of our own ;
  For porter, punch, and negus were not known.

v.

The noise and uproar of the scullery tribe,
  All pilfering and scrambling in their calling,
Was past all powers of language to describe—
  The din of manful oaths and female squalling :
The sturdy porter, huddling up his bribe,
  And then at random breaking heads and bawling,
Outcries, and cries of order, and contusions,
Made a confusion beyond all confusions ;

VI.

Beggars and vagabonds, blind, lame, and sturdy,
  Minstrels and singers with their various airs,
The pipe, the tabor, and the hurdy-gurdy,
  Jugglers and mountebanks with apes and bears,
Continued from the first day to the third day,
  An uproar like ten thousand Smithfield fairs ;
There were wild beasts and foreign birds and creatures,
And Jews and Foreigners with foreign features.

VII.

All sorts of people there were seen together,
  All sorts of characters, all sorts of dresses ;
The fool with fox's tail and peacock's feather,
  Pilgrims, and penitents, and grave burgesses ;
The country people with their coats of leather,
  Vintners and victuallers with cans and messes ;
Grooms, archers, varlets, falconers and yeomen,
Damsels and waiting-maids, and waiting-women.

VIII.

But the profane, indelicate amours,
  The vulgar, unenlighten'd conversation
Of minstrels, menials, courtezans, and boors,
  (Although appropriate to their meaner station)

Would certainly revolt a taste like yours; '
Therefore I shall omit the calculation
Of all the curses, oaths, and cuts and stabs,
Occasion'd by their dice, and drink, and drabs.

IX.

We must take care in our poetic cruise,
    And never hold a single tack too long;
Therefore my versatile ingenious Muse
    Takes leave of this illiterate, low-bred throng,
Intending to present superior views,
    Which to genteeler company belong,
And show the higher orders of society
Behaving with politeness and propriety.

X.

And certainly they say, for fine behaving
    King Arthur's Court has never had its match;
True point of honour, without pride or braving,
    Strict etiquette for ever on the watch;
Their manners were refined and perfect—saving
    Some modern graces, which they could not catch,
As spitting through the teeth, and driving stages,
Accomplishments reserved for distant ages.

XI.

They look'd a manly, generous generation;
    Beards, shoulders, eyebrows, broad, and square, and
        thick,
Their accents firm and loud in conversation,
    Their eyes and gestures eager, sharp, and quick,
Shew'd them prepared, on proper provocation,
    To give the lie, pull noses, stab and kick;
And for that very reason, it is said,
They were so very courteous and well-bred.

XII.

The ladies look'd of an heroic race—
    At first a general likeness struck your eye,
Tall figures, open features, oval face,
    Large eyes, with ample eye-brows arch'd and high;

Their manners had an odd, peculiar grace,
  Neither repulsive, affable, nor shy,
Majestical, reserved, and somewhat sullen ;
Their dresses partly silk, and partly woollen.

XIII.

In form and figure far above the rest,
  Sir LAUNCELOT was chief of all the train,
In Arthur's Court an ever welcome guest ;
  Britain will never see his like again.
Of all the Knights she ever had, the best,
  Except, perhaps, Lord Wellington in Spain :
I never saw his picture nor his print,
From Morgan's Chronicle I take my hint.

XIV.

For Morgan says (at least as I have heard,
  And as a learned friend of mine assures),
Beside him all that lordly train appear'd
  Like courtly minions, or like common boors,
As if unfit for knightly deeds, and rear'd
  To rustic labours or to loose amours ;
He moved amidst his peers without compare,
So lofty was his stature, look, and air.

XV.

Yet oftentimes his courteous cheer forsook
  His countenance, and then return'd again,
As if some secret recollection shook
  His inward heart with unacknowledged pain ;
And something haggard in his eyes and look
  (More than his years or hardships could explain)
Made him appear, in person and in mind,
Less perfect than what nature had design'd.

XVI.

Of noble presence, but of different mien,
  Alert and lively, voluble and gay,
Sir TRISTRAM at Carlisle was rarely seen,
  But ever was regretted while away ;

1*   Q

With easy mirth, an enemy to spleen,
    His ready converse charm'd the wintry day ;
No tales he told of sieges or of fights,
Of foreign marvels, like the foolish Knights,

XVII.

But with a playful imitative tone
    (That merely seem'd a voucher for the truth)
Recounted strange adventures of his own,
    The chances of his childhood and his youth,
Of churlish Giants he had seen and known,
    Their rustic phrase and courtesies uncouth,
The dwellings, and the diet, and the lives
Of savage Monarchs and their monstrous Wives :

XVIII.

Songs, music, languages, and many a lay
    Asturian or Armoric, Irish, Basque,
His ready memory seized and bore away ;
    And ever when the Ladies chose to ask,
Sir Tristram was prepared to sing and play,
    Not like a minstrel earnest at his task,
But with a sportive, careless, easy style,
As if he seem'd to mock himself the while.

XIX.

His ready wit and rambling education,
    With the congenial influence of his stars,
Had taught him all the arts of conversation,
    All games of skill and stratagems of wars ;
His birth, it seems, by Merlin's calculation,
    Was under Venus, Mercury, and Mars ;
His mind with all their attributes was mixt,
And, like those planets, wandering and unfixt ;

XX.

From realm to realm he ran—and never staid ;
    Kingdoms and crowns he won—and gave away
It seem'd as if his labours were repaid
    By the mere noise and movement of the fray :

No conquests nor acquirements had he made :
  His chief delight was on some festive day
To ride triumphant, prodigal, and proud,
And shower his wealth amidst the shouting crowd :

XXI.

His schemes of war were sudden, unforeseen,
  Inexplicable both to friend and foe ;
It seem'd as if some momentary spleen
  Inspired the project and impell'd the blow ;
And most his fortune and success were seen
  With means the most inadequate and low ;
Most master of himself, and least encumber'd,
When overmatch'd, entangled, and outnumber'd.

XXII.

Strange instruments and engines he contrived
  For sieges, and constructions for defence,
Inventions some of them that have survived,
  Others were deem'd too cumbrous and immense :
Minstrels he loved, and cherish'd while he lived,
  And patronized them both with praise and pence ;
Somewhat more learned than became a Knight,
It was reported he could read and write.

XXIII.

Sir GAWAIN may be painted in a word—
  He was a perfect loyal Cavalier ;
His courteous manners stand upon record,
  A stranger to the very thought of fear.
The proverb says, *As brave as his own sword ;*
  And like his weapon was that worthy Peer,
Of admirable temper, clear and bright,
Polish'd yet keen, though pliant yet upright.

XXIV.

On every point, in earnest or in jest,
  His judgment, and his prudence, and his wit,
Were deem'd the very touchstone and the test
  Of what was proper, graceful, just, and fit ;

A word from him set every thing at rest,
    His short decisions never fail'd to hit ;
His silence, his reserve, his inattention,
Were felt as the severest reprehension :

XXV.

His memory was the magazine and hoard,
    Where claims and grievances, from year to year,
And confidences and complaints were stored,
    From dame and knight, from damsel, boor, and peer
Loved by his friends, and trusted by his Lord,
    A generous courtier, secret and sincere,
Adviser-general to the whole community,
He served his friend, but watch'd his opportunity.

XXVI.

One riddle I could never understand—
    But his success in war was strangely various;
In executing schemes that others plann'd,
    He seem'd a very Cæsar or a Marius ;
Take his own plans, and place him in command,
    Your prospect of success became precarious :
His plans were good, but Launcelot succeeded
And realized them better far than He did.

XXVII.

His discipline was stedfast and austere,
    Unalterably fix'd, but calm and kind ;
Founded on admiration, more than fear,
    It seem'd an emanation from his mind ;
The coarsest natures that approach'd him near
    Grew courteous for the moment and refined ;
Beneath his eye the poorest, weakest wight
Felt full of point-of-honour like a knight.

XXVIII.

In battle he was fearless to a fault,
    The foremost in the thickest of the field ;
His eager valour knew no pause nor halt,
    And the red rampant Lion in his Shield

Scaled Towns and Towers, the foremost in assault,
  With ready succour where the battle reel'd :
At random like a thunderbolt he ran,
And bore down shields, and pikes, and horse, and man.

CANTO II.

I.

'VE finish'd now three hundred lines and more,
    And therefore I begin Canto the Second,
  Just like those wandering ancient Bards of Yore ;
    They never laid a plan, nor ever reckon'd
    What turning they should take the day before ;
  They follow'd where the lovely Muses beckon'd :
The Muses led them up to Mount Parnassus,
And that's the reason that they all surpass us.

II.

The Muses served those Heathens well enough—
  Bold Britons take a Tankard, or a Bottle,
And when the bottle's out, a pinch of snuff,
  And so proceed in spite of Aristotle—
Those Rules of his are dry, dogmatic stuff,
  All life and fire they suffocate and throttle—
And therefore I adopt the mode I mention,
Trusting to native judgment and invention.

III.

This method will, I hope, appear defensible—
  I shall begin by mentioning the Giants,
A race of mortals, brutal and insensible,
  (Postponing the details of the Defiance,
Which came in terms so very reprehensible
  From that barbarian sovereign King Ryence)
Displaying simpler manners, forms, and passions,
Unmix'd by transitory modes and fashions.

IV.

Before the Feast was ended, a Report
    Fill'd every soul with horror and dismay;
Some Ladies, on their journey to the Court,
    Had been surprised, and were convey'd away
By the Aboriginal Giants, to their Fort—
    An unknown Fort—for Government, they say,
Had ascertain'd its actual existence,
But knew not its direction, nor its distance.

V.

A waiting damsel, crooked and mis-shaped,
    Herself the witness of a woful scene,
From which, by miracle, she had escaped,
    Appear'd before the Ladies and the Queen ;
Her figure was funereal, veil'd and craped,
    Her voice convulsed with sobs and sighs between,
That with the sad recital, and the sight,
Revenge and rage inflamed each worthy knight.

VI.

Sir Gawain rose without delay or dallying,
    "Excuse us, madam,—we've no time to waste—"
And at the palace-gate you saw him sallying,
    With other knights, equipp'd and arm'd in haste ;
And there was Tristram making jests, and rallying
    The poor mis-shapen Damsel, whom he placed
Behind him on a pillion, pad, or pannel ;
He took, besides, his falcon and his spaniel.

VII.

But what with horror, and fatigue, and fright,
    Poor soul, she could not recollect the way.
They reach'd the mountains on the second night,
    And wander'd up and down till break of day,
When they discover'd, by the dawning light,
    A lonely glen, where heaps of embers lay ;
They found unleaven'd fragments, scorch'd and toasted,
And the remains of mules and horses roasted.

VIII.

Sir Tristram understood the Giants' courses—
 He felt the embers, but the heat was out—
He stood contemplating the roasted horses,
 And all at once, without suspense or doubt,
His own decided judgment thus enforces—
 "The Giants must be somewhere here about!"
Demonstrating the carcasses, he shows
That they remain'd untouch'd by kites or crows;

IX.

" You see no traces of their sleeping here,
 No heap of leaves or heath, no Giant's nest—
Their usual habitation must be near—
 They feed at sunset and retire to rest—
A moment's search will set the matter clear."
 The fact turn'd out precisely as he guess'd ;
And shortly after, scrambling through a gully,
He verified his own conjecture fully.

X.

He found a Valley, closed on every side,
 Resembling that which Rasselas [1] describes ;
Six miles in length, and half as many wide,
 Where the descendants of the Giant tribes
Lived in their ancient Fortress undescried :
 (Invaders tread upon each other's kibes)
First came the Britons, afterwards the Roman,
Our patrimonial lands belong to no man :

XI.

So Horace said—and so the Giants found,
 Expell'd by fresh invaders in succession ;
But they maintain'd tenaciously the ground
 Of ancient, indefeasible possession,
And robb'd and ransack'd all the country round
 And ventured on this horrible transgression,
Claiming a right reserved to waste and spoil,
As Lords and lawful owners of the soil.

---

[1] Prince of Abyssinia. See his Life, written by himself.

XII.

Huge mountains of immeasurable height
   Encompass'd all the level Valley round,
With mighty slabs of rock, that sloped upright,
   An insurmountable, enormous mound ;
The very River vanish'd out of sight,
   Absorb'd in secret channels under ground :
That Vale was so sequester'd and secluded,
All search for ages past it had eluded.

XIII.

High overhead was many a Cave and Den,
   That with its strange construction seem'd to mock
All thought of how they were contrived, or when—
   —Hewn inward in the huge suspended Rock,
The Tombs and Monuments of mighty men :
   Such were the patriarchs of this ancient stock.
Alas! what pity that the present race
Should be so barbarous, and depraved, and base !

XIV.

For they subsisted (as I said) by pillage,
   And the wild beasts which they pursued and chased :
Nor house, nor herdsman's hut, nor farm, nor village,
   Within the lonely valley could be traced,
Nor roads, nor bounded fields, nor rural tillage,
   But all was lonely, desolate, and waste.
The Castle which commanded the domain
Was suited to so rude and wild a Rèign:

XV.

A Rock was in the centre, like a Cone,
   Abruptly rising from a miry pool,
Where they beheld a Pile of massy stone,
   Which masons of the rude primeval school
Had rear'd by help of Giant hands alone,
   With rocky fragments unreduced by rule,
Irregular, like Nature more than Art,
Huge, rugged, and compact in every part.

XVI.

But on the other side a River went,
   And there the craggy Rock and ancient Wall
Had crumbled down with shelving deep descent ;
   Time and the wearing stream had work'd its fall :
The modern Giants had repair'd the Rent,
   But poor, reduced, and ignorant withal,
They patch'd it up, contriving as they could,
With stones, and earth, and palisades of wood ;

XVII.

Sir Gawain tried a parley, but in vain—
   A true-bred Giant never trusts a Knight—
He sent a Herald, who return'd again
   All torn to rags and perishing with fright :
A Trumpeter was sent, but he was slain—
   To Trumpeters they bear a mortal spite :
When all conciliatory measures fail'd,
The Castle and the Fortress were assail'd.

XVIII.

But when the Giants saw them fairly under,
   They shovell'd down a cataract of stones,
A hideous volley like a peal of thunder,
   Bouncing and bounding down, and breaking bones,
Rending the earth, and riving rocks asunder ;
   Sir Gawain inwardly laments and groans,
Retiring last, and standing most exposed ;—
Success seem'd hopeless, and the combat closed.

XIX.

A Council then was call'd, and all agreed
   To call in succour from the Country round ;
By regular approaches to proceed,
   Intrenching, fortifying, breaking ground.
That morning Tristram happen'd to secede :
   It seems his Falcon was not to be found ;
He went in search of her, but some suspected
He went lest his advice should be neglected.

XX.

At Gawain's summons all the Country came ;
  At Gawain's summons all the people aided ;
They call'd upon each other in his name,
  And bid their neighbours work as hard as they did.
So well beloved was He, for very shame
  They dug, they delved, entrench'd, and palisaded,
Till all the Fort was thoroughly blockaded,
And every Ford where Giants might have waded.

XXI.

Sir Tristram found his Falcon, bruised and lame,
  After a tedious search, as he averr'd,
And was returning back the way he came
  When in the neighbouring thicket something stirr'd,
And flash'd across the path, as bright as flame,
  Sir Tristram follow'd it, and found a Bird
Much like a Pheasant, only crimson-red,
With a fine tuft of feathers on his head.

XXII.

Sir Tristram's mind—invention—powers of thought,
  Were occupied, abstracted, and engaged,
Devising ways and means to have it caught
  Alive—entire—to see it safely caged :
The Giants and their siege he set at nought
  Compared with this new warfare that he waged.
He gain'd his object after three days wandering,
And three nights watching, meditating, pondering,

XXIII.

And to the Camp in triumph he return'd :
  He makes them all admire the creature's crest,
And praise and magnify the prize he earn'd.
  Sir Gawain rarely ventured on a jest,
But here his heart with indignation burn'd :
  " Good Cousin, yonder stands an Eagle's nest !
—A Prize for Fowlers such as you and me."—
Sir Tristram answer'd mildly, " We shall see."

XXIV.

Good humour was Sir Tristram's leading quality,
  And in the present case he proved it such ;
If he forbore, it was that in reality
  His conscience smote him with a secret touch,
For having shock'd his worthy friend's formality—
  He thought Sir Gawain had not said too much ;
He walks apart with him—and he discourses
About their preparation and their forces—

XXV.

Approving every thing that had been done—
  " It serves to put the Giants off their guard—
Less hazard and less danger will be run—
  I doubt not we shall find them unprepared—
The Castle will more easily be won,
  And many valuable lives be spared ;
The Ladies else, while we blockade and threaten,
Will most infallibly be kill'd and eaten."

XXVI.

Sir Tristram talk'd incomparably well ;
  His reasons were irrefragably strong.
As Tristram spoke Sir Gawain's spirits fell,
  For he discover'd clearly before long
(What Tristram never would presume to tell),
  That his whole system was entirely wrong ;
In fact his confidence had much diminish'd
Since all the preparations had been finish'd.

XXVII.

" Indeed !" Sir Tristram said, " for aught we know—
  " For aught that we can tell—this very night
" The valley's entrance may be clothed with snow,
  "And we may starve and perish here outright—
" 'Tis better risking a decided blow—
  " I own this weather puts me in a fright."
In fine, this tedious conference to shorten,
Sir Gawain trusted to Sir Tristram's fortune.

XXVIII.

'Twas twilight, ere the wintry dawn had kist
    With cold salute the mountain's chilly brow ;
The level lawns were dark, a lake of mist
    Inundated the vales and depths below,
When valiant Tristram, with a chosen list
    Of bold and hardy men, prepared to go,
Ascending through the vapours dim and hoar,
A secret track, which he descried before.

XXIX.

If ever you attempted, when a boy,
    To walk across the play-ground or the yard
Blindfolded, for an apple or a toy,
    Which, when you reach'd the spot, was your reward,
You may conceive the difficult employ
    Sir Tristram had, and that he found it hard,
Deprived of landmarks and the power of sight,
To steer their dark and doubtful course aright.

XXX.

They climb'd an hour or more with hand and knee ;
    (The distance of a fathom or a rood
Was farther than the keenest eye could see ;)
    At last the very ground on which they stood,
The broken turf, and many a batter'd tree—
    The crush'd and shatter'd shrubs and underwood—
Apprised them that they were arrived once more
Where they were overwhelm'd the time before.

XXXI.

Sir Tristram saw the people in a fluster ;
    He took them to a shelter'd hollow place:
They crowded round like chickens in a cluster,
    And Tristram, with an unembarrass'd face,
Proceeded quietly to take a muster,
    To take a muster, and to state the case—
" It was," he said, " an unexpected error,
Enough to strike inferior minds with terror ;

XXXII.

But since they were assembled and collected,"
  (All were assembled except nine or ten)
" He thought that their design might be effected;
  All things were easy to determined men.
If they would take the track which he directed,
  And try their old adventure once again,"
He slapp'd his breast, and swore within an hour
That they should have the Castle in their power.

XXXIII.

This mountain was like others I have seen;
  There was a stratum or a ridge of stone
Projecting high beyond the sloping green,
  From top to bottom, like a spinal bone,
Or flight of steps, with gaps and breaks between—
  A Copper-plate would make my meaning known
Better than words, and therefore, with permission,
I'll give a Print of it the next Edition.   .

XXXIV.

Thither Sir Tristram with his comrades went,
  For now the misty cloud was clear'd away,
And they must risk the perilous ascent,
  Right in the Giants' front, in open day:
They ran to reach the shelter which it lent,
  Before the battery should begin to play.
Their manner of ascending up that ridge
Was much like climbing by a broken bridge;

XXXV.

For there you scramble on from pier to pier,
  Always afraid to lose your hold half-way;
And as they clamber'd each successive tier
  Of rugged upright rocks, I dare to say,
It was not altogether without fear—
  Just fear enough to make brave people gay:
According to the words of Mr. Gray,
" They wound with toilsome march their long array."

XXXVI.

The more alert and active upward sprung,
    And let down ropes to drag their comrades after ;
Those ropes were their own shirts together strung,
    Stript off and twisted with such mirth and laughter,
That with their jokes the rocky echoes rung :
    Like countrymen that on a beam or rafter
Attempt to pass a raging wintry flood,
Such was the situation where they stood :

XXXVII.

A wild tumultuous torrent raged around,
    Of fragments tumbling from the mountain's height ;
The whirling clouds of dust, the deafening sound,
    The hurried motion that amazed the sight,
The constant quaking of the solid ground,
    Environ'd them with phantoms of affright ;
Yet with heroic hearts they held right on,
Till the last point of their ascent was won.

XXXVIII.

The Giants saw them on the topmost crown
    Of the last rock, and threaten'd and defied—
" Down with the mangy dwarfs there !—Dash them down!
    Down with the dirty pismires !"—Thus they cried.
Sir Tristram, with a sharp sarcastic frown,
    In their own Giant jargon thus replied,
" Mullinger !—Cacamole !—and Mangonell !
You cursed cannibals—I know you well—

XXXIX.

" I'll see that pate of yours upon a post,
    And your left-handed squinting brother's too—
By Heaven and Earth, within an hour at most,
    I'll give the crows a meal of him and you—
The wolves shall have you—either raw or roast—
    I'll make an end of all your cursed crew."
These words he partly said, and partly sang,
As usual with the Giants, in their slang.

XL.

He darted forward to the mountain's brow—
   The Giants ran away—they knew not why—
Sir Tristram gain'd the point—he knew not how—
   He could account for it no more than I.
Such strange effects we witness often now ;
   Such strange experiments true Britons try
In sieges, and in skirmishes afloat,
In storming heights, and boarding from a boat.

XLI.

True Courage bears about a Charm or Spell—
   It looks, I think, like an instinctive Law
By which superior natures daunt and quell
   Frenchmen and foreigners with fear and awe.
I wonder if Philosophers can tell—
   Can they explain the thing with all their jaw?
I can't explain it—but the fact is so,
A fact which every midshipman must know.

XLII.

Then instantly the signal was held out,
   To shew Sir Gawain that the coast was clear:
They heard his Camp re-echo with a shout—
   In half an hour Sir Gawain will be here.
But still Sir Tristram was perplex'd with doubt—
   The crisis of the Ladies' fate drew near—
He dreaded what those poor defenceless creatures
Might suffer from such fierce and desperate natures.

XLIII.

The Giants, with their brutal want of sense,
   In hurling stones to crush them with the fall,
And in their hurry taking them from thence,
   Had half dismantled all the new-built Wall.
They left it here and there, a naked fence
   Of stakes and palisades, upright and tall.
Sir Tristram form'd a sudden resolution,
And recommended it for execution.

XLIV.

" My Lads," he cried, " an effort must be made
  To keep those Monsters half an hour in play,
While Gawain is advancing to our aid,
  Or else the Ladies will be made away.
By mounting close within the palisade,
  You'll parry their two-handed, dangerous sway,
Their Clubs and Maces : recollect my words,
And use your daggers rather than your swords."

XLV.

That service was most gallantly perform'd :
  The Giants still endeavour'd to repel
And drive them from the breach that they had storm'd :
  The foremost of the Crew was Mangonell.
At sight of him Sir Tristram's spirit warm'd ;
  With aim unerring Tristram's falchion fell,
Lopp'd off his Club and fingers at the knuckle,
And thus disabled that stupendous Chuckle.

XLVI.

The Giant ran, outrageous with the wound,
  Roaring and bleeding, to the palisade ;
Sir Tristram swerved aside, and reaching round,
  Probed all his entrails with his poniard's blade :
His Giant limbs fall thundering on the ground,
  His goggling eyes eternal slumbers shade ;
Then by the head or heels, I know not which,
They dragg'd him forth, and toss'd him in the Ditch.

XLVII.

Sir Tristram, in the warfare that he waged,
  Strove to attract the Giants' whole attention ;
To keep it undivided and engaged,
  He rack'd his fiery brain and his invention ;
And taunted, and reviled, and storm'd, and raged,
  In terms far worse and more than I can mention.
In the mean while, in a more sober manner,
Sir Gawain was advancing with his banner.

XLVIII.

But first I must commemorate in rhyme
  Sir Tristram's dextrous swordmanship and might
(This incident appears to me sublime),
  He struck a Giant's head off in the fight:
The head fell down, of course, but for some time
  The stupid, headless trunk remain'd upright ;
For more than twenty seconds there it stood,
But ultimately fell from loss of blood.

XLIX.

Behold Sir Gawain with his valiant band ;
  He enters on the work with warmth and haste,
And slays a brace of Giants out of hand,
  Sliced downward from the shoulder to the waist.
But our ichnography must now be plann'd,
  The Keep or Inner Castle must be traced.
I wish myself at the concluding distich,
Although I think the thing characteristic.

L.

Facing your Entrance, just three yards behind,
  There was a Mass of Stone of moderate height,
It stood before you like a screen or blind :
  And there—on either hand to left and right—
Were sloping Parapets or Planes inclined,
  On which two massy Stones were placed upright,
Secured by Staples and by leathern Ropes,
Which hinder'd them from sliding down the slopes.

LI.

" —Cousin, those Dogs have some device or gin !—
  —I'll run the gauntlet—and I'll stand a knock—"
He dash'd into the Gate through thick and thin—
  He hew'd away the bands which held the block—
It rush'd along the slope with rumbling din,
  And closed the entrance with a thundering shock,
(Just like those famous old Symplegades
Discover'd by the Classics in their seas.)

I*   R

LII.

This was Sir Tristram—(as you may suppose)—
  He found some Giants wounded, others dead—
He shortly equalizes these with those ;
  But one poor Devil there was sick in bed,
In whose behalf the Ladies interpose :
  Sir Tristram spared his life, because they said
That he was more humane, and mild, and clever,
And all the time had had an ague-fever.

LIII.

The Ladies ?—They were tolerably well,
  At least as well as could have been expected :
Many details I must forbear to tell,
  Their toilet had been very much neglected ;
But by supreme good luck it so befell
  That when the Castle's capture was effected,
When those vile cannibals were overpower'd,
Only two fat Duennas were devour'd.

LIV.

Sir Tristram having thus secured the Fort,
  And seen all safe, was climbing to the Wall,
(Meaning to leap into the outer Court ;)
  But when he came, he saved himself the fall,
Sir Gawain had been spoiling all the sport,
  The Giants were demolish'd one and all :
He pull'd them up the Wall—they climb and enter—
Such was the winding-up of this adventure.

LV.

The only real sufferer in the fight
  Was a poor neighbouring Squire of little fame,
That came and join'd the party overnight ;
  He hobbled home, disabled with a maim
Which he received in tumbling from a height :
  The Knights from Court had never heard his name,
Nor recollected seeing him before—
Two leopards' faces were the arms he bore.

LVI.

Thus Tristram, without loss of life or limb,
  Conquer'd the Giants' Castle in a day ;
But whether it were accident or whim
  That kept him in the Woods so long away,
In any other mortal except him
  I should not feel a doubt of what to say ;
But he was wholly guided by his humour,
Indifferent to report and public rumour.

LVII.

It was besides imagined and suspected
  That he had miss'd his course by deep design,
To take the track which Gawain had neglected—
  I speak of others' notions, not of mine :
I question even if he recollected—
  He might have felt a moment's wish to shine ;
I only know that he made nothing of it,
Either for reputation or for profit.

LVIII.

The Ladies, by Sir Gawain's kind direction,
  Proceeded instantaneously to Court,
To thank their Majesties for their protection.
  Sir Gawain follow'd with a grand escort,
And was received with favour and affection.
  Sir Tristram remain'd loitering in the Fort ;
He thought the building and the scenery striking,
And that poor captive Giant took his liking.

LIX.

And now the thread of our Romance unravels,
  Presenting new performers on the stage ;
A Giant's education and his travels
  Will occupy the next succeeding page :
But I begin to tremble at the cavils
  Of this fastidious, supercilious age ;
Reviews, and paragraphs in morning papers—
The prospect of them gives my Muse the vapours.

LX.

"My dear," says she, "I think it will be well
    To ascertain our losses or our gains :
If this first sample should succeed and sell,
    We can renew the same melodious strains."
Poor soul ! she's had, I think, a tedious spell,
    And ought to be consider'd for her pains,
And keeping of my company so long—
A moderate compliment would not be wrong.

CANTO III.

I.

I'VE a proposal here from Mr. Murray,
    " He offers handsomely—the money down ;
My dear, you might recover from your flurry
    In a nice airy lodging out of town,
    At Croydon, Epsom, anywhere in Surrey ;
If every stanza brings us in a crown,
I think that I might venture to bespeak
A bed-room and front-parlour for next week.

II.

" Tell me, my dear Thalia, what you think ;
    Your nerves have undergone a sudden shock ;
Your poor dear spirits have begun to sink ;
    On Banstead Downs you'd muster a new stock,
And I'd be sure to keep away from drink,
    And always go to bed by twelve o'clock.
We'll travel down there in the morning stages ;
Our verses shall go down to distant ages.

III.

" And here in town we'll breakfast on hot rolls,
    And you shall have a better shawl to wear ;
These pantaloons of mine are chafed in holes ;
    By Monday next I'll compass a new pair :

Come, now, fling up the cinders, fetch the coals,
  And take away the things you hung to air,
Set out the tea-things, and bid Phœbe bring
The kettle up."—*Arms and the Monks I sing.*

IV.

Some ten miles off, an ancient abbey stood,
  Amidst the mountains, near a noble stream ;
A level eminence, enshrined with wood,
  Sloped to the river's bank and southern beam ;
Within were fifty friars fat and good,
  Of goodly persons, and of good esteem,
That pass'd an easy, exemplary life,
Remote from want and care and worldly strife.

V.

Between the Monks and Giants there subsisted,
  In the first abbot's lifetime, much respect ;
The Giants let them settle where they listed ;
  The Giants were a tolerating sect.
A poor lame Giant once the Monks assisted,
  Old and abandon'd, dying with neglect,
The Prior found him, cured his broken bone,
And very kindly cut him for the stone.

VI.

This seem'd a glorious, golden opportunity,
  To civilize the whole gigantic race ;
To draw them to pay tithes, and dwell in unity ;
  The Giants' valley was a fertile place,
And might have much enrich'd the whole community,
  Had the old Giant lived a longer space ;
But he relapsed, and though all means were tried,
They could but just baptize him—when he died.

VII.

And, I believe, the Giants never knew
  Of the kind treatment that befell their mate ;
He broke down all at once, and all the crew
  Had taken leave, and left him to his fate ;

And though the Monks exposed him full in view,
    Propt on his crutches, at the garden gate,
To prove their cure, and shew that all was right,
It happen'd that no Giants came in sight :

VIII.

They never found another case to cure,
    But their demeanour calm and reverential,
Their gesture and their vesture grave and pure,
    Their conduct sober, cautious, and prudential,
Engaged respect, sufficient to secure
    Their properties and interests most essential ;
They kept a distant, courteous intercourse ;
Salutes and gestures were their sole discourse.

IX.

Music will civilize, the poets say,
    In time it might have civilized the Giants ;
The Jesuits found its use in Paraguay ;
    Orpheus was famous for harmonic science,
And civilized the Thracians in that way ;
    My judgment coincides with Mr. Bryant's ;
He thinks that Orpheus meant a race of cloisterers,
Obnoxious to the Bacchanalian roisterers.

X.

Deciphering the symbols of mythology,
    He finds them Monks, expert in their vocation ;
Teachers of music, medicine, and theology,
    The missionaries of the barbarous Thracian ;
The poet's fable was a wild apology
    For an inhuman bloody reformation,
Which left those tribes uncivilized and rude,
Naked and fierce, and painted and tattoo'd.

XI.

It was a glorious jacobinic job
    To pull down convents, to condemn for treason
Poor peeping Pentheus—to carouse and rob,
    With naked raving goddesses of reason,

The festivals and orgies of the mob
  That every twentieth century come in season.
Enough of Orpheus—the succeeding page
Relates to Monks of a more recent age ;

XII.

And oft that wild untutor'd race would draw,
  Led by the solemn sound and sacred light
Beyond the bank, beneath a lonely shaw,
  To listen all the livelong summer night,
Till deep, serene, and reverential awe
  Environ'd them with silent calm delight,
Contemplating the Minster's midnight gleam,
Reflected from the clear and glassy stream ;

XIII.

But chiefly, when the shadowy moon had shed
  O'er woods and waters her mysterious hue,
Their passive hearts and vacant fancies fed
  With thoughts and aspirations strange and new,
Till their brute souls with inward working bred
  Dark hints that in the depth of instinct grew,
Subjective—not from Locke's associations,
Nor David Hartley's doctrine of vibrations.

XIV.

Each was ashamed to mention to the others
  One half of all the feelings that he felt,
Yet thus far each could venture—" Listen, brothers,
  It seems as if one heard heaven's thunder melt
' In music—! all at once it soothes—it smothers—
  It overpowers one—Pillicock, don't pelt !
It seems a kind of shame, a kind of sin,
To vex those harmless worthy souls within."

XV.

In castles and in courts Ambition dwells,
  But not in castles or in courts alone ;
She breathed a wish, throughout those sacred cells,
  For bells of larger size, and louder tone ;

Giants abominate the sound of bells,
  And soon the fierce antipathy was shown,
The tinkling and the jingling, and the clangour ;
Roused their irrational gigantic anger.

XVI.

Unhappy mortals ! ever blind to fate !
  Unhappy Monks ! you see no danger nigh ;
Exulting in their sound and size and weight,
  From morn till noon the merry peal you ply :
The belfry rocks, your bosoms are elate,
  Your spirits with the ropes and pulleys fly ;
Tired, but transported, panting, pulling, hauling,
Ramping and stamping, overjoy'd and bawling.

XVII.

Meanwhile the solemn mountains that surrounded
  The silent valley where the convent lay,
With tintinnabular uproar were astounded,
  When the first peal burst forth at break of day ;
Feeling their granite ears severely wounded,
  They scarce knew what to think, or what to say ;
And (though large mountains commonly conceal
Their sentiments, dissembling what they feel,

XVIII.

Yet) Cader-Gibbrish from his cloudy throne
  To huge Loblommon gave an intimation
Of this strange rumour, with an awful tone,
  Thundering his deep surprise and indignation ;
The lesser hills, in language of their own,
  Discuss'd the topic by reverberation ;
Discoursing with their echoes all day long,
Their only conversation was, ' ding-dong.'

XIX.

Those giant-mountains inwardly were moved,
  But never made an outward change of place :
Not so the mountain-giants—(as behoved
  A more alert and locomotive race),

Hearing a clatter which they disapproved,
  They ran straight forward to besiege the place
With a discordant universal yell,
Like house-dogs howling at a dinner-bell.

XX.

Historians are extremely to be pitied,
  Obliged to persevere in the narration
Of wrongs and horrid outrages committed,
  Oppression, sacrilege, assassination ;
The following scenes I wish'd to have omitted,
  But truth is an imperious obligation.
So—" my heart sickens, and I drop my pen,"
And am obliged to pick it up again,

XXI.

And, dipping it afresh, I must transcribe
  An ancient monkish record, which displays
The savage acts of that gigantic tribe ;
  I hope, that from the diction of those days
This noble, national poem will imbibe
  A something (in the old reviewing phrase),
" Of an original flavour, and a raciness ; "
I should not else transcribe it, out of laziness.

XXII.

The writer first relates a dream, or vision,
  Observed by Luke and Lawrence in their cells,
And a nocturnal hideous apparition
  Of fiends and devils dancing round the bells :
This last event is stated with precision ;
  Their persons he describes, their names he tells,
Klaproth, Tantallan, Barbanel, Belphegor,
Long-tail'd, long-talon'd, hairy, black, and meagre.

XXIII.

He then rehearses sundry marvels more,
  Damping the mind with horror by degrees,
Of a prodigious birth a heifer bore,
  Of mermaids seen in the surrounding seas,

Of a sea-monster that was cast ashore ;
Earthquakes and thunder-stones, events like these,
Which served to shew the times were out of joint,
And then proceeds directly to the point.

XXIV.

Erant rumores et timores varii ;
    Dies horroris et confusionis
Evenit in calendis Januarii ;
    Gigantes, semen maledictionis,
Nostri potentes impii adversarii,
    Irascebantur campanarum sonis,
Horâ secundâ centum tres gigantes
    Venerunt ante januam ululantes.

XXV.

At fratres, pleni desolationis,
    Stabant ad necessarium præsidium,
Perterriti pro vitis et pro bonis,
    Et perduravit hoc crudele obsidium
Nostri claustralis pauperis Sionis,
    Ad primum diem proximorum Idium
Tunc in triumpho fracto tintinnabulo,
    Gigantes ibant alibi pro pabulo.

XXVI.

Sed frater Isidorus decumbebat
    In lecto per tres menses brachio fracto,
Nam lapides Mangonellus jaciebat,
    Et fregit tintinnabulum lapide jacto ;
Et omne vicinagium destruebat,
    Et nihil relinquebat de intacto,
Ardens molinos, casas, messuagia,
    Et alia multa damna atque outragia.

XXVII.

Those Monks were poor proficients in divinity,
    And scarce knew more of Latin than myself ;
Compared with theirs they say that true Latinity
    Appears like porcelain compared with delf ;

As for the damage done in the vicinity,
 Those that have laid their Latin on the shelf
May like to read the subsequent narration,
Done into metre from a friend's translation.

XXVIII.

Squire Humphry Bamberham, of Boozley Hall
 (Whose name I mention with deserved respect),
On market-days was often pleased to call,
 And to suggest improvements, or correct;
I own the obligation once for all,
 Lest critics should imagine they detect
Traces of learning and superior reading,
Beyond, as they suppose, my birth and breeding.

XXIX.

Papers besides, and transcripts most material,
 He gave me when I went to him to dine ;
A trunk-full, one coach-seat, and an imperial,
 One band-box—But the work is wholly mine ;
The tone, the form, the colouring ethereal,
 " The vision and the faculty divine,"
The scenery, characters, and triple-rhymes,
I'll swear it—like old Walter of the " Times."

XXX.

Long, long before, upon a point of weight,
 Such as a ring of bells complete and new,
Chapters were summon'd, frequent, full, and late ;
 The point was view'd in every point of view,
Till, after fierce discussion and debate,
 The wiser monks, the wise are always few,
That from the first opposed the plan in *toto,*
Were over-borne, *canonicali voto.*

XXXI.

A prudent monk, their reader and librarian,
 Observed a faction, angry, strong, and warm
(Himself an anti-tintinnabularian),
 He saw, or thought he saw, a party form

To scout him as an alien and sectarian.
There was an undefined impending storm !
The opponents were united, bold, and hot ;
They might degrade, imprison him—what not ?

XXXII.

Now faction in a city, camp, or cloister,
    While it is yet a tender raw beginner,
Is nourish'd by superfluous warmth and moisture,
    Namely, by warmth and moisture after dinner ;
And therefore, till the temper and the posture
    Of things should alter—till a secret inner
Instinctive voice should whisper, all is right—
He deem'd it safest to keep least in sight.

XXXIII.

He felt as if his neck were in a noose,
    And evermore retired betimes from table,
For fear of altercation and abuse,
    But made the best excuse that he was able ;
He never rose without a good excuse,
    (Like Master Stork invited in the fable
To Mr. Fox's dinner) ; there he sat,
Impatient to retire and take his hat.

XXXIV.

For only once or twice that he remain'd
    To change this constant formal course, he found
His brethren awkward, sullen, and constrain'd,
    —He caught the conversation at a bound,
And, with a hurried agitation, strain'd
    His wits to keep it up, and drive it round.
—It saved him—but he felt the risk and danger,
Behaved-to like a pleasant utter stranger.

XXXV.

Wise people sometimes will pretend to sleep,
    And watch and listen while they droop and snore—
He felt himself a kind of a black sheep,
    But studied to be neither less nor more

Obliging than became him—but to keep
　His temper, style, and manner as before ;
It seem'd the best, the safest, only plan,
Never to seem to feel as a mark'd man.

XXXVI.

Wise Curs, when canister'd, refuse to run ;
　They merely crawl and creep about, and whine,
And disappoint the Boys, and spoil the fun—
　That picture is too mean—this Monk of mine
Ennobled it, as others since have done,
　With grace and ease, and grandeur of design ;
He neither ran nor howl'd, nor crept nor turn'd,
But wore it as he walk'd, quite unconcern'd.

XXXVII.

To manifest the slightest want of nerve
　Was evidently perfect, utter ruin,
Therefore the seeming to recant or swerve,
　By meddling any way with what was doing,
He felt within himself would only serve
　To bring down all the mischief that was brewing ;
" No duty binds me, no constraint compels
To bow before the Dagon of the Bells,

XXXVIII.

" To flatter this new foolery, to betray
　My vote, my conscience, and my better sense,
By bustling in the Belfry day by day ;
　But in the Grange, the Cellar, or the Spence,
(While all are otherwise employ'd), I may
　Deserve their thanks, at least avoid offence ;
For (while this vile anticipated clatter
Fills all their hearts and senses), every matter

XXXIX.

" Behoveful for our maintenance and needs
　Is wholly disregarded, and the course
Of our conventual management proceeds
　At random, day by day, from bad to worse :

The Larder dwindles and the Cellar bleeds !
  Besides,—besides the bells, we must disburse
For masonry, for frame-work, wheels and fliers ;
  Next winter we must fast like genuine friars."

XL.

As Bees, that when the skies are calm and fair,
  In June, or the beginning of July,
Launch forth colonial settlers in the air,
  Round, round, and round-about, they whiz, they fly,
With eager worry whirling here and there,
  They know not whence, nor whither, where, nor why,
In utter hurry-scurry, going, coming,
Maddening the summer air with ceaseless humming ;

XLI.

Till the strong Frying-pan's energic jangle
  With thrilling thrum their feebler hum doth drown,
Then passive and appeased, they droop and dangle,
  Clinging together close, and clustering down,
Link'd in a multitudinous living tangle
  Like an old Tassel of a dingy brown ;
The joyful Farmer sees, and spreads his hay,
And reckons on a settled sultry day.

XLII.

E'en so the Monks, as wild as sparks of fire
  (Or swarms unpacified by pan or kettle),
Ran restless round the Cloisters and the Quire,
  Till those huge masses of sonorous metal
Attracted them toward the Tower and Spire ;
  There you might see them cluster, crowd, and settle,
Throng'd in the hollow tintinnabular Hive ;
The Belfry swarm'd with Monks ; it seem'd alive.

XLIII.

Then, while the Cloisters, Courts, and Yards were still,
  Silent and empty, like a long vacation ;
The Friar prowl'd about, intent to fill
  Details of delegated occupation,

Which, with a ready frankness and good will,
 He undertook ; he said, "the obligation
Was nothing—nothing—he could serve their turn
While they were busy with this new concern."

XLIV.

Combining prudence with a scholar's pride,
 Poor Tully, like a toad beneath a harrow,
Twitch'd, jerk'd, and haul'd and maul'd on every side,
 Tried to identify himself with Varro ;
This course our cautious Friar might have tried,
 But his poor convent was a field too narrow ;
There was not, from the Prior to the Cook,
A single soul that cared about a book :

XLV.

Yet, sitting with his books, he felt unclogg'd,
 Unfetter'd ; and two hours together tasted
The calm delight of being neither dogg'd,
 Nor watch'd, nor worried ; he transcribed, he pasted,
Repair'd old bindings, index'd, catalogued,
 Illuminated, mended clasps, and wasted
An hour or two sometimes in actual reading ;
Meanwhile the belfry business was proceeding ;

XLVI.

And the first opening Peal, the grand display,
 In prospect ever present to his mind,
Was fast approaching, pregnant with dismay,
 With loathing and with horror undefined,
Like the expectation of an Ague-day ;
 The day before he neither supp'd nor dined,
And felt beforehand, for a fortnight near,
A kind of deafness in his fancy's ear :

XLVII.

But most he fear'd his ill-digested spleen,
 Inflamed by gibes, might lead him on to wrangle,
Or discompose, at least, his looks and mien ;
 So, with the Belfry's first prelusive jangle,

He sallied from the garden-gate unseen,
   With his worst hat, his boots, his line and angle,
Meaning to pass away the time, and bring
Some fish for supper, as a civil thing.

XLVIII.

The prospect of their after-supper talk
   Employ'd his thoughts, forecasting many a scoff,
Which he with quick reply must damp and balk,
   Parrying at once, without a hem or cough,
" Had not the bells annoy'd him in his walk ?—
   No, faith ! he liked them best when farthest off."
Thus he prepared and practised many a sentence,
Expressing ease, good-humour, independence.

XLIX.

His ground-bait had been laid the night before,
   Most fortunately !—for he used to say,
That more than once the belfry's bothering roar
   Almost induced him to remove away ;
Had he so done,—the gigantean corps
   Had sack'd the convent on that very day,
But providentially the perch and dace
Bit freely, which detain'd him at the place.

L.

And here let us detain ourselves awhile,
   My dear Thalia ! party's angry frown
And petty malice in that monkish pile
   (The warfare of the cowl and of the gown)
Had almost dried my wits and drain'd my style ;
   Here, with our legs, then, idly dangling down,
We'll rest upon the bank, and dip our toes
In the poetic current as it flows.

LI.

Or in the narrow sunny plashes near,
   Observe the puny piscatory swarm,
That with their tiny squadrons tack and veer,
   Cruising amidst the shelves and shallows warm,

Chasing, or in retreat, with hope or fear
  Of petty plunder or minute alarm ;
With clannish instinct how they wheel and face,
Inherited arts inherent in the race ;

LII.

Or mark the jetty, glossy tribes that glance
  Upon the water's firm unruffled breast,
Tracing their ancient labyrinthic dance
  In mute mysterious cadence unexpress'd ;
Alas ! that fresh disaster and mischance
  Again must drive us from our place of rest !
Grim Mangonel, with his outrageous crew,
Will scare us hence within an hour or two.

LIII.

Poets are privileged to run away—
  Alcæus and Archilochus could fling
Their shields behind them in a doubtful fray ;
  And still sweet Horace may be heard to sing
His filthy fright upon Philippi's day ;
  (—You can retire, too—for the Muse's wing
Is swift as Cupid's pinion when he flies,
Alarm'd at periwigs and human tyes.)

LIV.

This practice was approved in times of yore,
  Though later bards behaved like gentlemen,
And Garcilasso, Camoens, many more,
  Disclaim'd the privilege of book and pen ;
And bold Anuerin, all bedripp'd with gore,
  Bursting by force from the beleaguer'd glen,
Arrogant, haughty, fierce, of fiery mood,
Not meek and mean, as Gray misunderstood.

LV.

But we, that write a mere Campaigning Tour,
  May choose a station for our point of view
That's picturesque and perfectly secure ;
  Come, now we'll sketch the friar—that will do --
1*   s

" Designs and etchings by an amateur ;"
　" A frontispiece, and a vignette or two :"
But much I fear that aqua-tint and etching
Will scarce keep pace with true poetic sketching.

LVI.

Dogs that inhabit near the banks of Nile
　(As ancient authors or old proverbs say),
Dreading the cruel critic Crocodile,
　Drink as they run, a mouthful and away ;
'Tis a true model for descriptive style ;
　" Keep moving " (as the man says in the play,)
The power of motion is the poet's forte—
Therefore, again, " keep moving ! that's your sort ! "

LVII.

For, otherwise, while you persist and paint,
　With your portfolio pinion'd to a spot,
Half of your picture grows effaced and faint,
　Imperfectly remember'd, or forgot ;
Make sketch, then, upon sketch ; and if they a'n't
　Complete, it does not signify a jot ;
Leave graphic illustrations of your work
To be devised by Westall or by Smirke.

LVIII.

I'll speak my mind at once, in spite of raillery ;
　I've thought and thought again a thousand times,
What a magnificent Poetic Gallery
　Might be design'd from my Stowmarket rhymes ;
I look for no reward, nor fee, nor salary,
　I look for England's fame in foreign climes
And future ages—*Honos alit Artes*,
And such a plan would reconcile all parties.

LIX.

I'm strongly for the present state of things ;
　I look for no reform, nor innovation,
Because our present Parliaments and Kings
　Are competent to improve and rule the Nation.

Provided projects that true genius brings
  Are held in due respect and estimation.
I've said enough—and now you must be wishing
To see the landscape, and the friar fishing.

CANTO IV.

I.

A MIGHTY current, unconfined and free,
  Ran wheeling round beneath the mountain's
    shade,
Battering its wave-worn base ; but you might
    see
On the near margin many a watery glade,
Becalm'd beneath some little island's lee
  All tranquil, and transparent, close embay'd ;
Reflecting in the deep serene and even
Each flower and herb, and every cloud of heaven :

II.

The painted kingfisher, the branch above her,
  Stand in the sultry mirror fixt and true ;
Anon the fitful breezes brood and hover,
  Freshening the surface with a rougher hue ;
Spreading, withdrawing, pausing, passing over,
  Again returning to retire anew :
So rest and motion, in a narrow range,
Feasted the sight with joyous interchange.

III.

The Monk with handy jerk, and petty baits,
  Stands twitching out apace the perch and roach ;
His mightier tackle, pitch'd apart, awaits
  The grovelling barbel's unobserved approach :
And soon his motley meal of homely cates
  Is spread, the leather bottle is a-broach ;
Eggs, bacon, ale, a napkin, cheese and knife,
Forming a charming picture of still-life.

IV.

The Friar fishing—a design for Cuyp,
   A cabinet jewel—" Pray remark the boot ;
And, leading from the light, that shady stripe,
   With the dark bulrush-heads how well they suit ;
And then, that mellow tint so warm and ripe,
   That falls upon the cassock and surtout :"
If it were fairly painted, puff'd, and sold,
My gallery would be worth its weight in gold.

V.

But hark !—the busy Chimes fall fast and strong,
   Clattering and pealing in their full career ;
Closely the thickening sounds together throng,
   No longer painful to the Friar's ear,
They bind his fancy with illusion strong :
   While his rapt spirit hears, or seems to hear,
" *Turn, turn again—gen—gèn, thou noble Friar,*
Eleele—lèele—lèele—lected Prior."

VI.

Thus the mild Monk, as he unhook'd a gudgeon,
   Stood musing—when far other sounds arise,
Sounds of despite and ire, and direful dudgeon ;
   And soon across the River he espies,
In wrathful act, a hideous huge curmudgeon
   Calling his comrades on with shouts and cries,
" There—there it is !—I told them so before ;"
He left his line and hook, and said no more ;

VII.

But ran right forward (pelted all the way),
   And bolted breathless at the Convent-gate,
The messenger and herald of dismay ;
   But soon with conscious worth, and words of weight,
Gives orders which the ready Monks obey :
   Doors, windows, wickets, are blockaded straight ;
He reinspires the Convent's drooping sons,
Is here and there, and everywhere, at once.

VIII.

" Friends! fellow-monks!" he cried, ("for well you know
 That mightiest Giants must in vain essay
Across yon river's foaming gulf to go :)
 The mountainous, obscure and winding way,
That guides their footsteps to the Ford below,
 Affords a respite of desired delay—
Seize then the passing hour !"—the Monk kept bawling,
In terms to this effect, though not so drawling.

IX.

His words were these, " Before the Ford is crost,
 We've a good hour,—at least three-quarters good—
Bestir yourselves, my lads, or all is lost—
 Drive down this staunchion, bring those spars of wood ;
This bench will serve—here, wedge it to the post ;
 Come, Peter, quick! strip off your gown and hood—
Take up the mallet, man, and bang away !
Tighten these ropes—now lash them, and belay.

X.

" Finish the job while I return—I fear
 Yon Postern-gate will prove the Convent's ruin ;
You, brother John, my namesake ! stay you here,
 And give an eye to what these monks are doing ;
Bring out the scalding sweet-wort, and the beer,
 Keep up the stoke-hole fire, where we were brewing ;
And pull the gutters up and melt the lead—
Before a dozen aves can be said,

XI.

" I shall be back amongst you."—Forth he went,
 Secured the Postern, and return'd again,
Disposing all with high arbitrament,
 With earnest air, and visage on the main
Concern of public safety fix'd and bent ;
 For now the Giants, stretching o'er the plain,
Are seen, presenting in the dim horizon
Tall awful forms, horrific and surprising—

XII.

I'd willingly walk barefoot fifty mile,
  To find a scholar, or divine, or squire,
That could assist me to devise a style
  Fit to describe the conduct of the Friar;
I've tried three different ones within a while,
  The Grave, the Vulgar, and the grand High-flyer;
All are I think improper, more or less,
I'll take my chance amongst 'em—you shall guess.

XIII.

Intrepid, eager, ever prompt to fly
  Where danger and the Convent's safety call; ·
Where doubtful points demand a judging eye,
  Where on the massy gates huge maces fall;
Where missile volley'd rocks are whirl'd on high,
  Pre-eminent upon the embattled wall,
In gesture, and in voice, he stands confest;
Exhorting all the Monks to do their best.

XIV.

We redescend to phrase of low degree—
  For there's a point which you must wish to know,
The real ruling Abbot—where was he?
  For (since we make so classical a show,
Our Convent's mighty structure, as you see,
  Like Thebes or Troy beleaguer'd by the foe:
Our Friar scuffling like a kind of Cocles),
You'll figure him perhaps like Eteocles

XV.

In Æschylus, with sentries, guards and watches,
  Ready for all contingencies arising,
Pitting his chosen chiefs in equal matches
  Against the foe—anon soliloquizing;
Then occupied anew with fresh dispatches—
  Nothing like this!—but something more surprising—
Was he like Priam then—that's stranger far—
That in the ninth year of his Trojan war,

XVI.

Knew not the names or persons of his foes,
  But merely points them out as stout or tall,
While (as no Trojan knew them, I suppose)
  Helen attends her father to the wall,
To tell him long details of these and those?
  'Twas not like this, but strange and odd withal :
" Nobody knows it—nothing need be said,
Our poor dear Abbot is this instant dead.

XVII.

" They wheel'd him out, you know, to take the air—
  It must have been an apoplectic fit—
He tumbled forward from his garden-chair—
  He seem'd completely gone, but warm as yet :
I wonder how they came to leave him there ;
  Poor soul ! he wanted courage, heart, and wit
For times like these—the shock and the surprise !
'Twas very natural the gout should rise.

XVIII.

" But such a sudden end was scarce expected ;
  Our parties will be puzzled to proceed ;
The belfry set divided and dejected :
  The crisis is a strange one, strange indeed ;
I'll bet yon fighting Friar is elected ;
  It often happens in the hour of need,
From popular ideas of utility,
People are pitch'd upon for mere ability.

XIX.

" I'll hint the subject, and communicate
  The sad event—he's standing there apart ;
Our offer, to be sure, comes somewhat late,
  But then, we never thought he meant to start,
And if he gains his end, at any rate,
  He has an understanding and a heart ;
He'll serve or he'll protect his friends, at least,
With better spirit than the poor deceased ;

XX.

" The convent was all going to the devil
  While he, poor creature, thought himself beloved
For saying handsome things, and being civil,
  Wheeling about as he was pull'd and shoved,
By way of leaving things to find their level."
  The funeral sermon ended, both approved,
And went to Friar John, who merely doubted
The fact, and wish'd them to inquire about it;

XXI.

Then left them, and return'd to the attack :
  They found their Abbot in his former place ;
They took him up and turn'd him on his back ;
  At first (you know) he tumbled on his face :
They found him fairly stiff, and cold, and black ;
  They *then* unloosed each ligature and lace,
His neckcloth and his girdle, hose and garters,
And took him up, and lodged him in his quarters.

XXII.

Bees served me for a simile before,
  And bees again—" Bees that have lost their king,"
Would seem a repetition and a bore ;
  Besides, in fact, I never saw the thing ;
And though those phrases from the good old store
  Of " feebler hummings and a flagging wing,"
Perhaps may be descriptive and exact ;
I doubt it ; I confine myself to fact.

XXIII.

Thus much is certain, that a mighty pother
  Arises ; that the frame and the condition
Of things is alter'd, they combine and bother,
  And every winged insect politician
Is warm and eager till they choose another.
  In our monastic Hive the same ambition
Was active and alert ; but angry fortune
Constrain'd them to contract the long, importune,

XXIV.

Tedious, obscure, inexplicable train,
  Qualification, form, and oath and test,
Ballots on ballots, ballotted again;
  Accessits, scrutinies, and all the rest;
Theirs was the good old method, short and plain;
  Per acclamationem they invest
Their fighting Friar John with Robes and Ring,
Crozier and Mitre, Seals, and every thing.

XXV.

With a new warlike active Chief elected,
  Almost at once, it scarce can be conceived
What a new spirit, real or affected,
  Prevail'd throughout; the monks complain'd and grieved
That nothing was attempted or projected;
  While Quiristers and Novices believed
That their new fighting Abbot, Friar John,
Would sally forth at once, and lead them on.

XXVI.

I pass such gossip, and devote my cares
  By diligent inquiry to detect
The genuine state and posture of affairs:
  Unmanner'd, uninform'd, and incorrect,
Falsehood and Malice hold alternate chairs,
  And lecture and preside in Envy's sect;
The fortunate and great she never spares,
Sowing the soil of history with tares.

XXVII.

Thus, jealous of the truth, and feeling loth
  That Sir Nathaniel henceforth should accuse
Our noble Monk of cowardice and sloth,
  I'll print the Affidavit of the Muse,
And state the facts as ascertain'd on Oath,
  Corroborated by Surveys and Views,
When good King Arthur granted them a Brief,
And Ninety Groats were raised for their relief.

XXVIII.

Their arbours, walks, and alleys were defaced,
    Riven and uprooted, and with ruin strown,
And the fair Dial in their garden placed
    Batter'd by barbarous hands, and overthrown ;
The Deer with wild pursuit dispersed and chased,
    The Dove-house ransack'd, and the Pigeons flown ;
The Cows all kill'd in one promiscuous slaughter,
The Sheep all drown'd, and floating in the water.

XXIX.

The Mill was burn'd down to the water-wheels ;
    The Giants broke away the Dam and Sluice,
Dragg'd up and emptied all the Fishing-reels;
    Drain'd and destroy'd the Reservoir and Stews,
Wading about, and groping carp and eels;
    In short, no single earthly thing of use
Remain'd untouch'd beyond the convent's wall :
The Friars from their windows view'd it all.

XXX.

But the bare hope of personal defence,
    The church, the convent's, and their own protection,
Absorb'd their thoughts, and silenced every sense
    Of present loss, till Friar John's election ;
Then other schemes arose, I know not whence,
    Whether from flattery, zeal, or disaffection,
But the brave Monk, like Fabius with Hannibal,
Against internal faction, and the cannibal

XXXI.

Inhuman foe, that threaten'd from without,
    Stood firmly, with a self-sufficing mind,
Impregnable to rumour, fear, or doubt,
    Determined that the casual, idle, blind
Event of battle with that barbarous Rout,
    Flush'd with success and garbage, should not bind
Their future destinies, or fix the seal
Of ruin on the claustral Common-weal.

XXXII.

He check'd the rash, the boisterous, and the proud,
  By speech and action, manly but discreet ;
During the siege he never once allow'd
  Of chapters, or convoked the monks to meet,
Dreading the consultations of a crowd.
  Historic parallels we sometimes meet—
I think I could contrive one—if you please,
I shall compare our Monk to Pericles.

XXXIII.

In former times, amongst the Athenians bold,
  This Pericles was placed in high command,
Heading their troops (as statesmen used of old)
  In all their wars and fights by sea and land ;
Besides, in Langhorne's Plutarch we are told
  How many fine ingenious things he plann'd ;
For Phidias was an Architect and Builder,
Jeweller and Engraver, Carver, Gilder ;

XXXIV.

But altogether quite expert and clever ;
  Pericles took him up and stood his friend,
Persuading these Athenians to endeavour
  To raise a Work to last to the world's end,
By means of which their Fame should last for ever.;
  Likewise an Image (which, you comprehend,
They meant to pray to, for the country's good) :
They had before an old one made of wood,

XXXV.

But being partly rotten and decay'd,
  They wish'd to have a new one spick-and-span,
So Pericles advised it should be made
  According to this Phidias's plan,
Of ivory, with gold all overlaid,
  Of the height of twenty cubits and a span,
Making eleven yards of English measure,
All to be paid for from the public treasure.

XXXVI.

So Phidias's talents were requited
  With talents that were spent upon the work,
And every body busied and delighted,
  Building a Temple—this was their next quirk—
Lest it should think itself ill-used and slighted.
  This Temple now belongs to the Grand Turk,
The finest in the world allow'd to be,
That people go five hundred miles to see.

XXXVII.

Its ancient carvings are safe here at home,
  Brought round by shipping from as far as Greece,
Finer, they say, than all the things at Rome ;
  But here you need not pay a penny-piece ;
But curious people, if they like to come,
  May look at them as often as they please—
I've left my subject, but I was not sorry
To mention things that raise the country's glory.

XXXVIII.

Well, Pericles made every thing complete,
  Their town, their harbour, and their city wall ;
When their allies rebell'd, he made them treat
  And pay for peace, and tax'd and fined them all,
By which means Pericles maintain'd a fleet,
  And kept three hundred galleys at his call ;
Pericles was a man for every thing ;
Pericles was a kind of petty king.

XXXIX.

It happen'd Sparta was another State ;
  They thought themselves as good; they could not bear
To see the Athenians grown so proud and great,
  Ruling and domineering every where,
And so resolved, before it grew too late,
  To fight it out and settle the affair ;
Then, being quite determined to proceed,
They muster'd an amazing force indeed ;

XL.

And (after praying to their idol Mars)
   March'd on, with all the allies that chose to join,
As was the practice in old heathen wars,
   Destroying all the fruit-trees, every vine,
And smashing and demolishing the jars
   In which those classic ancients kept their wine;
The Athenians ran within the city wall
To save themselves, their children, wives, and all.

XLI.

Then Pericles (whom they compar'd to Jove,
   As being apt to storm and play the deuce)
Kept quiet, and forbad the troops to move,
   Because a battle was no kind of use;
The more they mutinied, the more he strove
   To keep them safe in spite of their abuse,
For while the Farms were ransack'd round the town,
This was the people's language up and down:

XLII.

" 'Tis better to die once than live to see
   Such an abomination, such a waste;"
"No! no!" says Pericles, "that must not be,
   You're too much in hurry,—too much haste—
Learned Athenians, leave the thing to me;
   You think of being bullied and disgraced;
Don't think of that, nor answer their defiance;
We'll gain the day by our superior science.'

XLIII.

Pericles led the people as he pleased,
   But in most cases something is forgot:
What with the crowd and heat they grew diseased,
   And died in heaps like wethers with the rot;
And, at the last, the same distemper seized
   Poor Pericles himself—he went to pot.
It answer'd badly;—therefore I admire
So much the more the conduct of the Friar.

XLIV.

For in the Garrison where he presided,
  Neither distress, nor famine, nor disease,
Were felt, nor accident nor harm betided
  The happy Monks; but plenteous, and with ease,
All needful monkish viands were provided;
  Bacon and Pickled-herring, Pork and Peas;
And when the Table-beer began to fail,
They found resources in the Bottled-ale.

XLV.

Dinner and supper kept their usual hours;
  Breakfast and luncheon never were delay'd,
While to the sentries on the walls and towers
  Between two plates hot messes were convey'd.
At the departure of the invading powers,
  It was a boast the noble Abbot made,
None of his Monks were weaker, paler, thinner,
Or, during all the siege, had lost a dinner.

XLVI.

This was the common course of their hostility;
  The giant forces being foil'd at first,
Had felt the manifest impossibility
  Of carrying things before them at a burst,
But still, without a prospect of utility,
  At stated hours they pelted, howl'd, and cursed;
And sometimes, at the peril of their pates,
Would bang with clubs and maces at the gates;

XLVII.

Them the brave monkish legions, unappall'd,
  With stones that served before to pave the court
(Heap'd and prepared at hand), repell'd and maul'd,
  Without an effort, smiling as in sport,
With many a broken head, and many a scald
  From stones and molten lead and boiling wort;
Thus little Pillicock was left for dead,
And old Loblolly forced to keep his bed.

XLVIII.

The giant-troops invariably withdrew,
  (Like mobs in Naples, Portugal, and Spain),
To dine at twelve o'clock, and sleep till two,
  And afterwards (except in case of rain)
Return'd to clamour, hoot, and pelt anew.
  The scene was every day the same again;
Thus the Blockade grew tedious: I intended
A week ago, myself, to raise and end it.

XLIX.

One morn the drowsy sentry rubb'd his eyes,
  Foil'd by the scanty, baffling, early light;
It seem'd, a Figure of inferior size
  Was traversing the Giants' camp outright;
And soon a Monkish Form they recognize—
  And now their brother Martin stands in sight,
That on that morning of alarm and fear
Had rambled out to see the Salmon-Weir;

L.

Passing the Ford, the Giants' first attack
  Left brother Martin's station in their rear,
And thus prevented him from falling back;
  But during all the Siege he watch'd them near,
Saw them returning by their former Track
  The Night before, and found the Camp was clear;
And so return'd in safety with delight
And rapture, and a ravenous appetite.

LI.

" Well! welcome,—welcome, brother!—Brother Martin
  Why, Martin!—we could scarce believe our eyes:
Ah, brother! strange events here since our parting—"
  And Martin dined (dispensing brief replies
To all the questions that the monks were starting,
  Betwixt his mouthfuls), while each friar vies
In filling, helping, carving, questioning;
So Martin dined in public like a king.

LII.

And now the Gates are open'd, and the Throng
  Forth issuing, the deserted Camp survey;
" Here Murdomack, and Mangonel the strong,
  And Gorboduc were lodged," and " here," they say,
" This pigsty to Poldavy did belong ;
  Here Brindleback, and here Phagander lay.'
They view the deep indentures, broad and round,
Which mark their posture squatting on the ground.

LIII.

Then to the traces of gigantic feet,
  Huge, wide apart, with half a dozen toes ;
They track them on, till they converge and meet,
  (An earnest and assurance of repose)
Close at the Ford ; the cause of this retreat
  They all conjecture, but no creature knows ;
It was ascribed to causes multifarious,
To saints, as Jerome, George and Januarius,

LIV.

To their own pious founder's intercession,
  To Ave-Maries, and our Lady's Psalter ;
To news that Friar John was in possession,
  To new wax candles placed upon the altar,
To their own prudence, valour, and discretion ;
  To reliques, rosaries, and holy water ;
To beads and psalms, and feats of arms—in short,
There was no end to their accounting for't :

LV.

But though they could not, you, perhaps, may guess ;
  They went, in short, upon their last adventure,
After the Ladies—neither more nor less—
  Our story now revolves upon its centre,
And I'm rejoiced myself, I must confess,
  To find it tally like an old indenture ;
They drove off Mules and Horses half a score,
The same that you saw roasted heretofore.

LVI.

Our Giants' memoirs still remain on hand,
   For all my notions, being genuine gold,
Beat out beneath the hammer and expand,
   And multiply themselves a thousandfold
Beyond the first idea that I plann'd ;
   Besides,—this present copy must be sold :
Besides,—I promised Murray t'other day
To let him have it by the tenth of May.

END OF CANTO IV.

T

MISCELLANIES.

FABLES FOR FIVE YEARS OLD.

FABLE I.

Of the Boy and his Top.

LITTLE boy had bought a Top,
The best in all the toyman's shop;
He made a whip with good eel's-skin,
He lash'd the top, and made it spin;
All the children within call,
And the servants, one and all,
Stood round to see it and admire.
At last the Top began to tire,
He cried out, "Pray don't whip me, Master,
You whip too hard,—I can't spin faster,
I can spin quite as well without it."
The little Boy replied, "I doubt it;
I only whip you for your good,
You were a foolish lump of wood,
By dint of whipping you were raised
To see yourself admired and praised,
And if I left you, you'd remain
A foolish lump of wood again."

Explanation.

WHIPPING sounds a little odd,
It don't mean whipping with a rod,
It means to teach a boy incessantly,
Whether by lessons or more pleasantly,

Every hour and every day,
By every means, in every way,
By reading, writing, rhyming, talking,
By riding to see sights, and walking :
If you leave off he drops at once,
A lumpish, wooden-headed dunce.

FABLE II.

OF THE BOY AND THE PARROT.

ARROT, if I had your wings,
I should do so many things.
The first thing I should like to do
If I had little wings like you,
I should fly to uncle Bartle.[1]
Don't you think 'twould make him startle,
If he saw me when I came,
Flapping at the window-frame,
Exactly like the print of Fame ?"
All this the wise old parrot heard,
The parrot was an ancient bird,
And paused and ponder'd every word.
First, therefore, he began to cough,
Then said,—" It is a great way off,—
A great way off, my dear :"—and then
He paused awhile, and cough'd again,—
" Master John,[2] pray think a little,
What will you do for beds and victual ?"
—" Oh ! parrot, uncle John can tell—
But we should manage very well.

---

[1] The late Bartholomew Frere, then Secretary to the Embassy at Constantinople.
[2] His nephew, the late Rev. John Frere, rector of Cottenham.
"John is at Blake's Hotel. He took much to trying to improve little John [his nephew] in all ways—teaching him to spell, read, and figure ; and writing short fables for his use—walking with him, talking to him, explaining, and exerting his attention in every way, with great calmness and kindness."—*Extract of letter to Bartholomew Frere, at Constantinople, from his mother,* 1812.

At night we'd perch upon the trees,
And so fly forward by degrees."—
—" Does uncle John," the parrot said,
" Put nonsense in his nephew's head?
Instead of telling you such things,
And teaching you to wish for wings,
I think he might have taught you better;
You might have learnt to write a letter:—
That is the thing that I should do
If I had little hands like you."

FABLE III.

OF THE BOY AND THE WOLF.

LITTLE boy was set to keep
A little flock of goats or sheep.
He thought the task too solitary,
And took a strange perverse vagary,
To call the people out of fun,
To see them leave their work and run,
He cried and scream'd with all his might,—
"Wolf! wolf!" in a pretended fright.
Some people, working at a distance,
Came running in to his assistance.
They search'd the fields and bushes round,
The Wolf was no where to be found.
The Boy, delighted with his game,
A few days after did the same,
And once again the people came.
The trick was many times repeated,
At last they found that they were cheated.
One day the wolf appear'd in sight,
The Boy was in a real fright,
He cried, " Wolf! wolf!"—The Neighbours heard,
But not a single creature stirr'd.
" We need not go from our employ,—
'Tis nothing but that idle boy."
The little boy cried out again,
" Help, help! the Wolf!"—he cried in vain.

At last his master went to beat him,
He came too late, the wolf had eat him.

THIS shews the bad effects of lying,
And likewise of continual crying ;
If I had heard you scream and roar,
For nothing, twenty times before,
Although you might have broke your arm, ⎫
Or met with any serious harm, ⎬
Your cries could give me no alarm, ⎭
They would not make me move the faster,
Nor apprehend the least disaster ;
I should be sorry when I came,
But you yourself would be to blame.

FABLE IV.

OF THE PIECE OF GLASS AND THE PIECE OF ICE.

NCE on a time, it came to pass,
A piece of ice and piece of glass
Were lying on a bank together.
There came a sudden change of weather,
The sun shone through them both.—The ice
Turn'd to his neighbour for advice.
The piece of glass made this reply,—
"Take care by all means not to cry."
The foolish piece of ice relied
On being pitied if he cried.
The story says—That he cried on
Till he was melted and quite gone.

THIS may serve you for a rule
With the little boys at school ;
If you weep, I must forewarn ye,
All the boys will tease and scorn ye.

FABLE V.

OF THE CAVERN AND THE HUT.

AN ancient cavern, huge and wide,
Was hollow'd in a mountain's side,
It served no purpose that I know,
Except to' shelter sheep or so,
Yet it was spacious, warm, and dry.
There stood a little hut hard by.—
The cave was empty quite, and poor,
The hut was full of furniture ;
By looking to his own affairs,
He got a table and some chairs,
All useful instruments of metal,
A pot, a frying-pan, a kettle,
A clock, a warming-pan, a jack,
A salt-box and a bacon-rack ;
With plates, and knives, and forks, and dishes,
And lastly, to complete his wishes,
He got a sumptuous pair of bellows.—
The cavern was extremely jealous :
" How can that paltry hut contrive
In this poor neighbourhood to thrive ? "
The reason's plain," replied the hut,
Because I keep my mouth close shut ;
Whatever my good master brings,
For furniture, or household things,
I keep them close, and shut the door,
While you stand yawning evermore."

IF a little boy is yawning
At his lessons every morning,
Teaching him in prose or rhyme
Will be merely loss of time ;
All your pains are thrown away,
Nothing will remain a day,
(Nothing you can teach or say,
Nothing he has heard or read,)
In his poor unfurnish'd head.

FABLE VI.

Showing how the Cavern followed the Hut's Advice.

HIS fable is a very short one :
The cave resolved to make his fortune ;
He got a door, and in a year
Enrich'd himself with wine and beer.

Mamma will ask you, can you tell her,
What did the cave become ?—A cellar.

FABLE VII.

By Master John's[1] desire, about the Rod and the Whip.

HE Rod and Whip had some disputes ;
One managed boys, the other brutes.
Each pleaded his superior nature,
The Goad was chosen arbitrator,
A judge acquainted with the matter,
Upright, inflexible, and dry,
And always pointed in reply :—
" 'Tis hard," he said, " to pass a sentence
Betwixt two near and old acquaintance ;
The Whip alleges that he drives
The plough, by which the farmer lives,
And keeps his horses in obedience,
And on this ground he claims precedence.
The Rod asserts, that little boys,
With nonsense, nastiness, and noise,
Screaming, and quarrelling, and fighting,
Not knowing figures, books, or writing,
Would be far worse than farmers' horses,
But for the rules which he enforces—
He proves his claim as clear as day,
So Whips and Goads must both give way."

---

[1] See Note 2, p. 278.

FABLE VIII.

OF THE NINE-PINS.

(Being a Fable for Six Years Old.)

NINEPIN that was left alone,
When all his friends were overthrown,
Every minute apprehending
The destructive stroke impending,
Earnestly complain'd and cried ;
But Master Henry[1] thus replied:—
" Are you the wisest and the best ?
Or any better than the rest ?
While you linger to the last,
How has all your time been past ?
Standing stupid, unimproved,
Idle, useless, unbeloved ;
Nothing you can do or say
Shall debar me from my play."

THE Nine-pins you perceive are men,
'Tis death that answers them again ;
And the fable's moral truth
Suits alike with age and youth.
How can age of death complain,
If his life has past in vain ?
How can youth deserve to last
If his life is idly past ?
And the final application
Marks the separate obligation,
Fairly placed within our reach,
Your's to learn, and mine to teach.

---

[1] The present Earl Cadogan.

A FABLE.

DINGY donkey, formal and unchanged,
Browsed in the lane and o'er the common
    ranged,
Proud of his **ancient** asinine possessions,
Free from the panniers of the grave professions,
He lived at ease ; and chancing **once** to find
A lion's skin, the fancy **took** his **mind**
To personate the monarch **of the wood ;**
And for a time the stratagem **held good.**
He moved with so majestical a pace
That **bears** and wolves and all the savage **race**
Gazed in admiring awe, ranging aloof,
Not over-anxious for a clearer proof—
Longer he might have triumph'd—but **alas !**
In an unguarded hour it **came to pass**
He bray'd aloud ; and **show'd himself an ass !**

THE moral of this tale **I could not guess**
Till **Mr.** Landor sent his **works to press.**

"Poetry **is** too sublime **for** my **comprehension, and I**
have just to put up with plain prose."

"Weel, Sir, ye speak like **a** sensible **man ; you're just**
the customer I like **to meet wi' ;** you'll **find on the perusal**
o' **my poems a** *fullness* of *expression* about **them, that**
you'll **no ken but that it's** prose you're **reading."—***The*
Laird of Logan.

AN APPEAL[1] TO THE PROFESSORS **OF ART** AND LITERATURE **IN THE** UNITED KINGDOM

ON BEHALF OF WALTER SAVAGE LANDOR, ESQUIRE; **CONCLUDING WITH A RESPECTFUL REPRESENTATION TO THE** ASTRONOMICAL SOCIETY.

YE **painters** and engravers! **hear my** call,
Sculptors and poets, artists one and all,
Let Shakespeare, Milton, Byron, Walter Scott,
Pitt, Fox, and Burke, and Canning **be** forgot:
——Pre-eminent in priggery supreme
Let Walter Savage Landor be your theme:
Neither a Tory, Radical, or Whig,
But an immaculate consummate prig!
——**Ye** Shaftesburys and prigs of elder time,
Less perfect, and of priggery less sublime,
In those Elysian fields where **now you tread**
Engaged **in** conversations with **the dead,**
With contemplation of the immortal **Plato,**
And admiration of the virtuous Cato,
And **other** mighty prigs renown'd in story;
Alas, **alas,** for your departed glory!
Here **Walter** Savage Landor comes to snatch
The laurel from the brows of all your batch!
Rise then, and with profound obeisance greet,
Bowing **at** Walter Savage Landor's feet!
And own yourselves (as needs you **must confess**) ⎫
In prose less prosy, and in priggishness,   ⎬
Beyond dispute, immeasurably less——   ⎭
But I proceed **too** fast. **It may** be **said**
That Walter Savage Landor **is not dead.**
'Tis well observed, and therefore **I return**
To speak a word to those it may concern——

---

[1] This "Appeal" was provoked by Walter Savage Landor's *Imaginary Conversations,* more especially by that between Mr. Pitt and Mr. Canning; Conversation III. vol. 4, p. 59 of the Ed. 1829—and **a diatribe on** Mr. Canning, for his conduct to Queen Caroline, **in** vol. 5, p. 195.

Painters and artists (as I said before)
I wish you to proceed on a new score.
Let Walter Savage Landor's glorious noddle
Be your exclusive, universal model.
Work! Work upon it! with renew'd delight, ⎫
Work! Work (I tell ye) morning, noon, and night, ⎬
That in shop-windows it may charm the sight, ⎭
Attracting every gaze ; eclipsing all ⎫
Modern celebrities, both great and small, ⎬.
Whiggish, Conservative, and Radical. ⎭
—Ye printsellers all! wherefore should ye deal
In lithographs of Wellington and Peel,
O'Connells, and Lord Melbournes, and Lord Johns?
List to my words! discard them all at once!
Compared, I say, with Walter Savage Landor ⎫
The most distinguish'd statesman and commander ⎬.
In future ages will be deem'd a gander. ⎭
Yes! Walter Savage Landor beats them hollow, ⎫
Away with them ; let wits and poets follow, ⎬
Let the great Landor be your great Apollo ; ⎭
Discard Lord Byron with his loose shirt-collar,
Our glorious Landor is a better scholar,
Riper, as Shakespeare has it, and completer,
And makes Hendecasyllables in metre
As good as any fifth-form boy could do,
Without false quantities, or very few ;
And tho' Lord Byron's peerage ranks him higher,
Yet Mister Landor writes himself " Esquire,"
And keeps a groom! [1] and boasts himself to be
A scion of heraldic ancestry,
Wearing a coat of arms upon his seal!
A circumstance which animates his zeal
Against a base plebeian prelacy,
Fellows without a genealogy!

---

[1] James Wilkins, the same person who learned Welsh from Mr.
Landor's Scullion, or *under cook*, is now living with me as my *head
groom*, in consequence of his rejection as a candidate for orders
which he had applied for at the suggestion of his former master (Mr.
Landor). I keep a stable boy besides (and if it should be in any way
interesting to the reader), it may be proper to inform him that both
of them wear *my crest* on the buttons of their Sunday liveries.—See
" Reflections on Athens at the Decease of Pericles," appended to
Pericles and Aspasia.

Poised on the cherub contemplation's wings, ⎫
His lordship sits blaspheming as he sings, ⎬
Cursing and damning all terrestrial things, ⎭
Feeling the persecution and malignity
Of providence ; but feeling it with dignity,
Such as befits a person of his quality, ⎫
Pursued by a predestinate fatality, ⎬
But an essential poet in reality. ⎭
Admitting, therefore, that his lines are grander
Than those of Mister Walter Savage Landor,
We still maintain that in another sense
Our Landor claims a first pre-eminence.
I should be sorry to be deem'd severe,
But Byron was a most licentious peer,
Leading, in fact, a dissipated life,
Without respect of widow, maid, or wife.
While Walter Savage Landor's immorality ⎫
Is mere imaginary classicality, ⎬
Wholly devoid of criminal reality. ⎭
Yet Walter Savage Landor in his way
Is often-times unutterably gay.
" *He frolicketh,*" and " *doth frolic,*" and in fine
(Adhering strictly to the classic line
With such methodic gambols as become
A classic Prig) Landor *is frolicsome:*
Quite a beau garçon, a consummate beau,
In the beau-monde two thousand years ago.
A perfect master of the *savoir-vivre.*
Un homme à bonnes fortunes, a gay deceiver.
In his own conduct cautious and correct,
But a decided rake in retrospect.
With classic ardour, rash and uncontroll'd,
With Lais and with Thais he makes bold,
The Harriette Wilsons of the days of old.
He loves a tête-à-tête with fair Aspasia,
And takes his daily lounge in the gymnasia ;
But his supreme delight is Alcibiades.
A rhyme, I want a rhyme for Alcibiades ; ⎫
There's none that I can think of, none but Pleiades. ⎭
And a more lucky rhyme I never met !
For it suggests a scheme I might forget.
One point is settled, that we must not squander,

While we possess a Walter Savage Landor,
Honour or praise on any man beside ;
Is he not Europe's wonder ? England's pride ?
Therefore, I say, let every means be tried
To immortalize the most immortal man ;
Let all true Britons do the best they can,
Whatever art can do with brass and copper,
Canvas and marble, will be just and proper :
Whilst we that manufacture prose and verse
In humble strains endeavour to disburse
Our debt of admiration ; and express
His high deserts by dint of letter-press ;—
But all is transitory—prose and verse,
Sculpture and painting—Wise astronomers !
" *In all things I prefer the permanent.*"
Could you not place our Landor in the firmament ?
Marble will decompose, and canvas moulder,
Before the world is many centuries older.
Moreover, in all likelihood, God knows !
Our compositions, whether verse or prose,
Compose them as we may, will decompose :
Even great Landor's deathless works may die.
Whereas, if you could place him in the sky,
Nothing that happen'd here need signify.
There he might shine in spite of the ravages
And devastations of invading savages,
Tranquil and bright ; whilst a benighted age
Profaned in filthy sort his mighty page.
Surely with all your curious observation
You might detect a vacant constellation ;
Or make another new one here or there,
Just as you did with Berenice's hair.
Pope ask'd the question once, and so shall I !
" Is there no bright reversion in the sky ? "
No reserved district ?   Nothing unallotted ?
Were all your predecessors so besotted
As to grant out a total hemisphere
Assign'd to the first claimants that appear
(Like that proud Pontiff the sixth Alexander).
Is nothing left for Walter Savage Landor ?
I should not wish for our heraldic scion
To stand a whole-length figure like Orion,

Perseus, and other astronomic giants ;
I merely think that by the kind compliance,
Favour and aid of an illustrious science,
Somewhere or other in the bounds of space
His glorious *inkstand* might obtain a place.
See what a list of articles appear
Establish'd in the southern hemisphere ;
Their own chronometers and telescopes
Canonized by your astronomic Popes !
With other objects that still less concern us,
A painter's easel, and a chemist's furnace,
A sculptor's tools and workshop in a lot,
A microscope, an air-pump, and what not,[1]
And, oh ! shall LANDOR'S INKSTAND be forgot.[2]
For Landor " scrawls not upon greasy platters,"
Nor such-like sordid sublunary matters ;
His paper and his ink are transcendental,
Warranted sempiternal, elemental,
His patent right in ink is a good rental,
His affidavit states that the true article
Does not contain a perishable particle.

P. S. AND N. B.

A NECESSARY caution to the buyer—
Counterfeits are abroad—please to enquire
For packets seal'd[3] and sign'd, " *Landor, Esquire.*"
The Aeidian fluid, ink of immortality,
The rest are frauds of an inferior quality.

P. S.

ON second thoughts, " *I must recall my groom,*
And add a postscript, tho' for want of room
It must be short—a warning was omitted
Which to the sons of science is submitted.
My dear Astronomers ! you must be sensible
That caution in this case is indispensable ;

---

[1] Horologium, telescopium, equuleus pictoris, fornax chemica, apparatus sculptoris, cela sculptoris, microscopium, antlia pneumatica.
[2] *Inkstandium Landorianum.*
[3] Observe the Landor arms, a Donkey Sejant Proper—armed fanged and langued—Escryvant Brayant.

—I feel I must confess—my doubts and fears,
From Landor's exaltation to the spheres.
Let it be done with care and circumspection ;
And don't proclaim a general election
Of candidates for the new constellation,
Or every star will hurry from his station :
The least of them that feels the least ambition
To change his place and better his condition
Will bustle and start forth in the confusion
Of a chaotic general dissolution,—
Depend upon it, we shall hear the sky
Re-echoing with an universal cry,
" Place us in *Landor's Inkstand* or we die.
—Yes, welcome chaos ! if we can attain
That high distinction, let it come again."

MODERN IMPROVEMENTS.

THE cumbrous pollards that o'ershade
    Those uplands rough with brakes and thorns,
The green-way with its track-worn glade,
    The solitary grange forlorn,
    The lonely pastures wild and drear,
The lowly dwellings wide apart,
Are whispering to the fancy's ear
    A secret strain that moves the heart.
No forms of grandeur or of grace
    In the rude landscape you behold,
But their rough lineaments retrace
    The features of the times of old :
They speak of customs long retain'd,
    Of simple, plain, primeval life,
They mark the little we have gain'd
    With all our study, toil and strife ;
Such England was to Shakespeare's eyes,
    So Chaucer view'd her as he roved,
In russet weeds of rustic guise,
    In homelier beauty more beloved.

Our ancient halls have left the land,
  Turrets and towers have pass'd away,
Arcades and porticoes were plann'd
  And these again have had their day:
Impatient, peevish wealth recalls
  The forms which she defaced before,
Unthrifty sires destroy'd the halls
  Which modern prodigals restore ;
Confounding England, Rome, and Greece,
  Each ancient and each modern race,
We dislocate with wild caprice
  All unities of time and place ;
Yet here attended by the Muse
  Let harass'd Fancy pause awhile,
And unpolluted yet peruse   ·
  This remnant of our ancient isle.

JOURNEY TO HARDINGHAM

TO VISIT THE REV. W. WHITER, OF CLARE HALL.

THE rude South-wester from his den
Comes raving o'er a range of fen ;
The window frame of massy cast,[1]
Unhinged, unpullied, never fast,
Trembles and jostles to the blast :
The drops still standing on the pane,
The shivering twigs that drip with rain,
The prospect of the distant plain
Obscure and undistinguish'd, furnish
No motive for cross-country journeys.
Besides—with waiting for the post—
The morning is already lost.
While Reason pauses to decide,
Let Fancy paint the future ride.
From famed Winfarthing's lonely pound
To Buckenham's huge mysterious mound,

---

[1] In the study at Roydon Hall.

How dull and dismal is the scene—
Dreary, monotonous, and mean.
Its ancient Common, wide and bare,
Dissected into straight and square,[1]
How cheerless and devoid of grace !
With painful interrupted pace,
The drooping Peasantry retire
Stumbling and staggering thro' the mire :
From scatter'd huts the transient rays
Betray their frugal evening blaze ;
The wintry sun's descending beam,
With chilly melancholy gleam,
Reflected from the stagnant drains,
Illuminates those endless lanes :
Such scenes absorb my thoughts and bring 'em
Prepared with joy to enter Hingham ;
Her stately steeple strikes the sight,
And cheerful sounds and lively light
My past antipathies requite ;
Again, afraid to miss the mark,
I plunge thro' turnings close and dark,
Immerging among trackless acres
I hope to light upon the Quaker's.[2]
The Quaker's—sure it must be so—
The stream lies glimmering there below,
Look on—the steeple stands in view—
The parsonage and the steeple too—
The clattering gate returning hard,
Announces guests within the yard ;
I see the worthy priest rejoice—
With open face and hearty voice,
His old acquaintance kindly hailing,
With hand outstretch'd across the paling.
Alighting now, we pass the hall
And view the parlour snug and small,
The fire of logs, the tapestry wall ;
Huge volumes prostrate on the floor ;
A parsonage of the days of yore.

---

[1] By a late enclosure.
[2] A Dissenter who went by that name, at the foot of whose garden
a little stream runs.

Our dinner ended, we discourse
Of old traditions and their source,
Of times beyond the reach of history,
Of many a mythologic mystery,
Of primitive records and acts,
Their traces and surviving facts,
Of tribes, of languages, and nations,
Of immemorial old migrations ;
Hence our digressive chat inquires
Of justices, divines, and squires,
Of births, and marriages, and deaths,
Enclosures of the neighbouring heaths,
Of ancient friends at Caius and King's,
And such-like sublunary things.
Again—we soar to the sublime,
On pinions of recited rhyme,
While you persuade me to proceed
With " Well," or " Very well, indeed ! "
A long continued recitation,
Epistle, fable, or translation,
Exhausting all my last year's stock,
Conducts us on to twelve o'clock.
So be it then—In spite of weather,
I'll take the good and bad together ;
So, George, put up of shirts a pair,
And bid them saddle me the mare.

IMITATION OF HORACE, LIB. I. EP. XI.

QUID TIBI VISA CHIOS, ETC.

DEAR BARTLE,[1]

OW does Turkey suit your taste,
Compared with it is Lisbon quite effaced,
Seville, and all the scenes we view'd together?
What sort of climate have you found, and
    weather ?
The fish, the figs, the grapes, and Grecian wine,
In real earnest, are they quite as fine

---

[1] See page 278, note 1.

As modern travellers have represented?
Inform us—are you joyous and contented,
Or are you sick of Dragomans and Turks,
Muftis, Bashaws, and all their wicked works?
And pine to visit our domestic scene,
Roydon and Finningham and Mellis' Green,
To pass a rainy winter afternoon
With Mr., Mrs. and the Misses Moon,
Till, like an affable convivial priest,
Returning late from his parochial feast,
Temple[1] diverts us from backgammon-playing,
With phrases of old Daniel Garrard's saying.
Next morning we must saunter out once more
To view the scenes so often view'd before.
The solemn features and commanding stare
Of ancient justices and ladies fair,
Which Rednall still preserves with loyal care,
Arranged in order round his parlour wall,
Poor emigrants from the deserted hall ;
Or prune with grave discussion and suspense
The rising saplings in the new-made fence ;
Or wander forth where Syret's wife deplores
The broken pantiles in her pantry floors;
Or eastward pass to that remoter scene
Where tracts of hostile acres intervene,
To look at Kersey's maid, and taste his ale,
And grieve to see the new-made plaister fail.
Then to return, and find at every station
Old topics, that revive the conversation,
Themes of complacency and consolation.
" That stream with proper care might overflow
The strip of pasture ground that lies below ;
Those trees have of themselves contrived to grow :
Those ancient chimneys have been well replaced,"
And "Temple's chancel has been tiled with taste."
Such joys as these attend on my return
To Roydon, from the place of date—Eastbourne.

August 23, 1812.

---

[1] The Rev. Temple Frere, late Prebendary of Westminster.

FRAGMENT.

IS the dominion of an abstract rule
Restricted to the Geometric School,
To be recognized there, and there alone,
Shall we conclude of sciences unknown
  *   *   *   *
Analogy forbids it. What is true
In an establish'd science, in a new
May be true likewise. Her reply would say,
" Must—absolutely must—not only may—
But struggle for yourselves, I point the way."
And what say we? shall our familiar guide
Hear her instructions scoff'd at, and denied?
Good old analogy that first supplied
Our infant world with elemental speech !
She, that in daily life descends to teach
With nature at her side, adult, and grown
And wise in an experience of our own,
What nature dictates, and analogy,
Shall we with peremptory pride deny?
Or shall we follow where she points the way,
A path of steep ascent and hard assay,
Yet leading to a summit clear and high,
Of boundless vision, in a cloudless sky,
Where nature's mighty landscape, unsurvey'd
By mortal eye, lies open and display'd.
  *   *   *   *   *

The Ideal ruling law, like words to deeds,
In numbers and geometry, precedes
The Concrete, Thought is there the lord and king,
The sovereign ; the mechanic subject thing
Is substance, practice, and experiment ;
And shall we deem, that intellect was lent
To light a single science? Have the rest
Lost their high caste, degraded and deprest
Irrevocably : doom'd to labour here
For fame and gain, in an inferior sphere,
Surveyor, architect, or engineer?
Is there no spirit of a loftier strain,
A Kepler or a Newton once again,

With light upon the chaos, to divide
And fix the mass of knowledge dark and wide,
With a divining hand, to seize the clue,
To keep the known conclusion full in view,
And work the problem till he proves it true ?
Must we for ever shrewd and worldly wise,
Confine ourselves to Solomon's advice,
To seek enjoyment, and escape from want,
To take our pattern from the labouring ant,
Where imitative nature emulates
The forms of understanding, and creates,
Devoid of intellect, her pigmy states,
A single soul in sundry forms combined,
A patriotic universal mind,
An instrumental nature, ever striving
For a fixt purpose, labouring and contriving,
United, orderly, coherent, still
Without a selfish aim or separate will,
With nothing individual?   Which is he,
The legislator master of the free,
The great preceptor, teaching from his tomb
A living multitude, that shall presume
To place his model for the rule of man.
In parallel with this, the simple plan
Fix'd and ordain'd for an inferior state,
Penultimate of man's penultimate ?
           *   *   *   *

With righteous or perverted will to take
Good simply as good—evil for evil's sake ;
Mischief in children—bold debauch in men
Exulting and approved—the pimping pen
That seeks to pander for a race unborn,
The unholy league that pours contempt and scorn
On every better purpose, industry
Perverse and servile, that descends to pry
In crevices of forgotten infamy,
With unrewarded toil, to canonize
The rakes and drabs of former centuries,
Their relics and remains.
These and a thousand other signs reveal
The existence of a pure unpurchased zeal,
Zeal in the cause of evil, that divests

The obedient mind of selfish interests,
And ranks them in the legendary list,
The martyrs of the great antagonist.
Enough of Evil—for the love of good
Misconstrued, scandalized, misunderstood,
Denied and hated—still that it exists
I feel and know—Deny it he that lists—
But grant it—and you see the human will
Working in eager chase of good or ill.
These rudiments of an ulterior state
Embarrass and bewilder with debate
Our human hive and ant-hill—as the wings
Unfledged are cumbrous and contentious things
To callow birds (that struggle in the nest
Naked and crowded), useless at the best.

    *   *   *   *

FRAGMENT II.

THE revelation of an element,
    Its accidents and forms—What else is meant
    By that establish'd phrase, "the visible world?"
    What but a single element unfurled
    And manifested to a single sense?
Is tangible creation more immense,
More multiform, than the domain of Light,
That visible creation which the sight
Holds as its empire through the ministry
Of light, its elemental sole ally?
The Almighty Wisdom and Power that could direct,
And with a single element effect
So vast a purpose, shall we dare deny
(What reason teaches and analogy)
That the same Wisdom and Power, working his will
With the like simple means, with the same skill,
In a like form and method might devise
All that a grosser sense can recognize?
No! the celestial Author and Creator
In those two volumes of the Book of Nature
Ordain'd for our instruction, represents,

By multiform but single elements,
One universe of sense, all that we know,
The visible world of instantaneous show
And tangible creation, hard and slow,
The last remaining inlet of the mind,
The dreary blank creation of the blind.
Nor is it vain what elder bards indite
Of Love self-born, and by inherent might
Emerged from chaos and primeval night.
Was this the form, which idle fancy sings,
With glowing cheeks adorn'd and glittering wings,
The classic idol and the modern toy,
A torch, a quiver, and a blinded boy?
Was this the sense? or does it represent
Some sovereign and controlling element,
Some impulse unapproachable by thought,
Some force that 'midst the eternal tumult wrought,
And this fair order from confusion brought ;
Established motion's substance, form, and weight,
The statutes of this earth's material state ?
—Suppose a single element the source
Of all attractive and impelling force,
That motion and cohesion are the extreme
United opposites upon the beam
Of Nature's balance, a magnetic whole,
Single itself, and one ; but pole to pole
Contrasted ; as the powers of heat and light
Stand each confronted with its opposite,
Darkness and cold ; not mere negations they,
But negatives with a divided sway,
Pressing—oppress'd—advancing—giving way.
Suppose then (as has been supposed before
By wisest men) that in the days of yore
There was a deeper knowledge, and a store
Of science more exalted and sublime,
Whose relics on the barren shore of time
Lie stranded and dispersed, retaining still
Intelligible marks of art and skill,
Of an intended purpose and appliance,
The scanty salvage of a shipwreck'd science
Submerged time out of mind! Kepler could draw
From these remains the mighty truth he saw
Of an harmonic, necessary law ;

Then with an indefatigable mind
Analogies incessantly combined
With a foreseen conclusion full in view
He work'd the problem till he proved it true.
Is there no spirit of a nobler strain,
A Kepler or a Newton once again,
With light upon the chaos to divide,
And fix the mass of knowledge waste and wide ;
For as " the crowd of trees conceals the wood,"
With all things known, with nothing understood,
Perplex'd with new results from year to year,
As on the puzzled Ptolemaic sphere
With cycles epicycles scribbled o'er,
Like ancient Philomaths we doze and pore :
Thus Ashmole, Lilly, shine in portraiture
(Dear to the chalcographic connoisseur) ;
While the wise nightcap and the Jacob's staff
Awe the beholder and conceal his laugh.
—If we despair then to decipher nature
With our new facts and novel nomenclature :
Those almanacks of science that appear
Framed and adjusted for the current year,
And warranted correct for months to come ,
If calculation fails to find the sum
(A formula to comprehend the whole)
Of countless items on the crowded scroll,
Corrected, re-corrected, and replaced,
Obliterated, interlined, effaced,
Blotted and torn in philosophic squabble,
And endless, unintelligible scrabble ;
If the huge labyrinth with its winding ways
Entangled in the inextricable maze,
The wilderness of waste experiment,
Has foil'd your weary spirits worn and spent,
Since every path is trodden round and tried,
—Trust for a moment a superior guide ;
The trembling needle or the stedfast star,
Some point of lofty mark and distant far,
These shall conduct you, whatsoe'er your fate,
At least in a decided path and strait ;
Not running round in circles, evermore
Bewilder'd and bewitch'd as heretofore :
Like the poor clown that robb'd the wizard's store }

Breathless and hurrying in his endless race,
With eager action, and a ghastly face,
By subtle magic tether'd to the place.
   Yet let us hope that something may befall!
That things will find their level after all!
That these atomic facts, ever at war,
Tumbled together in perpetual jar,
After a certain period more or less
Will ultimately form or coalesce.
So shall it be! Strife shall engender motion,
And kindle into life each tardy notion.
Keen disputants in a judicial fight,
Sparring with spurs of controversial spite,
In battle-royal shall decide the right.
Till truth's majestic image stands reveal'd
The sole surviving game-cock in the field!
—That venerable, old, reviewing phrase,
Threadbare and overworn—mark what it says,
The fashionable tenet of the time,
Tho' stale in prose, it may be hash'd in rhyme.
—When disputants, it says, with hasty zeal
Clash in hard discord like the flint and steel,
The sparks elided from their angry knocks,
Caught in a philosophic tinder-box,
Falling upon materials cut and dried,
With modest brimstone diligently plied,
And urged with puffs incessantly supplied,
As an atonement for the noise and scandal,
Will serve to light a scientific candle.
—But no!—the wrath of man never attains
To pure results, nor his ambitious pains,
Nor busy canvas, nor a learned league,
(Except in undermining and intrigue;)
In lonely shades those miracles of thought
Are brought to light. No miracles are wrought
To gratify the scruples or the whim
Of a contentious testy Sanhedrim.
" To satisfy just doubts," " to guide decision,"
For no such purposes, the mighty vision
Was ever yet vouchsafed sudden and bright,
Descending in a soft illapse of light.
Quenching its murky steam of filthy vapour,

It kindles at a touch the fumy taper.
  Let, then, a new progressive step be tried, ⎫
Since light and heat, it is not now denied, ⎬
Are agents, consubstantial and allied. ⎭
Now for this other power, which we must call
(Taking a single quality for all)
Attraction, or the power of gravity,
The power of motion, form, solidity,
Third person of the Pagan Trinity.
This power, then, of attraction, truly view'd,
Displays a likeness and similitude
With light, as a congenial kindred force ;
For common reason will concede, of course,
That all attractive forces great and small
Are retroactive and reciprocal ;
As when the mariners with trampling feet
In even cadence round the capstan beat,
Moving in order round the mighty beam,
To warp their vessel against wind and stream,
While the huge cable, with its dripping fold,
In weary coils incessantly enroll'd,
Drags forth the labouring vessel to the deep.
The point, then, we have conquer'd, and can keep.
As being drawn itself, the cable draws,
Tho' passive, it becomes a moving cause.
Take then at once the reason and the facts,
Light is attracted, therefore light attracts—
And though the nobler attributes of light
Have left this incident unnoticed quite,
And though we find its feebler efforts fail
Of mark'd effect on a material scale,
Unheeded and impalpable to sense,
Yet reason must acknowledge its pretence
Enough to range it in a kindred class
Though inefficient on the subject mass.
The facts and inferences fairly view'd,
With this result we finally conclude—
If ever Reason justly gave assent ⎫
To truths too subtle for experiment, ⎬
Then light is an attracting element, ⎭
And heat, its congener, will be the same,
A joint supporter of this worldly frame.

Nor these alone—but that attractive force
Described in the first lines of our discourse,
Whose nature and existence known of yore
Was but a portion of the secret store
Of Eastern learning, which the busy Greek,
Active and eager, started forth to seek,
Purchasing here and there a wealthy prize,
Amidst the ruins of the rich and wise,
The mighty sacerdotal monarchies,
Stupendous Egypt—Stately Babylon
By the barbarian Persian overthrown.
(The Chivalrous Barbarian in his line,
A gallant loyal warrior, but in fine
A fierce Iconoclastic Ghibelline !)
Such is the fact—our first historic page
—Herodotus—begins with a dark age,
An age of antient Empires overturn'd,
Records obliterated, temples burn'd,
Their living archives, all the learned class,
Methodically murder'd in a mass.
Hence like a sutler at a city's sack,
The wary Grecian pedlar fill'd his pack,
And cannily contrived to bring it back
With merchandize : such as a pedlar gets,
Remnants and damaged samples, broken sets,
Fragments of plunder, purchased or purloin'd,
Rich fragments but incongruously join'd.
    The scheme of Hutchinson was incomplete,
It stands without its complement of feet :
A tripod resting upon light and heat
His third supporter fails, limping and bare
Of evidence, his element of air.
His scheme then at the time was doom'd to fall,
Or left with lumber propt against the wall,
A maim'd utensil, destitute of use,
Obscure with dust of obsolete abuse—
The learned dust excited in the frays
Of Jacobite and Hanoverian days.
Newton and Cambridge and the Brunswick line,
And Dr. Clarke, and Gracious Caroline,
Match'd against Oxford and the right divine.

Whether, in fact, as all opinions mix,
They finally converge to politics,
Or shrewd intriguers had contrived to fix
On their opponents a disloyal stain,
Blind to the glories of so bright a Reign,
The name with Jacobite opinions link'd
With Jacobite opinions was extinct:
Each cultivated ornamental prig
Of hybrid form, a parson and a whig,
(A whig by principle or calculation,
A Christian Priest by trade and occupation)
Each smooth aspirant, loyal and correct,
Was bound in policy to shun the sect;
While of the sacred bench each righteous son,
Clayton and Hoadly, and meek Warburton,
Condemn'd them soul and body, blood and bone!
Meanwhile Sir Isaac's theory of attraction
Afforded universal satisfaction;
Applauded by the clerical profession
As friendly to the Protestant succession;
A sober well-affected theory
Which none but a nonjuror could deny—
A theory may be false or incomplete,
While the phenomena and the rules may meet;
Conceive (as was imagined formerly)
That vision is ejected from the eye
—You'll find the rules of perspective apply.
We judge from practice the physician's skill,
And let him choose what principles he will,
Bad theories may cure and good ones kill.
First then our drugs and aliments we see,
Dry, cold, or hot in some assign'd degree:
Next mathematic learning came in use,
The blood was clogg'd with particles obtuse:
Poisons were points which antidotes must sheathe,
Mechanic action made us move and breathe:
A chemic system rose upon its fall,
Acids and alkalis were all in all:
A change of argument, a change of style,
Mere speculative change, for all the while
The same prescriptions rested on the file,

And while the verbal argument endured,
The patients as before were kill'd or cured.
  A theory that enables us to plant
A tortoise underneath our elephant,
But wants a creature of some other sort
To serve us for our tortoise's support :
In other words, it teaches us the laws
—Of motion and attraction—not the cause.
The laws are undisputed, and we see
How punctually predicted facts agree ;
Meanwhile the cause unnoticed or denied
Is with a monstrous postulate supplied:
First we suppose that our terrestrial ball,
Launch'd forth with an enormous capital
Of motion—like a wandering prodigal
Without a stipend of in-coming rent,
In all his course of travel, has not spent
One stiver of the first allotted sum,
Nor ever will, for ages yet to come.
The quantum still remains as heretofore,
An unexhausted, undiminish'd store,
The same precisely, neither less nor more ;
An article of faith hard to digest,
If common sense and nature are the test,
Yet proselytes must bolt it, husk and bran,
And keep it on their stomachs if they can—
—No theory or conjecture, not a notion
Of the first causes of a planet's motion !
Whence it originates no creature knows,
But with a given impulse forth it goes ;
Attraction's laws prohibit it to roam,
And bind the wanderer to his central home ;
Else had the wretched orb been whirl'd away,
Far from the stars of night and beams of day,
A cheerless, endless, solitary way.
Rescued, and grateful for the glad reprieve,
It gilds the morn or decks the front of eve,
And winds a joyous uneccentric way
In the warm precincts of the solar ray :
Obedient system clears the bounds of space
From all that might retard the yearly race.

The same incessant circuit is pursued,
With the same force for ages unrenew'd,
And sages of the sacred gown conclude,
That independent of an acting cause,
The properties of matters, motions, laws,
Preserve the punctual planet in his sphere,
Ordain the seasons and bring round the year—
See here the lessons reverend gownsmen teach,
The proud result of Learning's utmost reach.

Since wisest moderns have approved it true,
We take it as a fact—Nothing is new.
No—not the boast of this new century,
Our busy science of geology;
The terms of parturition and of birth
Express the first development of earth.
" This habitable earth, cheerful and fair,
Heaved from the teeming depth to light and air ;"
This truth which Hutton's school has taught us newly
Where do we find it first?   In Moses truly !
You see the passage paraphrased and quoted,
In the two lines above with commas noted,
Much weaker than the original.   Again—
The wisest, in his time, of living men
Adopts the same expression, adding more,
How the protruded mountains pierced the core
Of secondary strata form'd before,
Even as a finger passing thro' " a ring,"
This truth was known unto the " sapient king—"
See Proverbs, chapter eight, verse twenty-five,
And try what other meaning you can give ;
Or take the converse ; to characterise
The sense proposed, and frame it otherwise,
In Hebrew words, clearer and more precise ;
And we shall hail you when the task is done
A better scholar than King Solomon—
—The Hetrurian priesthood knew the identity
Of lightning and of electricity.
Discovery or tradition !—Such things were
Sources of hidden knowledge, deep and rare
Before the days of Franklin and Voltaire.

1*   x

(In the good days of old idolatry,
And priestcraft ! undisturb'd by blasphemy)
—Or tell me ! By what strange coincidence
Is the same word employ'd in the same sense,
A single word that serves to signify
The electric substance and the Deity
Of storms and lightning (their Elician Jove) ;
Whom with due rites invoked from the dark clouds above,
The priest attracted downwards ! woe betide
The novice that presumptuously tried,
Ignorant of the ritual and the form,
To dally with the Deity of the storm ;
Like the rash Roman king, by the dread stroke,
Which his unpractised art dared to provoke,
Smitten and slain ; a just example made
For ancient sovereigns who might dare to invade
And tamper with the sacerdotal trade.

  In the vast depths of ocean far below,
Where neither storms disturb nor currents flow,
Fish would remain unconscious of the water :
And reason, if experience had not taught her
By the rude impulse of the changeful wind,
Mere common understanding would not find,
That air existed—Nothing here below
Unless it can be felt or make a show,
Is mark'd or heeded, nothing else we know.
If light were universally display'd
Without its opposites, darkness and shade,
Constant and uniform in operation,
It never would attract our observation.
  Suppose the case, and that it were denied
That light existed—how could we decide,
Or judge the question by what test applied ?
Strong Reason and superior Art perhaps,
Long labouring in a long continued lapse
Of ages, might at length attain to show
What infants from their first impression know :
—" Ever the same yesterday and to-day ; "
Powers that exhibit no phenomena,
(No signs of life in change or difference)
To the mere understanding and the sense,

Are non-existences ; but here again,
Can our acknowledged principles explain
All our acknowledged facts ? Do none remain ?
When causes are assign'd to their effects,
Will there be no *Lacuna*, no defects,
Nothing anomalous or unexplain'd ?
I doubt it—otherwise the point is gain'd ;
The point, I presuppose, that there exists
An unacknowledged power, that as it lists
Rules paramount in its domain of air,
Guiding its endless eddies here and there :
But whither or from whence the currents flow,
Their source or end our senses cannot show,
And science never has attain'd to know.

Darwin has sung in verse beyond compare,
That in the North, beneath the Frozen Bear,
A huge chameleon spits and swallows air.
In fact, an instantaneous formation,
And a precipitous annihilation
Of our aerial fluid seems implied
In facts not yet developĕd or denied.
As in a whirlpool's strife the waters flow,
Pressing in eager eddies as they go
Precipitously to the void below,
In their own giddy circle wheel'd and held
By mutual haste impelling and impell'd :
With a like action airy currents move
To some unseen and hasty void above.
Now mark a strong coincidence !—Compare
The whirlpool's centre with its spire of air
Drawn downwards ; and behold the waters move
From the smooth ocean's surface rear'd above
In fluid spires ! Phenomena like these,
The careless seaman, in the summer seas,
Views unalarm'd, the momentary play
Of nature's power, an innocent display.
But what a power is here ! how little known,
That not beneath the Frozen north alone,
As Darwin deem'd, but in the sultry zone
Exists and acts—an atmosphere destroy'd,
And the creation of an instant void !

What other explanation can be found?
You see the watery columns whirling round,
They rise and move while Gravitation's laws
Are modified by a suspending clause—
In fine, if all our explanations fail,
When neither reason nor research avail
To solve the difficulty, this remains
The fair result and guerdon of our pains—
That *ex absurdo* thus it might be shown
That Gravity has phenomena of its own.
Thus far at least we might presume to say—
Here is a power without phenomena,
And the phenomena of a power unknown,
If both can be combined and brought in one
We gain a point, and something may be done.
The mere suggestion sure may be permitted:
No damage is incurr'd, no harm committed,
If not, they both remain on their own score
Obscure and unconnected as before.

Now then, resuming what before was stated,
We seek to show the converse: Air created,
And a continued efflux generated,
Where seamen witness in a cloudless sky
A driving hurricane eager and dry,
Continuous fury—without pause or shift
Its unappeasable, impetuous drift
Scourges and harasses the main for hours,
For days, for weeks, with unabated powers,
The Spirit of the Tempest hurries by,
With hideous impulse, and a piercing cry,
A persevering wild monotony.
Shorn of her topmast, all her goodly pride
And rich attire of canvas stript aside;
In a bare staysail, with an abject mien,
The vessel labours in the deep ravine,
A watery vale that intercepts the sight,
Or in an instant hurried to the height,
Pauses upon the fluid precipice,
Then downward to the dark and deep abyss
Shoots forth afresh, and with a plunging shock
Achieves the leap of her Tarpeian rock.
Her joints of massy frame compactly clench'd,

With the tormenting strain are rack'd and wrench'd ;
The baffled mariners, forlorn and pale,
Beneath eternal buffet droop and fail.
—Yet strange it seems the while ! no signs are given ⎤
Betokening hope or fear—no vapour driven   ⎬
In quick career across the void of Heaven !   ⎦
Tranquil and calm and blank, the mighty space
Wears an unconscious and unruffled face
Impassive in sublimity serene,
Mocking our toil, smiling upon the scene !
And yet the strong commotion was foretold,
(The sign Archilochus beheld of old)
The crooked, wicked cloud that, creeping slow
Around the distant mountain's haughty brow,
Folded its angry wreath, settled and fix'd,
Coil'd in itself, unmoving and unmix'd,
—A talismanic atmospheric spell—
The wary seaman knew the signal well ;
The seal of wrath : and from the token drew
A timely warning, terrible but true—
—Will the known principles of any school,
Will hydrostatic laws, or those which rule
The motions of elastic fluids guide
Our judgment, or assist us to decide
On facts like these ?   Alas ! when all is said,
We seek a living power among the dead,
And struggle to draw water in a sieve.
The cause of such effects must act and live,
Subsisting as a separate element,
Not as a mere result and accident
A simple passive thing urged or controll'd
By change of cold to heat, or heat to cold,
The vassal of a fickle temperature,
But a distinct and active power of nature.

TO A LADY[1] WITH A PRESENT OF A WALKING STICK.

COMPLIMENT upon a crutch
Does not appear to promise much;
A theme no lover ever chose
For writing billet-doux in prose,
Or for an amatory sonnet;
But thus I may comment upon it.
Its heart is whole, its head is bright,
'Tis smooth and yielding, yet upright.
In this you see an emblem of the donor,
Clear and unblemish'd as his honour,
Form'd for your use, framed to your hand,
Obedient to your least command.
Its proper place is by your side,
Its main utility and pride
To be your prop, support, and guide.

TO PADRE RIGORD.[2]

THERE is here, you must know, an old poet,
Rigord, between eighty and ninety, formerly a
Jesuit. I went to call upon him, and when he
was told my name he pulled the following distich out of his pocket:—

Clarissimo viro Frere vati Anglo
Vates Melitensis octogenarius
Gallico ludens vocabulo.

---

[1] Jemima, Dowager Countess of Errol, to whom he was afterwards married.

[2] Louis Maria Rigord, born in Malta, May 4, 1739, educated in the Jesuits' College in Palermo. On the expulsion of the Jesuits from Sicily in 1767 he went to Rome. He translated Catullus into Italian, and wrote several pieces of poetry, both in Italian and Maltese. He died and was buried in Malta.—See sketch of his life prefixed to the translation of Catullus, printed in Malta, 1839.

Distichon.

Si Frer nos fratres in primo nascimur Adam,
Frer sic in Phœbo nos decet esse fratres.

He made a much better distich for Buonaparte :—

Napoleon jacet hic—nomen tibi sufficit unum.
Huic par nullus erat—non erit alter—abi.

I could not answer him except in Iambics, because he made the first syllable of *frater* short ; so I made these:—

ALOYSIO RIGORD, S. J. POETÆ MELETENSI.

Hic me carentem patriâ atque affinibus,
    Fratrem vocari non piget,
Ætate quippe major et meritis tuis
    Fratrem minorem respicis :
Longæve vates ! Quid salutanti tibi
    Faustum precarer vel mihi ?
Ut innocentes sicut hactenus dies
    In laude ducas publicâ ;
Gratusque amicis semper, atque animo vigens,
    Sæclum perenne compleas.
Mihi, precari fas sit, exemplo tuo,
    Quod Flaccus olim optaverat,
Sanam senectam nec carentem carminis
    Cum mente sanâ consequi.

Malta, Sept. 26, 1821.

THE BUBBLE YEAR.

MIGHT we not hope, with humble confidence,
That finally a benignant Providence
Will extricate the British nation
From her embarrass'd situation,
    And graciously dispense
An earthquake or a pestilence.
An earthquake would be far the best,
To set the question once for all, at rest ;
    Sinking the sister isle
    At least a statute mile,

With a low, subsiding motion,
Beneath the level of the German Ocean,
   There to suffer a sea change,
   Into something queer and strange :
Then *if* their " bones are coral made "
They may supply the British trade
With an important new commodity :
Besides, when each Papistic churl
Shall have his eye-balls turn'd to pearl,
When " those are pearls which were his eyes,"
   When each invaluable ball
Is fish'd to light by British enterprise
   And British capital,
To what a premium will the shares rise !

1825.

LINES ON ED. NUCELLA, ESQ., ÆT. 75.

DANCES ; GOES LONG JOURNEYS ; AND WALKS SIX MILES AN
HOUR FOR TWO HOURS DAILY.

SEE the spirit and the vigour
Of an aged hearty figure,
Fit to dance and fit to sing,
Fit for any kind of thing,
To be sober, to be sad,
To be merry, to be mad ;
Never weary or afraid,
Undejected, undismay'd,
With a manner and a tone,
A demeanour of his own,
Like a former age reviving,
Lingering among the living.

1833.

WRITTEN IN THE FLY-LEAF OF MR. POLLOK'S POEM, " THE COURSE OF TIME."

OBERT POLLOK, A.M ! this work of yours
Is meant, I do not doubt, extremely well,
And the design I deem most laudable,
But since I find the book laid on my table,
I shall presume (with the fair owner's leave[1])
To note a single slight deficiency :
I mean, in short (since it is call'd a poem),
That in the course of ten successive books
If something in the shape of poetry
Were to be met with, we should like it better ;
But nothing of the kind is to be found,
Nothing, alas ! but words of the olden time,
Quaint and uncouth, contorted phrase and queer,
With the familiar language that befits
Tea-drinking parties most unmeetly match'd.

1832.

SPAIN.[2]

LAS, alas ! for the fair land of Spain,
That noble and haughty nation, whose domain,
Stretch'd from the rising to the setting sun,
Are not her judgments even now begun ?
Is she not mark'd and seal'd, stamp'd with the
stain
Of unrelenting fiery persecution ?
And this the final hour of retribution

---

[1] Lady Hamilton Chichester.

[2] "I send you a fragment as a specimen of J. H. F.'s selection of words in the English language *adapted* to the subject, and as much as possible consisting of the letters most liquid and as little sibilatory as can be found.

"Ellen will remember Herr Clauden's strong feeling of words, whose sound meets the sense, such as 'massacre in masses,' &c."— *Extract of a letter from Mrs. William Frere, at Malta, to the Hon. Stephen Spring Rice.*

Fallen upon her ? her that we beheld
Roused into wrath unquenchable, unquell'd,
Disarm'd and circumvented and betray'd
With an unanimous outbreak undismay'd,
Daring him single-handed to the fight,
The fiend whose recreation and delight
Was massacre in masses ; at whose word
The multitudinous European herd,
A meaner Race,
Politic and refined, sordid and base,
Enlighten'd, scientific, and polite,
Courts, cabinets, and camps crouch'd in affright,
Nor was their cumbrous and unwieldy strength
Roused by the fierce example, till at length
They saw the new Sennacherib down cast,
Smitten and wither'd in the wintry blast
With all his legions : then the cry went forth
Summoning to the field the people north,
Swarming in arms, and the quick life and soul
That had excited Spain inspired the whole.
Then warfare in another form was seen,
   The strenuous effort—the people's strife,
And the tremendous tactical machine
   Moved on its mighty wheels instinct with life.

Malta, 1844.

HEXAMETERS.[1]

ALTA, sovereign isle, the destined seat and
    asylum
    Of chivalry, honour, and arms—the nursing
       mother of heroes,
    Mirror of ancient days, monumental trophy
       recording
All that of old was felt, or fear'd, or achieved, or attempted,

---

[1] "I send John [his nephew, the late Rev. John Frere] in return
some English Hexameters of my own of the right sort, without false
quantities, all about Malta—at least they begin about Malta."—
Letter from Mr. Frere to his brother Mr. Geo. Frere, March 1, 1824.

When proud Europe's strength, restored with the slumber
    of ages,
Roused and awoke to behold the triumphant impious em-
    pire
Throned in the East, and vaunting aloud with lordly de-
    fiance ;
When from the Euxine shore to the Caspian and to the
    southern
Vast Erythrean main to the Gulfs of Ophir and Ormus,
Lydia, Syrian Sion, and all the dominion eastward,
Which the old Assyrian controll'd, to the bounds of Imaus,
Bow'd to the Sultan's yoke : when slavery bitter and
    hopeless,
Hopeless and helpless, oppress'd the dejected lowly believers.
    Thence to the setting sun, where Mauritanian Atlas,
Chill'd with eternal snows in a boundless cheerless horizon,
Views the deserted plain where Carthage, briefly triumphant,
(Africa's only boast, the rival of Italy, Carthage,)
Claim'd for a while to command the subject world, and
    accomplish'd
That which destiny doom'd—her dark oblivion's annals
Torn and blotted in hate ; her policy, valour, and ancient
Glory reduced to a scoff ; with a proverb left to the pedant,
Thence enslaved and adorn'd with the toys of slavery—
    temples,
Palaces, arches, baths—till they, the remorseless, apostate,
Infidel enemy came to avenge that gaudy debasement,
Trampling in hate and scorn laws, learning, lazy religion,
Luxury, sumptuous art, antiquity. Woe to the vanquish'd !
Woe to the fields of Spain, to the towers of lordly Toledo,
Wealthy Valencia, proud Castile, and stately Granada !
    Woe to the Gascon tribes, to the mountain glens, to the
    lonely
Pyrenean abodes, to the herdsman and hunter and hermit ;
Even amidst your shades, your woody recesses, and inmost
Rocky ravines, shall the armed tide with hideous impulse
Rise and inundate all, pouring, precipitous, headlong,
Forth to the fields of France.

EXTRACT OF A LETTER [1]

From the Right Hon. J. H. FRERE, *written from Malta to Dr.* DAVY, *on the subject of a Natural Phenomenon recently discovered in the neighbourhood of the* Pietà.[2]

COMMUNICATED BY DR. DAVY[3] TO THE "EDINBURGH NEW PHILOSOPHICAL JOURNAL" FOR JANUARY, 1837.

YOU may recollect my attempt at forming a kitchen garden at the Pietà by levelling a piece of rocky ground at the top of the hill; it has led to a discovery which is very extraordinary, and which to every person who has visited it appears unaccountable.

Near the Carruba tree, which you may remember on your right hand at the top of the new flight of steps, a piece of rock had been left untouched for fear of injury to the tree; at length, however, we ventured to remove this last remnant of rock. It was found to rest on a body of clay, about twenty-seven feet in length, and (at the surface) about fifteen in width. As a welcome addition to the scanty

---

[1] From the "Malta Gazette," 26th July, 1836.

[2] Any persons who on a Sunday or *festa* may wish to visit the premises, will be admitted on applying to the gardener, *Giovanni Moretti, Vico Secondo, No. 2 Molo della Pietà.*

[3] DEAR SIR,—I am induced by the interest of the subject to send you an extract of a letter, published in the *Malta Gazette*, which Mr. Frere has been pleased to address to me, relating to certain geological appearances recently discovered in Malta. One important point of inquiry to which they seem to lead is, the connexion of the traces of human art with indications of great changes in the physical condition of the surface; and associated with other facts relative to Malta, they may possibly warrant the conclusion, that Malta was inhabited by man before the great catastrophe took place to which it owes its present form, and by which it may have been separated from the continent. The bone noticed by Mr. Frere in his letter, in the opinion of M. Clift, to whom I have submitted it, is probably a portion of the radius of a ruminating animal—perhaps a goat. I have examined it chemically, and have found it in composition very similar to the bone of the bone-breccia, which occurs in many parts of the shores of the Mediterranean, consisting chiefly of phosphate of lime, without any animal matter, and with a larger proportion of carbonate of lime than exists in recent bone.—*Dr. Davy in a letter to the Editor.*

collection of soil which had served to cover the rocks and stones, one half of the length and the whole of the width was excavated to the depth of about twelve feet; but in doing this, stones (one or two of them as big as a man's head) were found imbedded in the clay, evidently rounded by the action of water; others were found of a laminous texture, in which all the crevices and interstices were penetrated by the clay, shewing that this same clay (though it had now become so hard, and dense, and heavy, as to be with difficulty broken up by a strong man working with a pick-axe) must at one time have been in a fluid state, suspended probably in a body of turbid water.

Moreover, the sides of the rock, forming a sort of irregular funnel in which the clay was contained, exhibited on one side (the side which may be called concave, and which as we descended was found to be vaulted and overhanging) indications distinctly suggesting, even to an unpractised observer, the notion of their having been formed by a rotatory action of water; and that this rotatory action had probably originated in the rush of water to some great cavity below, forming a sort of whirlpool. Indications different in appearance, but equally bearing witness to the violent action of water, were observable on the opposite, or what may be called the convex side, the form of which might be described as resembling a portion of an inclined cylinder, or of a cone; striped, as it was found to be, from top to bottom, with deep longitudinal furrows, shewing that the direct downward rush of water must have taken place on this side, while on the opposite and concave side the rotatory action resulting from the contraction of the lower part of the rocky funnel had left its traces in a series of horizontal furrows.

It followed, therefore, as an obvious inference, that the funnel upon which we had entered, would be found to penetrate through the whole depth of the rock. The work, therefore, was continued, partly from curiosity and partly for the chance of finding water, till it was brought down to the level of the sea, a depth of sixty-three feet from the surface; when all further operations were stopped by the influx of water. But the existence of a continued cavity filled with clay, and extending in a downward direction below the surface of the water, was ascertained by the facility with which iron bars could be thrust down into it, for the water was not found at first, but flowed in gradually as soon as the fissures of the rock were left unobstructed by the removal of the clay.

If my report had ended here, it would hardly have been worth while to trouble you with it ; but the only organized substance which was discovered is a fragment of bone, which I send, in the hope that some of your scientific friends may be able to determine the genus or species of animal to which it belonged. It was found (after we had been at work about three weeks) imbedded in the dense and tenacious clay. But a more singular discovery was made a day or two after; a piece of hard and very heavy stone, about four inches in length, and two and a half in width. It was irregularly fractured at the back and at the edges, but on the other and larger side reduced to what may be called a smooth surface ; that is to say, smooth with the exception of the traces of the instrument which had been employed for the purpose of giving it an even surface ; these traces are very distinctly observable upon it. This stone, like many others which were found imbedded in the same clay, was covered with a black fuliginous varnish, a mark of authenticity which, if I had any suspicion of the good faith of the workmen, would have been sufficient to remove it. It was entrusted to a lapidary, who has carefully polished one of the edges, the rest of the stone being left in the state in which it was found, with its varnish untouched. He declares it to be what they call a *pietra dura* of the hardness of a jasper or hone.

Stones exactly of the same quality have been procured for me by favour of the lapidary above mentioned. They were found near St. Julian's, imbedded in a red earth. Having examined their natural fractures, none of them were found to bear any resemblance to the surface which I supposed to have been produced artificially.

Chalk is nowhere to be traced in the existing strata of the island, but nodules of perfect chalk occurred frequently in the clay; it is singular, however, that no fragment of flint has been found to accompany it. Another circumstance worthy of remark is this ; that a slip of the rock is distinctly perceptible, extending from top to bottom, at the extremity of the major axis of the whole cavity ; the rock itself being unbroken and perfectly solid till we descend to

the level of the sea, where we find it broken and disjoined
to such a degree as to have occasioned great difficulty, and
made many precautions necessary for the safety of the
workmen : this disruption must have been anterior to, or at
least contemporary with, the rush of turbid water in which
the clay was suspended, since in nearly all those places
where the rock is discovered to be in a broken and shat-
tered state, its interstices are found filled with this hard and
tenacious clay.   Another circumstance might be mentioned
in confirmation of the former conclusion that the whole of
this clay had been suspended in a torrent of turbid water.
It was found, that in lateral cavities (which would have
escaped the general rush and pressure of such a torrent)
the clay did not completely fill the whole of such cavities,
and was taken out in a loose granulated state.   There is
one circumstance which seems to imply a very long-con-
tinued action of water, or, more properly speaking, the same
action renewed after long intervals.   The rounded stones
above described, "one or two of them as large as a man's
head," must have been brought there by a torrent of
water ; but it is impossible that they could have remained in
the place which they were found to occupy, only twelve feet
from the surface, unless the turbid water had, at the time
when they were brought there, already deposited a mass of
mud firm enough to afford them support, and to prevent
them from being borne by their own weight to the bottom
of the cavity.

   I now come to a circumstance which, except to an actual
spectator, might make the statement and inferences above
mentioned appear wholly fallacious and incredible. Accordingly, even to an actual spectator, it has usually been the
last which I have pointed out.   I have said : "You see immediately beneath your feet the straight furrows stretching
downwards ; you see the horizontal furrows on the side
opposite ; in neither of them are there any salient parts ;
but every angle either in a downward or horizontal direction is worn and rounded off: you see further down little
niches and cavities worn out by the rebound of the water,
and becoming gradually deeper and more marked as you
descend to those parts where the rocky funnel is more
straitened, and where the resistance and reaction must
have been greatest ; in short, all the undoubted traces of a

rush of water pouring down the cavity from the side on
which we are standing. Now, let us turn round, and look
for the higher or equal level from which this rush of water
must have proceeded. It has ceased to exist ; you can see
nothing behind you but a declivity leading down to a branch
of the present harbour."

This, therefore, is one of the local enigmas which are of
frequent occurrence in geology, and which are usually (and
in the present state of science perhaps justly) overlooked by
those observers whose attention is more properly directed
to general and comprehensive facts.

The single circumstance, however, of the discovery of the
traces of human workmanship in the situation above described, is sufficient to place it in a distinct class. If the
frozen elephant of Siberia had been discovered two hundred
years ago, it would have given rise to a number of vain and
fanciful theories. It now finds its just and proper place ;
being classed apart, as a separate and (in our present state
of knowledge) an unaccountable fact, awaiting its solution
from such future discoveries as chance or science may produce, and which it may contribute to confirm or to illustrate.
In the same manner the discovery (which I have been endeavouring to describe), though not immediately available
for the solution of any question actually in discussion, or
even likely to be discussed for some time to come, appears
to me so singular and unusual as to deserve at least to be
distinctly authenticated and recorded. With this view,
wishing that scientific strangers who may happen to pass
this way should have an opportunity of visiting the spot
while the traces of everything are fresh and distinct, I hope
you will not think that I take an unwarrantable liberty with
your name, if what I have written is communicated to this
portion of the public in the easiest and most obvious way,
being printed with its Italian translation in the *Malta
Gazette.*[1]

---

[1] The following inscription was cut in the rock, over the entrance
to the cave :—

INGREDERE HOSPES

SUMMUM NATURÆ MIRACULUM VISURUS

VORAGINEM ASPICIES

DENSISSIMA DUDUM ARGILLA OPPLETAM :

EPITAPH ON LORD LAVINGTON,

GOVERNOR OF ANTIGUA, 1801-1809.

WRITTEN AT THE REQUEST OF LADY LAVINGTON.

ITH every part well acted—life enjoy'd,
And every talent to the last employ'd,
Here Lavington is laid; a people's grief
Consigns to memory their regretted chief.
    That easy vein of unaffected sense,
The wit devoid of effort or offence,
The cordial welcome and the smile sincere
To living memory long shall linger near.
    Not that they fear'd those traces to forget,
Their ready suffrage paid the general debt,
And gave this lasting form to long regret.

QUA EXHAUSTA
MANIFESTA TORRENTIS AQUÆ VESTIGIA
DETECTA SUNT
AB HAC BOREALI PARTE IRRUENTIS
UBI NUNC SCILICET SINUS MARIS EST
OLIM CONTINENS TERRA EXTITERAT:
QUO MAGIS MIRERE
IN TENACI ILLA ARGILLA
INTER SAXA
ROTANTIBUS AQUIS
TRITA ET ROTUNDATA
AD PROFUNDITATEM XV. PEDUM
DURIOR LAPIS INVENTUS EST
OPIFICIO HUMANO PROCUL DUBIO
ELABORATUS!
HOC TE NESCIRE NOLUIT
QUI HUNC LABOREM EXANTLAVIT
COMMODUMQUE TIBI INGRESSUM
EXCISA RUPE
PATEFECIT.
I. H. FRERE
NATIONE ANGLUS HUJUSCE INSULÆ
PER COMPLURES ANNOS INCOLA.
MDCCCXXXIX.

No, fix'd to future years they bid it stand,
A record of well-exercised command.
Strict and exact, though popular and kind,
Discordant virtues in a single mind ;
High principles with easy manners join'd,
A courtier's graces, but without his art ;
A patriot's zeal where faction had no part,
And manly virtues in a gentle heart.

EPITAPH ON LORD NELSON.

HE fragile texture of this earthly form,
    Which Death has stript aside and cast below,
Must never more be shaken by the storm,
    Nor worn with care, nor shatter'd by the
        foe.

At war's grim sacrifice in fire and blood
    My living presence never must preside ;
The keen pursuit across the trackless flood
    My watchful spirit never more must guide.

Britons, farewell !   Our country's utmost claim,
    My life, my labours all are past and paid ;
The tears of vain regret, the toys of fame,
    Are idle offerings to your champion's shade.

This only tribute to my memory give :—
    In all your struggles, both by land and sea,
Let Nelson's name in emulation live,
    And in the hour of danger think on me.

EPITAPH UPON THE DUQUE DE ALBUQUERQUE.

MPIGER, impavidus, spes maxima gentis Iberæ,
    Mente rapax, acerque manu bellator, avita
    Institui monumenta novis attollere factis ;
    Fortunâ comite, et virtute duce, omnia gessi :
    Nullâ in re, nec spe, mea sors incepta fefellit.
Gadibus auxilium tetuli, patriamque labantem
Sustentavi ; hæc meta meis fuit ultima factis :

Quippe iras hominum meritis superare nequivi.
Hic procul a patriâ vitæ datus est mihi finis,
Sed non laudis item ; gliscit nova fama sepulto :
Anglorum quod testantur proceres populusque,
Magno funus honore secuti, mæstitiâque
Unanimes. Æterna, pater, sint fœdera, faxis,
Quæ pepigi. Nec me nimium mea patria adempto
Indigeat, nec plus æquo desideret unquam.
Sint fortes alii ac felices, qui mea possint
Facta sequi, semperque benignis civibus uti.

EPITAPH ON THE REV. WALTER WHITER,[1]

AUTHOR OF THE "ETYMOLOGICON UNIVERSALE," ETC. ETC.

IF, wandering here, the learned or the wise
Should wish to view the spot where Whiter
    lies,
Here is his last abode ! and close beside
The simple dwelling where he lived and died.
For forty years an unpromoted priest,
In the world's estimate the last and least,
By genius and by learning placed above
The greedy, noisy, literary drove
Immeasurably high. Without a frown,
He views the busy press, the silly town,
And clouds of blockheads clamouring for renown.
The purpose of his life, its end and aim,
The search of hidden truth ; careless of fame,
Of empty dignities or dirty pelf,
Learning he sought—and loved it for itself.

    1834.

---

[1] See verses entitled "A Visit to Hardingham," *anteà*.

EPITAPH ON SIR VINCENT BORG,

IN THE CHURCH AT BIRCHIRCARA, MALTA.

D. O. M.
Eques Vincentius Borg
Afflictis et prope desperatis
Patriæ rebus
Cum adversus invadentium Gallorum
Contumelias
Inopino impetu Melitensium indignatio
Prorupit :
A concivibus hujusce pagi
Dux acclamatus
Postero die
Incredibili fiducia et fortuna
Cohortem CCC Gallorum
Fudit fugavitque
Ab inermi rusticorum multitudine
Fustibus et saxis oppressam :
Deinde melioribus armis instructus
Hostium eruptiones
Ab hac boreali parte
Donec ad deditionem redacti sunt
Constanter cohibuit :
Idem ut concives suos bello simul
Et fame afflictos invecto frumento
Sublevaret
Sortem universam
Quam in mercatura habuit
Vili pretio Siciliensibus addixit
Patrimoniumque gravi fœnore oneravit :
Vir tantis in patriam meritis
Pristinam simplicitatem et modestiam
Semper retinuit :
Per reliquam vitam, sanctitate morum,
In Deum pietate, in pauperes
Benevolentia
Præcipue notabilis
Hujusce Ecclesiæ fabricam

Summa liberalitate
Auxit et ornavit.
Obit XIII. Kal. Aug. MDCCCXXXVII.
Vixit annos LXIV
I. H. Frere Anglus scripsit
An. MDCCCXXXVII.

EPITAPH ON MR CANNING.

HILE sister arts in rivalry combine
For Canning's honour,—Sculpture and De-
sign,
Verse claims her portion ; a memorial line
Such as he loved ; and fittest to rehearse
His merit and his praises—Truth in verse.
The pride of Honour, and the love of Truth,
Adorn'd his age, and dignified his youth.
Approved thro' life, and tried with every test,
In power, in favour, in disgrace, confess'd
The first of his coevals, and the best.
Unchanged thro' life, from Childhood's early day,
Playfully wise, and innocently gay,
Ever the same ; with wit correctly pure,
Reason miraculously premature,
Vivid imagination ever new,
Decision instantaneously true,
A fervid and precipitated power
Of hasty thought, achieving in an hour
What tardier wits, with toil of many a day,
Polish'd to less perfection by delay.[1]
By nature gifted with a power and skill
To charm the heart, and subjugate the will:
Born with an ancient name of little worth,
And disinherited before his birth ;

[1] Or for these last four lines—

Invention preternatural, with a power
Of hasty thought, outstripping in an hour
What tardier wits, with wearisome delay,
Could scarce achieve, and toil of many a day.

A landless Orphan—rank and wealth and pride
Were freely ranged around him ; nor denied
His clear precedence, and the warrant given
Of nobler rank ; stamp'd by the hand of Heaven
In every form of genius and of grace,
In loftiness of thought, figure and face.
Such Canning was : and, half a century past,
Such all the world beheld him to the last :
Admired of all, and by the best approved,
By those, who best had known him, best beloved ;
His Sovereign's support and the people's choice, ⎫
When Europe's balance trembled on the poise, ⎬
Call'd to command by their united voice ; ⎭
Fate[1] snatch'd him from the applauding world ; the first
Omen of Europe's danger, and the worst.

ANOTHER ON THE SAME, SHOULD THE FORMER

BE CONSIDERED TOO LONG.

HILE sister arts in rivalry combine ⎫
　For Canning's honour, Sculpture and De- ⎬
　　sign, ⎪
　Verse claims her portion ; a memorial line ⎭
　Such as he loved ; and fittest to rehearse
His merit and his praises—Truth in verse.
Truth was his idol ; and the pride of truth
Adorn'd his age, and dignified his youth.
Ever the same ; with wit correctly pure,
Reason miraculously premature,
Vivid imagination ever new,
Decision instantaneously true.
By nature gifted with a power and skill
To charm the heart, and subjugate the will,
Admired of all, and by the best approved,
By those, who best had known him, best beloved ;

---

[1] Or "Death."

His Sovereign's support, and the people's choice, ⎫
When Europe's balance trembled on the poise, ⎬
Call'd to command by their united voice : ⎭
Fate[1] snatch'd him from the applauding world ; the first
Omen of Europe's danger, and the worst.

ANOTHER MORE CONCISE.

WAS destroy'd by Wellington and Grey.
They both succeeded. Each has had his day.
Both tried to govern, each in his own way ;
And both repent of it—as well they may !

LINES INSCRIBED IN ROYDON CHURCH,

*In Memory of his nephews, Temple and Griffith Frere, the
eldest and the youngest son of Temple and Jane Frere.
The elder was drowned when saving the life of a fellow-
student at Trinity College, Cambridge; and the younger
died in the fire which consumed the Vicarage House, at
Warfield, Berks.*

MANLY tender heart, a form and frame
    Heroical, the pride of all his race,
Their pride and hope in early youth he came
    An unexpected inmate of the place
Ordain'd for all that breathe on earth below.
    Exempted from the common ills of life,
No wearisome disease, painful and slow,
    No wild excess, nor youthful hasty strife,
Consign'd him to the tomb. The prompt endeavour
    Of a kind heart to succour and to save,
Darken'd our dawn of hope, and closed for ever
    His rising worth in an untimely grave.

---

[1] Or "Death."

Deem them not unprepared, nor overtaken
At unawares, whose daily life is pure.
God's chosen children never are forsaken :
His mercies and his promises are sure.

TABLET IN ROYDON CHURCH.

Richard Edward Frere, sixth son of Edward and Mary Anne Frere, born at Llanelly, Brecknockshire, 28th February, 1817, died at Rawul Pindee, Punjab, 18th November, 1842, Lieutenant in H.M. 13th Regiment Light Infantry.

HEROIC England, prodigal of life,
Sends forth to distant enterprise and strife
Her daring offspring : we must not repine
If, from the frozen circle to the line,
Our graves lie scatter'd : and the sole relief
For kindred sorrow and parental grief
Is, to record upon an empty tomb
Honour and worth, and their untimely doom.

LINES ON THE DEATH OF RICHARD
EDWARD FRERE.

WRITTEN FOR A MONUMENT PROPOSED TO BE ERECTED
BY HIS BROTHER OFFICERS.

IN early youth, with a determined heart,
I sought to study war's tremendous art ;
Thence all that studious hours or busy thought
Or rudimental discipline had taught,
To the true test of practice was applied,
For daily scenes of action proved and tried.
In our first enterprise, when Ghuzni fell,
I placed our colours on the citadel ;

Thence other toils and hardships were essay'd,
An unexampled siege and marches made
Twice to Cabool and homewards in a line
Of inexpugnable defiles—in fine,
We visited again that Indian flood
Improvidently pass'd, and gladly stood
In a secure and peaceable domain,
When a severer foe, disease and pain,
Approach'd, and in that hard assault I fell,
A soldier! having served and suffer'd well;
My duties all discharged, with a firm mind,
Tranquil and pure, and peaceably resign'd,
My course is closed; and if I leave a name
Unregister'd upon the rolls of fame,
Still my kind comrades' care may make it known,
Recording on a monumental stone
A gentle, generous spirit like their own.

Malta, 1843.

LINES

DESCRIBING THE ALTERED FEELINGS AND CHARACTER

OF THE APOSTLES BEFORE AND AFTER THE

EFFUSION OF THE HOLY SPIRIT.

"And he took * * * the twelve, and began to tell them what things should happen unto him."—*Mark* x. 32.

LAS, what words are these! we vainly thought,
When Israel's redemption should be wrought,
And David's ancient dynasty restored,
That we—the first disciples of the Lord,
Whom his own wise and understanding heart
Had chosen for himself, and class'd apart
From the promiscuous giddy multitude,
The gazing, empty crowd, fickle and rude,
Taught in his secret hours to feel the force
And unsuspected depth of his discourse:
On whose behalf, vouchsafing to perform
His mightiest miracle, he rebuked the storm—
On the lone waves, and at the midnight hour
That wondrous act of elemental power

Was wrought ; and the presumptuous challenge given
(The challenge to produce a sign from heaven)
Was answer'd—for our comfort and behoof!
To fix our faith affording us a proof
Of his assured divinity, denied
To the demand of Pharisaic pride !—
Ordain'd in pairs, on his own errand sent,
For works of love and mercy forth we went,
When, as our faith avail'd us, the distrest
Were heal'd, and evil spirits dispossest,
And our kind Lord, unused to show concern,
Rejoiced in spirit at our glad return.
Thus therefore, as distinguish'd and preferr'd
To the proud learned and the vulgar herd—
—We deem'd that his disciples and his friends
Might look in cheerful hope to loftier ends ;
That when the promised kingdom was his own,
With a deputed power, each on his throne,
We might preside, sitting in humble state
With our great Chief, gravely subordinate.

    And must it end in this ? must we behold
The sad result so fatally foretold ?
Our promised Saviour, our expected King,
Reduced to a rejected, abject thing !
Must we behold him baffled and defied,
Insulted and tormented—crucified ?

    Far other thoughts were ours, of happy days,
Of peaceful empire, glory, power, and praise,
Of all the nations of the world combined
Beneath the rule of an harmonious mind,
A divine spirit affable and kind.

    Must we behold him thus ? we that have seen
His tender and compassionating mien
When witnessing in others the distress
Of griefs in daily life lighter and less !

    All vanishes at once ! the long delusion
Of our mistaken hopes—fears and confusion
Must haunt our future years ! where shall we find
The firm support of his celestial mind,
For exhortation, comfort, or reproof ;
Dispersed, pursued, and scatter'd wide aloof
Without a master and without a friend, ..

Sinking in shame for his opprobrious end ;
Outcasts of every synagogue—the scorn
Of Jews and heathen—hated and forlorn !
   Such were the thoughts the poor apostles had,
Communing in their hearts, cheerless, and sad,
Weakness and faith united ! grief and love !
Till strengthen'd by the Spirit from above.

   "And suddenly there came a sound from heaven as of a rushing
mighty wind, and it filled all the house where they were sitting.
And there appeared unto them cloven tongues like as of fire, and it
sat upon each of them."—*Acts* ii. 2, 3.

The promise is fulfill'd ; we see and own
The force and action of a power unknown.
What in a thousand forms our weary mind
And feeble spirit, ignorant and blind,
In vain imaginings had turn'd and cast,
That mighty blessing is conferr'd at last :
(Dimly conceived as an expected good
Now thankfully received and understood)
That spirit which inures us to behold   ⎫
With a collected mind, tranquil and cold,   ⎬
All that alarm'd us or allured of old :   ⎭
Prospective rank and power, the public breath,
Censuring or applauding, chains or death ;
That Spirit which enables us to stand
In presence of the rulers of the land,
Aweless and unabash'd, with confidence
Unshaken, and spontaneous eloquence
Infused and prompted at the present hour ;
Or in the public place with the like power
To quell the raving, giddy multitude,
Pierced to the quick, dejected, and subdued,
With self-conviction of their past offence :
Thence eager all with ready penitence,
Imploring consolation and advice,
Pledged in remorse and shame to pay the price
Of their announced redemption ; to discard
Their former hopes and fears ; to disregard
Their ancient fix'd adherence to the rules
Of Pharisaic hypocritic schools,

Emancipated from the vulgar awe
Of subtle formalists and priestly law.
Nor these alone, but other gifts and powers,
Our Lord's bequests, are attributes of ours,
Authentic warrants of a power Divine
Confirm'd by many a wonder, many a sign,
Wrought in His name and in the public view,
Proving our faith and testimony true.
  The beggar crouching at the temple gate,
A cripple from the cradle, that had sate
With hand outstretching and imploring eye,
And an unvaried customary cry,
Known and habitual to the passers-by;
Him (for he saw the power of inward faith
Lodged in his heart) Peter accosts and saith—
" Of gold or silver or the coin you crave,
Nought we possess—we give you what we have :
Through faith in Christ our Lord, and in His name
Stand forth upon thy feet—cease to be lame."
'Twas done ! (Such miracles are witness'd still
Of a free grace adjuring a free will.
The cripples rise with an obedient start,
With a strong effort and believing heart).[1]
The great Apostle, with an outstretch'd hand,
Rears and assists, and teaches him to stand,
Plying his ignorant unpractised feet :
While—not to leave the blessing incomplete,
The loved disciple at his other side
Attends the novice to support and guide
Within the temple, where he never stood,
With heart elate, leaping and praising God.
Nor are there wanting to the later law
Severer signs such as our fathers saw
Quelling their rebel hearts with fear and awe :
The perjured hypocrite bereft of life,
With his prevaricating, sordid wife,
Firm and erect in steady perjury
They stand and in the twinkling of an eye
Struck by the deadly sentence, there they lie.
  Such are the powers conferr'd ; and for their use

---

[1] Jones of Nayland, Sermon VI., vol. iii. p. 347, ed. 1810.

Thus gifted and endow'd—can we refuse
Danger or toil or pain or hardship? No!
With a fix'd faith and purpose forth we go,
In face of a vain world, bound to proclaim
His mission, and atonement in His name.
Secure of our reward, sure to succeed,
And well content to suffer and to bleed.

Malta, 2nd April, 1840.

A FRAGMENT.

UR fancies figure a Divinity,
Like Fielding's squire, a Mr. Alworthy:
Easy, benignant, equitable, kind—
A sort of patron, suited to our mind;
(A kind of character we should revere
For an estated neighbour or a peer);
The qualities by fellow mortals praised,
Ad infinitum multiplied and raised,
Become our graven image in effect
By mortal handicraft advanced and deck'd.
Imagination, ever poor and blind,
Frames its own idol, after its own kind,
In its own likeness. We construct on high
A mighty form of human quality,
And worship the colossal effigy;
We puzzle and confuse our puny wits
To build an infinite with endless bits
As silly children use—we strive to fill
A mimic fountain of eternal will,
And form a puddle with our idle skill.
But deem not of the Deity as is meant
In daily phrase—good, wise, omnipotent:
No; nor all-wise, all-good; nor hope to span
That mighty compass with the speech of man.
Not entity, but essence, such is He
Beyond all measure, quality, or degree—
Power, wisdom, goodness in infinity,
In abstract. He, the Centre and the Source
Of the attributes of good, which vain discourse

Collects, concentrates—and, when all is done,
Reflects its idle mirror to the sun.
   With Him the past abides—the eternal past—
The future is fulfill'd—the first and last
Stand obvious to the immeasurable sense,
Mere digits in the vast circumference.
Through chinks and crevices we dimly trace
Existence in the forms of time and place ;
Predicamental loopholes, poor and small,
That bound our vision through the dungeon-wall :
The future, or the present, or the past,
The there or here—a simultaneous, vast
Infinite omnipresence—First and last
Centre in Him, the ineffably sublime,
Beyond all thought or language. If a crime—
I feel it or I fear it even thus,
In words of human usage to discuss
The Eternal Essence, and delineate
Infinitude—Shall the puny prate
Be suffer'd, which would limit and confine,
In an imaginary moral line,
The compass of eternal power and law ?
Shall human reason frame a rule to draw
Before its puny court the cognizance
Of a Divine eternal ordinance
With warrants of its own ?   Not more uncouth
The fines or forfeits in a barber's booth,
O, regulations in a billiard-room—
If quoted and applied to guide the doom
Of ermined judges in the learned hall
Bent on a serious plea—than those you call
Your axioms absolute and general.
   Or wilt thou call for archives and records,
Thy charter of existence, and the words
Which qualify the grant—with curious eye
Decyphering obsolete eternity ?
Canst thou peruse the content and declare
No covenant exists recited there
Of older date ?   No former forfeit due—
Mere aff mation ?   Can you prove it true ?
The Apostle shall reply—" Nay, what art thou,
Oh man, that with a bold and hardy brow

Arraign'd, and pleading in thine own defence,
Question and cross-examine Providence?
  To be consider'd as a fellow-creature
Seems a pretension of a modest nature,
But fails you when address'd to the Creator:
Justice you call for—justice let it be,
Such as inferior life receives from thee:
Your justice slays your vermin, and the fly
In pity saved, or left to drown or die,
Is the true pattern of a sinking spirit,
(In thorough parallel) its works and merit,
Of equal worth, whatever claims arise
Of just demeanour with his fellow-flies,
Moral effort, or struggling to be free,
And to crawl out by mere congruity—
Your aidance is gratuitously given;
Gratuitously,—like the grace of Heaven.

Pictâ, November, 1824.

TRANSLATIONS FROM "THE POEM OF THE CID."

The first, fifth and sixth of these translations were printed as an Appendix to the "Chronicle of the Cid, from the Spanish," by Robert Southey, Lond. 1808. pp. 437-468. The second, third, and fourth are now printed for the first time; and the argument at the head of Translation V. has been in consequence slightly altered. The original Spanish, which accompanied the former publication of the translations, is omitted, and in lieu of it reference is made to the lines of the "Poema del Cid," as published in Sanchez, "Coleccion de Poesias Castellanas anteriores al Siglo XV." Madrid, 1779.

[*Note of* 1872.]

TRANSLATIONS FROM "THE POEM OF THE CID."

I.

ARGUMENT.

The Cid being driven into banishment by the intrigues of his enemies, is accompanied by several of his friends and followers, for whom he undertakes to provide by carrying on a predatory war against the Moors. In the course of their adventures they surprise the Castle of Alcocer, but are soon after surrounded and besieged by a superior army. After some difference of opinion, the Cid yields to the wishes of his followers, and determines upon a sally, which is successful.

[From line 670 to 772.]

THEY fain would sally forth, but he, the noble Cid,
Accounted it as rashness, and constantly forbid.
The fourth week was beginning, the third already past,
The Cid and his companions they are now agreed at last.
" The water is cut off, the bread is well nigh spent,
To allow us to depart by night the Moors will not consent.
To combat with them in the field our numbers are but few,
Gentlemen, tell me your minds, what do you think to do ?"
Minaya Alvar Fañez answer'd him again,
" We are come here from fair Castile to live like banish'd men.
There are here six hundred of us, beside some nine or ten ;

It is by fighting with the Moors that we have earn'd our
  bread,
In the name of God that made us, let nothing more be said,
Let us sally forth upon them by the dawn of day."
The Cid replied, "Minaya, I approve of what you say,
You have spoken for the best, and had done so without
  doubt."
The Moors that were within the town they took and turn'd
  them out,
That none should know their secret ; they labour'd all that
  night,
They were ready for the combat with the morning light.
The Cid was in his armour mounted at their head,
He spoke aloud amongst them, you shall hear the words
  he said :
" We must all sally forth !   There can not a man be spared,
Two footmen only at the gates to close them and keep guard;
If we are slain in battle, they will bury us here in peace,
If we survive and conquer, our riches will increase.
And you, Pero Bermuez, the standard you must bear,
Advance it like a valiant man, evenly and fair ;
But do not venture forward before I give command."
Bermuez took the standard, he went and kiss'd his hand.
The gates were then thrown open, and forth at once they
  rush'd,
The outposts of the Moorish host back to the camp were
  push'd ;
The camp was all in tumult, and there was such a thunder
Of cymbals and of drums, as if earth would cleave in sunder.
There you might see the Moors arming themselves in haste,
And the two main battles how they were forming fast ;
Horsemen and footmen mix'd, a countless troop and vast.
The Moors are moving forward, the battle soon must join,
" My men, stand here in order, ranged upon a line !
Let not a man move from his rank before I give the sign."
Pero Bermuez heard the word, but he could not refrain.
He held the banner in his hand, he gave his horse the rein ;
" You see yon foremost squadron there, the thickest of the foes,
Noble Cid, God be your aid, for there your banner goes !
Let him that serves and honours it show the duty that he
  owes."
Earnestly the Cid call'd out, " For Heaven's sake, be still !"

Bermuez cried, " I cannot hold," so eager was his will.
He spurr'd his horse, and drove him on amid the Moorish
      rout ;
They strove to win the banner, and compass'd him about.
Had not his armour been so true he had lost either life or
      limb ;
The Cid call'd out again, "For Heaven's sake, succour him !"
   Their shields before their breasts, forth at once they go,
Their lances in the rest level'd fair and low ;
Their banners and their crests waving in a row,
Their heads all stooping down toward the saddle bow.
The Cid was in the midst, his shout was heard afar,
" I am Ruy Diaz, the Champion of Bivar ;
Strike amongst them, gentlemen, for sweet mercy's sake !"
There where Bermuez fought, amidst the foe they brake,
Three hundred banner'd knights, it was a gallant show :
Three hundred Moors they kill'd, a man with every blow ;
When they wheel'd and turn'd, as many more lay slain,
You might see them raise their lances and level them again.
There you might see the breastplates, how they were cleft
      in twain,
And many a Moorish shield lie shatter'd on the plain.
The pennons that were white mark'd with a crimson stain,
The horses running wild whose riders had been slain.
The Christians call upon Saint James, the Moors upon
      Mahound,
There were thirteen hundred of them slain on a little spot
      of ground.
Minaya Alvar Fañez smote with all his might,
He went as he was wont, and was foremost in the fight.
There was Galin Garcia, of courage firm and clear,
Felez Munioz, the Cid's own cousin dear ;
Antolinez of Burgos, a hardy knight and keen,
Munio Gustioz, his pupil that had been.
The Cid on his gilded saddle above them all was seen.
There was Martin Munioz, that ruled in Montmayor,
There were Alvar Fañez and Alvar Salvador :
These were the followers of the Cid, with many others more,
In rescue of Bermuez and the standard that he bore.
Minaya is dismounted, his courser has been slain,
He fights upon his feet, and smites with might and main.
The Cid came all in haste to help him to horse again ;

He saw a Moor well mounted, thereof he was full fain,
Through the girdle at a stroke he cast him to the plain :
He call'd to Minaya Fañez and reach'd him out the rein,
" Mount and ride, Minaya, you are my right hand,
We shall have need of you to-day, these Moors will not
      disband !"
Minaya leapt upon the horse, his sword was in his hand ;
Nothing that came near him could resist him or withstand ;
All that fall within his reach he despatches as he goes.
The Cid rode to King Fariz, and struck at him three blows ;
The third was far the best, it forced the blood to flow :
The stream ran from his side, and stain'd his arms below ;
The King caught round the rein, and turn'd his back to go,
The Cid has won the battle with that single blow.

II.

ARGUMENT.

*On the death of King Almudafar, his sons Zulema and
Abenalfange divided his dominions ; the former had the kingdom of Zaragosa, and put it under the protection of the Cid.
The latter had the kingdom of Denia ; and, as there began
to be great enmity between the brothers, Abenalfange was
helped by Don Pedro King of Aragon and Count Don Ramon
Berenger of Barcelona, who thereby became enemies of the Cid.
The Cid with* 200 *horsemen attacked the lands of Alcaniz, and
after that infested Huesca and Montalban.* Of this tidings
were taken to the King of Denia, and to the Count of Barcelona, who attack the Cid in a valley near the Pine-wood
of Thebar, are routed, the Count taken prisoner, and his
sword *Colada* taken by the Cid. The Count refuses all food,
and starves himself for three days, till the Cid promises
him and two of his followers their freedom if he eats a
hearty dinner, which he does, and obtains his freedom.

[From line 964 to 1089.]

THE news spread wide and far, it reach'd Count
     Ramon's ear,
The Count of Barcelona Don Ramon Beren-
     ger,
How the Cid Ruy Diaz was riding far and
near,

Plundering all the country.   The Count was bold and hot,
A proud and angry word was spoken on the spot :
" Ruy Diaz has offended us and evermore offends ;
He smote my kinsman in the court and never made
    amends ;
And here he comes to rob the Moors, my neighbours
    and my friends,
That pay me for protection, and live within my league.
I never join'd against him with faction or intrigue,
Or was his secret enemy, or defied him as a foe,
Or wrong'd him or attack'd him ; but since he wills it so,
And since he comes against us, against him we must go."
The Count with all his vassals is mustering strong and
    fast—
They throng in troops together and follow forth in haste,
Christian Knights and Franks, and Moors of every caste,
Riding in hot pursuit of the Champion of Bivar,
And there at length they found him, at the Pine-wood
    of Thebar ;
It was a three days' march before they reach'd so far.
    The Cid came with his plunder, a convoy large and good,
Descending from the mountain to a vale beside the wood ;
A summons there was sent him from the Count Berenger,
The Cid, when he received it, return'd a messenger—
" Tell the Count Berenger we mean to part from hence ;
We wish to part in peace, we never meant offence ;
Whatever gain we made was not at his expense."
    The Count, in haste and anger, replied—" It is not
    true ;
He shall now pay me for the past, and for the present
    too ;
I shall teach this outlaw the respect that is my due."
Wi' that the messenger return'd ; the Cid might fairly see
That he must risk a battle, it might no better be.
" Look to your baggage, gentlemen, set all the gear apart,
And arm yourselves for battle, we fight before we part.
Our enemies are here at hand with a mighty threat and
    boast,
The Count of Barcelona forsooth with all his host !—
Franks and Moors together, I know not which are most :
But since they come pursuing, and their intent is clear
To attack us as they find us, we'll fight our battle here :

They will be riding down the slope with a broken pace;
Our saddles are all firm and deep, well girded in their
     place,
And theirs are easy surcingles and saddles for a race.
You will not find among them one well arm'd cavalier;
A hundred of our number might fight them without fear:
Before they reach the valley let us meet them with the
     spear;
For one man that you strike three saddles will be clear.
We shall teach the Count Don Ramon Berenger,
With knighthood and with practice and proof of manhood
     sheer,
What kind of knights and what a chief he comes pursuing
     here,
To take our booty from us, the spoil we bought so dear!"
And now the noble Cid had finish'd his discourse;
His knights are ranged in order, each upon his horse.
The Franks come down the hill with a random course.
Just where the mountain ended, at the valley's source,
The Cid gave orders to his men to charge with all their
     force:
That order they perform'd with all their soul and heart,
With pennons and with lances so well they play'd their part,
Some are pierced and wounded, others beaten down,
The Count is taken captive, his host is overthrown,
His sword that was worth a thousand marks, the Cid has
     made his own,
The noble sword Colada that through the world was known.
He has adorn'd that mighty beard with honour and renown,
His beard, that as a banish'd man was left all overgrown—
The Count is taken with the Cid in close and steady ward
A surety for his creditors for them to watch and guard—
The Cid came from his tent, and at the door he stood,
His knights are crowding round him, all in a merry mood,
Right merry was the Cid, the spoil was rich and good.—
     For the service of the Cid a banquet was prepared,
Count Ramon would not eat of it, or pay the least regard;
They served the meat before him. He laugh'd at them
     again—
" I would not eat a morsel for all the wealth of Spain;
I would rather lose my life, and perish here outright,
Since such a set of ragged knaves have conquer'd me in
     fight."

The good Cid Ruy Diaz, these were the words he said :
" Eat and drink, Sir Count, of the wine and of the bread,
If you do as I advise you shortly may be free,
Else you can never hope a Christian land to see—
Be merry, Don Rodrigo—feast and make good cheer."
" I shall not eat a morsel ; I mean to perish here."—
They shared and pack'd the booty ; till the third day was
  past,
The Count continued still to famish and to fast.
They could not make him eat a morsel nor a crumb :
At length the worthy Cid said, " Come, Sir Ramon, come !
If ever you design to return to Christendom,
You needs must break your fast ; therefore if you'll agree
To eat a goodly dinner fairly and lustily,
With two companions of your choice, I promise all the three
To quit you from your prison, and leave you ransom-free."
The Count was joyful at the word, and answer'd cheerfully :
" Cid, if you mean it as you say, this way to ransom me,
As long as I shall live a marvel it will be."—
" Then come to dinner, Count, and when you've eat your
  fill,
You with your two companions may go whene'er you
  will ;
But for the booty that I gain'd, I mean to keep it still :
No not a farthing will I give of all the wealth you lost,
Your plea was overthrown in fight, and you must pay the
  cost ;
Besides, I want the goods myself, for the service of my
  host,
My ragged hearty followers, my safeguard and my boast ;
Thus we must live, till Heaven above has otherwise dis-
  posed,
Standing in anger of the king, with all the best and most
Of our inheritance and lands sequester'd and foreclosed ;
As is the wont of banish'd men, we needs must think it
  fair
To keep our troop together, with plundering here and there."
The Count was pleased, and call'd for water for his hands,
A bason with the banquet was brought at his commands ;
Two knights were with him, that the Cid released him
  ransomless ;
I warrant all the three were joyous at the mess.

Then spoke the noble Cid—" Sir Count, before we part,
You must perform your promise, and eat with all your
      heart,
Else I must keep you with me to whet your appetite."⎫
The Count replied—"The contract shall be fulfill'd aright;⎬
I promise you to do my part, and do it with delight."⎭
The noble-minded Cid stood smiling there beside
To see the Count at meat, so fast his hands he plied.
" An if it be your pleasure, Cid, now that our dinner's ⎫
      done,   ⎬
Give order for our horses, and let us hence be gone ; ⎪
Of all the meals I ever made this is the heartiest one."—⎭
Three palfreys were brought up to them, with saddles rich
      and fair,
With mantles and with housings of cloth and peltry rare.
The Count was in the midst, his knights on either side,
The Cid for half a stage would escort him on his ride ;—
" Farewell, Sir Count ! you leave me ransomless and frank;
I quit you with all courtesies ; and furthermore I thank
Your bounty for the booty you left with me behind ;
And if you should repent of it, or chance to change your
      mind,   •
And wish to mend your luck, whenever you're inclined,
Myself and my companions are easy folks to find :—
But if you leave me quiet, (as well, methinks, you may) ⎫
Your lands will fare the better ; and on a future day   ⎬
With your own goods or others perhaps I may repay."—⎭
" Cid, you may fairly boast, you're safe upon that head ; ⎫
For this year and the next my score is fully paid;   ⎬
And as for coming after you let nothing more be said." ⎭
    The Count went crowding on his pace, and looking fast
      behind
Pressing and urging onward, he doubted in his mind
The Cid might change his purpose. He little knew the
      Cid ;
That would have been a treason,—a thing he never did ;
He never would have done so base an act—not even
To purchase all the gold and treasure under heaven.

III.

ARGUMENT.

The Cid—after various successes, having won the city of Valencia, and having overthrown the King of Seville (who was ·sent with 30,000 men to besiege him) in the battle of Villa Nueva, in which every footsoldier shared 100 marks of silver—fearing lest his people who were now rich should return to their own country, took counsel with Alvar Fañez and others, when Minaya advised that proclamation should be made that no man should leave the city without permission of the Cid, on pain of losing all he had and being impaled. With this view the Cid orders an account to be taken of all his vassals, sends Alvar Fañez and Martin Antolinez with presents to the King Don Alphonso, beseeching him to let his wife and daughters join him,—re-makes Valencia into a bishoprick, and makes the pilgrim Don Jerom bishop. The king receives the messengers favourably, and orders that the ladies have a guard to escort them throughout his dominions, and restores the Cid and his followers to favour.

[From line 1266 to 1379.]

WISH for an account
    Of all my vassals here, their number and
        amount,
    Their grants of tenements and lands, Minaya,
        will you look
To mark their names in writing, and count them in a book—
—For the service of Valencia this shall be the law—
If any man shall leave it, to desert us and withdraw,
He shall resign and vacate his tenure, to divide
Among my followers here, that in the town abide,
That watch the city walls, and keep the country side."
    Minaya said—" The thing can easily be done."
He summon'd them to Court, they came there every one ;
He wrote their names in order, and made a fair account,
Three thousand and six hundred was the complete amount.
" Thanks be to God, Minaya, the troop was thinner far
When we rode forth as exiles from my manor at Bivar :
As we have prosper'd hitherto so shall we prosper still ;
Yet farther, if you like it, and if it suits your will,

I fain would send you forth for a message into Spain,
To see my Lord Alphonso my lawful king again.
A hundred goodly steeds for a present you shall bring,
A portion of the booty, to present them to the king.
Then you shall kiss his hands intreating earnestly
That he will condescend to set my wife and daughters free—
And for their coming with you, these words shall be the
    token;
The words they recollect, that heretofore were spoken:—
That the Cid's daughters and his wife, upon some future
    day,
As rich and mighty dames should ride in proud array
To meet their worthy father within some foreign land,
Where he should reign a conqueror in honour and com-
    mand."
" I'll do it," said Minaya, " with all my soul and heart."
He sets affairs in order preparing to depart,
With a hundred men-at-arms as an escort strong and fair; }
And a thousand marks of silver must Alvar Fañez bear }
To the Convent of San Pedro, for the good abbot there. }
  While thus they were discoursing, and mirth and hope }
    increased
A pilgrim came amongst them, from adventures in the East, }
A clerk of holy Church and shaven as a priest :
Don Jerom was his name, a person of discerning,
Courteous and discreet, and famous for his learning;
A worthy man besides, on horseback or on foot,
And thither was he come, for his errand and pursuit
Had been to join the Cid, that he might fight his fill,
Sword-in-hand among the Moors, to cut them down and
    kill.—
The Cid with his arrival was pleased and satisfied;
He takes Minaya Fañez to speak with him aside.
" Hear me, Minaya Fañez! in Heaven's name I say,
Of all that Heaven has bless'd us with, something we must
    repay:
And therefore of my conquest this shall be the fruit,
I'll make a bishop here, and a bishopric to boot ;
And this same good Don Jerom the bishop he shall be.
Where can we find in all our host a better clerk than he?
These will be goodly tidings, happy news and fair,
Reported in Castile at your arrival there."

Minaya was agreed ; the thing was done as said,
And therewithal Don Jerom was a bishop made,
Invested and endow'd with lands and yearly rent ;
And, oh ! what happy tidings thro' Christendom were sent,
In all the courts of Christendom, and every town of Spain,
That a bishop in Valencia was appointed once again.

Minaya took his leave, and forth in haste he prest
His journey through Valencia ; the country was at rest :
As for his other travel, I care not to recite
The stages that he made or where he stopt at night.
He rides inquiring for the king ; at last he comes to know,
" The king was at St. Fagunt a little while ago,
Meaning to go to Carrion, so people understood."
Minaya rode to Carrion, to find him if he could,
Ready with his present in case the king should pass ;
And there at once he met him returning from the Mass.
Behold Minaya Fañez, in presence of the crowd,
He knelt before the king and made his moan aloud :—
" The good Cid Ruy Diaz salutes you as is meet,
As a good vassal to his lord, kissing your hands and feet ;
He is driven from your kingdom, and he has lost your love,
Be gracious to him, good my Lord, for heaven's sake above ;
Though living as a banish'd man, yet hath he prosper'd well
Within the Moorish border, such tidings I can tell.
He has taken towns and lands and castles many a one,
Xerica and Almenar, Cebola, Casteion ;
He has taken Penna Cadella, the fortress and the hill, ⎫
He has taken Murviedro, which is far better still ; ⎬
He is master of Valencia and rules it at his will ; ⎭
He has made a bishop of his own, with mitre, ring, and
    pall ;
He has fought five battles in the field, and conquer'd in
    them all ;
Great is the wealth and booty that, by the will of Heaven,
The Cid hath purchased in the field, and largely hath he
    thriven ;
And here I bring your Grace a sample and a token,
In proof of his allegiance, and that the truth is spoken,—
A hundred noble coursers, strong and tall and fleet,
With saddles and caparisons, and all equipments meet ;
He sends his humble present, kissing your Grace's hands,
And owns himself your vassal in his lordship and his lands."

The king lift up his hand, made a cross upon his brow,
The Cid was grown, he thought, to power and wealth enow.
" As Heaven shall be my speed, Heaven and St. Isidore,
I like these tidings well from the Cid Campeador,
And I receive his present and thank him furthermore."
But the Count Garci Ordonnez, at his heart's inmost core,
The more the king was satisfied, was envious and sore.
" If the Cid conquers at this rate, if all is true that's said,
What has become of all the Moors? the people must be
　　dead."
The king said, " Hold your peace, and make no more ado;
The Cid has served me more and better far than you."
With that Minaya Fañez made a manly speech:—
" The Cid entreats your favour and fain he would beseech
Your warrant and your licence (if so your Grace should
　　please),
As for his wife and daughters to grant them their release,—
To take them from the convent whereat they now remain,
And bring them to Valencia, to see them once again."
　" It pleases me right well," the noble king replied:
" A convoy they shall have, where'er they pass or ride,
To defend them from dishonour or offence that may
　　betide
In all my country's bounds, up to the border's side:
But when they pass the border the charge will rest with
　　you,
To attend them and protect them, as is their right and due.
—Ye knights and nobles of the court, my vassals, hear ye
　　me!
Henceforth shall Ruy Diaz stand unimpeach'd and free;
I quit him from all forfeiture and other detriment,
And for his followers that have lost their heritage and rent
In favour of the Cid I grant it back again,
To enable them to serve him there in his new domain."
Minaya kiss'd his hand, and thank'd him for his grace.
Then spoke the noble king, with his smiling, manly face,
" Whichever of my vassals is minded to resort
To Valencia with the Cid may freely leave the court;
And he shall hold his lands unforfeited and free;
And I shall own his service as a vassalage to me."

IV.

ARGUMENT.

Alvar Fañez and Martin Antolinez, having taken leave of the King, go to the monastery of St. Pedro de Cardena, where Dona Ximena and her daughters were, and bring them to within three leagues of Valencia, where they are met by the Cid on his famous horse Babieca. He runs a career with him, and at the end of the course, alighting, goes towards his wife and daughters. Donna Ximena kneels to receive him ; he conducts them into Valencia, where they are received with great rejoicings. In the spring, Yusef, King of Morocco, sends an army against Valencia. The Cid shows his wife and daughters the Moors landing, and entering the gardens round the city. Alvar Salvador makes a sally, and drives the Moors back to their tents, but is himself taken prisoner. Next day, after early mass by the Bishop Don Jerom, who obtained the boon of being first in the battle, the Cid attacks the Moors, who are utterly routed, and wounds King Yusef, who escapes him. On his return to the city, the Cid declares his intention of giving the ladies attendant on his wife and daughters in marriage to his vassals, with a dowry out of the plunder of two hundred marks of silver to each of them. The King of Morocco's tent he reserves for the King Don Alphonso, and, in addition to his share of the booty, gives a tithe of his own fifth to the Bishop Don Jerom.

[From line 1602 to 1809.]

SHE knelt before the Cid there in the people's
  sight :
  " Cid, in a lucky hour were you girded as a
  knight ;
  Full often have you rescued me from injury
and wrong :
And now, sir, with Heaven's blessing, here I have brought
  along,
To glad you with their presence, your own dear daughters
  both,
Rear'd in noble nurture and of good health and growth."

The Cid embraced them all with pleasure and surprise ;
The tears for very joy were streaming from their eyes.
Then spake the noble Cid the words that you shall hear : ⎫
"Beloved and honour'd woman, and you, my children dear, ⎪
The pride and solace of my heart, my darlings, welcome ⎬
    here ; ⎪
    ⎭
Come hither to Valencia, the mansion and the land
That I have purchased for you !" They knelt and kiss'd
    his hand.
He took them to the palace in triumph through the town,
He show'd them from the tower the prospect looking down,
The city spread below, the cultivated plain, ⎫
The garden of Valencia, the paradise of Spain, ⎬
Stretching beyond the sight, the mountains and the main ⎭
Encompassing it round ; they lift their hands and eyes
To Heaven that had bestow'd so fair and rich a prize.
There were pastimes fair enow at the entrance of the town,
Of tourneying and riding and riving targets down,
And hurling darts and snapping spears that it was joy to
    see,
With songs and instruments among, and mirth and
    minstrelsy ;
The Cid with his companions has kept a noble court,
The while the winter lasted, in solace and disport.
    The winter is departed, for March is coming in :
And I must tell you tidings, the tidings that begin
To reach us day by day from parts beyond the sea, ⎫
From Africa and Morocco ; King Yusef there is he, ⎬
Ruling the mighty realm with strength and chivalry. ⎭
And the report has reach'd his ears of all the Cid has done,
Of towns and castles taken and battles fought and won :
The kingdom of Valencia he detains it as his own,
And owns no lord on earth, but holds from Christ alone.
    This Emperor of Morocco has assembled all his host :
And fifty thousand warriors are encamp'd upon the coast ;
They put themselves on shipboard and shortly cross the ⎫
    main, ⎪
They disembark in haste along the coast of Spain, ⎬
They move towards Valencia, and encamp upon the plain. ⎭
    The Cid has seen and heard it :—" I thank the Lord
    above !
All upon earth that I possess, with all the things I love,

Are here assembled round me, my children and my wife,
And this my goodly conquest achieved with toil and strife,
I never mean to leave it while I retain my life."—
—" But sure this Emperor, like a courteous gentle knight,
Has sent us out a pageant for our pastime and delight,
That I may bear a part in, in my wife and daughters' sight,
And attire myself for battle and enter in the fight;
That they may see with their own eyes the life we long
    have led,
In daily combat with the Moors, earning our daily bread."
He took the ladies up on high to the tower of the Alcazar,
They saw the Moorish camp in all the pride of war,
The banners and pavilions stretching wide and far.
" Cid,—for mercy's sake! what upon earth is this?"
—" Nothing at all, my worthy dame—nothing that comes
    amiss.
The Moors are arrived to greet you, their courtesy to pay,
With a present for your daughters against their wedding-day:
Remain, then, in the palace, or here in the Alcazar,
And never feel alarm'd if you see me join the war.
By the blessing of the Lord and of St. Mary bright
We shall prosper once again and conquer in the fight,
And with your presence here, and combating in your sight,
My heart feels larger than before—joyous, alert, and light."
  Now from the Moorish host, with the first dawn of day,
Their heavy drums began to thunder and to bray:
The Cid was joyous at the sounds—" there comes a noble
    day!"
The ladies all are trembling with terror and dismay:
The Cid look'd smiling on them with his hand upon his
    beard,
" Courage, noble ladies, there is nothing to be fear'd;
The drums there that are making the noises that are heard,
You should have them brought before you, within a fort-
    night' space,
To view their shape and make here in this very place:
We shall dispose them afterwards as the bishop may desire,
To remain for a memorial in the cathedral quire;
It is a vow recorded—a vow the Cid has made,
To present them for an offering, and it must needs be
    paid:"
Thus has he cheer'd the ladies, they felt no more afraid.

I*   A A

The Moorish cavaliers are advancing without fear,
They enter in the Huerta and approach the city near:
The watchman in the barbican has smitten on the bell,
The Christians are assembled, arm'd and accoutred well,
They sally forth in order with an eager fierce attack—
The Moors are broken with the shock, routed and driven
    back.
In the charge and the pursuit five hundred Moors were slain,
The Christians follow them in haste to the tents upon the
    plain,
But by their own mischance, ere they return'd again,
Alvar Salvador was left a prisoner to remain ;
The rest are all return'd that dine at the Cid's board.   ⎫
The adventures of the day they report them 'to their Lord: ⎬
The Cid has seen and heard it—he spake a merry word: ⎭
" Gentlemen, for this day's work our chance has not been ill,
To-morrow with God's blessing we shall do better still ;
Our Bishop, good Don Jerom, an early mass shall say
And give us absolution before the dawn of day.
Then we shall sally forth and assault them in the names
Of the Lord and his Apostle our worthy good St. James."
There was an answer all at once, one answer from the whole :
" With all our hearts," the knights replied, " with all our
    hearts and soul."
Minaya was in haste, and thus he spake his mind :
" Cid, since you so determine, leave six score men behind ;
Go forward with the rest, and let the battle join,
And God will send us succour on your side or on mine."
" Let it be so ! " the Cid replied. The night was coming on.
The Christians all were arm'd betimes, accoutred every one.
At the second cock-crow, before the dawn of day,
The Bishop Don Jeronimo was ready mass to say.
He sang the mass full solemnly in the cathedral quire,
And gave them absolution, perfect and entire.
" He that falls in battle, his face against the foe,
I make him clean of all his sins, his soul to heaven shall go.
And now, right worthy Cid, for the mass that has been
    chanted,
I shall require a boon and it must needs be granted.
—The foremost place in battle and the first stroke of the
    fight."
" Let it be yours," the Cid replied, " it is a claim of right."

They sally forth, arm'd and equipp'd, beyond the city wall:
The Cid is there amongst them, to arrange and order all:
Babieca, his good courser, bearing him gallantly,
Arm'd and attired for battle, a goodly sight to see!
A guard is left to keep the gates, men of high trust and
worth:
And now beyond the gates the banner is borne forth;
Thirty less four thousand was the number at the most
To encounter fifty thousand, such was the Moorish host.
They rush upon them all at once, without a thought of fear:
Minaya chose his time to charge the flank and rear.
The Moors with sudden onset, such was the will of Heaven,
Were broken and confused, and wide asunder driven:
The Cid with his spear in hand and sword so sharp and ⎫
good, ⎪
From the elbow to the point dripping down with blood, ⎬
The number that he slew was never understood. ⎭
He singled out King Yusef; the king durst not abide ⎫
So fearful an assault, but fast away 'gan ride ⎬
To the castle of Guyera, a palace fortified: ⎭
There was he safely lodged; but till he reach'd the place,
The Cid was foremost in pursuit, nor ever left the chase.
Now with his followers he returns, rejoiced and satisfied:—
He has gain'd a mighty booty, he has check'd the Moorish
pride;
And his courser, Babieca, has been fully proved and tried.
The plunder of the camp was plentiful and great— ⎫
Coin of gold and silver, and gold and silver plate, ⎬
And other riches more than they could estimate. ⎭
The Cid has left Minaya to take a just account,
Returning to Valencia before he would dismount;
An hundred knights were with him, he rode an easy pace,
Arm'd as he was before, all but his head and face.
There might his countenance be seen furrow'd with a
frown—
Sword-in-hand, upon his steed he enter'd in the town.
He has rein'd him up before the porch, there, where the
ladies stood
Ready to receive him. He spoke in merry mood:
" Welcome, welcome, ladies! we have purchased great
renown—
I have conquer'd in the field—and you have kept the town.

It shows the will of Heaven, that it hath pleased to bless
Your first arrival here with victory and success.
You see my courser reeking, my sword with slaughter red—
Such is the fashion among knights when Moors are slain
      and fled.
Pray God to spare my life for two years or for three,
Then gentlemen and knights shall salute you on their knee."
These words the Cid has spoken before he lighted down—
His daughters with their ladies, his dame of high renown,
Bent the knee before him and kiss'd his hand with tears—
" We live, sir, in your favour,—may you live these many
      years !"
Then passing onward from the porch, to the rich hall he
      goes,
Sitting amongst them, for a while, in silence and repose—
" Hoh ! Donna Ximena, my wife, it is a scheme of mine—
You never mention'd it yourself, but this is my design—
The ladies, your attendants, that have been brought to stay,
I mean to marry them forthwith to the vassals in my pay,
And to give each two hundred marks upon their wedding-
      day.
They have served a noble lady, folks in Castille will say—
—The marriage of our daughters for the present we delay."
They rose and kiss'd his hand; so, from the first report,
Till the Cid's promise was fulfill'd, great was the mirth
      and sport,
The gladness and rejoicing in the camp and in the court.
Minaya still was in the camp, busied all the day,
Reckoning and writing, and assorting all the prey,
And dealing with the shares of plunder and of pay.
The whole amount of wealth was more than I can say:
The tents and the pavilions, armour and rich array,
And horses without number running wide astray ;
Many became a prize to the native peasants round,
Yet, for the fifth part of the whole, there were fifteen
      hundred found
(The Cid's own proper portion), horses strong and sound.
The rest with their allotments were joyous and content,
From many a proud pavilion and many a costly tent,
Enrich'd with silken hangings and golden ornament.
The great imperial tent, that in the centre stood,
It rested on two pillars of gold and sandal-wood ;

It is order'd to be left untouch'd, perfect and entire.
" I mean it as a present for our own Lord and sire ;
When the King receives it no courtier will refuse
To credit our successes or cavil at the news."
Now to Valencia they return with a store of wealth in hold.
The Bishop Don Jeronimo, like a worthy priest and bold,
Was fairly wearied out and glutted with delight,
With a sword in either hand striking to left and right,
No man could reckon up or guess the numbers he had slain;
For his own portion he received the largest share of gain.
The Cid from his own fifth presented him the tithe—
Thus all were joyous in the town, confident and blythe.

V.

ARGUMENT.

*After the route of King Yusef and his army, the Cid
sends Alvar Fanez and Pero Bermudez with King Yusef's
tent and a present of two hundred horses to King Alfonso,
because the king had sent his wife and daughters when he
asked for them, and because of the honour which he had done
them. The king, when he saw the present, said that never
had so goodly a present been sent before to a king of Spain
by his vassals, and desired Alvar Fanez and Pero Bermudez,
when they took their leave, to tell the Cid that he had a great
desire to see him. The meeting was appointed upon the
Tagus. When it took place, the king, at the previous instigation of the Infants (whose family were his old adversaries)
asked the Cid to give his daughters in marriage to the
Infants of Carrion. The Cid in reply consents to place his
daughters "at the disposition of the king." The wedding
is celebrated at Valencia with the greatest possible splendour,
and the two young Counts remain at Valencia with their
father-in-law: their situation, however, is an invidious one;
some occasions arise in which their courage appears doubtful,
and the prudence and authority of the Cid are found insufficient to suppress the contemptuous mirth of his military
court. Accordingly they enter into the resolution of leaving
Valencia, but determining at the same time to execute a
project of the basest and most unmanly revenge, they request*

*of the Cid to be allowed to take their brides with them upon
a journey to Carrion, under pretence of making them acquainted with the property which had been settled upon them
at their marriage. The Cid is aware that their situation
is an uneasy one; he readily consents, takes leave of them
with great cordiality, loads them with presents, and at their
departure bestows upon them the two celebrated swords,
Colada and Tison. The Infants pursue their journey till
they arrive in a wilderness, where they dismiss their followers, and being left alone with their brides, proceed to
execute their scheme of vengeance by stripping them and
" mangling them with spurs and thongs," till they leave them
without signs of life: in this state they are found by a
relation of the Cid's, Felez Munioz, who, suspecting some
evil design, had followed them at a distance. They are
brought back to Valencia. The Cid demands justice. The
king assembles the Cortes upon the occasion. The Cid,
being called upon to state his grievances, confines himself
to the claim of two swords which he had given to his sons-
in-law, and which he now demands back since they have
forfeited their character. The swords are restored without
hesitation, and the Cid immediately bestows them upon two
of his champions. He then rises again, and upon the same
plea requires the restitution of the gifts and treasures with
which he had honoured his sons-in-law at parting. This
claim is resisted by his opponents: the Cortes, however,
decide in favour of the Cid, and as the Infants plead their
immediate inability, it is determined that the property which
they have with them shall be taken at an appraisement.*
This is accordingly done. The Cid then rises a third
time, and demands satisfaction for the insult which his
daughters had suffered : an altercation arises, in the
course of which the Infants of Carrion and one of their
partisans are challenged by three champions on the part
of the Cid.

[From line 3254 to 3401.]

 ITHIN a little space
There was many a noble courser brought
into the place,
Many a lusty mule with palfreys stout and
sure,
And many a goodly sword with all its furniture.

The Cid received them all at an appraisement made,
Besides two hundred marks that to the King were paid:
The Infants give up all they have, their goods are at an end,
They go about in haste to their kindred and their friend;
They borrow as they can, but all will scarce suffice ; ⎫
The attendants of the Cid take each thing at a price: ⎬
But as soon as this was ended, he began a new device. ⎭
" Justice and mercy, my Lord the King, I beseech you of
  your grace!
I have yet a grievance left behind which nothing can efface.
Let all men present in the court attend and judge the case,
Listen to what these Counts have done and pity my dis-
  grace.
Dishonour'd as I am, I cannot be so base,
But here, before I leave them, to defy them to their face.
Say, Infants, how had I deserved, in earnest or in jest,
Or on whatever plea you can defend it best,
That you should rend and tear the heartstrings from my
  breast?
I gave you at Valencia my daughters in your hand,
I gave you wealth and honours and treasure at command;
Had you been weary of them, to cover your neglect,
You might have left them with me in honour and respect.
Why did you take them from me, dogs and traitors as you
  were?
In the forest of Corpes, why did you strip them there?
Why did you mangle them with whips? why did you leave
  them bare
To the vultures and the wolves, and to the wintry air?
The court will hear your answer and judge what you have
  done.
I say, your name and honour henceforth are lost and gone."
  The Count Don Garcia was the first to rise:
" We crave your favour, my Lord the King, you are always
  just and wise!
The Cid is come to your Court in such an uncouth guise,
He has left his beard to grow and tied it in a braid,
We are half of us astonish'd, the other half afraid.
The blood of the Counts of Carrion is of too high a line
To take a daughter from his house, though it were for a
  concubine.
A concubine or a leman from the lineage of the Cid,
They could have done no other than leave them as they did.

We neither care for what he says nor fear what he may
    threat."
With that the noble Cid rose up from his seat:
He took his beard in his hand, " If this beard is fair and
    even,
I must thank the Lord above, who made both earth and
    heaven ;
It has been cherish'd with respect and therefore it has
    thriven :
It never suffer'd an affront since the day it first was worn.
What business, Count, have you to speak of it with scorn ?
It never yet was shaken, nor pluck'd away nor torn,
By Christian nor by Moor, nor by man of woman born,
As yours was once, Sir Count, the day Cabra was taken ;
When I was master of Cabra that beard of yours was
    shaken;
There was never a footboy in my camp but twitch'd away
    a bit :
The side that I tore off grows all uneven yet."
Ferran Gonzales started upon the floor,
He cried with a loud voice, " Cid, let us hear no more,
Your claim for goods and money was satisfied before :
Let not a feud arise betwixt our friends and you,
We are the Counts of Carrion, from them our birth we
    drew.
Daughters of Emperors or Kings were a match for our
    degree,
We hold ourselves too good for a baron's such as thee.
If we abandon'd, as you say, and left and gave them o'er,
We vouch that we did right, and prize ourselves the more."
The Cid look'd at Bermuez, that was sitting at his foot ;
"Speak thou, Peter the Dumb, what ails thee to sit mute ?
My daughters and thy nieces are the parties in dispute.
Stand forth and make reply, if you would do them right.
If I should rise to speak you cannot hope to fight."
Peter Bermuez rose, somewhat he had to say,
The words were strangled in his throat, they could not find
    their way ;
Till forth they came at once, without a stop or stay :
" Cid, I'll tell you what, this always is your way,
You have always served me thus, whenever we have come
To meet here in the Cortes, you call me Peter the Dumb.

I cannot help my nature ; I never talk nor rail ;
But when a thing is to be done, you know I never fail.
Fernando, you have lied, you have lied in every word :
You have been honour'd by the Cid, and favour'd and pre-
    ferr'd.
I know of all your tricks, and can tell them to your face :
Do you remember in Valencia the skirmish and the chase ?
You ask'd leave of the Cid to make the first attack .
You went to meet a Moor, but you soon came running
    back.
I met the Moor and kill'd him, or he would have kill'd you;
I gave you up his arms, and all that was my due.
Up to this very hour I never said a word.
You praised yourself before the Cid, and I stood by and
    heard,
How you had kill'd the Moor, and done a valiant act,
And they believed you all, but they never knew the fact.
You are tall enough and handsome, but cowardly and weak.
Thou tongue without a hand, how can you dare to speak ?
There's the story of the lion should never be forgot.
Now let us hear, Fernando, what answer have you got ?
The Cid was sleeping in his chair, with all his knights
    around,
The cry went forth along the hall, that the lion was un-
    bound,—
What did you do, Fernando ? like a coward as you were,
You slunk behind the Cid, and crouch'd beneath his chair.
We prest around the throne to shield our Lord from harm,
Till the good Cid awoke ; he rose without alarm ;
He went to meet the lion with his mantle on his arm ;
The lion was abash'd the noble Cid to meet,
He bow'd his mane to the earth, his muzzle at his feet.
The Cid by the neck and mane drew him to his den,
He thrust him in at the hatch, and came to the hall again :
He found his knights, his vassals, and all his valiant men ;
He ask'd for his sons-in-law, they were neither of them
    there.
I defy you for a coward and a traitor as you are ;
For the daughters of the Cid you have done them great
    unright,
In the wrong that they have suffer'd you stand dishonour'd
    quite.

Although they are but women, and each of you a knight, ⎫
I hold them worthier far ; and here my word I plight, ⎬
Before the King Alfonso, upon this plea to fight. ⎭
If it be God his will, before the battle part,
Thou shalt avow it with thy mouth, like a traitor as thou
　　　art."
Uprose Diego Gonzales and answer'd as he stood : ⎫
" By our lineage we are Counts, and of the purest blood ; ⎬
This match was too unequal, it never could hold good ; ⎭
For the daughters of the Cid we acknowledge no regret,
We leave them to lament the chastisement they met.
It will follow them through life for a scandal and a jest.
I stand upon this plea to combat with the best,
That having left them as we did, our honour is increased."
Uprose Martin Antolinez when Diego ceased :
" Peace, thou lying mouth ! thou traitor coward, Peace !
The story of the lion should have taught you shame at
　　　least :
You rush'd out at the door, and ran away so hard,
You fell into the cesspool that was open in the yard.
We dragg'd you forth in all men's sight, dripping from the
　　　drain ;
For shame, never wear a mantle, nor a knightly robe again !
I fight upon this plea without more ado ;
The daughters of the Cid are worthier far than you.
Before the combat part you shall avow it true,
And that you have been a traitor and a coward too."
Thus was ended the parley and challenge betwixt these two.
Assur Gonzales was entering at the door
With his ermine mantle trailing along the floor ;
With his sauntering pace and his hardy look,
Of manners or of courtesy little heed he took :
He was flush'd and hot with breakfast and with drink.
" What ho, my masters, your spirits seem to sink !
Have we no news stirring from the Cid Ruy Diaz of Bivar ?
Has he been to Riodivirna to besiege the windmills there ?
Does he tax the millers for their toll, or is that practice
　　　past ?
Will he make a match for his daughters another like the
　　　last ?"
Munio Gustioz rose and made reply :
" Traitor ! wilt thou never cease to slander and to lie ?

You breakfast before mass, you drink before you pray : ⎫
There is no honour in your heart, nor truth in what you say; ⎬
You cheat your comrade and your Lord, you flatter to betray : ⎭
Your hatred I despise, your friendship I defy.
False to all mankind, and most to God on high.
I shall force you to confess that what I say is true."
Thus was ended the parley and challenge betwixt these two.

VI.

ARGUMENT.

The king suppresses all further altercation, and declares that those only who have already challenged shall be permitted to fight. The time and place are fixed. The Cid being obliged to return to Valencia, leaves his Champions under the protection of the king. The Cid takes leave of the king. At the end of three weeks the combat is fought, and the three Champions of the Cid are victorious.

[From line 3516 to 3702.]

CRAVE your favour, my Lord the King, since things are settled so ;
" I have business at Valencia, and thither I must go.
Before the town was conquer'd it cost me pains enow."
The king lift up his hand, made a cross upon his brow :
" I swear by St. Isidro, the patron of Leon,
In all my realm beside there is not such a good baron."
The Cid leapt on his steed and rode him round the course, ⎫
He came up to the king and proffer'd him the horse— ⎬
" 'Tis the noble Babieca that is famed for speed and force, ⎭
Among the Christians nor the Moors there is not such ⎫
another one ; ⎬
My Sovereign Lord and Sire, he is fit for you alone : ⎬
Give orders to your people, and take him for your own." ⎭
The king replied, " It cannot be ; Cid, you shall keep your horse,
He must not leave his master, nor change him for a worse ;

The man that would take him from you, evil may he speed,
Our kingdom has been honour'd by you and by your steed.
A courser such as he is fit for such a knight,
To beat down Moors in battle, and follow them in flight."
Now they have taken leave, and broken up the Court,
The Cid goes with his champions to advise them and exhort:
"You, Martin Antolinez, and Pero Bermuez, you,
And you, Munio Gustioz, be valiant men and true:
When I am gone to Valencia let me have good tidings
     there."
Martin Antolinez replied, "Sir, what needs this care?
We are pledged in your behalf, we must do our best en-
     deavour;
You may hear that we are dead, but defeated never."
The Cid was joyful at the word, and quitted them anon;
He has taken leave of all his friends, and shortly he is gone.
The Cid goes to Valencia, the king to Carrion.
Three weeks had been appointed, and now they are past
     away,
The Champions of the Cid are ready at the day:
They are ready in the field to defend their master's right,
The noble king is with them, to protect them with his might.
They waited in the place for two days and a night,
Behold the Lords of Carrion where they appear in sight:
They are coming with an host of their kindred and their
     clan,
With horses and with arms, and many a valiant man;
If they could meet with them apart, or take them unaware,
In dishonour of the Cid to have slain his Champions there.
The thought was foul and evil, but yet they did not dare,
For fear of the King Alfonso that had them in his care.
That night they watch'd their arms, and past the hours in
     prayer;
The night is past and over, the day begins to break;
Great was the throng of folk who, for that battle's sake,
Flock'd in on every side, assembled for the fight,
And many a man of arms and many a wealthy knight.
There is the King Alfonso with all his power and might,
To keep down force and wrong, and to defend the right.
The Champions of the Cid are all of good accord,
They are arming themselves together, like vassals of one
     Lord.

The Infants of Carrion are arming themselves apart,
Count Garcia sits advising them, and keeps them in good
    heart.
They bring a plea before the king, and they pretend a
    right,
That those two trenchant swords should not be used in
    fight,
The swords Colada and Tison, which the Cid's champions
    wore ;
They repent of their imprudence when they gave them
    up before.
They were earnest in their plea, but they could not
    succeed ;
" You might have kept them for yourselves to serve you
    in your need ;
If you have other good ones, make use of them instead.
Infants of Carrion ! hear me and take heed :
You must approve your honour by some manly deed.
Go forth into the field, and show a valiant heart,
For nothing will be wanting upon the Champions' part.
If you are conquerors in the fight you will purchase great
    renown,
If you are beaten and disgraced, the fault will be your own,
For this business was your seeking, as has been seen and
    shown."
The Infants of Carrion are beginning to repent ;
The Lordship of Carrion with its honours and its rent,
Its mansion and its lands, they would have given all,
Could they command the past, to redeem it and recall.
    The Champions of the Cid, clad in their warlike weed,
The king is gone to see them and wish them well to speed.
" Sir, we kiss your hands as our good Lord and sire,
To have you judge and umpire is all that we require.
Defend us in all right, assist us not in wrong ;
The friends of the Lords of Carrion are numerous and
    strong,
We cannot guess their counsels, nor how they will behave.
To the good Cid, our master, the promise that you gave,
To defend us and protect us, this, Sir, is all we crave,
So long as right and justice are found upon our part."
".That will I," said the king, " with all my soul and heart."
Their horses are brought up to them, coursers strong and
    fleet,

They sign their saddles with the cross, and leap into the
    seat ;
Their shields are hanging at their necks with bosses broad
    and sheen,
They take their lances in their hands, the points are
    bright and keen,
A pennon at each lance, the staves were large and stout,)
And many a valiant man encompass'd them about.
They rode forth to the field where the barriers were
    set out.

The Champions of the Cid are agreed upon their plan,
To fight as they had challenged, and each to charge his
    man.
There come the Lords of Carrion with their kindred
    and their clan ;
The king has appointed heralds for avoiding all debate,
He spoke aloud amongst them in the field there where
    they sate.
" Infants of Carrion ! Attend to what I say:
You should have fought this battle upon a former day,
When we were at Toledo, but you would not agree ;
And now the noble Cid has sent these Champions three,
To fight in the lands of Carrion, escorted here by me.
Be valiant in your right, attempt no force or wrong ;
If any man attempt it he shall not triumph long:
He never shall have rest or peace within my kingdom
    more."
The Infants of Carrion are now repenting sore ;
The heralds and the king are foremost in the place,
They clear away the people from the middle space :
They measure out the lists, the barriers they fix :
They point them out in order, and explain to all the six :
" If you are forced beyond the line where they are fix'd
    and traced,
You shall be held as conquer'd, and beaten and dis-
    graced."
Six lances' length on either side an open space is laid,
They part the field between them, the sunshine and the
    shade.
Their office is perform'd, and from the middle space
The heralds are withdrawn, and leave them face to face.
Here stood the warriors of the Cid, that noble champion,

Opposite on the other side, the Lords of Carrion.
Earnestly their minds are fix'd each upon his foe ;
Face to face they take their place ; anon the trumpets
blow.
They stir their horses with the spur, they lay their
lances low,
They bend their shields before their breasts, their face to
the saddle-bow.
Earnestly their minds are fix'd each upon his foe.
The heavens are overcast above, the earth trembles below,
The people stand in silence, gazing on the show :
Bermuez the first challenger first in combat closed,
He met Ferran Gonzales, face to face opposed ;
They rush together with such rage that all men count
them dead,
They strike each other on the shield, without all fear or
dread.
Ferran Gonzales with his lance pierced the shield outright,
It past Bermuez on the left side, in his flesh it did not bite.
The spear was snapt in twain, Bermuez sat upright,
He neither flinch'd nor swerved, like a true stedfast knight,
A good stroke he received, but a better he has given ; ⎫
He struck the shield upon the boss, in sunder it is riven. ⎬
Onward into Ferran's breast the lance's point is driven, ⎭
Full upon his breastplate, nothing would avail ;
Two breastplates Fernando wore and a coat of mail :
The two are riven in sunder, the third stood him in stead,
The mail sunk in his breast, the mail and the spear-head,
The blood burst from his mouth that all men thought him
dead.
The blow has broken his girdle and his saddle-girth,
It has taken him over his horse's back, and borne him to
the earth.
The people think him dead, as he lies on the sand ;
Bermuez left his lance and took his sword in hand.
Ferran Gonzales knew the blade which he had worn
of old,
Before the blow came down, he yielded and cried,
" Hold !"
Antolinez and Diego encounter'd man for man,
Their spears were shiver'd with the shock, so eagerly
they ran.

Antolinez drew forth the blade which Diego once had
    worn,
Eagerly he aim'd the blow for the vengeance he had sworn.
Right through Diego's helm the blade its edge has borne,
The crest and helm are lopt away, the coif and hair are
    shorn.
He stood astounded with the stroke, trembling and forlorn,
He waved his sword above his head, he made a piteous cry,
"O save me, save me from that blade, Almighty Lord on
    high !"
Antolinez came fiercely round to reach the fatal stroke,
Diego's courser rear'd upright, and through the barrier
    broke.
Antolinez has won the day, though his blow he miss'd,
He has driven Diego from the field, and stands within
    the list.
I must tell you of Munio Gustioz, two combats now are
    done ;
How he fought with Assur Gonzales, you shall hear anon.
Assur Gonzales, a fierce and hardy knight,
He rode at Munio Gustioz with all his force and might ;
He struck the shield and pierced it through, but the point
    came wide,
It pass'd by Munio Gustioz, betwixt his arm and side :
Sternly, like a practised knight, Munio met him there.
His lance he levell'd stedfastly, and through the shield
    him bare ;
He bore the point into his breast, a little beside the heart ;
It took him through the body, but in no mortal part ;
The shaft stood out behind his back a cloth-yard and
    more ;
The pennon and the point were dripping down with gore.
Munio still clench'd his spear, as he pass'd he forced it
    round,
He wrench'd him from the saddle, and cast him to the
    ground.
His horse sprung forward with the spur, he pluck'd the
    spear away,
He wheel'd and came again to pierce him where he lay.
Then cried Gonzalo Assurez, "For God's sake spare
    my son !
"The other two have yielded, the field is fought and won."

MISCELLANEOUS TRANSLATIONS.

TRANSLATION FROM THE ILIAD.

LIB. IX. 308 TO 487.

Διογενὲς Λαερτιάδη, κ. τ. λ.

ISE and illustrious chief, Laertes' heir,
'Tis best my settled purpose to declare,
As reason and my fix'd resolves decide,
No more with vain discourses to be plied,
And baffled and beset from side to side :
For worse than hell the caitiff I detest,
Whose tongue belies the secret of his breast ;
Thus, then, receive mine answer, in the strain
That suits my character, broad speech and plain.
  Not he the king, nor any wiser Greek
Will prosper in his errand, if they seek
To win me to their purpose—for the meed
Of valour waits not upon warlike deed—
The coward and the brave alike succeed.
When I have labour'd hard and nobly fought,
When all is ended, it avails me nought
To pass my days in danger and in strife,
At every turn of war to stake my life ;
As the fond bird protects her infant brood,
Fatigued and fasting to provide them food,
I watch'd the Greeks : for them in arms I lay
Long weary nights that sleepless pass'd away,
And toil'd in tasks of bloodshed through the day.

Twelve island towns I took, eleven more
I storm'd and sack'd upon the Trojan shore ;
Large booty from them all I bore away,—
Atrides, in the camp here where he lay,
Received the whole, and, as it liked him best,
Dealt round a portion, and reserved the rest.
Each chief retains that portion as his own,
Mine, mine, he re-demands, and mine alone ;
He has her—let him surfeit with delight,
There let him pass the careless easy night,
With the fond partner that my soul held dear—
But tell me, then ! what purpose brought us here ?
Why are the tribes of Greece and Troy at strife ?
Forsooth for Menelaus and his wife—
The noble sons of Athens it should seem
Feel for their wives and women. Do they deem
That passion to their single soul's confined,
Or common to the hearts of human kind ?
Not so.—The wife or consort claims a part,
Endear'd and inward in each manly heart,
The heart of every worthy man and brave ;
And I loved her, though captive and a slave.
Now then, let him that scorn'd me and misused,
(Scorn'd in his turn, rejected and refused)
Forbear, for shame, no more resort to us,
But some more practicable point discuss ;
Let him with you, Ulysses, and the rest
Deliberate what means may promise best
To save his fleet and camp from being fired :
Great things has he achieved since I retired.
Has he not built a noble mound and wall,
Turrets and trenches, palisades and all ?
But all is little when the headlong might
Of murderous Hector urges on the fight.
When I was in the field his utmost reach
Was to the seven portals and the beach ;
Once, only once, he ventured to advance,—
He stood one onset, and escaped by chance.
But now those transient enmities are o'er,
The noble Hector is my foe no more.
And if the sight be worth your thought or care,
To-morrow you may view a prospect fair—

The ships and vessels crowding from the shore,
And lusty sailors stooping to the oar ;
The prows with garlands crown'd in joyous pride,
Stemming athwart the strong proponding tide ;
A three days' voyage, if our vows are heard,
We reach the shores of Phthia on the third.
The wealth that I relinquish'd there before,
To die despised on this accursed shore,
I shall again behold, and add thereto
Gold, brass, and comely captives not a few :
My lawful prize, the purchase of the sword ;
As for the boon he gave—your haughty lord
Has falsified his gift and borne her hence,
In my despite, with wrong and insolence—
So tell him, word for word, my plain reply
Aloud in public—that the common cry
May vindicate my wrongs—that every Greek
(Whene'er this tyrant lord again may seek
To pillage and dishonour him) may know,
And stand forewarn'd of what his actions show—
His fraud, his insolence, his love of pelf,—
This for the rest. For what concerns myself
The tyrant's impudence would scarce suffice
To meet me face to face ; no more advice,
Counsel, or aid shall he receive from me—
Enough ! more than enough ! so let him be,
Even as he is, mark'd by the fates' decree,
For speedy wrath, by the just hand of Jove,
Blasted with pride and madness from above;
His gifts I loathe—and hate the giver worse—
The poorest Carian born, that fills a purse,
Following his trade of mercenary war,
I deem a nobler chief, and worthier far—
I scorn, then, I reject, his gifts, his gold,
If they were doubled, trebled, ten times told—
With all that he possesses else or more—
No, not the piles of wealth amass'd of yore
In old Orchomenus, nor all the store
Of Thebes in Egypt, where a hundred gates
Pour forth their armies to the subject states—
Not these, nor all the wealth of land and sea
Shall ever reconcile your lord and me.

Till my full vengeance has its course, the last,
The sole requital of offences past.
His girls may equal Venus in their bloom,
Or Pallas in the labours of the loom,
Adorn'd with graces and with charms divine,
But never shall he see them wives of mine.
Some suitable alliance let him seek ;
Some other nobler, more distinguish'd Greek ;
For me, when all my wars are at an end,
If I return alive, with heaven to friend,
My father Peleus will himself provide,
Among the neighbouring chiefs, a proper bride :
Some daughter of the native nobles there,
Of goodly kindred and possessions fair,
That hold the cities of the plain in charge,
Or in their rocky castles live at large :
There, too, whatever girl may most attract
My fancy would be mine ; my mind, in fact,
Is turn'd to marriage and domestic life ;
A fair inheritance, a comely wife,
To live at ease with what the pains and care
Of Peleus have provided for his heir ;
For after all this life-blood in the breast
Of all possessions is the first and best ;
Not to be barter'd, countervail'd, or sold
For all that in the wealthy times of old
This town of Troy possess'd, before the day
That brought her power and treasure to decay ;
Or all that rocky Pythos holds immured,
For sanctuary, secret and secured ;
Flocks, herds, and coursers of a noble strain,
By force or fraud, we lose them and regain ;
But when the breath of life is past and gone,
No rescue serves, and ransom there is none.
This, too, my mother goddess has declared,
The double destiny by Jove's award,
Allotted to my choice, free to refuse,
Or to select at will the fate I choose.
If longer I remain and persevere
To prosecute the siege I perish here,
Leaving a name and memory behind
Renown'd among the races of mankind ;

Returning home a peaceful easy life
Awaits me, destitute of care and strife,
Compensating the loss of future praise,
With wealth and ease and length of happy days.
And truly the same counsel I should give,
For all my comrades to return and live,
And save your host and navy while you may.
The Trojan race are brave, and day by day
More desperate they manifestly fight,
With Jove's assistance and increasing might.
Now then return, and to the chiefs in court
Assembled make a full and fair report,
With this advice, moreover, sound and short,
To think of other means that may suffice
To save their army—for this new device,
This scheme of reconcilement to secure
My service at their need, is premature."

  He ceased—the chiefs, astounded at the force
And unabated wrath of his discourse,
Sat mute, till Phœnix, like a worthy Greek,
In pity for his friends, essay'd to speak,
The tears fast falling down his aged cheek.
"Since then, indeed, you mean, Achilles dear,
To leave the fleet and host in danger here,
Moved by the fiery pride and high disdain
That rules your spirit, how should I remain?
What should I do without you left behind,
When he, your father Peleus, old and kind,
Appointed me your guide the very day
We went to join the king, and came away
From his own house at Phthia, then were you
A youth unpractised in the world, and new,—
New to the wars, and to concerns of state,
Unused to public council and debate.
Therefore I went, appointed, you to teach
All stratagems of war and arts of speech,
To make you, what the world has known and seen,
The creature that you are and long have been.
And shall I leave you now, my son—not I,
Not if the Gods, to tempt me to comply,
Would make me young and active, and restore
My strength and spirit as it was before

When I abandon'd first my native place,
Flying an exile from my father's face.
Our strife too for a woman's cause began,
He view'd and chose and brought her home, his plan
To take her for a concubine to shame
My noble mother his own lawful dame ;
She therewithal with earnest prayer and strong
Entreated and besought me fast and long
To anticipate him—yielding to the son
She deem'd the damsel would detest and shun
The father. I complied, and it was done—
It was detected—and my father knew—
And ever, as his rage of passion grew,
He pray'd aloud, with grief and fury torn,
That never infant from my body born
Might press my arms or prattle at my knee—
Thus pray'd my sire, and thus the fates decree.
Then was my spirit moved with grief and pain,
As restless and indignant to remain
Under a father's curse, beneath his roof ;
Then, too, the friends and kindred wide aloof,
Came at a summons on my sire's behoof—
Kinsmen and cousins, all with long discourse,
To reconcile or keep me there by force ;
They feasted and caroused, the beeves and swine
Were slaughter'd, hoarded jars of racy wine
Drawn forth and emptied—thus the day was past ;
At night they watch'd by turns and kept me fast
Within my chamber, with a fire before
The threshold of my gate and at my door.
Thus nine continued days with guard and light
They watch'd me till the tenth and fatal night :
Then forth I burst and broke the chamber door,
And rush'd across the court and vaulted o'er
Th' enclosure, fence and all, fleeing amain
Straight forward thro' the broad Helladian plain :
There noble Peleus, with a kind good will,
Received me, favour'd and protected still,
Even as a cherish'd unexpected heir,
Appointing me possessions rich and fair,
Vassals and lands—there in a frontier place,
I dwelt and govern'd the Dolopian race :

And there, Achilles, with all pains and care
I nursed and rear'd and made you what you are.
And dearly did I love you, for your will
Was ever constant to be with me still;
Nor ever would you dine abroad or eat,
But I must mix the wine and carve the meat;
And often was my bosom drench'd with wine,
When you were seated on these knees of mine,
Coughing and heaving at an awkward sup,
When with your hands in mine I held the cup."

TRANSLATION FROM THE ODYSSEY.

LIB. XXI. 424 TO LIB. XXII. 42.

Τηλέμαχ', οὔ σ' ὁ ξεῖνος, κ.τ.λ.

ELEMACHUS, your choice was not misplaced
On men like me, nor has your guest disgraced
Your friendly roof. I did not labour long
To bend the bow, nor have I aim'd it wrong.
I feel my practice and my force the same.
Henceforth the noble suitors will not blame
The vigour of my arm and truth of aim.
But now the hour invites you to repair
To some slight banquet in the open air,
Anon to feast within with dance and song,
For joys like these to festive hours belong."
He knit his brow, his son the signal knew,
And the light sword across his shoulders threw,
And grasp'd his spear, and stood with youthful pride
Array'd for battle at his father's side;
Ulysses cast his tatters to the ground,
Sprung forth and seized the threshold at a bound,
Then showering down the glittering shafts around
From his full quiver, thus aloud he spake.
"Another trial, lords, I mean to make—
Unlike the last, for further proof I take

A point untouch'd by any marksman's skill,
If my force fail me not—and Phœbus will."
Then at Antinoüs his aim he took,
That stood, with careless air and easy look,
Fearless of fraud or force, secure of soul,
Just heaving from the board a mighty bowl;
He poised it in his hand, the cup was gold
With double handles of a massy mould;
Wafting it round, or e'er he quaff'd the wine,
Of death or danger what could he divine,
Or how imagine that a hand unknown,
Bold though he were, a stranger and alone,
Amidst his feasting friends should strike him dead?
Ulysses loosed the string, the shaft was sped,
It struck him through the throat, the grisly point
Peer'd out behind beside the spinal joint;
He sinks aside, his limbs their force forego,
From his loose grasp the goblet falls below,
With streams of spouting gore his nostrils flow,
The table is spurn'd down, a mingled flood
Pollutes the floor with meat, and wine, and blood.
The suitors rise in uproar round the hall,
And angry voices on Ulysses call.
"Stranger, this was a shrewd and evil shot,
The archer's prize no more shall be thy lot,
The vultures of this isle shall gnaw thy head,
The noblest chief of Ithaca lies dead."
They spoke unconscious of his dire intent,
As of a murder casual and unmeant;
But the stern chief abandoning disguise,
And fiercely looking round them thus replies:
"Traitors and dogs, you never dreamt before
To see me here return'd from Ilion's shore,
That, weak and helpless, in her husband's life,
With boisterous courtship have besieged my wife;
Grinding my household, and defiling all,
Careless whatever vengeance may befall
From righteous men or the just Gods on high—
But know, your doom is fix'd this day to die."

TRANSLATIONS FROM EURIPIDES.

THE DIRGE IN THE ALCESTIS.

Ὦ Πελίου θύγατερ, κ.τ.λ.—l. 435.

FARE thee well, good and fair, Pelias's noble heir,
  Thy course is done ;
 Good and gracious things betide thee,
 In the dark mansion that must hide thee
  From yon fair sun.
The Sovereign of the Realm, and he that at the helm
 Steers in the murky stream his dusky wherry,
(Wafting the feeble sprites that flit below,)
  Shall hear and know,
 That never did a nobler spirit pass
  The Infernal Ferry.
 Firm and fond, far far beyond
 The best of woman-kind that have been ever ;
  Whilst here on earth above,
  Thy constant worth and love
 Shall form the theme of emulous endeavour,
Wherever minstrels sing—or where they strike the string :
 Whether in Sparta's ancient state austere,
  When the revolving year
Brings round the high Karneian festival,
And the moon's awful and full-orbed ball
  Fills and illumines all :
Or where proud Athens hails the festive day,
With pomp and art and prosperous display.

HERCULES FURENS.

Μὴ σὺ νουθέτει, κ.τ.λ.—l. 855.

THE Demon of Madness is represented as having a certain feeling of justice and right, averse to exercising her power, but at the same time having a pleasure in it. She has been remonstrating with Iris, who answers:

Iris. Don't remonstrate, Juno's order justifies you, never fear,
You've a warrant for your errand, and you come, commission'd here,
For a sudden execution, not to parley and debate.
  Lyssa. Heaven and earth I call to witness. I protest and invocate
Every power that sees and hears us, and the sun's all-viewing eye,
To record that, as a vassal, on compulsion I comply.
Since the fates have so decreed it, and you bring me tied and bound,
Train'd to chase the prey before me, like a huntsman with a hound,
Here I go then!—Nor the tempest, nor the deep earth-quaking shock,
Nor the speed of angry lightning, nor the bolt that splits the rock,
With a fiercer haste and heat shall hurry than shall I to seize
And overturn and storm the breast and brain of Hercules.
First, I mean to slay the children, nor shall he—the father —he,
Know the deed his hands are doing, till I leave his spirit free.
—Now the storm begins to shake him—life and death are in debate,—
—Look before you—there! behold him—lowering at the palace-gate—
Mark the turn his eyes are taking—and the forehead, bending low,
Breathing hard and angry like the bull that meditates a blow—
Invocating earth and hell, and all the dreary powers below.

There you stand entranced and idle ! I shall rouse and shake
    ye soon—
Hand in hand, a surly partner dancing to a bloody tune.
—Iris, hence! to fair Olympus, speed aloft your airy flight.—
I proceed within the palace—creeping onward out of sight.

FROM EMPEDOCLES.[1]

ΠΕΡΙ ΚΑΘΑΡΜΩΝ.—Frag. 77 & 78.

Ω φίλοι, οἳ μέγα ἄστυ, κ.τ.λ.

RIENDS! kinsmen! inmates of the noble town,
Whose rocky-planted turrets guard and crown
Old Agrigentum's memorable seat ;
Famous for courteous cheer and converse sweet,
My fellow-citizens !—I greet you well :
Within your gentle precincts here I dwell,
An earthly sojourner, but honour'd more
Than ever human mortal was before,
Even as a visible Deity ; with a crown,
With garlands and with fillets falling down,
With such a pomp of ornament, I meet
Your daily gaze, and move along the street.
When to the neighbouring city, as befals,
My progress leads me, far without the walls,
The multitude flock forth and crowd the way,
Men, women, old and young, in long array,
Eager in admiration or concern,
To know, what it imports them most to learn,
Of omens, expiations, prophecies,
Or politic advisements, deep and wise,
Or means of public safety for defence
Against the wasting power of pestilence—
Oh, poor pre-eminence ! how mean ! how base !
Amidst this earthly, transitory race,
To boast of worldly power, or name, or place.

---

[1] "Memorie sulla Vita e Filosofia d' Empedocle Gergentino di Domenico Scina." Palermo, 1813. Vol. ii. p. 248.

FROM THE SAME.[1]

ΠΕΡΙ ΦΥΣΕΩΣ.—Frag. 75.

'Αλλὰ θεοὶ τῶν μὲν μανίην, κ.τ.λ.

UORUM stultitiam Superos compescere par est
Quod precor, utque aliis concedant rite min-
                                    istris,
Ore pio puri latices effundere veri:
At te, Musa decens, niveis quæ pulchra lacertis
Carminis excelso e curru moderaris habenas,
Te precor, humanis si quid concredere fas sit
Auribus, ut mecum peragas sine fraude gubernans
Inculpatarum vestigia sancta rotarum ;
Nec te Gloria rivalis de tramite cogat
In vetitam transire viam, dum fervida plausu
Præteragit, fulgente premens latus ardua curru :
Tu castum officium cautè timideque ministra :
Nec te præmia destituent, quæ maxima semper
Debita victori sapientia porrigit ultro,
Si quis ad excelsam enisus pervenerit ædem.
Sed tamen omnimodis et ab omni parte cavendum est;
Neve oculo tu crede, nec auri, ne dolus insit ;
Nec stupeas populi rumoribus, at simul audis
Infantum balbas voces audire putato :
Sensibus humanis neve hilum crede quod usquam
Sensu animi mentisque acie complectier æquum est.

MESSINA, *Feb.* 1821.

FROM CATULLUS.

CARM. III.—*Lugete, o Veneres,* &c.

E Venuses and Cupids all,
        And all polite, well-bred,
Ingenious persons, hear my call !
        My lady's sparrow,—he is dead,
And therefore you must drop a tear :
He was so nice a little dear—

---

[1] Vol. ii. p. 244.

Such a darling, such a love ;
Round the room, about, above,
He used to flutter and to hurry,—
Then he came, in such a flurry,
Flying to my lady's breast,
Lodging in it like a nest,
Like an infant with a mother ;
He would not leave her for another ;
He would not move, he would not stir,
Nor chirp for any but for her.
And now, they say, that he must go,
For ever, to the shades below,
Where not a creature, I can learn,
Was ever suffer'd to return.
O nasty, spiteful, ugly death,
    To be so peevish and absurd,—
    To take that dear, delightful bird,
Down to your odious shades beneath ;
O dismal and unhappy case,—
Poor Lesbia's eyes and lovely face
Are flush'd with weeping, vex'd and red,
Since her unlucky bird is dead.

CARM. IV.—*Phaselus ille*, &c.

STRANGER, the bark you see before you says,
That in old times, and in her early days,
She was a lively vessel that could make
The quickest voyages, and overtake
All her competitors with sail or oar ;
And she defies the rude Illyrian shore,
And Rhodes, with her proud harbour, and the seas
That intersect the scatter'd Cyclades,
And the Propontic and the Thracian coast,
(Bold as it is) to contradict her boast.
She calls to witness the dark Euxine sea,
And mountains that had known her as a tree,
Before her transformation, when she stood
A native of the deep Cytorian wood,
Where all her ancestors had flourish'd long,
And, with their old traditionary song,

Had whisper'd her responses to the breeze,
And waked the chorus of her sister trees.
Amastris! from your haven forth she went,
You witness'd her first outset and descent,
Adventuring on an unknown element.
From thence she bore her master safe and free
From danger and alarm, through many a sea;
Nor ever once was known to lag behind,
Foremost on every tack, with every wind
At last, to this fair inland lake, she says,
She came to pass the remnant of her days,
Leaving no debt due to the Deities,
For vows preferr'd in danger on the seas:
Clear of incumbrance, therefore, and all other
Contentious claims, to Castor or his brother,
As a free gift and offering she devotes
Herself, as long as she survives and floats.

CARM. X.—*Varus me meus,* &c.

ARUS, whom I chanced to meet
The other evening in the street,
Engaged me there, upon the spot,
To see a mistress he had got.
She seem'd, as far as I can gather,
Lively and smart, and handsome rather.
There, as we rested from our walk,
We enter'd into different talk—
As, how much might Bithynia bring?
And had I found it a good thing?
I answer'd, as it was the fact,
The province had been stript and sack'd;
That there was nothing for the prætors,
And still less for us wretched creatures,
His poor companions and toad-eaters.
" At least," says she, " you bought some fellows
To bear your litter; for they tell us,
Our only good ones come from there."
I chose to give myself an air;
" Why, truly, with my poor estate,
The difference wasn't quite so great

Betwixt a province, good or bad,
That where a purchase could be had,
Eight lusty fellows, straight and tall,
I shouldn't find the wherewithal
To buy them." But it was a lie;
For not a single wretch had I—
No single cripple fit to bear
A broken bedstead or a chair.
She, like a strumpet, pert and knowing,
Said—" Dear Catullus, I am going
To worship at Serapis' shrine—
Do lend me, pray, those slaves of thine !"
I answer'd—" It was idly said,—
They were a purchase Cinna made
(Caius Cinna, my good friend)—
It was the same thing in the end,
Whether a purchase or a loan—
I always used them as my own;
Only the phrase was inexact—
He bought them for himself, in fact.
But you have caught the general vice ⎫
Of being too correct and nice, ⎬
Over curious and precise; ⎭
And seizing with precipitation
The slight neglects of conversation."

CARM. **XXXI.**—*Peninsularum Sirmio, &c.*

F all the famous isles and promontories, .
From the sun's up-rise to his setting glories,
Of all that Neptune's liquid arms surround,
In oceans or in midland waters found,
The fairest and the best, to thee I call—
Sirmio, the gem and jewel of them all.
How gladly I revisit and review
Thy wonted scenes, and scarce believe it true,
After so long a journey, past and o'er,
From Hellespont and the Bithynian shore,
To find myself amidst your walks once more.
How sweet it is to lay aside the load
Of foreign cares within one's own abode,

1*   C C

And with free heart and unencumber'd head
To couch ourselves in our accustom'd bed ;
That single moment overpays our pain—
Sweet Sirmio, receive me once again,
And with thy smiles thy old possessor greet.
   And ye, fair waters of the Lydian Lake,
   Salute me with such mirth as ye can make,
And roll your laughing billows at my feet.
   Let all be glad and cheerful for my sake.
     1805.

CARM. XXXIX.—*Egnatius quod candidos,* &c.

EGNATIUS has a certain pride that centres
   In his white teeth; he smiles at all adventures:
   He goes, like other people, to attend
   And countenance the trial of a friend :
   The orator insists and perseveres ;
The audience and judges are in tears ;
When in the midst of his pathetic style,
Egnatius sympathises with a smile.
Following a widow to the funeral pile
Of her last child, he cannot choose but smile :
Without a thought of person, time, or place,
He wears a constant smile upon his face :
In business, in distress, in haste, in sadness,
It looks like a disease, a kind of madness :
(Though not a witty madness or refined)—
A madness in degree, though not in kind,
And therefore all his friends must speak their mind.
—My dear Egnatius, if your birth had been
At Tiber, Rome, or in the space between ;
Were you a Susian fat or Umbrian poor,
A Volscian, or a Lanuvinian boor,
Sharp-tooth'd and eager at your meals and labours;
Or a Cisalpine, like my friends and neighbours ;
Of any nation, tribe, or race, in short,
That scour their teeth and gums in cleanly sort,
I still should disapprove that constant smile,
It shows a silly, poor, affected style.—
But in his native Celtiberian land,

Your Celtiberian, as we understand,
Time out of mind cleanseth his jaws and bone,
Each for himself, with urine of his own,
Reserved and hoarded from the day before ;
And therefore calculated on that score,
The whiteness of your teeth seems to imply
A steady, copious use of chamber-lye.

1810.

CARM. LXI.—*Collis o Heliconei*, &c.

ATULLUS, at the marriage of his friend Manlius, in addition to his services as a poet, had
undertaken an office suited to his character
as a lively, humorous young cavalier, namely,
to maintain discipline among the assembled
rabble ; presiding, according to Swift's description, as
master of the ceremonies to the mob—

" To hurrah the blackguard boys,
And keep them in subjection."

He takes his station accordingly at the door of the palace
of the bride's family, proceeding at first in his proper character as poet, with the customary invocation to Hymen,
which is continued to the end of the eighth stanza. He
then, as manager and director, calls to the chorus of
maidens, inviting them to perform their part. They commence their invocation (apparently in a great fright) very
poorly and prosaically, hesitating and hurried, but improv-
ing as they proceed. This is more strongly expressed in
the original ; the tone of hurry and rapidity is, however,
to a certain degree, represented in the translation. The
chants of the maidens being concluded, the poet, as prolocutor of the mob, expresses their impatience by a summons to the party within. He then turns round to pacify
his constituents by a tacit appeal to the delicacy of their
feelings, describing the tears and agitation of the bride, to
whom he addresses, at the same time, a consolatory stanza
(the XXth). We must suppose that, from his station at
the door, he could command a view of the interior, either
from its being left ajar, secured by a loose chain, or having

a wicket-window in one of the upper panels, like the miser's door in Hogarth's print of " Beer Street."

The stanzas which follow (XXI. to XXVI.) belong to the common town-minstrels (what we should call the " City Waits "), who, of course, would not fail in their services and attendance on such an occasion.   It has been observed elsewhere, that the imitation of their vulgar style gives the poet an opportunity of good-humoured banter at the expense of his friends.   And here it should also be remarked, that, although the varieties of style and character are sufficiently indicated at their first introduction, it is not by any means easy to define the precise point at which they terminate ; for the poet will be found in many passages (unconsciously, as it were, or as if weary of the disguise) departing from his assumed style, and relapsing into his own natural elegance.

The poet again, in his office of manager and director, having looked within doors, gives notice that the nuptial procession is formed.

I.

You that from the mother's side
Lead the lingering, blushing bride,
      Fair Urania's son—
Leave awhile the lonely mount,
The haunted grove and holy fount
      Of chilling Helicon.

II.

With myrtle wreaths enweave thy hair—
Wave the torch aloft in air—
      Make no long delay :
With flowing robe and footsteps light,
And gilded buskins glancing bright,
      Hither bend thy way.

III.

Join at once, with airy vigour,
In the dance's varied figure,
      To the cymbal's chime :
Frolic unrestrain'd and free—
Let voice, and air, and verse agree,
      And the *torch* beat time.

IV.

Hymen, come, for Julia
Weds with Manlius to-day,
    And deigns to be a bride.
Such a form as Venus wore
In the contest famed of yore,
    On Mount Ida's side ;

V.

Like the myrtle or the bay,
Florid, elegant, and gay,
    With foliage fresh and new ;
Which the nymphs and forest maids
Have foster'd in sequester'd shades,
    With drops of holy dew.

VI.

Leave then, all the rocks and cells
Of the deep Aonian dells,
    And the caverns hoar ;
And the dreary streams that weep
From the stony Thespian steep,
    Dripping evermore.

VII.

Haste away to new delights,
To domestic happy rites,
    Human haunts and ways ;
With a kindly charm applied,
Soften and appease the bride,
    And shorten our delays.

VIII.

Bring her hither, bound to move,
Drawn and led with bands of love,
    Like the tender twine
Which the searching ivy plies,
Clinging in a thousand ties
    O'er the clasping vine.

IX.

Gentle virgins, you besides,
Whom the like event betides,
    With the coming year ;

Call on Hymen ! call him now !
Call aloud ! A virgin vow
   Best befits his ear.

X.

" Is there any deity
More beloved and kind than he —
   More disposed to bless ;
Worthy to be worshipp'd more ;
Master of a richer store
   Of wealth and happiness ?[1]

XI.

" Youth and age alike agree,
Serving and adoring thee,
   The source of hope and care :
Care and hope alike engage
The wary parent sunk in age
   And the restless heir.

XII.

" She the maiden, half afraid,
Hears the new proposal made,
   That proceeds from Thee ;
You resign and hand her over
To the rash and hardy lover
   With a fix'd decree.

XIII.

" Hymen, Hymen, you preside,
Maintaining honour and the pride
   Of women free from blame,
With a solemn warrant given,
Is there any power in heaven
   That can do the same ?

XIV.

" Love, accompanied by thee,
Passes unreproved and free,
   But without thee, not :

---

[1] The tone of hesitation and hurry is still more strongly marked in the Latin.

Where on earth, or in the sky,
Can you find a deity
    With a fairer lot?

XV.

" Heirship in an honour'd line
Is sacred as a gift of thine,
    But without thee, not :
Where on earth, or in the sky,
Can you find a deity
    With a fairer lot?

.

XVI.

" Rule and empire—royalty,
Are rightful, as derived from thee,
    But without thee, not :
Where on earth, or in the sky,
Can you find a deity
    With a fairer lot?"

The poet is here in his office as manager of the mob,
mediating between them and the gentlefolks within. In
stanza XVII. he speaks as the prolocutor of the rabble
outside.

XVII.

Open locks ! unbar the gate !
Behold the ready troop that wait
    The coming of the bride ;
Behold the torches, how they flare !
Spreading aloft their sparkling hair,
    Flashing far and wide.

XVIII.

Lovely maiden ! here we waste
The timely moments ;—Come in haste !
    Come then. . . . Out, alack !
Startled at the glare and din,
She retires to weep within,
    Lingering, hanging back.

XIX.

Bashful honour and regret
For a while detain her yet,
    Lingering, taking leave :

Taking leave and lingering still,
With a slow, reluctant will,
　　With grief that does not grieve.

XX.

Aurunculeia, cease your tears,
And when to-morrow's morn appears,
　　Fear not that the sun
Will dawn upon a fairer face,—
Nor in his airy, lofty race
　　Behold a lovelier one.

The town minstrels are here introduced; they begin
with the same image which the poet had already employed
in his proper person.

XXI.

Mark and hear us, gentle bride;
Behold the torches nimbly plied,
　　Waving here and there;
Along the street and in the porch,
See the fiery-tressed torch
　　Spreads its sparkling hair.

XXII.

Like a lily, fair and chaste,
Lovely bride, you shall be placed
　　In a garden gay,
A wealthy lord's delight and pride;
Come away then, happy bride,
　　Hasten, hence away!

XXIII.

Mark and hear us—he your Lord,
Will be true at bed and board,
　　Nor ever walk astray,
Withdrawing from your lovely side;
Mark and hear us, gentle bride,
　　Hasten, hence away!

XXIV.

Like unto the tender vine,
He shall ever clasp and twine,
　　Clinging night and day,

Fairly bound and firmly tied ;
Come away then, happy bride,
    Hasten, hence away !

XXV.

Happy chamber, happy bed,
Can the joys be told or said
    That await you soon ;
Fresh renewals of delight,
In the silent fleeting night
    And the summer noon.

The poet appears again in his office of manager, and in
the next stanza authorizes the commencement of the
Fescennine Songs.

XXVI.

Make ready.   There I see within
The bride is veil'd ; the guests begin
    To muster close and slow :
Trooping onward close about,
Boys, be ready with a shout—
    "Hymen ! Hymen ! Ho !"

XXVII.

Now begins the free career,—
For many a jest and many a jeer,
    And many a merry saw ;
Customary taunts and gibes,
Such as ancient use prescribes,
    And immemorial law.

XXVIII.

"Some at home, it must be fear'd,
Will be slighted and cashier'd,
    Pride will have a fall ;
Now the favourites' reign is o'er,
Proud enough they were before,—
    Proud and nice withal.

XXIX.

" Full of pride and full of scorn,
Now you see them clipt and shorn,
    Humbler in array ;

Sent away, for fear of harm,
To the village or the farm,—
    Pack'd in haste away.

XXX.
" Other doings must be done,
Another empire is begun,
    Behold your own domain !
Gentle bride! Behold it there !
The lordly palace proud and fair :—
    You shall live and reign

XXXI.
" In that rich and noble house,
Till age shall silver o'er the brows,
    And nod the trembling head,
Not regarding what is meant,
Incessant uniform assent
    To all that's done or said.

XXXII.
" Let the faithful threshold greet,
With omens fair, those lovely feet,
    Lightly lifted o'er ;
Let the garlands wave and bow
From the lofty lintel's brow
    That bedeck the door."

XXXIII.
See the couch with crimson dress—
Where, seated in the deep recess,
    With expectation warm,
The bridegroom views her coming near,—
The slender youth that led her here
    May now release her arm.

XXXIV.
With a fix'd intense regard
He beholds her close and hard
    In awful interview :
Shortly now she must be sped
To the chamber and the bed,
    With attendance due.

XXXV.

Let the ancient worthy wives,
That have pass'd their constant lives
    With a single mate,
As befits advised age,
With council and precaution[1] sage
    Assist and regulate.

XXXVI.

She the mistress of the band
Comes again with high command,
   · " Bridegroom, go your way ;
There your bride is in the bower,
Like a lovely lily flower,
    Or a rose in May."

This is evidently the characteristic language of the old gossips, "bonæ senibus viris cognitæ bene fœminæ," but as before observed it is difficult to mark the point at which it ends.

XXXIX.

" Ay, and you yourself in truth
Are a goodly comely youth,
    Proper, tall, and fair ;
Venus and the Graces too
Have befriended each of you
    For a lovely pair.

XL.

" There you go ! may Venus bless
Such as you with good success
    In the lawful track ;
You that, in an honest way,
Purchase in the face of day
    Whatsoe'er you lack."

XLI.

Sport your fill and never spare—
Let us have an infant heir
    Of the noble name ;

---

[1] Precautions against enchantments or the evil eye.

Such a line should ever last,
As it has for ages past,
      Another and the same.

XLII.

Fear not! with the coming year,
The new Torquatus will be here,
      Him we soon shall see
With infant gesture fondly seek
To reach his father's manly cheek,
      From his mother's knee.

XLIII.

With laughing eyes and dewy lip,
Pouting like the purple tip
      That points the rose's bud;
While mingled with the mother's grace,
Strangers shall recognise the trace
      That marks the Manlian blood.

XLIV.

So the mother's fair renown
Shall betimes adorn and crown
      The child with dignity,
As we read in stories old
Of Telemachus the bold,
      And chaste Penelope.

XLV.

Now the merry task is o'er
Let us hence and close the door,
      While loud adieux are paid:
" Live in honour, love and truth,
And exercise your lusty youth
      In matches fairly play'd."

CARM. XCI.—*Non ideo Gelli, &c.*

ELLIUS, it never once was my design,
In all that wretched, tedious love of mine,
To treat you as a worthy man or just,
Alive to shame, susceptible of trust,
In word or act true, faithful, or sincere;
But since that idol which my heart held dear

Was not your sister, niece, or near of kin,
The slight inducement of so small a sin
As broken faith to a confiding friend,
Would scarce, methought, allure you to descend
From those proud heights of wickedness sublime--
Giant ambition that aspires to climb
The topmost pinnacles of human guilt :—
—To make the mistress of your friend a jilt
Appear'd too poor a triumph.   I was blind ⎫
To that perpetual relish which you find   ⎬
In crimes of all degrees and every kind.   ⎭

TRANSLATION FROM LOPE DE VEGA.

Madre, unos ojuelos vi
Nigros,[1] alegres y bellos, &c.

UCH a pair of black eyes as I saw yesterday—
So lively, so sparkling, so gentle and gay !
Dear mother, such things they were seeming
        to say ;
They so taunted and teased betwixt earnest
        and play ;
They gave me such pleasure, so mingled with pain,
And oh! I am dying to see them again !

Lisbon, 1802.

FROM THE SPANISH OF GONZALO DE BERCEO.

" *Vida de San Millan,*" Stanzas 57, 63-65, 77 and 78.[2]

E walk'd those mountains wild, and lived within
        that nook
For forty years and more, nor ever comfort
        took
Of offer'd food or alms, or human speech or
        look ;
No other saint in Spain did such a penance brook.

---

[1] " Verdes" in the original.   See " Tesoro de los Romanceros y Cancioneros Españoles," &c.   Paris, 1838, p. 284.
[2] The order of the stanzas is changed in the translation.   Sanchez,

And there I saw, myself, for so the chance befell,
Upon the mountain ledge, beside a springing well,
A hermitage of stone, a chapel and a cell,—
It is not yet destroy'd; he built it, as they tell.

For many a painful year he pass'd the seasons there,
And many a night consumed in penitence and prayer—
In solitude and cold, with want and evil fare,
His thoughts to God resign'd, and free from human care.

Oh, sacred is that place, the fountain and the hill,
The rocks where he reposed, in meditation still ;
The solitary shades, through which he roved at will,
His presence all that place with sanctity did fill.

In every act a saint, in life's every feature,
Of controverted points no teacher or repeater ;
Call'd by the voice of God, from the first hand of nature,
From childhood to his end, a pure and holy creature.

He is sent for by the bishop, and comes to the town.

In such guise as he could, and in such poor array,
Where or whence he had it, in truth, I cannot say,
He came down from the hills, and went forth on his way,
The road across the plain, to where the city lay.

There, leaning on his staff, he enter'd in the town,
His eyes upon the earth, his forehead bending down ;
His beard was deep and large, his locks all overgrown,
So strange and rude a form they ne'er had seen anon.

"Coleccion de Poesias Castellanas anteriores al Siglo XV," vol. ii.
p. 120. Madrid, 1780.

FROM THE "DIANA" OF MONTEMAYOR.

> Murió mi madre en pariendo,
>   Moça hermosa y mal lograda:
> El ama que me dió leche
>   Jamas tuvo dicha en nada, &c.[1]

Y mother died to give me life—
    I was born in sorrowing;
The very nurse that tended me
    Was a poor ill-fated thing.
So have I been all my life,
In courtship and in marrying:
Love, so seeming sweet at first,
    Left behind a secret sting;
Sireno plighted me his faith,
    And went, forsooth, to serve the king;
My father gave me to a churl,
    For such wealth as he could bring,
Would he had given me to the grave,
    With a shroud instead of a wedding-ring!
Jealousy couches by my side,
    From bed-time to the fair morning.
When I wake he watches me;
    When I rise he is on the wing—
Jealousy pursues my path,
    To the fold and to the spring.
Jealousy besets me so,
    That I can neither laugh nor sing:
I can neither look nor speak
    For fear of false interpreting.
His countenance is never gay,
    Always sour and threatening;
His looks still peering on one side—
    No voice but angry muttering;
If I ask him what he ails,
    He never answers anything.

---

[1] Libro quinto, fol. 136, ed. Antwerp, 1580. The rhyme throughout the original is on the syllable "ada," as the translator makes it
on "ing."

TRANSLATION OF THE "ROMANCE DEL REY DE ARAGON."

Miraba de Campo Veijo,
El Rey de Aragon un dia, &c.

THE King of Aragon look'd down
From Campo Veijo, where he stood,
And he beheld the Sea of Spain,
Both the ebb-tide and the flood.

He saw the galleys and the ships—
How some set sail and others enter ;
Some were sailing on a cruise,
And others on a merchant's venture.

Some were sailing to Lombardy,
And some to Flanders, far away:
And, oh, how bright were the ships of war,
With swelling sails and streamers gay !

He saw the city that spread below—
Royal Naples, that noble town !
And the three castles, how they stood,
On the great city looking down:

The new castle and the Capuan,
And St. Elmo, far the best—
Like the sun at the noon-day,
It shone so bright above the rest.

The King stood silent for a while,
He gazed and wept at his own thought—
Oh, Naples, thou'rt a princely purchase,
But thou hast been dearly bought !

Many brave and loyal captains
You had cost, ere you were won ;
Besides a dear and valiant brother,
Whom I grieved for like a son,—

---

[1] From the "Silva de varios Romances." Barcelona, 1684.

Knights and gallant gentlemen,
  Whose like I ne'er shall see again,
Of soldiers and of other subjects,
  Many, many thousands slain;

Two-and-twenty years you cost me,
  The best of my life that are pass'd away;
For here this beard began to grow,
  And here it has been turn'd to grey.

Madrid, 1804.

LINES WRITTEN AFTER VISITING THE

MONASTERIES AT CATANIA.

" Li Beati singulari
Son poi mi li Regolari;
Va vidite a li Cunventi,
Ca su tutti ben contenti."—*Vivu Mortu.*

ONKS and holy clerks profest
Lead the sweetest and the best,
The securest life of all.
Look within the convent wall,
See the countenances there
Unannoy'd by worldly care,
Unaffected happy faces,
With the features and the traces
Of habitual tranquillity:
With the joyous affability
That bespeaks a heart and head
Undisturb'd at board and bed.
Studious hours and holy rites
Occupy their days and nights;
Study, learning, and devotion,
Leading onward to promotion;
Here discreet and trusty Friars
Rule the Brotherhood as Priors;
Some are known as casuists,
Theologians, canonists;
One among them, here and there,
Rises to the prelate's chair.

I*

Thence again his parts and knowledge
Fix him in the sacred college,
With the robe of Cardinal ;
Last—the topmost point of all—
The majestic throne of Pope
Stands within the verge of hope :
That supreme and awful state,
Which the noble and the great
With devout obeisance greet,
Humbly falling at his feet.

Messina, *Feb.* 9, 1821.

TRANSLATION FROM FAUST.

Act III.   Scene VII.

Mephistopheles.

BUT I withdraw myself.   I see
You've visitors of quality.
   Martha. Come, get your best-bred answer
     ready,
My dear, he takes you for a lady.
   Margaret. 'Tis the good gentleman's good nature,—
I'm a poor harmless simple creature,
I've neither jewels, silk, nor lace ;
I've nothing but my silly face.
   Martha. Ah! dress and jewels are not all,
But there's a style, an air withal,
An elegance—
   Meph.   Well, if I may,
I'm glad that I'm allow'd to stay.
   Martha. And what's your errand, tell me, pray?
   Meph. My worthy dame, if I could choose,
I should have brought you better news :
But 'tis a promise, after all,
Your husband begg'd of me to call.
To give his best respects, he said,
And to acquaint you—He was dead.

Martha. What, dead! dear honest soul! And I—
I sha'n't survive it. I shall die.
    Marg. Good worthy mother, don't distract
Yourself.
    Meph. The melancholy fact
Is as I mention'd.
    Marg. Well, I vow,
For my part it would kill me now,—
I never should look up again.
    Meph. Pain follows pleasure—pleasure pain.
    Martha. But how? when did it happen? Say!
    Meph. Your husband lies in Padua,
In a fair churchyard open'd newly,
Enclosed and consecrated duly,
In the best spot that could be found,
Accommodated under ground.
    Martha. You've brought me something, I suppose?
    Meph. Yes, when his life drew to a close
He trusted me with a commission
Of costly charge : his last petition,
As a memorial of the dead,
To have five hundred masses said.

Dec. 1835.

ÆSOP'S FABLE OF THE FROGS.

FROM LA FONTAINE.

THE Frogs time out of mind
    Lived uncontroll'd.
    Their form of government was undefined,
        But reasons, strong and manifold,
    Which then were given,
Induced them to demand a King from Heaven.
    Jove heard the prayer, and to fulfil it,
    Threw them down a Log or Billet :
The Prince arrived with such a dash,
    Coming down to take possession ;
Frogs are easy to abash,
    Their valour is diluted with discretion,—

In a word, their hearts forsook them :
        That instant they dissolved the Session,
Choosing the shortest way that took them
        Down to the bottom of the Bog,—
Not one remained to cry, "God save King Log."
There was an ancient flap-chapp'd Peer,
                Nobly born
                Of the best spawn ;
        At first he kept aloof from fear,
        Waiting the close of all this storm,
        Till things should take some settled form—
                Like a great vassal
                In his castle,
                With full-blown bags,
Intrench'd with lofty bulrushes and flags.
A wish to gain the sovereign's ear
        Made him draw near ;
He saw him where he lay in state   ⎫
        With a solidity and weight   ⎬
        That bespoke him truly great.   ⎭
Then came a shoal in quest of posts and charges,
Much like our ancient courtiers with their barges,
        They ventured barely within reach,—
        The Chancellor discharged a speech :
They waited for his majesty's reply,—
They waited a long, tedious, awkward space,
        Then stared each other in the face,
                And drew more nigh,—
        Till growing bolder,
        They leap'd upon the back and shoulder
                Of their Stadholder.
The worthy monarch all that while
Was never seen to frown or smile,
He never look'd, he never stirr'd,—
He never spoke a single word,
                Bad or good.
        It seem'd as if he never heard
                Nor understood.
The Frogs, like Russian nobles in such cases,
Reading each others' meaning in their faces,
        Proceeded to the monarch's deposition,—
        This act was follow'd by preferring

A new Petition
For a new Prince more active and more stirring.
　　The prayer was heard;
　　To make quick work,
　Jove sent them down the Stork,
　First cousin to the Secretary Bird.
His forte was business and despatch:
　　At the first snatch
He swallow'd the Polonius of the Pool;
Then following Machiavelli's rule,
He fell upon the poor Marsh-landers,
Conscribing all that he could catch,
Trampling them down into the mud,
Confiscating their guts and blood,
Like a French Prefect sent to Flanders.
The wretched Frogs in their despair
　　　　　Renew'd their prayer;
And Jove in answer thunder'd this decree,—
　　"Since you could not agree
　　To live content and free,
I sent you down a King of the best wood,
　　Suited to your pacific brood;
　　Your foolish pride
　　Set him aside;
This second was intended for a curse,—
Be satisfied—or I shall find a worse."

1810.

TRANSLATION FROM PROSPER AQUITANUS.

"Hinc arbitrium per devia lapsum
Claudicat," &c.—*De Ingratis*, lib. 3, v. 21, *seq.*

THE bewilder'd will
　　Wanders in ways uncouth and stumbles still,
　　Never at rest, but ever in the wrong,
　　Yet eager, indefatigable, strong;
　　Within the labyrinthine circle bound,
In every path of error pacing round,

Vain hope, illusive confidence attend,
And guide the victim to his destined end,—
Frantic he rushes on forbidden ground,
Falls in a snare and rises with a wound.
Nay, more, to the distracted fallen will,
The grace that saves and heals appears to kill,
Suspending life and motion if applied.
No wonder—if a madman in his pride
Chases the kind physician from his side,
Loth to relinquish what his fever'd brain
Suggests of rank and power, to sink again
In weakness, want, and salutary pain.
   See the primeval artifice renew'd,
The very fraud of Eden which imbued
The streams of life with poison.   Oh, beware,
Heed not the subtle snake—avoid the snare,
Let not the flattering whisper tempt you now,
To feed on venom from the faded bough,—
Faded and broken, blighted at the fall,
Think not the evil diet will recall,
And nourish the Divine similitude,
The angelic form.   So pestilent and crude,
It feeds their angry tumour, throbbing rife
In the proud flesh, and from the fruits of life
Drives them with loathing horror—forth they flee,
And with a rabid instinct shun the Tree.

Pietà, *Nov.* 1821.

TRANSLATIONS OF SOME OF THE PSALMS OF DAVID.

IT would certainly be a great gratification to the curiosity of learning, and a most delightful indulgence to the imagination, which loves to transfer itself into the remotest times; if we could, by any means, attain to read and understand the Psalms of David, as they were read and understood and recited by the Minstrels and Singers of his own time. But for a Christian, seeking only his own edification, it is surely more profitable to meditate upon them as they were expounded by our Saviour and His Apostles, in their application to His own person and ministry, and to the events of His Church. That many of these events are still future, has been the opinion of the best theologians of our Church (as, for instance, Bishops Horne and Horsley); that they cannot be far distant, is the apprehension of many learned and devout persons now living ; to invest the awful images of antient prophecy, contained in the Psalms appropriated to our principal festivals, in suitable forms of austere and simple poetry, has been the attempt of the unworthy Author.

PSALM I.

LESSED is He—the man that hath not walk'd
In the counsel of the reprobate, nor talk'd
With Sinners in the broad and beaten way :
Nor, with unsanctified and haughty sway,
Throned in the magisterial chair, presumed
To censure and condemn what God hath doom'd.
But his delight is in that blessed Law—
To find it holy, pure, and free from flaw :
His task, his recreation, his delight,
Both Even and Morn, and in the depths of Night.
So shall he prosper,—flourishing and free,
Like to the natural or the mystic tree,
Fast by the living waters ; bringing forth
In his due season fruits of kindly worth,
Alms and oblations : while his very leaf[1]
Shall whisper of repentance and belief
Moved by the Spirit of heaven, and vocal made,
A living tongue,—it shall not fall nor fade.
Not so the ungodly.—When the winds arise
To scatter their inventions worldly wise,
Wafted in wild opinion to and fro,
With their atomic chaff,—away they go.
Therefore the curious spirits, idly bold,
Rash, sinful, insolent, shall stand controll'd,
With their exploded postulates uncouth,
In the firm Synod of eternal Truth.
  The Lord is over all,—to mark and know
The spirit and heart and mind of all below;
He 'stablishes and confirms the good,—and ever
Confounds the unrighteous in their vain endeavour.

---

[1] Leaves are metaphorically used to signify speech, language.

PSALM II.

EASTER DAY.

HY do the nations rage and storm in vain
With insurrection furious and profane ;
And lo,—the Monarchs of the world are met!
Their ranks are muster'd, and their council
    set ;
Princes and people—all with one accord
United in revolt against their Lord ;
Against the Lord, and his anointed Son ;
The purpose and design is ever one ;
Whether tyrannic, or tumultuous,—still
Enthroning earthly Wisdom, Power and Will.
    The last prerogative of human pride
Claim'd and avow'd,—to cast the bonds aside
Which fetter human action ;—to be free
From Him the Almighty Eternal Enemy!
" Come—let us break the chain, and rend away
These links of mental slavery "—Thus they say.—
He that abides in Heaven, surveys awhile
Their hideous uproar, with an awful smile ;
Till wrath divine,—long slumbering and supprest,
Rouses at length,—and each rebellious breast
Quell'd and appall'd,—attends the vast decree
Vouch'd in a voice of angry majesty.
" Yet shall He reign,—and He shall rule ye still
Anointed and enthroned on Sion's hill."
He comes !—" I come, the Teacher and the King,
The Lawgiver ; Jehovah's word I bring."
He saith to me,—" Mine only Son ! this day
Begotten, avow'd and born ; demand and say ;
Ask and obtain the privilege of birth ;
All tribes and tongues, and every realm of earth !
Thou shalt control them with the Rule of Right ;
As with an iron rod ; to rive and smite

The reprobate ; and like the potter's ware
Scatter asunder Empires here and there."
Therefore be timely wise, O ye the Chief
Of earthly powers!—Obedience and Belief
May yet avail you ; but the time is brief ;—
The warning is gone forth ;—the event is near ;
Be wise and learned ;—Serve the Lord in fear !
Princes and Kings of earth salute the Son
With reverence, ere the tempest is begun ;
The storm of fiery wrath, whose angry blaze
May snatch you wandering in forbidden ways ;
If it be roused and kindled ; bless'd are all
That with a trembling hope await the call.

Psalm XXI.

ASCENSION.

E shall rejoice, O Lord our rightful King,
  Exulting in thy succour, conquering
  The eternal enemy with Thy strength and aid.
  —Sin, Death, and Sorrow, and Pain are captive
      made—
His heart's desire thou grantest him—the scope
Of every supplication, prayer and hope !
With bounty, and love, and favour overflowing,
With blessing thou preventest him ; bestowing
On his anointed head, the regal ring
Incorruptible, as Conqueror, Priest and King !
The gold thereof is perfect ; purified,
Tormented in the furnace, proved and tried.
   Life was the boon he sought ; yet not to live
Alone ; but life eternal didst thou give :
Great is his glory and praise, achieved at length
In Thy salvation, with thy power and strength.
Thy countenance shall gladden him ; and display
A second self ; with delegated sway
Co-ordinate ; a fountain, and a store,
Of Mercy, and Hope, and Grace for evermore,

For all the nations! For his faith was tried;
For that his trust in Thee was testified;
Thy mercy shall maintain him on the throne,
Time without end, unshaken and alone!
　　King! Conqueror!—in thy wrath thou shalt arise
And thy right hand shall reach thine enemies
With ready vengeance—as the flames and heat,
That round the vaulted furnace rave and beat,
Enkindling and devouring all within;
Thy judgments shall consume the sons of sin,
The fuel of wrath, outrageous, fiery, rife,
With inextinguishable fury and strife .
Kindled to self-destruction; branch and root
Thou shalt eradicate them!—seed and fruit
Exterminated!—neither name nor place
Left upon earth—nor memory, nor trace!—
For why? the malice of their hearts was bent
Against Thy kingdom and name;—The vain intent
Is baffled, and recoils;—Thy vengeful bow,
Arm'd and upraised, is visible below!—
Stunn'd and amazed, the thunder of the string
Strikes on their ear, Thy shafts are on the wing!
O Lord, our succour in that fearful hour,
Exalt Thyself in Thine own strength and Power;
　　So shall we praise Thy blessed name, and sing
Our Conqueror and Deliverer, Lord and King.

Psalm XXII.

GOOD FRIDAY.

Y God, my God, look on me! why dost thou
In agony and distress forsake me now,
Forlorn of help from thee?—my daily cry
Goes up before thy throne, O Lord most high!
Incessant,—instant,—from the dawn of light,
And in the restless watches of the night:
But Thou remainest, stedfast, holy, pure,
Righteous, unchanged, and Thy decrees endure

Eternally predestined, truly and well,
O Thou, the glory and praise of Israel!
Our Fathers hoped in Thee ; they cried and pray'd
For help ; and Thou didst grant them present aid ;
They trusted and were holpen ;—as for me,
A worm and not a man—the last degree
Of deep debasement, ignominy, and scorn,
Oppresses me overwhelm'd and overborne—
An outcast of the people, a mark, a stock
For vulgar tongues and lips to taunt and mock ;
Saying, " He trusted in his God to save him,
Let God then interpose, if God will have him"—
Yes—Thou art He—that from my mother's womb
Deliver'dst me to light,—my trust,—on whom
Whilst laid at rest upon the nursing breast,
My thoughts and hopes were daily and hourly dwelling : ⎫
Father and Lord in mercy and might excelling,   ⎬
Whose glory and praise my lips were ever telling,   ⎭
Leave me not here abandon'd and alone ;
For trouble is hard at hand, and help is none !
   The bestial herd[1] of Basan close me round,
In boisterous outrage, with a savage sound
Of rage and outcry, like the lion's howl,
And eyes and gestures eager, fierce and foul—
And there I stand amongst them ! silent, slow,
Weak as the very water ; faint and low ;
My bones are out of joint ; my heart within
Melts as the wax ; my lips and tongue begin
To shrivel and wither with the parching breath—
And thou shalt bring me to the dust of death !—
The bloody dogs,[2] the unclean, are in the crowd !
With the hypocritic Elders stern and proud—
My feet and hands are pierced, and every bone
Naked and bare, and counted one by one !
In empty wonderment they gather round,
Gazing upon me, watching every wound !—
My garments are shared out—my vest unrent
Staked as a prize, with ribald merriment !—

---

[1] A race of animals, clean, according to the Law, but of a savage and violent nature—the Jewish Rulers.
[2] The unclean dogs, the Roman soldiers—of Gentile race.

But be not Thou far from me, O God my strength!
Father and Lord! incline thine ear at length—
Haste Thee to help me; save my soul from scath
Of fiendish rage; and thine appointed wrath,
The sword of Eden brandish'd early and long!—
So shall I praise Thee with a joyful song
Of victory and redemption; and proclaim
Thy justice and Thy mercies and Thy name
Amongst the brethren—Ye that fear the Lord!
Sons of the chosen seed! with one accord
Magnify and praise his name, with love and awe!
Sons of the covenant and of the law!
Children of Jacob and of Israel!
For ye can witness well,—that he the Lord—
Hath not abhorr'd—nor shunn'd the deep infliction,
That dreadful interdiction undergoing,
His tears in anguish flowing, and his cry
Were heard and seen on high; the Almighty face
Was turn'd to pity and grace,—and pardon given,
And ratified in heaven!—A louder voice
Shall summon to rejoice, a congregation
From many a tribe and nation; wider far;
From where the appointed star
Leads forth the mystic eastern Sages hoar;
E'en to the silent, shady, western shore;
The guests are marshall'd, and the banquet spread,
With heavenly wine and bread—The bread of life!
Without restraint or strife, or fear, or sadness,
In singleness of heart, with love and gladness;
A company which death shall not dissever—
They share the food which leads to life for ever.

Lastly, the extremest tribes and every race
Of the World's utmost space,
Spelling aright,—the words of truth and light
Through dark confused tradition long abused,
Shall turn anew;—to recollect the true
Saviour—and Sacrifice,—and Child of Heaven,
—The great primeval Hope and Promise given!

The Lord is Ruler; every Realm of earth
His heritage of birth, is claim'd and held

Subdued and quell'd—beneath his awful sway ;
Princes and kings obey ; the noble and great,
Sages and Chiefs of State, with humble cheer
Attend the table in fear ; or serve and wait :
Bashful and late, the sad rejected Seed,
From guilt and error freed, return at length ;
To be renew'd in strength, a mighty nation ;
Again accounted as a generation,
Enroll'd and register'd before the Lord,
Upon the great record ;—to testify
Of the Most High ; the deeds which he hath done ;
Pardon and grace with mighty struggles won,
And glory and rule ordain'd ; for him the anointed
Amidst a race pre-destined and appointed.

Psalm XLV.

CHRISTMAS DAY.

Y thoughts burst forth, even as a boiling
     spring ;
As a full flowing course of ready writing ;
From the deep source inditing,
The glory and praise of our anointed King:

Thy form, O King ! is fairer, and thy face,
Than the degraded, earthly, fallen Race ;
Thy lips are full of Wisdom, Truth, and Grace ;
For He, the Lord, hath blessed thee for ever.
Gird and prepare thee for the great endeavour ;
Gird and prepare the sword upon thy thigh,
        O Thou Most High !
        With glory and majesty
Ride prosperously forth, with pity and ruth,
Justice and Mercy, Righteousness and Truth,
The strength of thy right hand shall counsel thee ;
Framing the final Covenant and Law,
The Mystic Bow ; the work of wonder and awe,
Which hands almighty alone, can bend and draw.

From the tremendous string,
What fearful echoes ring,
Touches and tones of the celestial weapon:
To those that gather round,
Thy faithful followers found,
With no discordant sound they rise and deepen:
While through the world are seen
The winged volleys keen,
Shattering its frail defences, piercing, rending.
Incessant on the mingled host descending,
A living shower of flame, each fiery dart
Sped with unerring aim, to search the reins and heart.

Thy throne, O God! for ever and for ever,
Is fix'd—nor years, nor earthly time, shall sever
The sceptre from thy grasp—Our King our God!
Just is thy sceptre, righteous is thy rod!
For in thy secret heart, and inmost sense,
Hatred of sin, deep hatred, and intense
Was proved in shame, and agony, and distress
Triumphant in the zeal of righteousness.

Therefore even he thy God, with regal unction
Of grace and gladness, to thy rightful function
Hath raised thee, with supreme investiture—
Anointed, consecrated, holy, pure,
Inaugurate in perfect majesty;
A visible earthly present Deity!
From the rich unguent shed
Upon thy sacred head,
A wide perfume is spread—thy robes of state
Waft odours, that proclaim
From whence the tribute came;
In just obedience from the wise and great,
Proud halls, and ivory domes of Eastern kings,
Have sent their precious things,
To gladden thee with homage and adore;
Myrrh, nard, and cassia from the spicy shore;
Such gifts as soothed thine infant heart before.

Daughters of Kings, of comely garb and hue,
Stand in attendance due—Thy Bride and Queen

Pre-eminent is seen, in stately vesture,
In stature, form, and mien, in princely gesture
And comeliness of look surpassing all ;
Within the regal hall preferr'd to stand,
At thy right hand, distinct in rich array,
Rich with the gold of Ophir, purified,
Refined, and fully tried with hard assay.
Hear and attend, O Daughter ! Bride ! and Queen !
Mark and attend !—forget what thou hast been :
Thy name, thy nation, and thy father's house,
Thy customary vows, and wonted duty ;
So shall the king have plensure in thy beauty :
Him shalt thou worship, honour'd and adored
With other rites, thy Saviour and thy Lord !

Yet She too with her offering shall be seen,
The tributary Queen, Daughter of Tyre ;
That with her ample hire, and worldly dower ;
Sagacious of the coming hour, had wrought ;
And pearls of price with thrifty purchase bought ;
And placed with wary trust her wealthy store,
Where neither moth nor rust corrupt for evermore.

Behold in royal pride
The glorious happy bride,
In woven gold magnificently drest ;
Her gorgeous outer robe and inner vest
With mystic forms imprest ;
Forms which the painful needle long had wrought
With subtle labour to perfection brought.

Yet see with livelier air
Her young companions fair,
Harmless and joyous, innocent of care,
Fearless of fraud or guile, guiltless of malice,
With sportive easy cheer, and airy sallies,
They pass the court, and enter at the Palace ;
    A fair approval meeting ;
    Applauded and received with kindly greeting.

Think, then, no more of thy ancestral glory,
The Sages and the Saints of ancient story.

Prophets and Kings—look to the future race,
Ordain'd to nobler things—A wider space
Of empire and command, in other times,
Stretching in ample climes unknown before.

For me, thy Name and praise for evermore
Shall be my theme—a song for future days,
When thy supreme and undivided claim
Of empire every realm of earth shall bless,
And magnify and confess Thy mighty name.

PSALM LXVIII.

WHIT-SUNDAY.

ET God arise!
And let his enemies
Be scatter'd and dispersed!
The unrighteous, reprobate, profane, accursed!
Let them that hate him flee before His face;
As when the winds of Heaven, with easy chase,
Pursue the smoky blot that taints the sky
        (In vain aspiring high,
Rising and reeking from this earthly spot),
The feeble fumes that waver and dissever,
Vanish at once away dissolved for ever;
Or as the mass of wax within the fire
Sinks shapeless and dissolved, thy fervent ire
Shall melt their hearts with horror and dismay;
So shall they perish, shrink, and waste away;
The righteous shall behold it, and rejoice
Before the Lord, with cheerful heart and voice:
Praise ye the Lord in his ineffable name
Jah; the maintainer of this earthly frame;
Ruling and riding on the wheeling sphere
Like a strong horseman; curbing its career,
Bound through the barren empty tracts of space:
Thy providence and power shall also trace
A path before Thee, through the tracts of time:
And marshal forth the eventful march sublime,

Pacing the void of blank futurity—
God shall accomplish it.   The Father He
Of all the destitute ; to save and bless
The widows, the forlorn, the fatherless,
The solitary souls inured to chains
Planting them forth among the pleasant plains
To dwell in happy families and tribes ;
But other destiny and abode prescribes
For the rebellious, barren, hard and bare,
With hunger and cold, with scanty and evil fare.

Lord, when thou wentest forth, their mighty and dread
Sovereign and Chief; their covenanted Head ;
Rescuing the sons of Jacob from distress ;
When thou didst march amidst the wilderness,
Veiling thy glories in an earthly tent ;
The solid earth did quake ; the firmament
Stood shrouded and appall'd ; seeming to weep,
Blotting the soil with heavy drops and deep
—Drops of atoning sorrow from above—
And Sinai's mighty Rock was seen to move,
Bowing his antient hoary form sublime,
Mysterious, rooted in the abyss of time.
But on Thine heritage, Thou didst diffuse
A gracious shower of heavenly and holy dews ;
Cheering the famish'd hearts forlorn and weary ;
Appointing in the desert parch'd and dreary,
A place of rest, a plenteous habitation
For Thine own flock, Thy chosen congregation—
God gave the word—a mighty multitude
Moved forth at once, with faith and hope endued ;
Invested in the panoply divine ;
Train'd and array'd in saintly discipline ;
—A noble army of Martyrs—forth they went,
That (with the sound and sight, and summons sent)
Kings and embattled hosts in panic haste
Fled headlong—wide apart dispersed and chased ;
Enriching humble households with the spoil
Of Heathen pride ; without fatigue or toil,
Sharing at home the gain of godliness.
Long have ye lain in torture and distress,
The furnace of affliction ; soon to rise,

Lustrous as gold or silver, with the dyes
That wander o'er the changeful Dove and deck
Her silver wings, and gold-enamell'd neck :
Bright, pure, and ever welcome, such as she,
Heralds of peace and safety shall ye be.
 In the full triumph, Salmon's western height
Shines forth, enrobed in pure and snowy white,
The token of victory—proud Basan stands
Far eastward, overlooking heathen lands
With lofty ranges of superb ascent,
Lordly, majestical, magnificent,
Sources of health, and living springs of life,
Each in his region—but forbear the strife,
Ye mighty and haughty Mountains ! be not moved
Though Sion's hill be chosen and approved
Even as the saintly Sinai was before,
More honour'd, better loved, and cherish'd more—
Even as at Sinai, there the Lord shall be,
The Lord of Hosts, with might and majesty,
With fiery ministers, and cars of flame
Myriads of myriads—with a loud acclaim
In Heaven and Earth—the Lord is risen on high !
Destroying Death, leading captivity
Captive and bound ; large ransom doth he give
Even for his enemies to be saved and live
To praise and honour Him—here His throne and place
Are 'stablish'd—hence he deals His gifts of grace
In kingly largess—hence He shall subdue
The rugged-headed, rude, rebellious crew,
Perverse and hard, marring their shaggy crown
With His harsh sceptre, bruised and beaten down—
" Yet once again," the Lord hath said—" once more,
As from the field of Basan heretofore,
Will I lead forth my people ransom-free,
Rescued from labour and captivity
From the overwhelming multitudinous sea
To the rich purchase of fair victory,
Their promised land." Thy feet shall print the ground
With bloody traces—thy familiar hound
Shall tinge his tongue with carnage.—Pomp and state,
Praises and hymns, upon Thy triumph wait,
Conqueror and Lord, and leader of the tribes !

As holy pure magnific use prescribes.
First in the march the solemn singers go,
Mounting in even rank, and cadence slow ;
The thronging Minstrels crowd the rear below ;
And in the midst, a goodly troop and fair,
With the light timbrel toss'd and waved in air,
Are seen ascending on the sacred hill,
With happy virgin voices pure and shrill.
Praise ye the Lord in holy congregations,
Praise ye the Lord aloud among the nations,
Your kindred Chief, the stream from Jacob's well;
The Scion of the root of Israel—
    There might the little Benjamin preside,
Their humble early Ruler—or the Pride
Of princely Judah with his Peers of State,
Or from remoter regions, grave and great,
Councillors, Sages, Rulers, many a one,
Wise Nepthali, the wealthy Zabulon :
But he the Lord hath sent thee forth in strength,
Strengthen, O Lord, Thy work ; assert at length
Thine own dominion ; what Thy power hath wrought
Fix and confirm it, to fulfilment brought :
That other Kings and Chiefs may bend the knee,
Prone and adoring ; suppliant to Thee
With offer'd tribute for Thy temple's sake :
When in Thy wrath Thou shalt rebuke and break
The multitude of Spearmen, and the Beast,
Hideous and huge in loathly bulk increased,
That haunts the sultry Memphian River's edge,
Weltering and battening in the bristled sedge ;
The people of Priests, the formal haughty line,
That with the clinking silver glance and shine,
The dull idolaters of Calves and Kine—
Then shall the Lords and Chiefs of Egypt stand
And stretch before Thee the submissive hand
In supplication and surrender due :
And Ethiopia's Queen shall turn anew,
To worship in thy precincts ; to behold
Thy rich array, the pomp of power and gold ;
And marvels of Thy wisdom widely told—
Sing to the Lord, ye realms of Earth, O sing
The praises of your King, in Heaven abiding,

Upon the wheeling spheres in glory riding
Before all ages, years, or earthly time,
Eternal and sublime ; He sendeth forth
An image of his worth ; the Eternal word,
Our delegated Lord, a mighty voice,
Bidding his Saints rejoice ; proclaim and tell
That here in Israel, the Lord hath placed
His temple and throne, and with His presence graced
This land alone—His power and majesty
Stretches above the sky, but Israel !
Within thy sacred cell, to daunt thy foes ;
What awe does it disclose, what terrors carry,
Enshrined and shrouded in thy Sanctuary !
   —Chaunt forth in loud accord
   The glad triumphant word—
Praised be the Lord for ever. Praise the Lord.[1]

PSALM XC.

EFORE the solid mountains were upraised,
Heaved from the teeming earth to light and air.
Or that firm surface of the land appear'd,
Or habitable earth, cheerful and fair,
Thou, Lord, abidest, ever first and last,
The Eternal Future and the Eternal Past.
Sovereign and Judge ; in thy predestined plan,
Extinguishing the feeble race of man ;

---

[1] Ep. Heb. c. xii. v. 18,—"For ye are not come to the *mount* that might be touched, and that burned with fire, nor unto blackness and darkness and tempest, but ye are come unto *Mount Sion* and unto the city of the living God, the heavenly Jerusalem, and unto an *innumerable company of Angels to the general Assembly and Church of the First born.*" Here we see that St. Paul follows the order of association observable in this Psalm from v. 7 to 11, again (v. 26) in the same chapter he returns to the interpretation of the 8th verse of the same Psalm, as implying the abolition of the Ceremonial Law.

   "Long have ye lain in torture and distress."

   "Sensus patet," says Cocceius, "si jaccatis in camino, in furno, in igne πειρασμοῦ."

Again the word is utter'd—Turn again,
Inhabitants of earth; children of men!
Yes! for a thousand years are, in Thy sight,
As a brief interval passing away,
Like the neglected hours of yesterday,
Or unregarded watches of the night.
  Thy floods have overborne them; and they seem,
Their whole existence, memory, name, and place,
All vanish'd like a vision in a dream—
Sunk and extinct, an unremember'd race.
As the fresh grass, that in the summer air
Flourishes rank and free, lusty and fair,
It waxes wanton in its growth of pride;
But the destroyer comes at even-tide,
With his fell weapon; there it lies at length,
Stript of its beauty and strength,
Wasted and dried.

JUDGES.

CHAP. V. v. 9—13.

I LOVE the noble and the great,
  The learned and the wise,
Ready to rouse and animate,
Ready to share the common fate,
  The common enterprise:
Join me, then, with frank accord,
Join to praise and bless the Lord.

Ye that on pacers snowy white,[1]
Are wont to ride, a comely sight—
  Or on the judgment-seat
Sit with a grave and steady cheer,
Or move majestic and severe,
  Thoughtful and awful, in the street.

---

[1] The word rendered in our version, v. 10, "*speak*" is rather, as it is translated Gen. xxiv. 63, "*meditate.*" In the original it does not begin the sentence.

Let your daily duties cease—
Noisy debates and petty pleas,[1]
For drawing water from a well;
Proclaim aloud in Israel
Jehovah's judgments and decrees,
 The statutes of Jehovah's reign,
His bounty to the villages,[2]
 The vassals of his own domain;
Proclaim them where this people wait
As suitors at the city gate.

Rouse, rouse thee, Deborah, raise
Loud and high the song of praise;
Barak, in thy manly worth,
Son of Abinoam, stand forth,
A captive and a refugee,[3]
Advanced to power and victory,
Henceforth appointed to command
Among the nobles of the land:
For me, Jehovah will afford
Counsel and succour: He, the Lord,
Will prosper and direct by me
The mighty chiefs of victory.

---

[1] The word "*archers*," v. 11, expresses numbers of vexatious altercations, which the elders were employed in hearing and judging.

[2] His bounty, &c.
The vassals, &c. The original is "his own district of villages," *i.e.* inhabited places undefended by walls, trusting in the defence of the Most High.

[3] The translation is, "lead thy captivity captive," and "then he made him that remaineth," which in the original is expressive of the exaltation of Barak from a condition of oppression and obscurity.

ECCLESIASTES.

Chap. VII. *v.* 6.

THE mirth of fools, somewhere the preacher
   says,
Is like the crackling thorns when in a blaze ;
So unsubstantial are their liveliest joys,
 Made up of thoughtless levity and noise :
Though at the first the mantling flame looks bright,
'Tis but a momentary glare of light,
With nothing solid to sustain the fire,
It quickly sinks, and all their joys expire.

  1801.

END OF VOL. II

CHISWICK PRESS :—PRINTED BY WHITTINGHAM AND WILKINS,
TOOKS COURT, CHANCERY LANE.